SELLING

RANDOM HOUSE
BUSINESS DIVISION New York

SELLING
Personality
Persuasion
Strategy

Walter Gorman
The University of Tennessee at Martin

First Edition

98765432

Copyright © 1979 by Random House, Inc.

All rights reserved under International and Pan-American Copyright Conventions. No part of
this book may be reproduced in any form or by any means, electronic or mechanical, including
photocopying, without permission in writing from the publisher. All inquiries should be
addressed to Random House, Inc., 201 East 50th Street, New York, N.Y. 10022. Published
in the United States by Random House, Inc., and simultaneously in Canada by Random House
of Canada Limited, Toronto.

Library of Congress Cataloging in Publication Data

Gorman, Walter P.
    Selling: personality, persuasion, strategy.

    Includes index.
    1. Selling. I. Title.
HP5438.25.G67   658.8   78–24193
ISBN 0–394–32198–7

Manufactured in the United States of America

Acknowledgments

Fig. 1.2 Courtesy of the Upjohn Company.

Table 1.2 From: Executive Compensation Services (1978). Reprinted with permission of AMACOM, a division of American Management Associations.

Fig. 1.4 From: Executive Compensation Services (1975). Reprinted with permission of AMACOM, a division of American Management Associations.

Fig. 1.5 From: Executive Compensation Services (1978). Reprinted with permission of AMACOM, a division of American Management Associations.

Fig. 2.2 Courtesy of the Burroughs Corporation.

Fig. 2.3 Courtesy of the NCR Corporation.

Fig. 2.5 Courtesy of the Hamilton Electronics Corporation.

Table 3.1 From CASE ANALYSIS AND BUSINESS PROBLEM SOLVING by Kenneth E. Schnelle. Copyright © 1967 by McGraw-Hill, Inc. Used with permission of McGraw-Hill Book Company.

Fig. 3.2 From: CONTEMPORARY MARKETING by Louise E. Boone and David L. Kurtz. Copyright © 1974 by the Dryden Press, A division of Holt, Rinehart and Winston, Inc. Reprinted by permission of Holt, Rinehart and Winston, Inc.

Fig. 3.3 Reprinted with permission of Macmillan Publishing Co., Inc., from *Diffusion of Innovations* by Everett M. Rogers. Copyright © The Free Press 1962.

Fig. 4.1 With permission. From *Webster's New World Dictionary,* Second College Edition. Copyright © 1978 by William Collins + World Publishing Co., Inc.

Fig. 4.2 From Louis F. Basinger, *The Techniques of Observation and Learning Retention,* 1973. Courtesy of Charles C Thomas, Publisher, Springfield, Illinois.

Fig. 5.1 © 1954 by the Board of Trustees of the University of Illinois.

Fig. 6.1 From SALESMANSHIP: MODERN VIEWPOINTS ON PERSONAL COMMUNICATION by Steven J. Shaw and Joseph W. Thompson. Copyright © 1960 by Holt, Rinehart and Winston, Inc. Reprinted by permission of Holt, Rinehart and Winston and Joseph W. Thompson.

Fig. 6.2 Adapted by permission of the publisher from Dudley Bennett, "Transactional Analysis in Management," *Personnel,* January/February 1975, pp. 34–36; and also from "MBO: Appraisal with Transactional Analysis" by Heinz Weihrich. Reprinted with permission of *Personnel Journal* © copyright April 1976.

Fig. 6.4 From: A. H. Maslow, "A Theory of Human Motivation," *Psychological Review,* Volume 50, 1943, pp. 370–396. Copyright 1943 by the American Psychological Association. Reprinted by permission.

Fig. 6.5 From: John Howard, MARKETING MANAGEMENT: ANALYSIS AND PLANNING, rev. ed. (Homewood, Ill.: Richard D. Irwin, Inc. © 1963), p. 36.

Fig. 6.6 From: Philip Kotler, "Behavioral Models for Analyzing Buyers," as reprinted from the *Journal of Marketing,* Volume 29, No. 4, October 1965, published by the American Marketing Association. Reprinted with permission of the American Marketing Association.

Fig. 6.7 From: C. Glenn Walters, CONSUMER BEHAVIOR: THEORY AND PRACTICE, rev. ed. (Homewood, Ill.: Richard D. Irwin, Inc. © 1974), p. 87.

Fig. 7.1 Adapted from Wroe Alderson, MARKETING BEHAVIOR AND EXECUTIVE ACTION (Homewood, Ill.: Richard D. Irwin, Inc. © 1957), pp. 35–97.

Fig. 7.5 Courtesy of John Deere Company.

Fig. 7.6 Courtesy of The Procter & Gamble Company.

Tables 9.1 and 9.1a Reprinted by permission from Sales & Marketing Management magazine. Copyright 1973.

Table 10.1 Summary table of basic selling strategies, adapted from Thomas F. Stroh, *Salesmanship* (Irwin, 1966), pp. 161–256.

Fig. 10.2 Courtesy of John Deere Company.

Fig. 11.2 Reprinted by permission from Sales & Marketing Management magazine. Copyright 1977.

Fig. 11.4 Courtesy of the NCR Corporation.

Fig. 14.1 Reprinted by permission of Southern Company Services, Inc., September 1978.

Fig. 15.3 Reprinted by permission from Sales & Marketing Management magazine. Copyright 1976.

Fig. 16.1 Courtesy of The Procter & Gamble Company.

Fig. 16.5 From: Executive Compensation Services (1978). Reprinted with permission of AMACOM, a division of American Management Associations.

Photos

1.1 Karsh, Ottawa
1.2 Courtesy, Xerox Corporation
1.3 Courtesy of Barry Cook and *Sales & Marketing Management*
2.1 Dennis Brack/Black Star
3.1 (photos a–d) Sepp Seitz/Woodfin Camp & Assoc.
4.1 Courtesy of William H. Baker
8.1 Alex Webb/Magnum
8.2 Dan Brinzac/Peter Arnold, Inc.
9.1 James H. Karales/Peter Arnold, Inc.
10.1 James H. Karales/Peter Arnold, Inc.
10.2 Courtesy, 3M Corporation
13.1 Hugh Rogers/Monkmeyer Press Photo
13.2 Laimute Druskis
14.1 Burt Glinn/Magnum

Advisor's Foreword

A new era is emerging in marketing as the 1980s approach. It is best described as the era of the marketing communicator. The huge array of products and services, the complex customer demands, and the intensive competition for markets have created a need for individuals who can provide a sense of order to the marketplace. Men and women who can tie business and its markets together through effective communication will be needed more than ever. At the forefront of this new generation of marketing communicators are those involved in personal selling. In spite of all of the marvels of mass electronic communication, there is still no substitute for the persuasive personality of the individual in face-to-face communication with the customer.

But to be effective in personal selling, a high level of competence is required, just as it is for any other profession. Professor Gorman's *Selling: Personality, Persuasion, Strategy* was written to help the student achieve this high level of competence. This exciting and lucidly written text covers all the basic principles needed to lay a foundation for the development of effective personal selling skills. Illustrative examples and episodes presented throughout the text capture the tempo and flavor of personal selling as it takes place in the real world. Professor Gorman has also integrated success theory and personality development into the personal selling process. The emphasis placed on understanding the buyer, selling environment, and selling techniques further underscores his innovative and thorough treatment of personal selling as a major marketing force, which offers growing challenges and opportunities as we approach the 1980s.

As the advisor in marketing for Random House, I am proud to be associated with this exciting and innovative text.

Bert Rosenbloom
Drexel University

To my wife, Susie Lee Edmonds,
and daughters, Susie Lee and Marjorie Ellen

Preface

Success in personal selling depends on the total personality and not just a knowledge of standard selling techniques. Practicing sales managers and trainers have long realized that while a thorough understanding of tested selling methods is a significant part of the persuasive profile, much more is needed to build sales professionals capable of projecting favorable corporate images and influencing sophisticated buyers. Accordingly, many practitioners have incorporated personality-building elements into their instructional programs—elements such as success and attitude training, self-image building, transactional analysis, and nonverbal communication training. Previously, college sales texts have underemphasized or omitted the many personality-building techniques. A new text seemed needed for sales students, one which would blend these exciting but neglected ideas with the best parts of the traditional approach. Accordingly, this text was written to harmonize techniques and strategies with personality development, so that sales students might move toward their full potential in selling. In the tradition of persuasion, the first chapter uses selling techniques to interest and motivate students. The last chapter explains important procedures for finding and getting the "right" selling job. Techniques for developing learning, listening, creative, and memory skills are included to help the persuasive personality mature. Chapters on special selling situations should help students match their qualifications with market opportunities. A chapter on selling environments is offered, in keeping with the "total preparation" theme of the text. Part I focuses on personal development; Part II emphasizes tested techniques and strategies, climaxing in the face-to-face meeting of the sales representative and the prospect; and Part III centers on the long-range career considerations of sales aspirants.

While a sales text should contain an abundance of challenging ideas, it should, above other kinds of books, be clearly expressed and inviting. An important goal in writing was to provide substance with simplicity—an idea-filled text, written in understandable English, with the intended informality of a "you" approach. Many examples, illustrations, figures, cartoons, special listings, and multiple subheads are featured to give the book openness and warmth. The closing clock illustrated in Chapter 13 exemplifies this spirit of exposition. The end-of-chapter incidents (short cases and role situations) are intended to help students preexperience real selling problems. While many short examples of selling situations are incorporated under the chapter headings, slightly longer situations are relegated to the incidents. This is done in order to maintain clear organization and continuity without interruption of thought in the main copy. A glossary is included for better understanding of selling terminology, and an index is furnished for easy subject reference. The teaching aids package is unique and should contain a new dimension for added visualization, easy assimilation, and longer retention of text ideas.

The text was written to provide a new and more realistic direction for the academic preparation of students for selling careers, but it also expands traditional techniques to form a more complete presales foundation. If it points students in the right direction for a successful career in sales, then its purpose will have been accomplished.

WALTER GORMAN

In Appreciation

I am deeply grateful to the people who helped me with the development of this text. William Bennett of the University of Alabama, Professor Lynn Robinson of the University of South Alabama, Keith Weisinger of the Burroughs Corporation, and Phil Williams—who taught me so much about selling—contributed many of the basic ideas and philosophies that are the substance of this book.

I wish especially to thank my reviewers: Professors Benjamin J. Cutler of Bronx Community College; Peter Doukas and John D. Christesen of Westchester Community College; Abraham Baum of the City University of New York; Charles M. Futrell of Texas A & M University; Louis Black of Manhattan Community College; Joel Podell, Jonas Falik, and Abraham Axelrud of Queensborough Community College; and Tom Noble of the University of Tennessee at Martin—all of whom provided valuable encouragement and guidance. I wish to thank Professor J. Dale Molander of the University of Wisconsin at Oshkosh, who tested the text in his classroom and provided direction as well as encouragement. Professor Bert Rosenbloom of Drexel University will always be appreciated for his excellent input.

Without Paul Donnelly, College Department Business Editor at Random House, the text would not have been possible. It is difficult to express my deep appreciation for his competent captaincy of this undertaking. I would also like to thank Deborah Connor, College Department Manuscript Editor at Random House, for her expert and tireless work to improve the image and the copy. Thanks also for her patience with an author who should have been better schooled in English grammar. Thanks to Liz Danks, Assistant Editor, for helping to coordinate so much of everyone's effort; Brent Collins for his advice; and John Sturman for his valuable efforts. The Random House College Design Department is due special commendation for its careful contributions.

Thanks to my Dean, Dr. William H. Baker of the University of Tennessee at Martin, for continually furnishing encouragement and support; and to Dr. Gary D. Dicer, Chairman of the Department of Business at the University of Tennessee at Knoxville, for allowing me to teach there in the summer and enjoy the expanded facilities of the university library.

How much more difficult manuscript preparation would have been without the help of Guy Moore, my student assistant; Genease Mays, reference librarian; Leah Grubbs, who tested and made suggestions about the readability of the manuscript; and Connie Cantrell, who helped me meet the typing deadlines. Thanks to Joe Baker, Vickie Armstrong, Elizabeth Hammer, and Sherilyn Ratliff for typing the manuscript; and to David Tanguay and Ron Gifford for contributing valuable art sketches.

WALTER GORMAN

Contents

Part III

Insuring Future Opportunities 385

Detailed Contents

Part III

INSURING FUTURE OPPORTUNITIES   385

SELLING

Personal Preparation

The ability to persuade others is a vital attribute in a free-enterprise economy, but to realize your persuasive potential will require more than just a knowledge of selling methods and techniques. You will need an ability to communicate and a persuasive personality that projects a positive selling image. Chapters in this part are designed to help you evaluate career opportunities in persuasion, explore the informational and attitudinal requirements for success in selling, build a persuasive personality, learn communications theory, understand buyers, and become aware of selling environments. All units will focus on your personal development, to enable you to meet persuasive opportunity.

Career
Opportunities

A knowledge of persuasive techniques combined with a persuasive personality is power—especially in a free-enterprise economy. Persuasive power can be used to:

- Sell products
- Win elections
- Marry sweethearts
- Free the accused
- Convert sinners
- Help gain world peace
- Get your ideas across
- Help you get promoted
- Ease your relationships with people many times a day

Jimmy Carter, Billy Graham, Bob Hope, Golda Meir, Karl Marx, and Fidel Castro are examples of persuasive personalities. A detailed look at people who have used the power of persuasion is in the best tradition of salesmanship. If you can be convinced that the persuasive personality is a major reason for financial success, you will be motivated to get the most out of this text.

5

EXAMPLES OF SUCCESS THROUGH PERSUASION

Persuasive Men

H. Ross Perot was employed by IBM in Dallas as a computer sales representative, after active duty with the Navy during the Korean War.[1] He gained recognition early, and in his fifth year he reached his annual quota by the first three weeks in January. His success led to a promotion to a desk job in the Dallas corporate office. Feeling that he was out of the mainstream of selling opportunity, he quit his desk job with IBM and decided to use his persuasive ability to fill a need that was then neglected by the computer industry. In June 1962, when he was 32, Perot founded Electronic Data Systems with $1,000 of his own savings and unused time from an insurance company's computer. On a contract basis, his service organization provided computerized record keeping for clients and utilized computer time that had previously been wasted. He bought excess computer time wholesale and persuaded business executives to buy it from him at retail. No longer did businesses have to rent or buy their own computers to have access to information from modern data processing equipment. In 1968, after great initial success, he put Electronic Data Systems stock on the market and retained 9 million shares for himself. When the stock rose to $23 a share during the first day's trading, he became a multimillionaire overnight. In 1970, with the stock selling at $150 per share, he was worth over a billion dollars[2]—at least on paper.

**Photo 1.1
H. Ross Perot**

[1] Charles Moritz (ed.), *Current Biography* (New York: Wilson, 1971), pp. 322–324.
[2] *Ibid.*

Barry Rand sold for Xerox while studying at Stanford University. He was promoted rapidly to sales manager, branch sales manager, area manager, and full manager of the North Virginia branch. Under his leadership, the branch became number one in its region and number five in the country for Xerox in just one year.

Harlan Sanders was financially prepared to retire on the income earned by his small restaurant in Corbin, Kentucky. The restaurant was valued at one time at $164,000. His specialty was fried chicken, and Duncan Hines had even recommended his restaurant. When the highway on which the restaurant was located was rerouted, Sanders went bankrupt. His only income at age sixty-five was his $105 monthly Social Security check. However, he did have two important things—his chicken recipe and the determination to sell the idea. He traveled through Ohio and Indiana, sleeping in his ten-year-old Ford by night and demonstrating his chicken process by day. Although after two years he had sold only five franchises, he persisted in trying to sell his idea. Suddenly, his sales began to boom. Today, Kentucky Fried Chicken is one of the largest fast-food franchises in existence, with thousands of outlets worldwide. "Colonel" Sanders sold his business in 1964 to a Nashville businessman and a Louisville attorney for $2 million.[3] Perhaps he sold too cheaply!

Arthur George Gaston learned about the power of persuasion early in life. As a child, he charged his playmates buttons for the privilege of using his backyard swing. He then sold the buttons to neighborhood women. When he needed capital during his days as a laborer, he sold peanuts and loaned his earnings to fellow laborers for interest. Gaston founded the Smith and Gaston Burial Society and the Booker T. Wash-

[3] "Chicken Colonel," *Newsweek*, July 25, 1966, p. 79.

ington Insurance Company. Both became the beginning of a network of businesses, and by 1972 Gaston's holdings were estimated at $24 million.[4]

Persuasive Women

Barry Cook, daughter of a Navy officer, moved often during her school years. She learned to adjust to new people and to new environments. She graduated from the University of California in 1966, where she had developed a talent and affinity for debating and public speaking. After a year as a systems support representative for a competitive company, she joined Honeywell Information Systems as a technical salesperson. In 1974 she became the first woman to join Honeywell's President's Club, one of Honeywell's highest honors.[5] She maintains that to teach technical aspects of information systems to executives who are unfamiliar with the products, you must avoid making them feel uncomfortable about their lack of knowledge. In February 1978 Barry Cook was a National Account Manager, selling to important accounts from Honeywell's San Francisco branch.[6]

Photo 1.3
Barry Cook

[4] Arthur George Gaston, Sr., *The Ebony Success Library,* vol. II (Chicago: Ebony Johnson, 1973), pp. 84–87.

[5] Sally Scanlon, "Manage Sales . . . Yes, she can," *Sales and Marketing Management,* vol. 118, no. 8 (June 13, 1977), pp. 33–39.

[6] Barry Cook, telephone interview, February 8, 1978.

Sara Breedlove Walker, daughter of poor farmers, was born near Delta, Louisiana. She moved to St. Louis and discovered a formula to style black women's hair. The product was called "the Walker method." Sara Walker used persuasion to sell her method door-to-door, and she gained both customers and agents. She founded the Madame C. J. Walker Manufacturing Company and became president and sole owner. Her enterprise distributed her products throughout the United States and the Caribbean. She became one of the first black women millionaires before she died in 1919.[7]

One Big Deal

An ambitious vice-president of the Southern Premium Company quit his job in Atlanta so he could use his knowledge about trading stamps to make money quickly. His timing was excellent. Aware of the success of trading stamps in Georgia, he persuaded the executives of Malone and Hyde (grocery wholesalers headquartered in Memphis) and other interests of the Big Star chain to let him supply Big Star supermarkets with a stamp plan. He founded the Quality Stamp Company in Memphis and hired J. R. Mann to "sell up" (sell to all eligible prospects) other supermarkets and small businesses in the Malone and Hyde trade area. Soon, Memphis and the surrounding area had hundreds of merchants giving Quality Stamps. After about three years, he sold his interest in Quality Stamps to Malone and Hyde and retired to Florida with a fortune.[8]

Many Deals Add Up

Joe Girard sold 1,208 Chevrolets to *individual* customers in 1972. He was ranked the number one automobile sales representative for seven straight years.[9] He worked as a sales representative for Merollis Chevrolet in Detroit, employing two assistants to scout prospects and one assistant to handle the extensive paperwork resulting from those sales. Although he paid $25 for referrals from satisfied customers, the secret of his success was in his short, customer-oriented sales presentation. If he didn't make a sale in twenty minutes, he would go on to the next prospect. He tried to give his prospects the best deal in town, and he chose to rely on volume business. He worked only six to eight hours a day, five days a week, and

[7] Edward T. James, Janet Wilson James, and Paul S. Boyer, *Notable American Women 1607–1950: A Biographical Dictionary,* vol. III (Cambridge, Mass.: Belknap Press, 1971), pp. 533–534.

[8] J. R. Mann, personal interview, Montgomery, Alabama, April 1976.

[9] "Autos Joe," *Newsweek,* July 2, 1973, pp. 62–64.

spent much of the remaining time with his family in Grosse Pointe, not far from the home of Henry Ford II. In the early 1970s, he made about $160,000 per year.

Look Around You

James A. Crews, Jr., a successful former sales student of the author, sold books door-to-door to help support himself during college. At this writing he is sales director of the Varsity Company, manages over 700 salespersons, and enjoys a very high income. Investigate the progress of recent graduates of *your* college who have begun a selling career. You should also find out how many financially successful people in your community have made their fortunes in persuasive occupations and specifically in personal sales.

CONTRIBUTING TO SOCIETY THROUGH PROFESSIONAL SELLING

Obviously, success should not be defined only in terms of money. People should not feel satisfied with their occupation if their efforts do not contribute to the prosperity of others within their community. For centuries, and particularly during the Middle Ages, people believed that sellers of merchandise were parasites. Trading nations like Venice and Spain, however, became very wealthy, and more recent thinking has revealed that the persuader *is* a contributor. The social science of economics shows that products have greater utility and afford greater satisfaction in the possession of someone who has real need for the product. Thus, by using persuasion, a salesperson can create ownership satisfactions. Although selling has been identified with slick practices because of a few who have used unethical selling tactics, the image of the salesperson is changing. There is now a better understanding of the sales-person's role as contributor to society and a realization that selling talents help support a free-enterprise system. A sales representative is:

- A change agent for progress
- A promoter of mass-production economies
- A promoter of other economic activities
- A creator of customer satisfaction
- A professional in the system

A Change Agent for Progress

Anthropology (the study of people and their cultures) demonstrates that "change agents" have been responsible for societal progress. Change agents persuade other members of their group to accept new cultural tools and better ways of doing things. The sales representative's role, then, is that of change agent—to speed the acceptance of new products that offer advantages over existing products and to improve the standard of living of all cultural members. Pioneers like Cyrus McCormick, who invented and sold the reaper; Isaac Singer, who introduced the sewing machine to the American household; and Henry Ford, who marketed the motor car to the average American, are greatly responsible for the high standard of living enjoyed in this country. However, it must be pointed out that no matter how useful an invention is, it is worthless to society if it is not accepted.

Today, good sales representatives can contribute even more to the economy than the pioneers contributed to their economies. Many pioneers lived at a time when the market would readily accept new manufactured goods. Today, competition is keener, and older products are more entrenched. Continued progress may be dependent on introducing better products to the market. Many factories manufacture products which can't be sold by advertising alone. The cumulative effect of those plants going out of business would have a negative effect on the economy. As you read this, sales representatives are persuading buyers to use new and more efficient equipment and services to run their factories and households. Without personal selling, many customers would buy less, and a reduction in available goods and services would lead to higher unemployment.

A Promoter of Mass-Production Economies

At one time shopkeepers made *and* sold their products at one location. As a result, they had firsthand contact with their market. Later, the Industrial Revolution demonstrated that mass production could result in great economic savings, since assembly lines could turn out large quantities of uniform multiple units. Large-capacity machinery further added to mass production. Big operations provided greater savings for the producer and less expensive products for the consumer. However, markets had to be sought—sometimes far away—to keep the factories in full operation. A separation between maker and buyer resulted. Sales forces had to be created to reach business prospects and bridge market distances.

Today, the separation between manufacturer and market is increasing rather than decreasing. There is a growing need for salespeople to communicate and "fit" a standardized product to a customer's needs. Without the help of salespeople, large operations would not have an adequate market for their goods and would not be able to increase profits. The expense of employing a sales force is a high-yield investment.

A Promoter of Other Economic Activities

Selling not only helps introduce new products into the market, it also promotes innovation. And by making innovations profitable, it promotes product improvement. The sales representative constantly reminds production research about market needs and the necessity for more competitive products. All of the firm's activities depend on sales. The levels of production, hiring, financing, and purchasing depend on how many units of the product can be sold in the marketplace. Because selling focuses on persuading people rather than producing products, companies using scientific calculations to figure production costs may be willing to pay a premium to the salesperson whose worth cannot be evaluated on the calculator.

A Creator of Customer Satisfaction

Personal selling adds to the enjoyment of goods and services by increasing the buyer's satisfaction level. Do you remember an automobile or article of clothing that was well sold to you? The salesperson's knowledge and assurances added a further dimension to the enjoyment of your purchase. Has a salesperson ever told you something about a product that has helped you to take better care of it and, consequently, to increase its useful life? If you are better informed and better assured, you are better satisfied as a customer. Thus, the product is worth more to you. Sales representatives in estate planning (insurance) and accounting-systems selling, to name two examples, act as consultants (advisers) to individuals and small businesses. The advice of sales professionals has saved many small firms from bankruptcy.

A Professional in the System

With longer training periods, higher standards of conduct, and more exacting standards of selection, the image of the salesperson is changing. This is partly due to the increasing complexity of the products themselves and to the realization by executives that sales representatives who meet buyers face-to-face influence the customer's image of the company. Consequently, highly qualified sales representatives are being hired to sell products such as investments and complex industrial machinery. Selling is acquiring a more professional image because more intelligent people are entering the field, training periods are longer, and standards of admission are tighter. Corporations are searching for problem solvers who can think both technically and strategically. The greater the problems and the money involved, the greater the need for polished, professional, and intelligent graduates.

Certified life underwriters, licensed real-estate brokers, industrial equipment salespeople, and sales engineers are helping refurbish selling's image. The professional salesperson is closer to the professional lawyer or doctor than to the huckster attracting trade on the sidewalk. Because of the current emphasis on prospect cultivation and the complexity of the market, a new sales professional is developing with higher ethical standards and service attitudes. The public is beginning to recognize men and women in sales as professional consultants rather than "peddlers."

KINDS OF SELLING OPPORTUNITIES—THE DIVERSITY OF SALES WORK

Everybody Sells

Persuading is a universal activity, and it plays a role in everyone's daily life. Since the American free-enterprise system is not coercive, and since most people do not *have to* accommodate us, we find ourselves constantly using persuasion to get what we want:

- Children try to persuade parents.
- Traffic offenders try to persuade judges.
- Teachers try to persuade students.
- Students try to persuade teachers.
- Buyers try to persuade sellers.
- Applicants try to persuade employers.
- Employees try to persuade supervisors.
- Supervisors try to persuade employees.

Even the physician, the politician, and the accountant depend on selling talents to promote their ideas. Everyone must sell to advance.

Personal Selling Is Open to Everyone

The variety of selling opportunities offers a chance to nearly every type of positive personality. Even introverts capable of complex thinking are urgently required for certain complicated or technical sales jobs. While their personalities might benefit from more openness, it is their ability to think and resolve buyer problems that is most important to many companies. Almost anyone with average intelligence who is willing to make minor personality adjustments can find opportunities to make an exceptionally good living in sales.

One of the reasons selling is so profitable is that many young people have developed a false image of selling and have left the field open to others. As a ten-year-old boy I sold a popular magazine door-to-door. That experience led to an incorrect belief that all selling was on that level. Many people have had an unsuccessful experience with low-level selling. Because they have incomplete information about available opportunities in sales occupations, they search elsewhere for jobs. Thus, the number of persons seeking sales work is limited and this increases the rewards for those who do go into the field.

Types of Selling Situations by the Extent of Closing Effort Required

The special challenge of personal selling is to secure definite commitments from prospects—that is, closing the sale. *Support sales representatives, order-taking sales representatives, order-getting sales representatives,* and *innovative sales representatives* are classified by the amount of closing effort required in their job.

Support Sales Representatives. Support sales representatives do not use persuasive techniques as a main function of their jobs. Their primary goal is to help buyers locate merchandise and to advise buyers on the use of the product. Repair personnel, for example, may sell repair and operating supplies only in conjunction with machinery maintenance. Technical representatives may accompany order-getting and innovative salespeople to explain the operation of equipment to the prospective buyer. They rarely solicit big ticket orders alone.

Order-taking Sales Representatives. Order-takers deal with prospective customers who have previously established needs. Order-takers, such as milk and potato chip route drivers, serve customers on a predetermined route. Order-taking salespersons take care of stock, display products, and answer questions about merchandise. They also use suggestion selling to create wants for other products. In other words, they suggest to the customer that additional units or kinds of goods should be bought.

Order-getting Sales Representatives. Order-getting sales representatives stimulate wants and directly or indirectly ask for the order. They systematically search out customer problems and help prospects make up their minds by solving a problem with a company product. They must find the prospect's real needs and translate needs into wants. The order-getter usually goes to the prospect and initiates the interview. He or she must have self-confidence, a positive self-image, and a knowledge of persuasive techniques. While order-takers primarily serve customers who know what they want, order-getters use standard techniques to persuade prospects who are uncertain about their needs.

Innovative Sales Representatives. The salesperson who uses imagination and creativity and interjects new ideas into the sales situation is innovative. The innovative salesperson develops new ways to use the product and approach buyers. This type of salesperson can be distinguished by an ability to close accounts that order-getters could not close using conventional means and tested procedures. Innovative or creative salespersons approach each sales situation in an organized way. They examine all aspects of relationships and make adjustments easily. They must be concerned about future sales building and long-range strategy. They must have detailed knowledge about the product, the prospect's need situation, and the competitive environment. This knowledge should be combined with experience, persuasive competence, and intuition to result in consistent and sustained selling. The innovative salesperson is always in demand to handle complex selling problems and difficult closing situations.

Types of Selling Situations by Firms Employing

Salespersons sell tangible and intangible products at every level of distribution. They can be classified into *retail, wholesale, manufacturer's,* and *intangible* sales representatives according to the nature of the employing business. *Retail sales representatives* are expected to be patient, helpful, and friendly. They are sometimes thought of as order-takers who do not receive high salaries. However, managers of retail stores, successful store owners, and retail salespersons who work on a bonus or commission basis are creative closers and often command exceptional incomes. *Wholesale sales representatives* make sure that buyers are adequately supplied with needed items. They also see that stock is displayed attractively and that store managers are informed about new items. They must be friendly, dependable, and helpful. Personality is especially important in wholesale selling. *Manufacturer's sales representatives* range from order-takers who service a route to innovative salespersons who sell complex industrial equipment and train other salespersons. Sales engineers who sell technical products, detail sales-

Figure 1.1 Classifications of Selling Jobs

Types by Employer Served	Description
Retail sales representative	Sells to the ultimate consumer and usually sells at an established place of business. Many jobs for salespeople are in this category.
Wholesale sales representative	Sells to customers in the field. Many are service sales people who check stocks and set up displays.
Manufacturer's sales representative	An order-getting salesperson, usually with extensive training and knowledge. Job can involve complex problems and may result in sizable rewards.
Intangible sales representative	A salesperson who does not have a tangible product and therefore must create images in the minds of prospects.

Types by Extent of Closing	Description
Support sales representative	Provides technical and advisory assistance. Not usually involved in closing.
Order-taking sales representative	Serves customers who know what they want. Uses suggestion selling methods.
Order-getting sales representative	Serves customers who are uncertain about their needs. Uses persuasive selling methods.
Innovative sales representative	Uses imagination and creativity in addition to the standard selling methods.

persons who call on doctors and other professional customers, and missionary salespersons who train dealer sales personnel are examples of people with jobs with high requirements and high rewards. *Intangible sales representatives* must create images (pictures) in the minds of prospects. They may sell life insurance, investments, or consulting services and must be sincere, self-assured, and professional. (See Figure 1.1 for summary classifications of selling jobs.)

The Nature of the Sales Job—Other Duties Besides Selling

Most sales representatives spend a majority of their time accomplishing vital marketing duties other than face-to-face selling. The time spent *traveling* varies with the nature of the product, the distance between prospects in the market, the salesperson's territory, and the work attitude of the individual sales representative. In most high-level selling, the salesperson goes to the prospect. Even salespersons with city territories may have to travel hundreds of miles a week. Since prospects can seldom be seen as soon as sales representatives arrive, they must *wait* patiently and productively. Time must be spent *routing and planning* to achieve maximum efficiency. Industrial specialty salespersons must make *studies* of prospect problems, write *proposal letters* outlining solutions to prospect problems in detail, *install equipment,* and *train operators* in the use of equipment. Some salespersons must *program* the machines they sell.

Sales representatives have a *reporting* obligation. Since most sales representatives work independently, they must furnish accounts of their activities for feedback and analysis. They may be expected to attend *trade fairs* and demonstrate equipment or services. Sometimes sales representatives *collect money from accounts* that have become delinquent. Salespersons are expected to *study and learn* about new applications and new company products. They must *attend sales meetings* to learn new strategies and to learn to work as a team in promoting company products. Senior sales representatives and supervisory sales representatives may be expected to *train other salespersons.* Manufacturer's missionary salespersons, for example, may act as sales managers to dealer sales representatives who sell the products on another channel level. Salespersons are expected to write letters, entertain prospects, send advertisements, and carry out many auxiliary functions in addition to making prospect presentations. Most good sales representatives, however, spend as much time as possible in direct interviews with prospects. Their quota is reached by closing deals, and this usually occurs in the presence of the prospect. (See Figure 1.2 for an example of job specifications and a training program for a salesperson.)

Figure 1.2

 THE UPJOHN COMPANY
MEDICINE...DESIGNED FOR HEALTH...PRODUCED WITH CARE

DOMESTIC PHARMACEUTICAL SALES   *An Equal Opportunity Employer*

8952 11/77

Job Specification – Pharmaceutical Representative

Nature of Work	Provide information on company products and policies, verbally and by use of literature to: physicians, pharmacists and other licensed practitioners in private practice, institutions and industrial concerns. The objective is to obtain product specification and sales where applicable, and at the same time develop and maintain good professional relations for the company.
Functions of Job	***Physicians*** Call on each physician in the territory to present products and literature, tailoring the presentation to fit the specialty or special interest of each physician. The objective: obtain product specification on prescriptions and product sales where feasible.
	Pharmacists Call on each pharmacy in the territory as often as necessary to provide product information, check stocks, encourage stocking new items, sell special product promotions, encourage the use of various merchandising aids such as window and counter displays, watch credit and encourage prompt payment of invoices; contact new stores opening in the territory to add to the customer list.
	Other Practitioners Call on dentists and other licensed practitioners as time permits, handling them in the same manner as the physician, with the product presentation tailored to fit the special interest of each individual.
	Hospitals Call on hospitals in the territory to present products and literature to staff physicians, residents and interns, again tailoring the presentation to fit special interests; acquaint staff nurses with products; contact the pharmacist. The objective: obtain product specification and maintain adequate product inventory in the pharmacy.
	Industrials Call on industrial firms which maintain an industrial health department with a physician in charge. The objective: sales of products which are used in such plants.
Requirements	***Academic Training*** Baccalaureate Degree desirable. A background in pharmacy or life science is beneficial. Continued study of company-provided product and medical information is required.
	Experience Qualifications None required (work in a pharmacy, other retail stores, or direct selling experience is helpful).
	Personal Requirements Good physical condition; neat and well groomed; good posture and bearing; ability to think and talk clearly and concisely; present own ideas; good natured and presonable; energetic and enthusiastic.
	Initiative And Resourcefulness Must use initiative in planning calls, tailoring product presentation to practitioner's individual interest, locating new physicians and stores. Be resourceful in budgeting time, gaining audience with physicians and pharmacists, and handling problems which may arise.
Responsibilities	Responsible for adequate preparation, through study and organization, for both sales and detail calls; for proper maintenance and judicial distribution of personal stock of literature and samples; for a neat, well-organized and properly stocked "detail bag". In the pharmacy: for checking stocks, presenting product information, deals and promotional material; watching credit,

collections and encouraging prompt payment of invoices. For a thorough knowledge of material in the catalog and sales manual; for promptly executing the various reports requested; for creating and maintaining good professional relations, and conduct at all times becoming a representative of The Upjohn Company.

Training Program–Pharmaceutical Representative

The Upjohn training program begins the day new representatives are hired and comes to an end only when they relinquish their final assignment at retirement. This program is designed to help prepare the representatives to successfully accomplish whatever challenge or responsibility they are called upon to face. The major emphasis in both time and effort involves actual performance by the trainee in the physician's office, the hospital and the pharmacy. The program is essentially a four phase operation which is carried out in the sales area office, the national learning center, the field, and at the home office in Kalamazoo, Michigan. The following outline highlights the sequence of events and principal activities. Timing is flexible and the program is adjusted to the personal requirements of each individual.

Sales Area Office Training

Several weeks are devoted to this phase of the training program. Under the direction of the area sales manager and the distribution center manager, new representatives are enrolled, briefed on the mechanics of the job and the operations of the sales area office, receive initial disease and product information, and their territory supplies.

Initial Home Office Training

This portion of training takes place under the leadership of national sales trainers and consists of several weeks of intensive activity at The Upjohn Company's Learning Center in Kalamazoo, Michigan. Using the latest educational techniques, the new representative touches everything from product knowledge and application to role playing in sales situations. The trainee will use films, videotapes, programmed learning, listening training and small group sessions to help develop the problem-solving attitude required in professional selling. With the guidance of the sales trainers, the representative will embrace all phases of sales from retail merchandising of nonprescription products to hospital sales. Also included is a tour of the Company's research, production and office facilities.

Field Training

A minimum of three weeks is utilized for this phase of the training program, which is completed under the guidance of the district manager. The locale is the territory to which the new representative has been assigned. This is essentially a "laboratory" application of the subject matter presented in the sales area and national learning center. It involves both demonstration and actual practice–demonstration by the district manager with the new representative as observer and performance by the representative with the district manager as advisor.

Subsequent Home Office Training

After approximately 18-24 months in a sales territory, and at periodic intervals thereafter, representatives return to the Home Office in Kalamazoo, Michigan for one-week seminars and workshops under the leadership of the Sales Training Unit. A review of pharmacy, practical physiology and therapeutics, and additional product information occupy much of the time. Films, group discussions and question-and-answer sessions are an important part of these conferences.

After returning to the territory, the representative is kept up to date on products, policies and the latest medical developments through regular sales area conferences. All training programs have been formulated with one purpose in mind: to help representatives accomplish whatever goals they set for themselves within the company structure.

EVALUATING SELLING AS A CAREER

There will be a need for professional persuaders as long as the free-enterprise system exists. Fundamental questions are: Does a career in personal selling constitute a rewarding lifetime occupation? Do advantages outweigh disadvantages? While the answers depend somewhat on the individual, every student should at least consider a selling career as one of the possible choices. A career in personal selling offers:

- The outlook of many high-paying openings
- Excellent opportunities for financial success
- Possibilities for rapid advancement
- Freedom
- Personality development
- The chance to work with people
- The excitement of traveling
- Continual learning

Employment Opportunities

The outlook for future openings in high-paying sales jobs is very good. Table 1.1 provides statistical data to chart the projected growth of

TABLE 1.1   OUTLOOK FOR SELECTED SALES OCCUPATIONS

OCCUPATION	EMPLOYMENT 1974	PROJECTED EMPLOYMENT 1985	PERCENT GROWTH 1974–1985	AVERAGE ANNUAL INCREASE	GROWTH	REPLACE-MENTS
Underwriters	470,000	536,000	15.0	19,400	6,400	13,000
Manufacturer's salesworkers	380,000	387,000	2.4	9,500	800	8,700
Retail-trade salesworkers	2,800,000	3,175,000	15.1	190,000	38,000	152,000
Securities salesworkers	100,000	130,000	31.9	6,100	2,900	3,200
Wholesale-trade salesworkers	770,000	883,000	15.0	30,000	10,000	20,000
Real-estate salesworkers	400,000	480,000	21.8	28,500	7,800	20,700

Source: *Occupational Projections and Training Data, 1976*, Bulletin No. 1918, U.S. Government Printing Office, U.S. Department of Labor, Bureau of Labor Statistics, pp. 31, 38–40.

selected sales occupations through 1985. The average-annual-increase figure includes the dual effects of growth (from an increase in total employment) and replacements (from retirements and other types of turnover).

As you can see, there are many yearly openings in each category due to both growth and turnover. While these classifications were selected to represent interests of college-trained sales aspirants, most wholesale salesworkers have not had college training. The majority of securities sales representatives, however, have had a college education. Experienced securities salesworkers averaged $21,000 in 1972, while beginning manufacturer's salesworkers could expect $9,000. Experienced manufacturer's salesworkers earned between $16,000 and $32,000.[10]

Financial Opportunities

The financial rewards of selling vary greatly and depend on factors such as:

- The difficulty and complexity of selling problems
- The sophistication of personality required
- Closing creativity required
- The risk or security involved in the job
- The compensation system
- The future outlook of the employing firm
- The social status of the job
- The amount of travel and relocation involved

Persons interested in selling careers must realize that college training is not as necessary in jobs where there are fewer problems, less challenge, and easier selling. The greater the problems and the more complicated the products, the greater the rewards. Jobs that require salespersons to project a corporate image and meet with high officials demand exceptional intelligence and polish. These jobs consequently pay more. Salespersons who depend on commissions and bonus arrangements rather than on salaries generally make more money. Salespersons willing to travel, relocate, work longer hours, or sell products of questionable social value may also be able to earn more money. Firms whose future outlook is highly dependent on business cycle fluctuations may have to promise more to attract competent sales representatives. With these reservations in mind, and realizing that compensation varies among types of sales jobs more than in most other fields, look at the following general data.

[10] *Occupational Outlook Handbook, 1974–1975 Edition,* Bulletin No. 1785, U.S. Government Printing Office, Department of Labor.

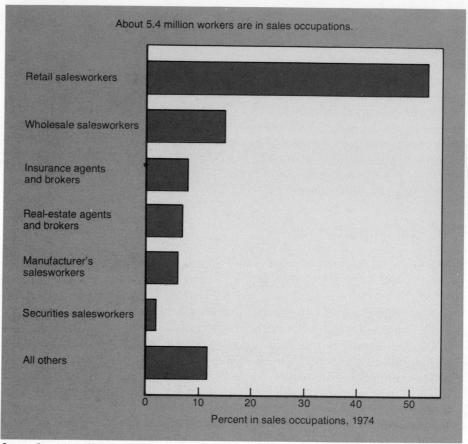

About 5.4 million workers are in sales occupations.

Retail salesworkers

Wholesale salesworkers

Insurance agents
and brokers

Real-estate agents
and brokers

Manufacturer's
salesworkers

Securities salesworkers

All others

Percent in sales occupations, 1974

Source: *Occupational Outlook Handbook,* 1976–1977 Edition, Bulletin no. 1875, U.S. Government Printing Office, U.S. Department of Labor, Bureau of Labor Statistics.

Figure 1.3   Distribution of Sales Occupations

In 1977, college graduates selling consumer goods and services averaged $11,040, an increase of 6.9 percent over the previous year. Those selling industrial goods and services averaged $12,600, an increase of 3.8 percent. Masters of Business Administration graduates with nontechnical undergraduate degrees averaged $16,920, while Masters graduates with technical undergraduate degrees averaged $18,038. New graduates with bachelor degrees in sales-marketing could expect to be hired at an average of $12,636.[11]

More important than starting salaries are salaries of sales representatives

[11] Abbot, Longer & Associates, college recruiting report, 1977. In "Salesmen's Annual Compensation," *Sales & Marketing Management,* 120, no. 3 (February 27, 1978), 69.

who have been in the field for several years. Table 1.2 summarizes sales representatives' annual compensation for consumer and industrial products. Note that sales representatives selling industrial products consistently average more than those selling consumer products. Those on

TABLE 1.2 SALES REPRESENTATIVES' ANNUAL COMPENSATION BY TYPE OF REPRESENTATIVE

Salesman level	CONSUMER PRODUCTS			INDUSTRIAL PRODUCTS		
	1977	1976	% Change	1977	1976	% Change
Sales trainee						
Straight salary	$10,675	$10,620	+ 0.5%	$12,217	$12,047	+ 1.4%
Salary plus incentive						
Salary	11,400	10,633	+ 7.2	11,722	11,000	+ 6.6
Incentive	1,300	1,400	− 7.1	2,178	1,640	+32.8
Total	12,333	11,933	+ 3.4	14,222	12,980	+ 9.6
A and B salesmen*						
Straight salary	14,175	13,867	+ 2.2	17,427	16,660	+ 4.6
Salary plus incentive						
Salary	14,550	12,967	+12.2	15,114	14,722	+ 2.7
Incentive	3,150	2,367	+33.1	3,495	2,994	+16.7
Total	18,350	16,750	+ 9.6	19,714	17,933	+ 9.9
Senior salesmen†						
Straight salary	22,350	14,700	+52.0	21,624	20,493	+ 5.5
Salary plus incentive						
Salary	18,783	16,350	+14.9	19,343	18,124	+ 6.7
Incentive	5,017	3,900	+28.6	5,357	4,335	+23.6
Total	24,250	21,100	+14.9	23,571	23,171	+ 1.7
Sales supervisor						
Straight salary	25,625	20,800	+23.2	26,161	22,500	+16.3
Salary plus incentive						
Salary	23,033	20,300	+13.5	23,678	21,133	+12.0
Incentive	4,967	3,550	+39.9	6,122	5,067	+20.8
Total	27,433	23,500	+16.7	29,644	26,653	+11.2

Note: Some differences between years reflect changes in the organizations that reported data. It should also be noted that in the "salary plus incentive" category, the "total" compensation will not equal the sum of the "salary" and "incentive" components because not all respondents provided information for each of the components.
Source: American Management Associations, *Executive Compensation Service.*

* *Salesmen grade A:* "regular" salespersons who have little or no selling experience except that which has been acquired in the company sales training program. *Salesmen grade B:* salespersons who have broad knowledge of the company's products and services and who sell in a specifically assigned territory. They develop new prospects.
† *Senior salesmen:* Salespersons with the highest level of selling responsibility.
Source: Sales & Marketing Management, 120, no. 8 (February 27, 1978), 66.

incentive compensation plans also average more than those on straight salary. It is important to remember that this table includes many types of salespersons and those with and without college training. Sales representatives in high-level selling jobs will obviously earn a higher salary.

Figure 1.4 shows how salespersons' compensation has fared through a severe recession, while Figure 1.5 charts actual increases for salespersons on various rungs of the promotional ladder. The student should compare these statistics with those for other occupations in the same time period. Also consider salaries that reflect both college and noncollege backgrounds.

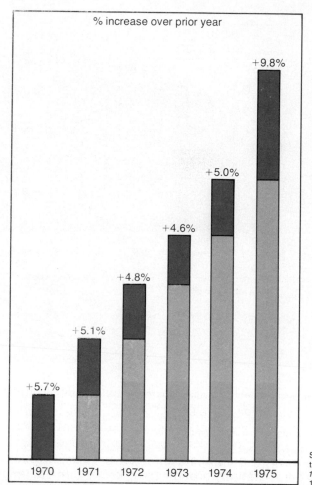

% increase over prior year

+9.8%

+5.0%

+4.6%

+4.8%

+5.1%

+5.7%

1970   1971   1972   1973   1974   1975

Source: American Management Associations, *Executive Compensation Service 1975*. In *Sales & Marketing Management*, 116, no. 2 (February 9, 1976): 41.

Figure 1.4 Compensation Gains Accelerate

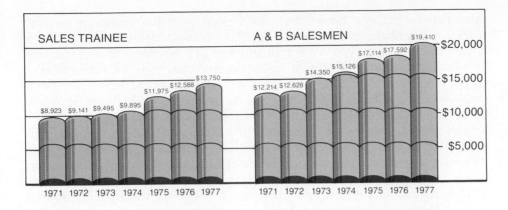

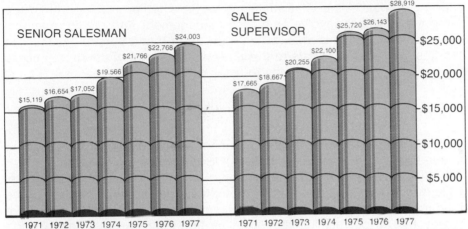

Note: Salaries plus commission incentives. Figures apply to consumer goods, industrial goods, and "other," that is, insurance, services, transportation, and utilities.

Source: American Management Associations, *Executive Compensation Service*. In *Sales & Marketing Management*, 120, no. 3 (February 27, 1978): 62.

Figure 1.5   How Salesmen's Total Compensation Is Growing

Advancement

A typical promotional route is junior sales representative, sales representative, senior sales representative, zone sales manager, sales manager, vice-president in charge of sales and marketing, and president. Junior sales representatives are generally considered on-the-job trainees. Most people in this apprentice category are not experienced or knowledgeable enough to justify their compensation through their profitability at this point. After the juniors are given a territory and work mostly on their own, they are usually considered full-fledged sales representatives. Senior sales representatives have most often been with the company several years. They have proven their profitability and been entrusted with important accounts. When a significant part of their formal duties involves training and supervising junior salespersons, they may be formally recognized as assistant sales managers or zone sales managers. A sales manager or sales branch manager may be promoted to vice-president and perhaps to president. Often, field sales representatives doing well in their territories are reluctant to take desk jobs. Since desk jobs may require relocation or even a cut in compensation (from commission to salary), they may refuse the promotion. Many field sales representatives prefer better territories as a reward for exceeding their quotas and not promotion.

Nevertheless, many top executives have come up through the selling ranks. Many top corporate executives and board members believe that selling experience is a vital qualifying variable for promotion. Most top corporate positions involve employee management and public relations, and sales experience is an excellent indication that a person has learned to adjust and accommodate to the views and feelings of others. Success in sales also indicates an ability to listen to others.

Freedom

Some people are suited by temperament to spending long hours doing detailed figure work behind a desk. Some even enjoy working with machines and numbers more than dealing with new personalities. Others, while they may tolerate desk work, prefer to be outside the company office building, free from routine and confinement. Sales representatives are usually free to do most of their own routing; call on prospects of their choosing; plan their own strategy; and, within the confines of spending their time in marketing activity, do what they feel is best to solicit business. The typical salesperson contacts dozens of people each day and faces situations that are anything but routine.

Personality Development

Since success in sales requires the development of an attractive and persuasive personality, salespersons acquire and develop those traits that promote acceptance by other people. They learn to put themselves second (subjugate their personalities) and to let prospects express feelings and enjoy being the center of attention. Sales representatives learn to be sympathetic listeners and to sparkle with optimistic enthusiasm. By adjusting personality to the needs of others, they sell both self and product. Thus, personality develops consciously and unconsciously under the challenge of financial reward.

People-Oriented

There is great satisfaction dealing with and learning from people. Since we are all social beings, many sales representatives find their work challenging and enjoy the variety of people they meet. Personal contacts made in selling often carry over into social life. It is helpful to have a wide range of friends and acquaintances, since they often add to selling potential by referring new prospects.

Traveling and Learning

It is interesting to meet new people and to see what is going on in the sales territory every day. Sales professionals selling accounting systems, insurance sales representatives, and investment salespersons, to name a few, have an opportunity to learn about the "inside" of major business operations. Nearly every sales representative benefits from the learning experience that comes from involvement in customer problems and personal contacts. Many sales representatives find the traveling aspects of their job and the interaction with a variety of people exciting.

Although the above advantages are significant, selling is not without its disadvantages:

- It is hard work.
- It is sometimes psychologically difficult.
- It may require relocation and time away from home.

Hard Work

A branch manager in Memphis always asks new sales applicants if they are looking for a "job" or a "position." If the applicant says position, the manager ends the interview by explaining that he does not have any positions to offer—just hard work. While sales work is varied, it often requires physical stamina and persistent effort. It may require driving in traffic and lifting heavy products. It may require study, research, and concentration. It requires calling on a maximum number of prospects and taking adequate time to prepare for and interview each prospect. Other selling duties must also be done correctly. Sales representatives are usually free to work as long and as hard as necessary to sell as much as they want to sell.

Psychologically Difficult

Sales representatives may have to take a certain amount of abuse from prospects who are testing the salesperson's personality. In a sales situation, the prospect may bring up objections or may attempt to irritate the salesperson to determine the truth about the product and the sales-person. In fact, the sales situation may be thought of as a contest, with the prospect increasing conflict and the sales representative attempting to minimize conflict. Salespersons must be able to take on the under-standing role. They must restrain any inclination to be argumentative, overbearing, or self-assertive. The prospect, on the other hand, is under no such restraint. If prospects wish to defer the displeasure and risk of decision making, they may avoid and discourage sales representatives. Consequently, they may not treat salespersons in a socially graceful manner. Persons particularly sensitive to criticism, who take the probing of prospects personally, may find that they are too "thin-skinned" to enjoy selling. Fortunately, most prospects are understanding and nice. The few that try to take advantage of their superior bargaining position are the exception and not the rule in high-level selling. Most prospects value the knowledge and professionalism of sales representatives. Just as the surgeon must overcome an aversion to bad accident cases, the sales representative must overcome an aversion to an occasional emotional confrontation, since emotions accompany decision pressure.

Relocation and Time Away from Home

Many sales jobs, such as real estate, insurance, and city territorial assignments, do not involve extensive travel or relocation. The market for industrial goods, however, may be concentrated in one area, or it may be highly scattered, depending on the good. Usually, corporate selling entails some out-of-city travel. For certain items like pollution control systems, extensive air travel may be required. Some people have deep roots in a community in terms of friends and family. Depending on the product, sales aspirants wishing limited mobility may have to make money and promotion sacrifices later in their careers. Promotion with many corpo-rations means relocating, since corporations like to foster experience in their top personnel and local openings are often limited.

The Non-Employee-Oriented Firm

Some corporations have been known to take advantage of salespersons by "milking" their best years and releasing them when they are middle-aged or older and can no longer relate to prospects because of their age. Insurance firms have been known to hire agents, expecting them to get discouraged and quit the straight commission job after they have sold up friends and contacts. Other high-pressure companies will raise quotas almost to the point of impossibility to pressure even successful sales agents out of the job. Certainly, most firms realize that trained, producing sales representatives are their most valuable asset. The more training a salesperson has, the more investment the company has in the person. The sales aspirant should therefore be sure to determine the potential employer's philosophy by finding out policies and talking to fellow employees.

SUMMARY

Persuasive power, a vital force in a free-enterprise system, has been used by many in their climb to financial success. Personal selling (which is persuasive power directed toward moving products) contributes to society by helping maintain the level of effective demand, allowing the economies of scale and specialization, encouraging innovation, and creating consumer satisfaction. Selling is becoming more of a professional activity because of the need for market cultivation and the desire to project a more favorable company image. Almost anyone wishing a selling career can find a place, since there is a wide variety of selling opportunities available. However, special rewards are awaiting creative thinkers with attractive personalities who can solve prospect problems and move a firm's products. Career sales offers freedom, personality development, a chance to work with people, and the growth afforded by continual learning. Selling, however, is hard work and sometimes it is psychologically difficult. It may require relocation and extensive traveling. Everyone should learn about selling, because persuading is a part of everyday life.

REVIEW QUESTIONS

1. What common elements do you find in the examples of success through persuasion?

2. Justify the role of sales representatives in a free-enterprise system by listing their contributions to the economy.

3. What factors contribute to the sales representative's professional image?

4. Compare and contrast order-takers with innovative sales representatives.

5. What is a missionary sales representative?

6. A prospective salesperson should look for a sales job with a company that has products that are easy to sell. Comment.

7. What are the differences between door-to-door selling and computer selling?

8. What do salespersons do besides talk to prospects?

9. What are the advantages and disadvantages of selling as a career?

APPLICATION QUESTIONS

1. Give examples of situations that you might encounter today where you could use persuasion to good advantage.

2. Would you rather work for a retail, wholesale, or manufacturing firm? Why?

3. Find two examples of successful persons in selling. Explain how or why you think they became successful.

INCIDENTS

1–1

Joe and Larry are talking about entering the community college next year and their prospective majors.

Larry: Joe, I wish you would major in sales with me.

Joe: Why? You'll be sorry you took that sales stuff. Why don't you take accounting, like me? There isn't much demand for salesmen here.

Larry: How about Old Man Simons and his furniture store? He's got the biggest house in town, and he made it all with his store. He didn't have any more than I have, when he started out.

Joe: Yeah, but what kind of business would fit in here now that isn't already here?

Larry: Well, I was just telling you what could be done. I would probably start out working for some outfit like L&R Distributors. I understand Don Pettit, who has been selling for them for only three years now, made over $20,000 last year.

Joe: Yes, Larry, but that guy is never home and travels all the time.

Larry: There were some insurance recruiters at the college last spring, and Tom Crawley went with them for a salary of $700 a month while he's in training. He figures he'll make $30,000 a year in five years. There is money in it no matter how you look at it. Uncle Dan says so.

Joe: Insurance men don't do as well, though. When they get old, all the prospects are young and they have sold to all their friends. Besides, you're going to have to leave this rinky-dink place to get the big money.

Larry: Well, I like it here, but it would be exciting to live in Chicago or San José or Memphis or someplace big like that. I could come back and see you and the folks. I just don't care for a desk job in accounting where I can't move around.

Joe: What makes you think accountants sit and figure all the time? They get paid steady and well. There's a need for good accountants even here. Don't you remember the time we tried to sell those Christmas cards and what a drag that was? I made up my mind then that I wouldn't get mixed up in selling again. We wore ourselves out and got little except a hard time.

Larry: All selling isn't like that. That figure work in accounting isn't my bag. Besides, with no football scholarship next year, I can co-op in the outlet store, earn money, and find out whether I like selling or not. You'll have to wait a year to get part-time accounting money.

Joe: To each his own. At least, I'll be able to make a steady living.

QUESTIONS

1. What are some important factors Larry and Joe are not considering?

2. If you were Larry, what would you have told Joe?

3. Do you know any sales success stories that you could share?

1–2

John Flemming is four months away from graduating from Jackson State College. He is majoring in marketing and has a "B" average. He has a good personality and has been treasurer of the Marketing Club. John is presently considering a job with a nationally known cereal manufacturer. He has interviewed a personnel director of the firm, and the director indicated that John would be very favorably considered for the opening. The official said that John could start at $750 per month straight salary during a six-month training program that would involve a month's special training at the home plant. He was told that he should make about $13,000 the second year, and after four years he would have an excellent chance to become a manager with a salary approaching $20,000. Higher management levels would be compensated more, of course, and the personnel director gave John examples of several young men in upper management who were drawing salaries of over $30,000 per year. John was told that advancement usually meant relocation and that about 600 miles of traveling each week with one overnight could be expected. The job would involve service selling to retailers within a 200-mile radius of a major city. John would be expected to set up displays, help with store openings, and sell other products that are secondary lines to the cereal. The company is among the top four cereal manufacturers and has an excellent national reputation.

Would you take this job? Why or why not?
Analyze the opening in terms of its good and bad features.
What do you think of the compensation expectations?
What other things would you like to know before you would commit yourself?
Would you take a job without making other comparisons?

1–3

Denby Brandon was popular in high school and was president of the student body in his senior year at Southwestern at Memphis. He always seemed to be interested in other people and to have time to listen. Thinking that he would go into teaching, Denby continued his education and received a master of arts degree from Duke University in 1952. In that same year he moderated *Your Future Unlimited,* a Memphis local television program designed to help young people evaluate different careers. He also began his career as a life insurance underwriter. In 1955 his television series won the Sylvania Award for the best locally produced television series in the nation. But, he was to leave that behind in 1957. Because of his personality and great determination to succeed, he excelled in selling life insurance and quickly became a member of the Million Dollar Roundtable. In 1957, he accepted a general agency with Pan American Life Insurance Company and began to select and train a superior sales force scientifically.

Denby is president of Denby Brandon Enterprises, located in the Denby Brandon Building in Memphis. He is a partner in the Sabra Company, a director of Mem-Phys Corporation, and the owner of the Hazelwood Company. He raised the Pan American Agency in Memphis from seventy-fifth place in sales in the nation to first place in just four years (1957–1961). The agency's sales contribution has enabled it to win the award for being the outstanding agency in the Pan American Insurance Company. He has achieved an exceptionally low rate of salesperson turnover, because most of his salespersons are successful. Two of his famous talks are "Power for Your Purpose" and "The Secrets of Leadership." Both are on 33⅓ rpm records. He is a popular speaker in the Memphis area. He is proud to be a Certified Life Underwriter and a practicing salesman. He started with little except the ability to understand people and make them like him, a good mind, and real determination.

Would you be interested in a career like this?
In what other fields could you start from scratch financially and become extremely successful in less than a decade?

2 Strategic Selling Knowledge

The opportunities discussed in Chapter 1 can be translated into success by those prepared to meet the challenge. The following chapters are designed to give you the knowledge and direction you need to take advantage of selling opportunities.

Effectiveness and poise in selling situations are promoted when you have: (1) a broad educational background that gives you confidence in talking to people in the areas of *their* interests; (2) specialized training in representing the company and selling the company's specific products; (3) a willingness to improve yourself through self-development methods; (4) an understanding of persuasive techniques; and (5) the ability to recognize the strategic information you should have in order to use persuasive techniques effectively. A broad educational background comes from taking courses in many academic areas, having good reading habits, and having a variety of work experiences. The company for which you work should train you to apply specific selling principles needed for their product line. The remaining three requisites will be examined in this text. Chapters 3 through 7 of Part I include ideas designed to help you become successful, develop your selling personality, understand prospect thinking, and become aware of selling environments. Part II contains descriptions of tested selling techniques that can be applied to any field of persuasion. Part III deals primarily with career advancement.

This chapter features a discussion of basic strategic information every sales representative should know before interviewing customers. Strategic planning requires a knowledge of strategy-guiding definitions and a recognition of what information should be acquired to perform the selling function competently. The following areas will be analyzed:

- Strategy-guiding definitions
- Knowledge of the company and its products
- Knowledge of pricing, discounts, and buying arrangement alternatives
- Knowledge sources

STRATEGY-GUIDING DEFINITIONS

Definitions are needed to guide a salesperson's general approach to and mental preparation for selling. *Strategy* is the overall or coordinated plan for achieving goals. *Planned strategy* can be formulated from definitions that suggest the best methods for reaching selling goals. Strategic plans can be compared to basic definitions. If there are any incompatibilities between the plans and the definition, the salesperson can replan or redefine. The definition of a market, for example, is people who have a need or want for the product and who have the ability to buy it. By searching the territory for people with these qualifications, the salesperson can learn which products in the product line have the best chance of success and which products should be sold to particular prospects. The definition can be used to *qualify* or evaluate each potential prospect, because money, needs, and wants are the important elements in buying decisions.

Marketing

Marketing includes those activities that are necessary to assure that the right goods and services are moved efficiently to customers through the right routes, at the right price, and using the right promotional combination (see Figure 2.1). Personal selling strategy must be coordinated with other parts of the total marketing effort, such as pricing, delivery, and distribution elements. Your selling strategy must be compatible with advertising and other promotional decisions. In formulating strategy, the sales representative should be conscious of other marketing efforts by the firm so that all selling plans are coordinated for maximum market impact. The sales message, for example, should never contradict an advertising message. It should support any favorable statements made about the product in advertising media.

Customer Orientation

Customer orientation means focusing primary attention on satisfying the needs and wants of customers at a profit. If the firm is to survive and grow, all firm employees and all operations should reflect this philosophy. As a salesperson, it is especially important for you to remember that your primary function is to serve customers profitably. Every transaction should benefit both the seller and the buyer. Furthermore, buyers must always sense that you have a genuine interest in their needs.

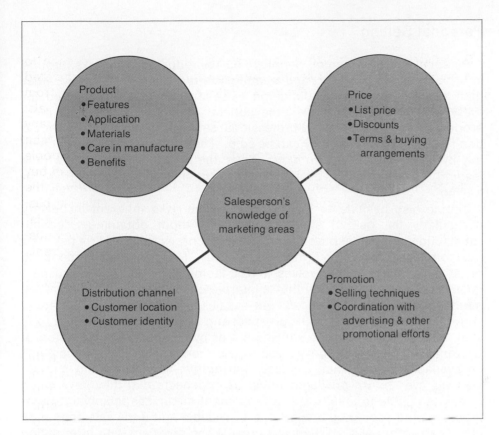

Figure 2.1 Salesperson's Knowledge of the Marketing Mix

Persuasion

Persuasion is an open appeal, either rational or emotional, to influence someone into action or belief.[1] Particular attention should be paid to the word *emotional* in this definition. Expensive items usually cannot be sold to individuals without arousing some level of emotion. Parting with money or making a decision affecting one's position in the firm is an emotional experience for most people. Even selling industrial goods requires recognizing emotional motivations in buyers. It is extremely hard to persuade someone to buy, unless there is at least a tinge of excitement stimulated in the sales interview. This is why enthusiasm is so vital in selling—it stirs the prospect's feelings.

[1] *Webster's New World Dictionary* (New York: World Publishing, 1966), p. 1092.

Personal Selling

Personal selling is *leading* people to buy by reducing their risks through information and assurances and creating an atmosphere of harmony rather than conflict. A separate definition of selling might be formulated for every product type. However, the general definition suffices for most products and reflects today's professional selling approach. Most people don't want to admit that they can be sold. They prefer to believe that they buy by making up their own mind. Thus, the sales representative who is *leading* the customer has established the proper interview atmosphere for buying.

People also hesitate to buy because of the *risks* inherent in buying, particularly the risk of spending money without obtaining adequate satisfaction. Industrial buyers who make purchases for their firm risk their positional standing in the firm when they buy. People have a tendency to resist any change that involves a risk factor. The more the prospect receives positive *information* that is interpreted as beneficial, the more the mental risk barrier is reduced. As a sales representative, you should suggest positive benefits to the prospect and overbalance any buying risks with the risks of losing the satisfaction of ownership. The definition of personal selling should remind you to use the prestige of your company, its available maintenance services, warranties, and, in certain circumstances, even return privileges to *assure* prospects that they have much to gain and little to lose. A trial arrangement minimizes financial loss for the buyer and should be offered if it is available and if the sale cannot be closed any other way. When you provide the prospect with information and assurances, you should remember to inspire confidence and create excitement about the idea of ownership.

The sales confrontation is a conflict-of-interest situation. The salesperson is interested in persuading prospects to spend their money, and the prospects are interested in keeping their money until they are sure they are gaining the best value. You must set a congenial atmosphere for the interview. You can create *harmony* by establishing rapport with the prospect, by being a good listener, and by making sure the prospect views you as a friend instead of an antagonist. Gaining from an argument is so rare in selling that it is best never to argue. This does not mean that you cannot challenge direct attacks on your honesty, integrity, or your firm's reputation. Many prospects view the sales interview as a "game," and unless salespersons subjugate their own personality, retain poise, and supply convincing information about solving the prospect's problems, they will be penalized and lose the sale. Therefore, this definition of selling reflects the core philosophy of this text and suggests the proper attitude for serving today's sophisticated markets.

Company Knowledge

Prospects want to know about the company standing behind the product they buy. Facts about its history, its size, its place in the industry, and its policies furnish needed assurances. The company is of particular interest to several types of customers: those who buy expensive industrial equipment that requires expert installation and servicing; those who buy products that may have to be returned; and those who purchase intangibles such as life insurance or consulting services, where firm expertise is important in obtaining the desired results. Bankruptcy in the case of an industrial-equipment company could mean improper maintenance support and loss of trade-in values, while mismanagement of an investment portfolio could mean loss of the capital invested.

The sales representative's morale, confidence, and efficiency are affected by understanding the system within which he or she works. A knowledge of the firm's history can make you feel proud and give you a sense of identification with an important tradition. It is important for a Burroughs sales representative to know, for example, about the role of Burroughs as developer of the adding machine and the corporation's commitment to the data-processing industry (see Figure 2.2, p. 40).

A sales representative should know company employees by name, particularly higher officials in the corporation, people concerned with order processing, and supporting service personnel. Knowing the names of superiors can save you embarrassment and promote your advancement. Knowing the names of order processors can facilitate communication and expedite service and delivery to customers. Acquaintance with support personnel can foster a team spirit in serving customers.

The sales representative is an agent of the company and must understand its policies and rules. Many salespersons have the power to bind their company legally, so they must be aware of corporate policies regarding offers to the buyer. Most companies have policy manuals to assure integrity in dealing with their publics. Prospects are especially interested in price and discount policies, credit policies, delivery policies, and rules about returning merchandise. This information is outlined in most policy manuals.

Product Knowledge

The product is more than a physical object (hardware). It is a "total package" that includes the purchasing environment, delivery, credit,

Burroughs had its beginning in St. Louis, Missouri, in 1886 with the first production of the adding machine by its predecessor, the American Arithmometer Company. Our worldwide operations began very shortly thereafter, with the formation of the first overseas subsidiary in England in 1896, and the first overseas manufacturing plant in Nottingham, England, in 1898.

In 1904, the Company moved its United States operations to Detroit, Michigan, which has been the location of its World Headquarters ever since.

Burroughs products have grown from the original adding machine to a broad range of data processing equipment and services. Our products include large, medium, and small-scale computer systems; business mini-computers; peripheral equipment; terminal products and systems; data preparation products; small application machines; program products; business forms and supplies; custom products, and electronic components.

Today, we are a major company in the data processing industry—an industry which some predict will be the largest in the world by the end of this century. We are a worldwide company employing over 48,000 people. We have engineering and manufacturing facilities in nine countries, and our products are supplied in more than 120 countries.

Burroughs growth has been particularly rapid in recent years, as illustrated by our financial progress. Since 1963, worldwide revenue has grown from $391 million to $1.284 billion. During the same period, net income has risen from $8.5 million to $115.9 million.

Burroughs World Headquarters in Detroit is located on a site that has been the Company's home since 1904.

Source: *Burroughs in Brief*, a company publication to acquaint customers and other interested publics with the history and products of the Burroughs Corporation. Burroughs Corporation, Detroit.

Figure 2.2   A Brief History of the Burroughs Corporation

installation, training in usage, warranties, advertising, maintenance, and other services. The product is the entire unit offering to the consumer— the sum total of satisfactions the buyer expects to derive from its use. The physical object, if one exists, is meaningful only in terms of the satisfaction it provides. The product plus all its services is known as the *offering*.

Why Product Knowledge Is Important. The key ingredient to professionalism in selling is knowledge of the product. Expert buyers such as engineers and purchasing agents complain that vague knowledge of the product is a great weakness of many sales representatives. Buyers often have to justify purchasing products in detail, and they are unable to do so if the salesperson lacks knowledge about the product. Medical doctors sell medical services, and if they don't know the product, their patients are in danger. Even a deficient selling personality may be overlooked if the salesperson is an expert in understanding how the product can be applied to prospect needs. If you, as a sales representative, project confidence and enthusiasm based on product knowledge, the prospect will gain confidence in the offer. Given full information on the product, the prospect can visualize the ideal use of the product and overcome the risk barrier. In addition, salespersons who confront the silent type of prospect never need to be at a loss for words. They can make a smooth presentation based on product information and specifics instead of generalities. The mark of the unprofessional salesperson is a loss for words or constant use of meaningless adjectives like ''wonderful,'' ''outstanding,'' and ''terrific.'' As a salesperson, you will be asked the most searching questions about your product offering, and ignorance will keep you from closing many sales. If you sell a line of complex products requiring diligent study, product knowledge may be your greatest challenge (see Figure 2.3, p. 42). Some companies completely revamp their product lines every few years to keep up in the frantic technology race and to provide a real competitive advantage.

Manufacturing Facts. The prospective buyer may appreciate information about research, the quality of input materials, the care taken in manufacturing, the skilled labor involved, tests the product can stand,

"*That price is for our stripped down model. With options including tinted nose cone, chrome finish, and our super Deluxe T-67 rocket engine, the price is $7,500,000.00 complete. Tax and license not included.*"

Reprinted from *The Saturday Evening Post* © 1976 The Curtis Publishing Company.

All customers, particularly expert buyers, are interested in important details about the product.

New NCR 399 accounting computer can function as an independent data processing system or as a satellite to larger computers. During 1972 various peripheral units were released, making the 399 one of the most versatile products ever developed by NCR.

The accounting data-process computer is complex and requires diligent study by the salesperson to understand its features, operations, and applications.

Source: *NCR Annual Report*, 1972, p. 6.

Figure 2.3

quality control standards, and other data reflecting the product's value. Many products go into production only after careful research indicates they have a relative advantage over existing offerings. The results of this research can be used to show the potential customer the special benefits incorporated into the item.

Materials used in manufacturing processes are of interest to prospective customers, because they affect the product's durability and performance and indicate its resistance to rust, temperature changes, and other detrimental environmental elements. Zenith stresses care in manufacture and skilled labor input, by advertising the craftsmanship embodied in its television sets. All the precautions taken to make and test the product should be explained to convey the idea of quality construction. For example, prospects who might question the quality of less expensive screws made abroad might accept the results of breaking-strength tests, as proof of the screws' durability as component parts. Quality-control standards also affirm the manufacturer's commitment to excellence. Purchasing agents prefer to buy from sellers with formal quality control.

If companies can prove their manufacturing experience through evidence of government contracts or long-term pioneering in the field, buyers may be impressed. An office-equipment corporation gained much of its experience in computers by making units for the space missile program. It was able to use this experience to enter the highly competitive data-processing computer market. This type of background information helps give the salesperson confidence in the offering and in the company, and both are crucial to attitude.

Product Features. The product or service itself is the focal point of the sales interview. Prospective buyers are interested in a product's characteristics and how these characteristics or features can benefit them. The salesperson who goes into an interview with inadequate product knowledge may not be able to answer the prospect's questions. Few things can end an interview faster than loss of confidence in the salesperson. Both enthusiasm and confidence stem from product knowledge. While it is important to know all features and characteristics of a product, it is imperative to know those advantages that differentiate your product from competition. Competition can actually help you sell by creating prospect interest in the product, in general. If you can show the superiority of your particular offering, you have potential for a sale. Statements like the following explain why the customer should choose your product: "This machine is 30 percent faster than any other machine on the market," or "You simply press this button to change the program on this machine, while other machines require a separate control unit for each separate application," or "Because this equipment has a special feature that allows you to print an original ledger and statement, you don't have to handle expensive and messy carbons. Your customers will be impressed with their clear copy of the invoice."

All *performance* features of your product should be discussed, because you can never be certain what will be important to the customer. Nearly every product has performance features:

- Paint sellers talk about coverability, durability, and spreadability.
- Fuel merchants speak in terms of power ingredients and additives.

- Do-it-yourself floor advertisers broadcast ease of application.
- Tissue-commercial creators demonstrate softness qualities.
- Insurance companies stress fast payments of claims.
- Food brokers use shelf life and nutritional value.
- TV dealers mention color and repair accessibility.

Some performance features of machinery and equipment are capacity, speed of operation, ease of operation, flexibility in application, operating-materials costs, infrequency of repair, operator skill needed, safety features, and low maintenance requirements.

Other facts about the total offering can be equally important. Customers who take their time making up their minds still expect to get *delivery* as soon as possible. The salesperson should be very honest about how long delivery takes and should make every effort to get the purchased item to the buyer within the promised time limits. *Warranties* reduce buying risks and should always be mentioned in sales presentations. Many appliances and machines have a service warranty, and usually, when the warranty expires, the customer may purchase a service contract on a yearly basis. When competition has indicated that its equipment doesn't need to be repaired as frequently as the equipment you are selling, you can counter with the fact that your *service contract* for each year is no higher than your competitor's (if this is true). When you sell products to middlemen for resale, *consumer advertising* may be a significant feature in your product offering. Merchants who are concerned with inventory turnover and profits want to know the extent and quality of advertising and promotional materials backing the product sales.

Often, *Consumer Reports* or other research from *independent research firms* may compare your product favorably to competition. For selling purposes, this "unbiased" information can be regarded as a part of the product's total offering.

The *price* will probably be the most asked about part of your offering. Some sales representatives have so many products to sell that they have to refer to price lists, and prices of certain raw materials and industrial goods fluctuate frequently, requiring new lists nearly every day. Naturally, it is better if you can make an offer and close the sale without having to refer to your price list. But for special orders, you must have the price list with you (see Figure 2.4).

Buyers often want a selection, so you should be able to explain how the product offered fits into the total line of products you sell and why alternative products offered by the company might also be needed by the customer. You should also tell the prospect about all the features of the product and not just the features that solve the particular problems indicated as important by the prospect. Buyers may want to trade in or sell the product later, or they may need the product for other applications

Figure 2.4   Price List* The Jan-Chem Company
Price Schedule (Institutions)—1–1–79 through 3–31–79

Jan-Towels (paper towels) 12 rolls	$ 3.00	dozen

NON-AEROSOL SPRAY CANS

Jan-Pure, Disinfectant and Deodorant	27.00	dozen
Jan-Oven-Baking Surface Cleaner	24.50	dozen
Jan-Surface Clean (all purpose)	21.00	dozen
Jan-Gleem, Glass Cleaner	20.00	dozen
Combo-Jan, Deodorant, Disinfectant, and Cleaner	22.00	dozen
Jan-Ceptic, Toilet Bowl Antiseptic	20.00	dozen
Jan-Sting Insecticide, Bees and Wasps	33.00	dozen
Jan-Kill, Insecticide	30.00	dozen
Jan-Cide, Ant and Roach Insecticide	33.00	dozen
Jan-Shine, Furniture Polish	28.00	dozen
Jan-Alum, Aluminum Polish	23.50	dozen
Jan-Panel, Paneling Renew	21.00	dozen
Jan-Elec, Electric Contact Cleaner	38.00	dozen
Jan-Strip, Paint Stripper	32.00	dozen
Jan-Degreaser	33.00	dozen
Jan-OGT, (oil, grease, and tar remover)	37.00	dozen
Jan-Back, Chalkboard Cleaner	24.50	dozen
Jan-Wax, Vinyl Wax	27.00	dozen
Jan-Vin, Vinyl Cleaner	23.00	dozen
Jan-Porce, Porcelain Cleaner	21.00	dozen

FLOOR FINISHES

Jan-Acril, Acrylic Finish (55-gallon drums†)	6.00	gallon
Jan-Gym (55-gallon drums†)	7.50	gallon

DRUM CONTAINER CLEANSER

Jan-Detergent (general) (55-gallon drums†)	5.00	gallon

HAND CLEANER

Jan-Moist Waterless (24–30 ounces)	42.00	case

SPECIAL DEALS

1 case of Jan-Moist with any $2,000 purchase
1 dozen Jan-Pure with any 5-drum–purchase floor finish

* Fictitious price list
† Ask about our discount schedule for large purchases.

in the future. The total capabilities of the product reflect its maximum potential value and help tip the scales in favor of buying. As mentioned before, some equipment is so flexible and has so many possible applications that knowing about its total use is almost impossible. Computer capabilities, for example, are limited by the human mind's inability to discover and program all jobs that the machines might accomplish. However, every salesperson is expected to know the common applications and capabilities of each unit in the entire line.

Strategic Use of Features. Features should be used to show prospects *how* they can satisfy their wants and solve their specific problems. A key selling strategy is finding out what prospective buyers want and convincing them that your product can fill their needs. You may know all the technical qualities and scientific virtues of your offering, but you must convince buyers that they will benefit from each product feature. An air conditioner, for example, may have a 15,000 BTU capacity and a sealed motor. This may be meaningless unless the buyer is convinced that it can cool a vacation cottage and does not have to be oiled. An outboard motor with 50 horsepower becomes meaningful if the potential customer learns that it can pull two skiers at 35 miles per hour. A removable printing element on a typewriter means the type can be changed easily and quickly and cleaning is much simpler. Benefits that competition cannot match are the most forceful selling points.

The good sales representative learns and uses magic phrases in such a way that prospects can visualize themselves using the product and deriving maximum satisfaction from it. Words are the tools of the selling trade, and every product has special words associated with it that cast it in a special light. Often, selling phrases can be found in advertising copy or in other company publications, but sometimes, the salesperson must learn them from experience. Examples of selling phrases are:

- Air-cooled means you are ready to go and you don't need antifreeze.
- Sleeping on a Sealy is like sleeping on a cloud.
- Gives you finished pictures in sixty seconds.
- The kind of boots the real cowboys wear.
- Just turn the knob to change the job.
- Goes from 0 to 60 in six seconds.
- Lucite turns you loose.
- All you add is love.
- Finger-licking good.
- Shake and bake.
- Squeezably soft.

Notice that nearly every one of these phrases translates some feature into a benefit. Notice also that each suggests a picture of the buyer using the product under ideal circumstances.

Certain words other than those used in key phrases must also be learned. Above all, the salesperson does not want to hint, by using poorly selected words, that the product has certain weaknesses. Words like "cheap" and "substitute" should not be used in association with most products. Learning the right sequence of words and phrases to convince the prospect is also important. Finally, the salesperson should learn and use the vocabulary used in the business. This shows that the salesperson is a part of the industry and speaks the language of the trade.

To fit benefits to prospect problems, you must know how prospective buyers can use the product to their best advantage. Salespersons selling minicomputers, for example, sell the "hardware" only in connection with accounting system ideas that will improve the prospect's data processing. Systems sales representatives have to study good mechanized accounting operations and know more than their prospects to justify a recommended change of procedure. Because many buyers look to the professional salesperson for consulting advice, the salesperson has to know how the product will fit into the operation of each customer. If you recommend the wrong product in your line, and if the customer discovers you had a more appropriate product for his or her operation, you may lose that account in respect to future sales. It is impossible to know too much about the product, its benefits, and its applications.

Competitive Product Knowledge. Foreign and domestic competition has increased in nearly every industry over the last few years. It is now even more important for sales representatives to know what offers are being made to their prospects by other sales representatives. If you sell, you need to know almost as much about the competition as you do about your own product. You need to know features, benefits, delivery time, warranties, maintenance requirements, services, competitive strategy, and prices. Many large companies analyze competitive products. They collect information about strengths and weaknesses just as coaches send out scouts to find out about the plays of the other team before devising a game plan for that opponent. Competitive information is relayed to salespersons at sales meetings, conventions, and through special firm memorandums. Even if the company you work for is small, you can learn much about your competition from your customers, your fellow sales representatives, and from advertisements. Salespersons should be wary, however, of information given by prospects. In an effort to make a deal, prospects may stretch the truth, or they may be mistaken about the competitive offer. In trying to get the best bargain, prospects may quote a price lower than the competitive salesperson actually offered, or they may be comparing the price of a competitive product of lower quality to a price you quoted on an item of higher quality.

KNOWLEDGE OF PRICING, DISCOUNTS, AND BUYING ARRANGEMENT ALTERNATIVES

The basic attitude of your firm's executives toward price and price concessions will affect your selling strategy. The following discussion of basic pricing, discounts, and buying arrangements is designed to show you possible alternatives in price and price offering.

Basic Pricing

Mature products are sold on a market basis, an above-market basis, or a below-market basis. If your prices are above competition, you have to prove a relative advantage in your offering—you have to sell quality. If your prices are below competition, you should emphasize price in your presentation and remember that your firm may expect more sales volume from you. If your price is competitive and your offering is just about the same as your competitor, you should emphasize your personality and your company's reputation. New products are either sold on a skimming or penetration price strategy. "Skimming" means selling at high prices to elite buyers and lowering the prices later to tap additional buyers. Plain plastic ball-point pens sold for $15 each when they were first introduced. Great care must be taken to select prospects and to sell the innovation's unique characteristics. Sometimes new, mass-produced products are priced to penetrate the market. This means the product is expected to be sold "en masse" and the innovating company's market share (portion of the market) is to be enlarged or maintained. In this case, volume can be gained by spreading the information by telephone or direct mail and cultivating a broad range of prospects. Specific price policies and psychology are beyond the scope of this text, but persons contemplating going into business for themselves should know many pricing alternatives. Price is a central consideration in the minds of most buyers.

Discounts

Every buyer expects a discount, since most firms give quantity, trade, or cash discounts. Quantity discounts are given to a buyer for purchasing in multiple units or bulk. They must be given strictly according to company schedules or legal trouble may follow. The pattern of agencies, from producer to consumer, through which goods must move is termed the marketing channel. Trade discounts are given to wholesalers and retailers because of their position in the marketing channel. A bigger trade discount goes to the wholesaler. Make sure that you classify the buyer's channel position correctly. Cash discounts are given for paying bills before certain dates, but to the buyer they are seen as reductions in list price. Discounts reduce risks by reducing the cost of the product. Sometimes advertising allowances or special services are given with purchases. Again, it is important that company policy be strictly followed to avoid legal problems.

Buying Arrangements

Many buyers have a definite need for the product and can mentally justify buying it; however, they may not have the money. The buyer in bad financial condition obviously needs profits or cost-saving products

THE SATURDAY EVENING POST

"And now I suppose you're wondering if you can afford it."

Reprinted by permission of the artist, Joseph Zeis.

The salesperson should know all buying terms that make the product affordable to the prospect.

more than the buyer with large cash reserves. Most large concerns can offer several options to pay for equipment. It is imperative for you to know these options or for you to be able to direct the buyer to a bank plan or financial concern that lends money. Some corporations are stricter than others as to which customers will be extended credit. The salesperson must coordinate selling plans with the credit manager's policies. Usually, durable goods can be purchased on an installment plan, or they can be rented. The buyer will want to know about interest charges, and you must be able to figure out accurately what the monthly payments will be. If your calculations of the monthly payments are accidentally too small, buyers may cancel the order when they find out the price is higher. If your calculations of the installment payments are too large, they may not buy from you in the first place. Some buyers would rather rent equipment, because rent can be deducted as a cost of doing business and may mean important tax savings, while total equipment costs can be deducted only in part—one year of depreciation. In justifying the deal, monthly benefits may be directly compared to monthly costs, or the amount of time in which cost-saving equipment can pay for itself (payback) may be an important consideration. Some sales representatives can control price by offering seconds or demonstrators, by allowing more or less for trade-ins, or by offering used products. Remember, your firm wants you to be a profitable member of the sales team. Avoid making too many concessions too early. The prospect to whom you sold your low-priced, "fighting brand" may have needed and wanted the first-line product, and price is forgotten long before a durable product needs to be replaced.

KNOWLEDGE SOURCES

To be efficient, sales representatives need quick access to information sources. Knowing where to find needed information saves time, promotes learning, and frees the mind to store those important facts that must be recalled during the interview. A wealth of information can be obtained from company literature, sales meetings and conferences, outside material, personal sources, and careful observation.

Company Literature

Many companies, particularly large companies, publish policy manuals; sales-training texts; product-information manuals; visual-aids materials, such as charts and diagrams; newsletters; advertising copy; annual reports; research reports; and other matter designed to supply the salesperson with fast information. Each company varies the format of these references, and smaller companies usually provide fewer publications. Beginning salespersons should make a special point to locate everything the company has that will help them learn the business. This may not be easy, since most companies have sources in many different places and not in a centralized library.

New trainees should spend hours looking through the manuals to select information they might use and become thoroughly familiar with each source. They should read about the firm's historical heritage, philosophies, and role in the industry. They should look into employee policies that affect them, such as retirement, vacations, sick leave, and compensation regulations. They should study the company's order-handling, price, discount, credit, returns, allowance, service, and complaint-handling policies. These policies represent the company's experience in dealing with its publics, and they insure that employees will handle recurring situations uniformly and legally.

Some manuals or publications will also contain in-depth product information. Detailed chemical, mechanical, or descriptive product analyses may be available to give beginners insight into product composition and benefits. Salespersons should locate and study charts, diagrams, and other visual aids available for learning and selling. Competitive product information may also be found in current company newsletters. Annual reports contain trends, products, and the future direction of the company. Product and market research may be available on request, and advertisements such as the one shown in Figure 2.5 (p. 52) are often on display racks in the sales office.

Sales training texts may be part of a formal training course. These materials embody the company's experiences in salesperson-customer relationships and contain product information, role-playing situations, sample sales presentations, cases, and ways to handle common problems. This helps the trainee adjust previous information and experience to the special problems of selling the specific company offering.

Sales Meetings and Conferences

Sales meetings are usually held when calling on prospects is least productive. This varies with particular sales situations. In the game of selling, sales meetings may be considered strategic half-time meetings designed to tie the sales force together, discuss selling strategy, and assess goal accomplishments. New information is often introduced about company and competitive products, and selling experiences are shared. Yearly sales conferences are usually more formal meetings, where company experts offer explanations of new corporate commitments, new applications, new products, and revised selling strategy.

the "MIGHTY MIKE" MODEL MM5

PORTABLE SUPER-POWERED LOUDSPEAKER

HAMILTON ELECTRONICS CORP.

* Engineered for extra powerful voice projection—to be heard as far as half a mile away. Exceptional clarity and "understandability"!

* Ruggedly built for outstanding durability and dependability. Highly resistant to impact, all outdoor climatic conditions, constant heavy duty usage.

* Compact, easy to carry, weighs only 3½ lbs. Built-in pistol type grip and carrying strap included.

* 15 Watt output power—solid state transistorized. Provides instant operation—no warm up.

* Detachable dynamic cardioid microphone, protective microphone cover, plus extension cable with "on-off" switch, and batteries.

* Volume control knob permits increase or decrease of "loudness" as desired.

Bell Diameter: 9¾";
Length: 16½".
Weight: 3½ lbs.

Don't compare the MIGHTY MIKE with ordinary portable loudspeaker systems! Engineered and constructed expressly for outdoor and emergency use, this unit provides extra powerful voice projection — to be heard above the din of any crowd — in any field — up to a ½ mile distance! Lightweight and compact—it travels anywhere and so ruggedly built — steel and molded plastic — it resists impact, all weather conditions — dust, dirt, sand, etc. like no other unit on the market today!

INSTANTLY CONVERTIBLE TO PORTABLE PUBLIC ADDRESS SYSTEM

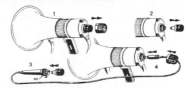

The "MIGHTY MIKE" can be instantly converted into a portable PA System by simply removing the microphone module and inserting the microphone extension cable. (See Fig.) Note: The microphone extension cable is (optional)

HAMILTON ELECTRONICS CORP.

2003 West Fulton Avenue, Chicago, Illinois 60612 / 312-421-5442

Figure 2.5

Outside Material

Useful noncompany materials can be found in libraries, trade association offices, magazine articles, media advertisements, competitive annual reports, and publications of other companies. Public and university libraries contain census data with details about territories and markets, books on selling, and current magazine articles concerning the industry, products, trends, and selling in general. Reference librarians, periodical guides, and card catalogues will help you find what you need at the library. Many books on success theory, magazines for sales representatives, and sometimes even tapes, records, and films may be examined. Secretaries in trade association offices collect information about the industry that may include competitive comparisons and standings (market share) of firms.

Sales & Marketing Management magazine and *Industrial Distribution* are designed for sales representatives. *Sales & Marketing Management* covers selling costs, comparative salaries, current selling methods, territorial potential indexes, and other important data. *Industrial Distribution* is of particular interest to the industrial salesperson. *Consumers Research Bulletins* and *Consumer Reports* give detailed comparisons of competing consumer products and make purchase-decision recommendations to customers. If your product is favorably compared and recommended by either of these supposedly unbiased sources, you can use the source to help sell your prospects. Media advertisements show the selling benefits of competitive products, while competitive annual reports feature the progress and new offerings of competitors. The Bell Telephone Company furnishes booklets on telephone selling techniques. The Success Motivation Institute at Waco sells tapes and records on success theory. For a fee, private research corporations like Nielsen will furnish company sales trends.

Personal Sources

Sales managers, fellow sales representatives, customers, repair personnel, competitors, and others can be good information sources. You should ask people questions and keep your ears open. Sales managers are expected to know the answers or to know where to find them. Senior sales representatives can give junior sales representatives information and pointers on technique. There is no substitute for watching an innovative salesperson get an order from a prospect. Customers are the best source of information on customer problems and often on competitive selling techniques and offerings. Repair personnel know when the old product is wearing out and can tell you facts about the product you should know. Even competitive salespersons may give you information about customers they can't serve. Almost anybody can help you prospect, if you know how to ask questions and listen.

Careful Observation

You can get a vast amount of information by watching other sales representatives sell, looking for changes in the territory that could lead to new prospects (see Photo 2.1), and observing prospects' environment and body movements for clues about their interests and attitudes. Although each sales personality is different, a clearer concept of the sales interview interaction is gained from following the strategy of a senior salesperson in action. Machine sales representatives who do not watch their territory for new construction or fire damage are missing an important source of prospects. The insurance sales representative who does not clip marriage and birth announcements may not be observing carefully. More will be said about observing prospects' environment and body movements in later chapters.

Photo 2.1
The salesperson should learn to observe changes in the territory. What opportunities to sell products will result from the construction of this new building?

This chapter was written to help you identify the areas of knowledge and self-development that are important to a successful selling career. More specifically, it was designed to show you what basic information must be acquired before you can formulate selling strategy effectively. The sooner you can set your learning and development goals, the faster you can progress. Then, you will be able to assimilate more from the text, from your formal education, from your social experiences, and from the company environment.

The requisites for good selling are a broad educational background, specialized training in selling the company's products, a disposition toward self-improvement, a knowledge of selling techniques, and an awareness of what basic information is necessary for selling strategy. Definitions can help guide selling strategy. By knowing the definition of *marketing,* you can help coordinate selling strategy with other parts of the marketing effort. By knowing the definition of *consumer orientation,* you can increase your awareness of the importance of both profits and consumer satisfaction. By knowing the definition of *persuasion,* you can remind yourself that both emotion and reason are important in selling appeals. And by knowing the definition of *selling* you understand that *leading* (not driving) people to buy, by reducing their risks, in a harmonious atmosphere, is the desirable approach.

The aspiring salesperson should also know what specific facts must be learned about the company, the products, the competition, the price, and the buying terms before interviewing prospects. Prospects may be vitally interested in the financial strength, market position, technical experience, policies, and reputation of the company. They are interested in the total product—the total of satisfactions that can be gained from using the product. While technical product features are important to expert buyers, all buyers want to know the details about what the product can do to satisfy their specific needs. Buyers should always be told about the competitive advantages of the product. In this regard, the salesperson should study the product features, the prices, the services, and the policies of competition to be able to offer ethical comparisons and to devise strategy to win the sale. All customers want to know about price and many about buying terms. Buying arrangements, discounts, and rental arrangements can help induce customers to use your product.

Strategic information can be found in company literature, at sales meetings and conferences, in noncompany publications, by asking knowledgeable persons, and by careful observation. Policy manuals, product manuals, and advertising can reveal much product information. Notes taken in sales meetings and conferences may also be valuable. Libraries have a variety of sources of information about markets and competitive operations, and customers and competitive advertising can furnish much about competition. If you know what important strategic information you need to learn when you take a job with a company, you will be able to find it, learn it, and use it faster and more effectively.

REVIEW QUESTIONS

1. Define the following terms and explain how each can guide and help the salesperson:
   a. Market
   b. Customer orientation
   c. Persuasion
   d. Personal selling
   e. Offering

2. List ways the salesperson can create harmony and reduce the conflict-of-interest situation in an interview.

3. In what ways can the sales representative reduce the risks of the buyer—that is, through what specific types of information and assurances?

4. What does a product include in terms of the total offering?

5. Give three reasons why product knowledge is so important.

6. What are the important facts the salesperson should know about the product offering to give the prospective buyer full information?

7. What is the best way to prevent competition from winning your prospect?

8. Why is it permissible to name the competitor in a television advertisement but not permissible to do it during a sales interview?

9. What are the differences between quantity, trade, and cash discounts?

10. Explain the ways in which buyers can obtain merchandise without paying cash for the whole amount?

11. What are the three basic pricing strategy levels for mature products?

12. New products may be sold by "skimming" or "penetrating the market." Explain these two alternatives.

13. Describe the kinds of company literature available to the salesperson.

14. Where might you find the following information:
    a. Characteristics of your customers
    b. Company policy on pricing
    c. Solving selling problems
    d. Company history
    e. Product analysis
    f. Books on success theory in selling

APPLICATION QUESTIONS

1. Evaluate the following: Industrial buyers are also emotional buyers, because their position in the firm is affected by important purchases. But, they must always justify product purchases to themselves and others through rational buying criteria or motives.

2. What manufacturing facts might a prospect want to know about a cash register? a computer? a CB radio?

3. List the magic words and phrases that show benefits and suggest pleasant uses of each of five currently advertised products.

4. Make up original phrases for Wall-O-Vision, a TV that projects pictures on a screen.

INCIDENTS

2–1

David Donelson is looking at a new car on the lot—here comes salesman James Longodds.

James:	That's a nice car, isn't it? It's our deluxe model.
Donelson:	It should be, at that stickor price.
James.	If you think that's high, we have one inside for about $500 more that has all the extras.
Donelson:	What does this little knob here on the dashboard do?
James:	I'm not sure. If you'll wait a minute, I'll go in and ask the sales manager.

Donelson:	That's O.K. It unlocks the trunk.
James:	If we gave you $400 off of list, would you buy it today?
Donelson:	I don't know what it has on it yet. What kind of city mileage does this one get?
James:	Oh, about sixteen miles per gallon, but it should do twenty on the road, I think.
Donelson:	What kind of engine does it have?
James:	Do you mean what cubic-inch displacement? That's in one of the manuals inside.
Donelson:	I see. It's here on the sticker.
James:	Pretty color, isn't it?
Donelson:	Does it come in a medium green?
James:	We only have two greens, forest and moss. But I don't think we have any on the lot.
Donelson:	*(starting the car)* It sounds good. How do you adjust the seat?
James:	I'm not sure. Isn't there a little lever on the side? By the way, I'm James Longodds. I'm sorry I don't know more about this model, but I've just been working here a month.
Donelson:	James, I'm David Donelson, coowner of this dealership.

QUESTIONS

1. Evaluate James' knowledge of strategic facts that would have helped him sell the product.

2. What should he have known about the product before attempting to sell it?

3. Should he have made it a special point to meet the coowner before now?

2–2

Marjorie Jowers is a manufacturer's representative who specializes in selling women's apparel for clothing manufacturers on a commission basis. In the clothing industry, it is common to allow department stores and other buyers to purchase on credit up to a certain amount. The "line of credit" or credit limit depends on the merchants' financial condition and credit standing. Halperin's Department Store is one of Marjorie's best customers and has always enjoyed a good credit rating. Marjorie persuaded Sam Halperin to buy a line of ladies' coats on credit for $30,000, which was $5,000 over the store's credit limit with Claybaugh Manufacturing Company. Claybaugh granted the extra $5,000 credit to Halperin's, after Halperin returned a fully answered, detailed questionnaire about the store's financial condition. Unfortunately, Halperin's had a very disappointing fall season, and the coats didn't sell too well. Sam Halperin didn't pay his bill to Claybaugh on the due date but planned to pay it five days late after Saturday's sales revenues came in. The new credit manager with Claybaugh sent a very short and tactless letter to Sam Halperin the day after the due date. The letter read:

Dear Mr. Halperin:

As you know, Claybaugh allowed you to exceed your credit limit on the purchase of the $30,000 worth of ladies' coats. We demand this sum forthwith. To delay further would jeopardize your credit rating, and if payment is not tendered within ten days from the date of this letter, legal proceedings will be instituted.

Sincerely,

Albert Whittle, Credit Manager
Claybaugh Manufacturing Company

Mr. Halperin called Marjorie long distance and explained the situation. He could not understand the attitude of Claybaugh's credit manager, since he had been just a little late before with another manufacturer but had been treated courteously by the other supplier. Marjorie is over 200 miles away and has a full schedule of prospects.

How should she handle the situation?

2-3

Hubert Steen reported for work at the branch sales office of the American Office Machine Company four weeks ago. The branch manager introduced him at that time to the other salespersons and company personnel, gave him some of the manuals, and told him to try to prepare himself for selling machine accounting systems. He has studied the manuals, watched the repair personnel fix equipment, and helped deliver some equipment when asked to do so. Everyone seems so busy, and Hubert is perplexed. Few people ask him to do anything, and Ron Johnson, the branch manager, is busy and seems to have forgotten all about him. He's tired of looking at the manuals, because much of the equipment is so complicated. Having just graduated from college, he's anxious to go out and sell. He has tried to stay out of the way, but he really doesn't know how to prepare himself further. He doesn't have a territory yet, and only four times has a senior sales representative asked him to go on a call. Of course, he is drawing a straight salary until after his formal training in Chicago, which doesn't start for six months.

If you were Hubert, what would you do?
How would you spend your time?
What do the branch manager and the others expect him to do?

3 Success Theory

Success in selling takes more than just a knowledge of facts and common selling practices. It depends heavily on attitude and other personality factors. The next few chapters are designed to give you information that will help you become a successful salesperson rather than a salesperson with just a mechanical knowledge of selling procedures. There is a need to relate to sales experience and to build on it, and a significant part of sales experience is success theory.

Success theory is a collection of principles that has been built using success ideas of outstanding men and women. The basic assumption is that anyone who follows the advised techniques and philosophies with the proper faith and self-discipline can achieve success, wealth, fame, rank, or the accomplishment of other personal goals. Books, records, and speeches on success ideas have been marketed to practicing salespersons for millions of dollars. The problem is that often good ideas have been hidden in a forest of obvious and conflicting suggestions, vague statements, and repeated slogans. The discussion of success theory in this text is the result of sifting through success literature for dominant ideas. As you will see, much of the core of success theory is *personality factors*. While this chapter will treat the major success elements, the next chapter will focus on personality development. A review of the larger body of success theory indicates ten key elements:

- Goal definition
- Methodology and planning
- Attitude
- Awareness of dynamics
- Motivation and self-image building
- Questioning and listening
- Dominant-theme focus
- Enthusiasm
- Personality development
- Persuasiveness

61

Copyright 1976, Universal Press Syndicate.

GOAL DEFINITION

Goal definition (expressing major purposes in concise guiding statements) is so fundamental that most success theorists emphasize it. However, it is widely violated in practice. Determining precise definitions of objectives early provides both direction and motivation. Napolean Hill, in the classic *Think and Grow Rich,* writes that purpose is the basis for getting anything done. A person can achieve whatever he or she "conceives and believes."[1] He suggests that after definite major goals are written down in detail, they should be repeated aloud morning and night with future success visualized.[2] Writing and reviewing major goals focuses both conscious and subconscious efforts on achieving them. The writing out of yearly, weekly, and daily goals on index cards frees the mind for accomplishing those goals.

While well-directed efforts result in achieving most purposes, setting the *right* objectives and selecting the most important subobjectives can be difficult. The sales representative should spell out objectives in detail with regard to sales, demonstrations, interviews, services, collections, and product knowledge. More will be written about objectives in later chapters. However, pursuing these goals alone is a narrow approach. The

[1] Napolean Hill, *Think and Grow Rich* (New York: Hawthorn, 1967), p. 31.
[2] *Ibid.,* pp. 77–78.

sales representative who is success-oriented should be interested in balanced physical, mental, and spiritual development. Strength and health are important assets, and the salesperson without stamina and vitality cannot be as effective as the person who enters the interview with a vibrancy based on a vigorous physical condition. Mental outlook and positive thinking are emphasized throughout success theory, and having definite learning goals helps assure growth, optimism, and confidence. Spiritual development is a basis for high-level motivation and healthy personality adjustment. According to such success theorists as Norman Vincent Peale[3] and W. Clement Stone,[4] guilt, frustration, worry, and an unhealthy self-image, which destroy so many salespersons, can be overcome by a healthy spiritual life.

Success in achieving the wrong goal can be a greater problem than failure to achieve the right goal. Too many sales representatives have "succeeded" only to realize that their efforts have been wasted on an unworthy objective. While early decisions on goals are important, it is essential for salespersons to have enough prior information and experience to set goals that will be worthwhile and productive. People fail, too, because their goals conflict, they are unwilling to decide which goals are important, and they hesitate to unify their efforts into one basic purpose. It is important to realize from the very beginning that accomplishing most goals requires sacrifices of time and effort. The price to be paid must be predetermined as part of the goal-defining process.

METHODOLOGY AND PLANNING

Mathematics, statistics, accounting, and other step-by-step method courses are designed to facilitate planning. In athletics, the player who follows tested methods of procedure has a good chance to excel, because few are willing to do this. In selling, study and practice of the tested methods for prospecting, routing, approaching, answering objections, and closing sales increase the chances for success. A planned effort is more organized and unified than an unplanned approach.

Good method may be superior to high intelligence in reaching goals. Industrialist Charles Schwab is reported to have sent consultant Ivy Lee a $25,000 check for the following simple idea: "At the beginning of each day determine what are the really essential things you should do. You'll

[3] Norman Vincent Peale, *Enthusiasm Makes the Difference* (Englewood Cliffs, N.J.: Prentice-Hall, 1967), pp. 60–83.

[4] W. Clement Stone, *The Success System That Never Fails* (Englewood Cliffs, N.J.: Prentice-Hall, 1962), p. 117.

get more accomplished if you organize your tasks, doing them one at a time in the order of their importance."[5] While this type of goal organizing is an excellent way to begin planning, many fail because they do not consider a wide range of alternate goals before selecting the best route to their objectives. The concept of expanding your choice of goals for selection depends on both method and intelligence and might be called *breadth of consideration.* Going to other people who know and asking for information is a way of expanding choices. Committee discussions can expand your range of alternatives. The following methods and ideas are also designed to increase the number of choices to be considered and to aid in the selection of the right choice:

- Schnelle's Complex Problem-Solving Method
- The creative process
- Learning methods
- Systems thinking

Schnelle's Complex Problem-Solving Method

Schnelle's Complex Problem-Solving Method encourages the use of maximum thought, concentration, and alternative consideration. Salespersons run into complex problems every day. A complex problem is a problem or group of problems that requires predicting what will probably happen in the future. Selecting an employer, making a creative sales proposal on insufficient knowledge, or even deciding on weekly routing plans can be complex problems. Schnelle recommends that the most important problem or the one easiest to solve be singled out of the problem cluster and approached separately. Perhaps the biggest difficulty is identifying the right problem to solve first. The following steps are recommended:

1. Statement of the problem
2. Statement of the facts
3. Statement of alternative courses of action
4. Advantages and disadvantages of alternative courses of action
5. Evaluation of advantages and disadvantages
6. Certainty of occurrence of advantages and disadvantages
7. Selection of the best alternative

[5] Alfred Armand Montapert, *Success Planning Manual* (Englewood Cliffs, N.J.: Prentice-Hall, 1967), p. 5.

**TABLE 3.1   ANALYSIS OF ALTERNATIVE NUMBER 1—TAKE A
JOB WITH THE XYZ COMPANY***

ITEM	Advantages CERTAINTY VALUE	CHANCE OF OCCURRENCE	ADJUSTED VALUE
Better-than-average salary	$10,000	0.8	$ 8,000
Good chance for advancement	8,000	0.7	5,600
Good management	4,000	0.9	3,600
Long training program	5,000	1.0	5,000
Executive customers	3,000	1.0	3,000
Good fringe benefits	2,000	1.0	2,000
Bonus arrangements	6,000	0.5	3,000
Value of advantages			30,200

ITEM	Disadvantages CERTAINTY VALUE	CHANCE OF OCCURRENCE	ADJUSTED VALUE
Much traveling	$ 8,000	0.9	$ 7,200
Product weak	15,000	0.7	10,500
Excessive pressure	10,000	0.8	8,000
Possible bad territory	10,000	0.4	4,000
Relocation	6,000	0.6	3,600
Value of disadvantages			33,300
Net disadvantage of alternative			(2,100)

8. Implementing the selected course of action
9. Comparing expected with actual results of the decision[6]

Steps 5 and 6, assigning values and chance of occurrence, can involve educated guessing. But, if you can force yourself to make the assignments, the procedure is not difficult. Assigning a monetary value means expressing the negative or positive value of the advantage or disadvantage in terms of money. Chance of occurrence is expressed as 1.0 for something that is certain to occur, 0.5 for something you feel has a fifty-fifty chance of occurring, and 0.1 if the chance of occurring is one out of ten. As you can see from the table, the alternative advantages and disadvantages are arranged in terms of dollar value and summated to give a total value. Table 3.1 is based on the Schnelle procedure and is an analysis of *one* alternative in career selection. In actual practice, several of these alter-

[6] Kenneth E. Schnelle, *Case Analysis and Business Problem Solving* (New York: McGraw-Hill, 1967), pp. 1 ff.
* Based on Schnelle's method

natives would be evaluated and compared. By using step-method models such as this, it is possible to approach the problem logically and to consider relevant alternatives. It is not mandatory that the alternative with the greatest positive money value be selected, but it is important that all aspects of the problem be thought out and evaluated. How well the goal path determination procedure is followed depends largely on the breadth of consideration given each detail and how real the planner makes the value assignments.

The Creative Process

Innovative salespersons must be able to use their creative facilities to the fullest to come up with new ideas and strategies. An understanding of the creative process aids inventiveness. The process involves four separate stages the *preparatory stage,* the *digestive stage,* the *incubation stage,* and the *illumination stage.*[7]

The Preparatory Stage. To be creative you must build a good general store of knowledge and be sensitive to the needs of others. In addition, it is important to accumulate facts and data concerning a specific problem while keeping an open mind. At this point there should be no attempt to put the information into neat categories, make judgments, or think deeply about the data. Creativity in making a sales proposal is enhanced by knowledge of the prospect's business problems and operations and by knowledge of product features and benefits. Putting yourself in the prospect's place by thinking in terms of his or her interests should complete the preparation.

The Digestive Stage. The next step is to work over the information and material gathered and sort it into many kinds of meaningful combinations. Attempt to uncover relationships among facts, and let the mind suggest different choices without passing any judgments. Consider *all* the possibilities and combinations, no matter how unreasonable one may seem. In a word, *meditate* on the knowledge you have.

The Incubation Stage. This stage involves giving your subconscious a chance. Put the problem out of your mind; do something else; rest on it. The subconscious organizes and suggests solutions to data input, even while you sleep or while your conscious mind is engaged in other thinking.

[7] C. H. Sandage and Vernon Fryburger, *Advertising Theory and Practice* (Homewood, Ill.: Irwin, 1975), pp. 289–291.

a. Preparatory intake of information

b. Digestion of the information

c. Incubation of the information

d. Illumination—write it down and act on it

The Illumination Stage. Suddenly the right idea will hit you—the solution will present itself. Maybe this will happen when you are eating supper or mowing the lawn. Insight comes when all the mentally stored elements come together into a recognizable whole that transfers from the subconscious into the conscious.[8] This stage is dependent on the other stages, however, and it is the preparatory input stage that is perhaps the most important. (See photos 3.1a–d.)

[8] *Ibid.*

Learning Methods

Many students who are not of superior intelligence excel because they understand how to learn. Others break learning rules and fail to realize their potential. Since sales representatives must be learners to succeed, you should be aware of techniques that help you save time in acquiring knowledge. To spend time looking over study material with your eyes while your mind is far away is rationalizing, not learning. Learning is *the art of asking yourself questions and providing the answers*. If the questions are comprehensive and realistic, this forces you to think about the material. Some forms of "motorization," such as writing, organizing, or saying the material to be learned aloud, aids retention. Repetition is important for remembering the answers to questions you have asked yourself. Also important is constructing a logical framework on which you can hang all the elements to be learned and see all the parts in their correct relationships with each other.

For greater learning efficiency, periods of rest must be alternated with periods of concentration. The subconscious, which works during rest, must be allowed to work. Learners who work hour after hour or all night without rest are not using their time to best advantage. A tired mind loses much of its ability to recall and organize. Giving yourself a reward after each thirty- or forty-minute period may help. A positive attitude is essential. Attitude is perhaps the most important factor in learning besides intelligence. Many learners are mentally blocked from understanding material simply because they suggest to themselves that they are unable to master the material. Of course, a quiet atmosphere containing few distractions, good lighting, and firm study furniture is helpful. Organizing and summarizing the material at the end of each study period initiates review and again forces you to repeat the answer and think more about the material. Finally, goal setting and planning on index cards, including time scheduling, are relevant to productive learning. Allow at least 10 percent reserve time, since some learning projects take longer than you might estimate (see Figure 3.1).

Systems Thinking

A system is a group of parts (like an automobile engine) combined to accomplish a certain purpose. The systems thinker reasons in terms of the total relationships among the parts of the system and considers the effects of any introduced change on all elements in the system. Champion chess players *systematize* their strategy and visualize the many possible moves that comprise the game plan. The amateur pool player shoots one shot at a time without regard to the next shot, while the professional looks

Figure 3.1   Index-Card Planning

STEP 1:
List activities. Then number each according to order.

```
             Things to do Monday

  1    Get brakes fixed on car
  7    Call John Davis (real estate broker)
  4    Mail package to California
  5    Mail film to Chicago
  8    Return books to library
 10    Study for product exam
  6.   Call on scheduled accounts
  3    Proposal for Callis Company
  2    Check air accommodations to Florida
  9    Get secretary's birthday present
```

STEP 2:
List in order. Then check off when completed.

```
             Things to do Monday

 ✓   1.  Leave car at garage - ride with Bill
 ✓   2.  Call airlines office (Florida)
 ✓   3   Write proposal letter - Callis Company
 ✓   4   Put California package in office mail
 ✓   5   Put Chicago film in office mail
 ✓   6   Call on scheduled accounts
**   7   Call John Davis from office BUT CALL TOMORROW
 ✓   8   Drop by library on way home
 ✓   9   Drop by gift shop on way home
 ✓  10.  Study for exam.
```

ahead stategically and makes sure the cue ball winds up in place for succeeding shots. The systems-thinking physician foresees the effects of the medicine given to cure one body system on all body systems. The excellent thinker in every situation thinks in terms of the total effect of any planned action. Innovative salespersons must accordingly think beyond the direct effects of actions and contemplate secondary and long-range effects. They must view the prospective buyer in the buyer's operating system, which is the buyer's company. The market must be viewed as a related group of prospects, and the sales representative must realize that selling to key people in a community will influence the ability to sell to other prospects and possibly start a snowballing effect. The sales representative must view his or her product line as a system of products and determine how this system might be sold to fill a corresponding system of buyer needs. Representatives, like chess masters, must anticipate competitive moves and counter those moves strategically. Representatives must also be aware that their firm is a system operating toward the common goal of profits, and they should realize that all sales actions affect this overall system and their positions in it. Systems thinking, then, involves taking a total view of one's problems and opportunities and thinking beyond it, by evaluating the effects of a planned series of moves on every component of the system.

Using Models. A great aid to systems thinking is the model. A model is a simplification of a real thing, intended to clarify the important relationships between its parts. Models can be expressed mathematically, verbally, or physically. A model train is a physical model, which may help a young boy understand more about railroading and the systems involved. A graph is a model that an insurance sales representative can use to explain to his or her prospects the relationships between Social Security and insurance needed to produce a given retirement income for an elderly widow. A securities sales representative may dramatize the long-run upward trend in stock values by a model showing the overall rise in the Dow Jones Index over the past several decades. The sales representative assumes the role of teacher in communicating complex information, and simple models that outline important relationships can facilitate these explanations.

ATTITUDE

An attitude is a tendency to respond in a certain way. Attitudes grouped together in consistent patterns make up traits, and traits are a major part of total personality. While attitudes will be treated again in the next

Salesmen must think positively to succeed.

chapter and throughout the book, an overview is necessary because of the special emphasis placed on attitudes by success theorists. Napolean Hill and W. Clement Stone's book *Success Through a Positive Mental Attitude* is indicative of the importance placed on attitudes.[9] Many attitudes are treated, but five stand out in success theory:

- An attitude of faith
- A service attitude
- A team attitude
- A self-improvement attitude
- An efficiency-improvement attitude

An Attitude of Faith

An attitude of faith is primary. There must be a belief in the product, a belief in the company, and a belief in yourself. Faith is promoted by constantly suggesting success to the subconscious mind.[10] Salespersons entering the interview with a defeatist attitude convey to the prospect the idea that something is wrong with the proposal to buy or that the value of the product is low. The cowardly sales representative, in fact, is the theme of many comedy characterizations on television. The prospect becomes infected with pessimism and embarrassment instead of excitement about the product and doesn't buy. Realistic optimism often fulfills its own prophecy in selling, and belief is one of the strongest motivational forces.

[9] Napolean Hill and W. Clement Stone, *Success Through a Positive Mental Attitude* (*Englewood Cliffs, N.J.: Prentice-Hall, 1960*), *pp. 17–20.*

[10] Hill, *Think and Grow Rich, op. cit.,* p. 71.

A Service Attitude

Frank Bettger states that a service attitude is the most important secret of salesmanship. He advises: "Find out what the other fellow wants and then help him find the best way to get it."[11] Marketing writers call this same idea the marketing concept. It may be defined (like consumer orientation) as serving consumers' needs and wants at a profit. A retail druggist in Tuscaloosa, Alabama, who would go out of his way to help any customer, is an example. Sometimes he would deliver prescriptions ten miles away at no extra charge. He was always cheerful, but more than that, he was always interested in his customers' problems. He was very successful, and although he took a great deal of personal time with his customers, he managed three drug stores in Tuscaloosa. A flour sales representative told his dealer customers that the price of flour would probably be lower in a few days, and they should hold off buying in quantity until then. Wouldn't you buy your flour from such a person? The personal touch of being the prospect's friend reveals the salesperson's sincerity and supplies the competitive edge in many situations. In selling, it is important to build long-term relationships.

A Team Attitude

Good sales representatives must also have a team attitude and work well with others to advance company interests. Sales representatives can expect failure when their company and their customers sense they are only out for themselves. The player on the basketball team may score more points if he or she plays as an individual, but five players working smoothly together and assisting each other are necessary for professional championships. You should carry out whatever management asks cheerfully, coordinate customer service with repair people and other members of the corporate team, and work well with the buyer's personnel. Good relationships with other sales representatives in prospecting, making proposals, or even team interviewing will insure your being able to get help when *you* need it. Never say anything bad about other corporate members, because even if it doesn't get back to them, you may think that is has, and this may affect your relationship with them.

A Self-Improvement Attitude

Sales representatives should develop a positive and persistent self-improvement attitude. Jack Lacy, a famous sales trainer, tells the story of

[11] Frank Bettger, *How I Raised Myself from Failure to Success in Selling* (Englewood Cliffs, N.J.: Prentice-Hall, 1949), p. 53.

a man who completely reshaped his personality within a few years. He rose from complete failure in selling to outstanding success. Lacy concludes that he has known thousands who have successfully remade their personalities.[12] Certainly, the person with a poor personality and poor selling habits has a distinct handicap in sales work. There must be a change before full selling potential is realized. While experience in selling serves to improve these factors, persons with a planned program of self-improvement progress faster and enjoy the additional benefits sooner. Specific self-improvement methods are discussed in Chapter 4.

An Efficiency-Improvement Attitude

In business there are four attitudinal "sets" (preparations) that improve efficiency and promote profits: (1) A consciousness of wasted capacity; (2) An expectation of simplifying transactions;[13] (3) The application of the "principle of postponement;"[14] and (4) The acquisition of additional products in the mix. An awareness of and attempts to use these efficiency-promoting concepts are keys to work improvement.

Wasted Capacity. In every sales operation there is wasted time, equipment, and space potential (capacities). The waiting time that salespersons spend before seeing the prospect, for example, can be utilized in learning or strategy planning or some other necessary work. Sales representatives who don't show the buyer how to get maximum use of their products may cause prospect dissatisfaction or lose a future sale. Many salespersons, having additional space in their automobiles or open space in their stores, have promoted new products, and with little additional costs, they have increased profits. Whenever there is additional, unutilized potential, an opportunity exists. Every sales representative should be prepared to look for these opportunities to utilize existing assets more efficiently.

Simplifying Transactions. Sales representatives are in business to cause transactions or get orders. Transactions that require many hours of negotiations are not simple and may prevent the sales representative from closing other deals in the territory. Anything that makes transactions simpler or repetitive in nature and cuts down on negotiations or bargaining time makes marketing more efficient. Consider the modern supermarket,

---

[12] Jack Lacy, "Secrets of a Winning Sales Personality," recording (Chicago: Businessmen's Record Club, 1961).

[13] Wroe Alderson, *Marketing Behavior and Executive Action* (Homewood, Ill.: Irwin, 1957), pp. 296–304.

[14] *Ibid.*, pp. 423–427.

where housewives can buy a basketful of groceries in less than thirty minutes because of the routinizing factors—self-opening doors, shopping carts, wide aisles, traffic patterns, displays, point-of-purchase advertising, self-service, branding, and fast checkout. Vending machines, mechanical coin changers, speaker systems in drive-ins, price tags, prepackaged foods, charge plates, installment credit, and guarantees are all designed to make the transaction more routine or easier.[15] Many of these simplifying devices have resulted in marketing fortunes. Together they have allowed the American retailing system to become the most efficient in the world. Simplifying transactions is not only an opportunity for those in business for themselves, but it is an attitudinal "set" the salesperson should have to facilitate territorial operations. Sales proposals, establishing friendships with prospects, providing avenues for prospects to contact you when your services are needed, visual aids, advertising pieces, checklists for making surveys of prospects' problems, and dozens of other methods reduce negotiations and save selling time (which is money). You should look for ways to save negotiating time while not lessening your effectiveness. This should become such a part of your nature that it becomes an attitude toward better strategy.

Principle of Postponement. Product adjustments for the customer should occur as late as possible in the marketing process or should be postponed to allow for the reduction of marketing risks, since every change that makes a product more suitable for a specific group of customers makes it less suitable for other customers.[16] This is why initialed water glasses are not etched until the customer buys them. Inventory problems are reduced from not having to carry thousands of different glasses. This allows automobiles to be mass produced and still have the custom features that so many different buyers want, since dealers can make changes at the dealership after customers express their exact desires. Alterations in the retail shop have simplified clothes marketing. Mixing paint to customer specifications has enabled dealers to carry a much smaller primary stock with color pigments mixed in at the point of purchase. Sales representatives should be aware of this principle and be prepared to customize their product for each buyer or to modify their sales presentation, or adjust it to the particular needs of their prospects.

Expanding the Line Offered. Sales representatives who have many products to offer their customers during a call may fulfill many needs. They therefore have a better chance of making a sale and selling more per successful interview. Since the salesperson must travel and wait to see

---

[15] *Ibid.,* pp. 296–304.
[16] *Ibid.,* pp. 423–427.

the prospect anyway, why not have a broad assortment of products to offer to utilize valuable selling time more fully? While it may be more efficient to have a number of products, there are limiting factors. Too much choice may confuse the prospect. Sales representatives may not be able to focus attention on all products during the interview. They may also be spread too thin and lack product knowledge factors if the products are complex or creative selling is involved. The salesperson should be set to see the opportunities and the limitations of expanded-line possibilities.

In summary, Charles Roth, a well-known sales author, comments that the main attitudes necessary for success are a genuine love of other people, optimism, and enthusiasm. He also contends that most attitudes can be learned.[17] When sales representatives use positive attitudes to solve prospect problems, they promote harmony and create a buying atmosphere.

AWARENESS OF DYNAMICS

Prediction of and adjustment to a changing environment are essential to success and survival. Successful persons study trends and cycles and plan ahead to meet opening opportunity. Failures tend to view circumstances as unchanging, aiming their efforts where the target *was*. Product life cycle, diffusion theory, trend analysis, and opportunity cycles all indicate the responsibility of sales representatives to determine change patterns and redirect efforts toward a constantly moving target. Change promotes new occasions for sales and closes up old markets.

Product Life Cycle

A detailed study of product life cycle is beyond the scope of this text, but it is important that sales representatives who sell products understand the basic pattern. In the first place, the death rate of new products is well over 50 percent. Don't get taken in by a smart promoter who wants you to sell a new product that has little relative advantage over existing products. Because consumers are creatures of habit, they have learned to buy their present assortments of products, and only something very special will make them change. Overoptimism about new products is a marketing trap many experience. A new product has to have a strong

---

[17] Charles B. Roth, *The Secrets of Success Encyclopedia* (New York: McGraw-Hill, 1965), pp. 5–34.

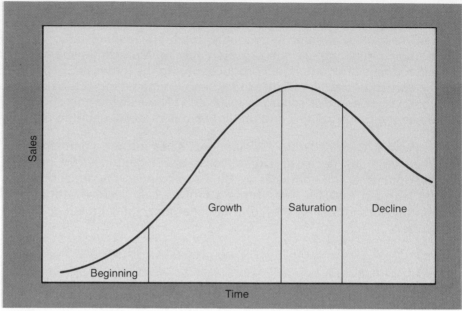

Source: Based on Louis E. Boone and David L. Kurtz, *Contemporary Marketing* (Hinsdale, Ill.: Dryden Press, 1974), p. 148.

Figure 3.2 Product Stages

advantage over existing products and fit in culturally to be widely accepted. Products move through four stages: a beginning stage, a growth stage, a saturation stage, and a decline stage (see Figure 3.2). In the beginning stage, the price/satisfaction ratio is poor, and few customers are willing to try the untried. Sales are slow. Costs of production are high because the good cannot be mass produced; prices are high; and production problems have not been solved. In the growth stage, sales increase at an increasingly rapid rate, competitors jump in, production costs and prices are lowered through mass production, product features are copied—lessening differences, and profits are greatest. Products are easiest to sell during this stage, and because of the greater-than-average profits of the pioneering firms, companies are willing to develop and market new products even while realizing the risks involved. In the saturation stage the market absorbs the product until it is overloaded, and competitors lower prices and profits. Because sales become increasingly hard to make, many inefficient firms fail. In the last stage, total industry sales decline, many firms leave the market, and only efficiently producing firms remain with moderate or poor profits. Seasonal cycles and business cycles also affect sales during the life of the product.

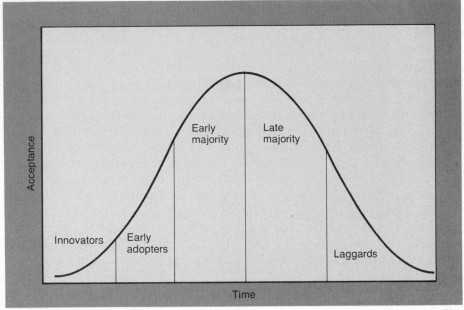

Source: Everett M. Rogers, *Diffusion of Innovations* (New York: Free Press, 1962), p. 162.

Figure 3.3   Diffusion-of-Innovations Curve

Diffusion Theory

More important to the salesperson is what is happening to the composition of the market as the product moves through the life cycle (see
Figure 3.3). Diffusion theory describes the direction of these changes.[18]
New products spread into the market in the manner of a bell-shaped
curve—slowly at first, then at an increasingly rapid rate, up to a peak rate
when the majority of the market is accepting them, and at a decreasing
rate. The speed with which new products spread into the market depends
on the nature of the market (the kind of prospective buyers) and the
product's characteristics. Products are accepted faster in "modern" areas
like New York than they are in "traditional" places like small, rural,
conservative areas. Products that have a strong relative advantage, that
are culturally compatible, that can be tried without much money outlay,
and that are simple and easy to understand speed over the diffusion curve
faster than those without those characteristics.[19]

[18] Everett M. Rogers, *Diffusion of Innovations* (New York: Free Press, 1962), pp. 1 ff.
[19] *Ibid.*

Innovators are the first group of acceptors or buyers. Innovators are likely to be wealthier, have higher incomes, be younger, be more educated, be more socially active, be more cosmopolite (oriented to the whole world rather than to the local social system), and be more willing to take risks than later buyers.[20] If the jet set characterizes the first group of buyers, the second group, the early adopters, might be called the city fathers. This group consists of local community leaders who are not quite as wealthy, educated, or young as the first group. The early majority and the late majority represent 68 percent of adopters. These groups exhibit fewer of the innovators' characteristics. Finally, laggards are the class who hold out longest and do not accept (buy) products, even when the products have strong relative advantages. This group is composed of poorer, less educated, older, and socially more isolated individuals than the previous groups. The dynamics described by this theory should alert you to possible changes in your customer composition and in opportunities to sell your product. The theory also explains why many people wait until they see others buy to reduce their own risks and to feel more assured about the product.[21]

Trend Analysis

An eye for dynamics requires an awareness and an understanding of important trends affecting possible sales of your product. The population of the United States is constantly increasing, but, because of a decline in the birthrate due to recessions and overpopulation concern, certain age groups (such as teen-agers graduating from high school in 1980) are underpopulated. Consumers born after World War II during the baby boom are currently in the market for houses and other nest-building products. Shifts in population from the Northeast to Florida, California, and Texas affect markets. Movements of industry toward pockets of cheaper labor in the South also affect sales of some products. Inflation is fostered by deficit spending. Greater cyclical swings also result from governmental overspending.[22] Women's liberation, consumerism, and raw material shortages affect markets. You should study trends affecting your company and products so that you can visualize what future opportunities may exist.

[20] *Ibid.*

[21] *Ibid.*

[22] Jesse Levin, "Budget Deficits and Inflation," *Financial Analyst Journal,* 30, No. 4 (July–August 1974), 44–46.

Opportunity Cycles

A useful concept is opportunity cycles, or, the view of cycles and change in terms of opportunity for the individual. This concept stresses the need for good timing in meeting favorable circumstances. Opportunity for the sales representative is based on the cycle of the industry and the firm selected. If you select a firm or product headed for prosperity, you will be swept along toward success with the current. On the other hand, if the opportunity is diminishing because of unfavorable environmental changes, you can fail in spite of an intelligent effort. People have made millions promoting trading stamps and certain fast-food franchises when they were on the "up" side of the opportunity cycle. Now, since the main current of opportunity has slackened, it is more difficult to promote new businesses in these fields. Fortunes are being lost by promoters entering markets that are already oversaturated. This does not mean that salespersons should change their jobs after establishing themselves in a firm whose cycle is slightly declining. To salespersons already committed to a business, this concept can be translated into taking advantage of trends within their territory and within their product offerings. The college student of selling should view the prospective job market in the light of the firm's ability to provide opportunity in the present and in the future. We live in an era of change, which requires constant adjustment to new circumstances.

MOTIVATION AND SELF-IMAGE BUILDING

Sales representatives should possess confidence and quiet dominance. Expecting success in closing sales promotes enthusiasm, persuasiveness, and, consequently, signed orders. Salespersons can increase motivation levels and build self-image by: (1) increasing their knowledge of the product, selling techniques, and prospects; (2) using self-suggestion and positive thinking; and (3) visualizing the objective. Napolean Hill, after studying the lives of hundreds of successful persons, concluded that confidence building through positive self-suggestion and visualization of goals is very important for success.[23] Health improvement through exercise and sensible living, dress, and grooming can enhance self-image. Overmotivation (over-drive), however, can destroy health and undermine poise. The power within an individual to move other people to action is promoted by a confident self-image. A tactful, self-assured personality inspires positive prospect response.

[23] Hill, *Think and Grow Rich, op. cit.,* pp. 52–77.

QUESTIONING AND LISTENING

Success theorists agree that proper questioning and listening techniques are important in being well received by customers and learning about their particular problems. Sales representatives can ingratiate themselves to the prospect by asking intelligent questions, listening, and adjusting responses to the prospect's personality and needs. Questions can be used in every phase of prospect confrontation. Good persuaders do not argue with prospects but attempt to reduce the natural conflict-of-interest situation that exists in bargaining, by listening. The idea in persuasion is to adjust to the prospect rather than require the prospect to do any adjusting other than agreeing to the sales proposal. Prospects will usually hear you if you listen and adjust to their needs first.

Ralph Nichols explains that listening principles are neglected in the educational process and has several suggestions for developing the art of listening.[24] He identifies branding subjects as uninteresting, criticising the talker, allowing the mind to wander, pretending attention, avoiding the difficult, and reacting to emotional words as bad listening practices. He suggests that guessing what the speaker will say next, determining supporting ideas, and mentally summarizing what has been said are practices that will improve the ability to listen and learn.[25] Listening can be the strongest type of persuasive activity, and the patience to remain silent and receive feedback often separates the pro salesperson from the amateur.

DOMINANT THEME FOCUS

Jack Lacy calls it the "hot button," Frank Bettger calls it the "key issue," and Denby Brandon calls it the "law of attention and focus." However, all advise the successful salesperson to use the strategy of determining and focusing on the most important buying motive. This gives the sales representative's efforts the unity and direction that come from simplicity. Persuaders should emphasize key selling benefits in such a dramatic way that prospects can visualize themselves enjoying the product. Many feel that success is often dependent on stressing the important determinants without getting enmeshed in unimportant details. When focusing on a dominant theme to drive toward a goal, the important concept is to alternate periods of effort with periods of rest. In a sales presentation,

[24] Ralph G. Nichols, "Listening Is Good Business," *Management of Personnel Quarterly*, 1, no. 2 (Winter 1962) 2–9.

[25] *Ibid.*

this allows response to and reflection about the prospect's ideas. In most work progress is fostered by laying aside the project and approaching it later, refreshed and with increased determination. Denby Brandon calls this work-rest-work idea the "law of alternation."[26]

ENTHUSIASM

Enthusiasm aids persuasion because it commands attention, creates interest, stimulates motivation, stirs emotion, and promotes action. Few people buy anything unless their emotions are aroused, and few are aroused emotionally about a product unless you show *eager interest* in your own offering. To generate enthusiasm, Norman Vincent Peale advises that one key is to begin deliberately behaving in a confident manner, as if you were able to meet situations and personal confrontations easily.[27] He also recommends that sales representatives believe in the importance of their work to the economy and take pride in their vocation.[28] While enthusiasm can be generated by just deciding to be enthusiastic, it is also promoted by belief in and knowledge about the product, personal health, a positive self-image, an increase in speech tempo, dramatic gestures, and the introduction of other exciting action into the presentation. Enthusiasm must be mixed with sincerity for maximum effect. Overdone enthusiasm, however, can easily lead to offensive high-pressured presentations.[29]

PERSONALITY DEVELOPMENT

When competing deals are otherwise balanced in the prospect's mind, the personalities of competing salespeople usually make the difference. Personality factors, in fact, are primary in affecting job tenure, promotion, and other important areas of human acceptance. Most prospects, depending on their self-images, prefer extroverted, happy, intelligent-sounding salespeople who have personal warmth, remember names, and appear genuinely interested in the prospect's conversation and problems. Per-

[26] Denby Brandon, "Power for Your Purpose," recording (Memphis: private label, 1964).

[27] Peale, *op. cit.*, p. 20.

[28] *Ibid.*, p. 39.

[29] *Ibid.*, p. 38.

haps foremost in the long list of mental, physical, and emotional virtues affecting persuasion is the communication of genuine concern for other people. Personality development will be treated in detail in the following chapter. But you must realize that the impression you make on other people is more than half of the success equation, and personality modification is possible and practical. Some of my academically weaker students who have good personalities have been more successful than academically talented graduates who nursed self-centered tendencies.

PERSUASION

Persuasion and salesmanship are almost synonymous. Persuasion is the opposite of forced coercion and essential to success in a democratic society. Persuasion theory will be treated in detail in Chapter 5, but no complete presentation of success elements could be advanced without a consideration of this vital component.

SUMMARY

Success theory is characterized by emphasis on goal-directed planning, development of positive personality attributes, and principles of interpersonal communication. Specific goal definitions guide and motivate. Good methodology combines with intelligence to produce superior performance. Systems thinking adds a new dimension to problem consideration by stressing the interrelationship of all parts of a problem. Positive attitudes assure you of being ready to respond correctly when the occasion demands action. Recognizing dynamics and trends allows prediction and encourages the formulation of strategy to hit moving markets. Motivation furnishes the power to accomplish. A confident self-image sets a proper interview tone. Questioning and listening methods promote two-way communication between you and your prospect and reduce the conflict-of-interest situation. Dominant-theme emphasis keeps you on a straight track toward the goal. Enthusiasm stirs the prospect to buy. Personality development improves the receptivity of your customers. Knowledge of persuasion oils the sales-closing machinery. In aggregate, success theory is a foundation for good selling and it is built by practitioner experience.

1. What are the ten key elements to success?

2. Give three rules for proper goal definition.

3. What are common mistakes people make with regard to goal definition?

4. Define "breadth of consideration."

5. Describe Schnelle's Complex Problem-Solving Method in detail.

6. Explain the creative process. What four steps are involved?

7. Explain each of the four suggested attitudinal "sets" that are helpful in improving efficiency. Cite a circumstance in which each might be used.

8. Using your text as a guide, trace a product through the life cycle. Show how the kind of prospect interested in the product might change over time.

9. List ways (according to the text) that you can develop motivation. Enthusiasm.

APPLICATION QUESTIONS

1. Nominate two other success elements (other than those given) that you feel belong in the group.

2. Write out your goals for the rest of the day and cross them out when you complete each one.

3. Using Schnelle's methodology, evaluate a career alternative.

4. Analyze your study methods. Write five ways you feel you might improve your study habits.

5. Relate the creative process to selling by indicating three situations where it might be used.

6. Using football or some other sport, explain the difference between a coach or player who uses systems thinking and one who does not.

7. Give an example of a retail salesperson who exemplified a service attitude.

8. In what ways might salespersons eliminate negotiation time without hurting their chances to sell?

9. Income and population trends are mentioned in the text. What additional trends may be of concern to the alert salesperson?

10. Examine three businesses using the opportunity-cycles concept.

11. Which of the listening problems mentioned in the text do you feel you need to correct?

12. Who has the best personality that you know of? Why?

INCIDENTS

3–1

Wayne Spenser, age twenty-four, is talking to Mary Kraft, age forty-three. Both sell real estate for the Golden Key Agency.

Mary: Hi, Wayne, what's the matter?

Wayne: Mary, I'm thinking about getting out of this business. My sales have been poor lately, and I guess I'm a failure at selling real estate. Prices are so high nobody can afford it.

Mary: You shouldn't think about quitting, Wayne. Sure we've had a slump during the recession, but all those young nest builders are out there, and they need homes. Stick with it. You have what it takes.

Wayne: I don't think so anymore. Mr. Keyes called me in and wanted me to set a goal for two houses per month. You know that in this business there just isn't any way to know what you can do. He wanted me to break down how many showings I plan to do each week and organize my prospecting. I have never done that before, and I don't intend to start now. I've always played it by ear.

Mary: Wayne, let me show you what I do. See? I make it a point to show at least five houses a day, and I call my prospects a day ahead to arrange my appointments.

Wayne: Where do you get all those prospects?

Mary: Well, besides the ones assigned to me by Mr. Keyes, I advertise in the newspaper myself, and I have about a dozen friends who keep their ears open for me. One of them works for Welcome Wagon, and several live in big apartment complexes.

Wayne: That's too much organization for me. Besides, I'm tired of Old Man Keyes always pushing . . .

Mary: He's not so bad, Wayne. He's been under a lot of pressure lately because sales have been down for the agency.

Wayne: Aw, Mary, real estate isn't any good. I've never fit into this agency. Anyway, the other salespeople are not friendly. Say, let's go down to the coffee shop and have a cup. There is nothing else to do.

Mary: I'd like to, but Mrs. Rachels wants me to show her a house and there she is now. You'd better stay with it, Wayne. Great days are coming . . .

Wayne: You can say that because you sold three houses last month. I guess I'm just not cut out to be a salesperson.

QUESTIONS

1. What problems do you see in Wayne's success philosophy?

2. Analyze this conversation in terms of success theory.

3-2

Carl Delman has just taken over his father's prosperous tennis shop and sporting-goods store. He has had to leave college with only six credit hours lacking because the senior Delman died suddenly of a heart attack, and Carl's mother and younger sister felt incapable of running the operation. The store has two employees, one who meets the customers and another who strings the rackets and repairs golfing equipment. The store has enjoyed a 20-percent increase in sales in the last two years, and Carl's father was in the process of building a new display room, 20 × 20 feet, when he died. The room is now finished. Carl wants to dismiss the salesman and has told the racket stringer that he wants to run the business "just like his father." Carl has brought in his best friend from school to help him meet the public. Sales have dropped within the last month, and some of Carl's father's customers have been hesitant to accept him. He has learned that some of them have even taken their business elsewhere. He doesn't know what to do with the spare room, since the racket repairman knew only that his father planned to put in a line of bicycles. Carl plans to leave it vacant for a while, except for minor storage.

Using Schnelle's Complex Problem-Solving Method, analyze this case. What would you advise Carl to do to make a continuing success of his father's business?

4 Personality Development

Personality, a key success element in selling, is the mirror that reflects your attitudes and attributes and helps determine how prospects will respond to your persuasive appeals. A good personality affects your ability to sell by *positively* influencing the response of prospective buyers to your presence and thus increasing your chances of achieving personal goals. It is also necessary that you understand personalities other than your own, to adjust to the needs of others. If you can improve your personality—and you can—you should be able to translate the more positive reactions from your customers into increased earnings and a happier work experience. Salespeople with good personalities also enjoy greater promotion opportunity, have more job tenure, and have better working relationships with other members of the corporate team.

Many writers indicate that personality can be changed to great advantage. Jack Lacy, the famous sales trainer, records that personality can be improved dramatically through persistent efforts. He claims to know thousands of salespeople who have increased their abilities to project a favorable image to others.[1] Frank Bettger, the internationally known insurance salesman and writer, reviews his own successful transformation, which involved a deliberate plan to change his weaker attributes.[2] Dale Carnegie's book on personality development has sold millions of copies.[3] And Dr. Maxwell Maltz, a plastic surgeon, has provided a clear explanation of a relatively new approach to help you realize your personality

[1] Jack Lacy, "Secrets of a Winning Sales Personality," recording (Chicago: Businessmen's Record Club, 1961).

[2] Frank Bettger, *How I Multiplied My Income and Happiness in Selling* (Englewood Cliffs, N.J.: Prentice-Hall, 1954).

[3] Dale Carnegie, *How to Win Friends and Influence People* (New York: Simon and Schuster, 1964).

87

potential in his book, *Psycho-Cybernetics.*[4] Ideas from these and many other sources will be examined in this chapter, to help you discover important keys to self-fulfillment. A practical approach to personality understanding and development requires a look at:

- The self-image approach to change
- The trait-development plan
- Observing and remembering

THE SELF-IMAGE APPROACH TO CHANGE

The Cybernetic Model

People like Maxwell Maltz[5] and Ben B. Smith[6] have popularized a concept of personality change that can be valuable to you in selling and in public-relations work. Human cybernetics is an important key to personality change, because it furnishes a positive model, is optimistic about the chances for improving your ability to relate to others, and is a logical method backed by evidence. According to cybernetics, the mind is like an amazingly efficient computer that is instructed or "programmed" in accordance with an individual's conscious thoughts (see Figure 4.1).

[4] Maxwell Maltz, *Psycho-Cybernetics* (Englewood Cliffs, N.J.: Prentice-Hall, 1960), p. 1 ff.

[5] *Ibid.*

[6] Ben B. Smith, *The Magic of Self-Cybernetics* (New York: Frederick Fell, 1971).

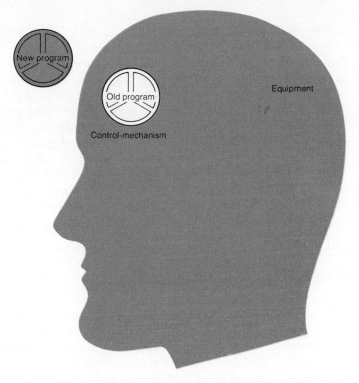

New program

Old program

Equipment

Control-mechanism

In cybernetics, we must reprogram our mental-control mechanism, just as a new program tape reel is put into a computer to meet a new situation. The dictionary defines *cybernetics* as "a science dealing with the comparative study of the operations of complex electronic computers and the human nervous system."

Source of definition: *Webster's New World Dictionary of the American Language*, Second College Edition (New York: World Publishing, 1978), p. 351.

Figure 4.1 The Cybernetic Model

Each time we experience and solve a problem, we "write" a program. That is, we instruct our mind with a particular solution pattern. This pattern may be used time and again to meet similar circumstances. We simply draw up the old "program" from our subconscious and use it when we come in contact with the "new" circumstance. Of course, we may modify the old program from time to time. We learn from experience to change, but sometimes experience is a bitter teacher. Experiential learning not only takes time, but the punishment for failure is unpleasant and sometimes painful. Lost sales, for example, are expensive. Maltz contends that "synthetic experience" or imagined experience is almost as effective a teacher as real experience. The mind and body respond just as if the experience were "real."[7] It is basically through synthetic experience that we can reprogram our mental machinery without the cost of actual trial and error and better adapt our personality to our needs.

[7] Maltz, *op. cit.*, p. xi.

A Goal-Directed Mechanism

The marvelous mental equipment that we have is a goal-directed mechanism. If we program our minds with thoughts of failure, the whole mechanism is instructed to produce failure, and our mental resources will bring this about. If we instruct it with belief in success, it will respond accordingly and marshal all of our faculties to produce success.[8] This model reinforces the *power of positive thinking* espoused by Norman Vincent Peale.[9] It is compatible with the Judeo-Christian teachings on the power of faith. Because this mechanism is a goal-directed apparatus that works in an efficient but mysterious way to fulfill our instructions, it is essential that goals be *visualized in detail,* verbalized, written down, and continually reviewed. This kind of emphasis gives clear programming instructions to our "computer," which takes the visualized goal object, such as making 125 percent of quota, and produces real results.

Problems with the Old Self-Image

Because we continually use old programs when meeting new situations, we severely limit our capabilities. Sometimes our parents have programmed us with negative thoughts. Your mother or father may have continually reminded you of your lack of some specific ability and convinced you to the point where you were unsure of that ability and lacked confidence. If you ever have to work very much in the area of that weakness it will be necessary for you to reprogram that inhibition. It is permissible under cybernetics to admit failure in a test or in a specific selling circumstance, but it is destructive to suggest to yourself continually that you *are* a failure, or that you will always fail in a certain area. Some students freeze up when any kind of mathematical model is shown on the board. They tell themselves that "math is not their bag" and inhibit their minds from accomplishing the solution simply and logically. Similarly, salespeople can program themselves negatively, concluding that they are not cut out for selling. The truth is that you couldn't lift your hand off your desk if you suggested to your mind that you couldn't do it, and you believed that you couldn't. Maltz reports that while persons practicing basketball free throws from the line physically improved their ability to make shots by 24 percent, persons who went through the motions mentally only (imagining that they were shooting the ball) were able to improve 23

[8] *Ibid.,* p. 12.

[9] Norman Vincent Peale, *The Power of Positive Thinking* (Englewood Cliffs, N.J.: Prentice-Hall, 1964).

percent. A third group, which practiced neither physically nor mentally, showed no improvement.[10]

One of the most debilitating problems of salespeople is lack of confidence or just plain fear. "Hot doorknobs," or fear of being rejected, can keep you from visiting your best prospects. Cybernetics has an answer for this, too. Negative feedback, which can be so useful in getting you on course to your goal, can also stop you altogether.[11] The problem is that you are dwelling on the possibilities of failure instead of the possibilities of success. You are issuing to your mind a self-fulfilling prophecy. Finally, you may tell yourself that you are not cut out to be a salesperson and label yourself as a failure in any kind of public-relations work. The concept of "purpose tremor" shows how and why people "lock up" in certain situations—such as, when attempting to thread a needle, the thread gets close to the eye of the needle and your hand shakes, or when an attempt is made to pour liquid into a small test-tube opening and the same thing happens. Your hand shakes because you are trying too hard and overreacting by being too careful. Many students experience this on important tests. Salespeople who are overly concerned about making a good impression usually make a poor one, because they act self-consciously and nervously. Overconcern can jam the mechanism,[12] but if the stress can be transformed and used positively, it can work *for* you. Turning some slight tension during the interview into enthusiasm may create excitement and arouse enough emotions to promote the proper buying atmosphere. Much worse than the salesperson with "purpose tremor" is the salesperson who projects an unenthusiastic attitude.

Reprogramming

The answer to the problems of fear, anxiety, and stress is *reprogramming*. The main keys to reprogramming are belief, synthetic experience, and goal visualization.

Belief. People have been known to accomplish amazing feats under stress or hypnosis. We have all heard about people being able to lift objects several times heavier than they normally could, during a fire or a wreck or some other traumatic event that immediately reprogrammed their belief out of necessity. We have also heard how people under hypnosis can imagine pain to such an extent that their bodies react exactly as if the stimulus were real and not imagined. The four-minute mile was once a

[10] Maltz, *op. cit.*, p. 32.
[11] *Ibid.*, pp. 17 ff.
[12] *Ibid.*, pp. 154–198.

"*Inferior people have inferiority complexes,
superior people have superiority complexes.
It's as simple as that.*"

Cybernetics is
believing in yourself.

Reprinted from *The Saturday Evening Post* © 1974 The Curtis Publishing Company.

mental barrier to athletes who believed that running it under four minutes was impossible. There is a story about a man who was locked in a refrigerated railroad car in Russia. He kept a log of his experiences with a piece of chalk, which he used on the car wall. He described, legibly at first, the decreasing temperature in the car as the trip wore on. Finally, in an almost unintelligible scribbling at the base of the wall, he wrote of the terrible sensations of freezing to death. They removed his body, but the amazing thing was that the refrigeration in the car was off. It was only slightly cool. The man's body had responded to his mental suggestions, and his body died.

Synthetic experience. Synthetic experience had become a reality for the man locked in the railroad car. When salespersons can reprogram their minds with positive beliefs and be free from the inhibiting fears of failure, the potential for success is amazing. Athletes under hypnosis have been known to be 25 percent stronger without the inhibition of negative belief.[13]

Synthetic experience (sometimes expressed in other words) is advocated by many success theorists. Jack Lacy stresses the importance of imagining

[13] *Ibid.*, p. 50.

the interview. Salespersons can visualize the interview in their minds, and positively suggest mental pictures of themselves answering objections, making an effective demonstration, and effecting closing methods.[14] This kind of mental practice can pay big dividends and properly program that "servomechanism" without the penalties of losing order after order to gain experience. You might call this imaginative planning, and it can be applied to job interviews, installations, speaking, and many other selling activities.

Goal visualization. Goal visualization has already been covered, but how is "purpose tremor" handled? To perform well in a crisis, you should have practice under less stressful conditions. Stress should be translated into aggressive rather than defensive attitudes, and the crisis should be evaluated in its true perspective.[15] Often, people blow up consequences out of proportion. If the sale is lost, there will be other sales. Dwell on your successes and glance at your failures only long enough to get feedback and see what went wrong.[16] Dwell on the present, practice gradualism by slowly building up to a hard job, and attempt to postpone angry reflexes until they blow over. According to cybernetics, you will live up to your self-image.

A Spiritual Dimension

Many success writers, including Maxwell Maltz, emphasize a spiritual-moral dimension of personality development. Norman Vincent Peale contends that a deep faith in God is the primary factor behind sustained enthusiasm.[17]

W. Clement Stone, Chairman of the Board of the Combined Insurance Company, built a fortune from persuasion. He sees prayer as a success aid in all fields and writes, "Regardless of one's beliefs, prayer from a psychological viewpoint is beneficial in crystallizing one's ideas toward an objective and developing a stimulating internal force."[18] Cybernetically, people who believe in a personal, all-powerful God with whom they can communicate, have a self-image of being supported by this power, and they often have a special approach to success and personality development.

[14] Jack Lacy, *op. cit.*

[15] Maltz, *loc. cit.,* pp. 187–204.

[16] *Ibid.,* p. 26.

[17] Norman Vincent Peale, *Enthusiasm Makes the Difference* (Englewood Cliffs, N.J.: Prentice-Hall, 1967), p. 35.

[18] W. Clement Stone, *The Success System That Never Fails* (Englewood Cliffs, N.J.: Prentice-Hall, 1962), p. 117.

THE TRAIT-DEVELOPMENT PLAN

Frank Bettger credits much of his personality development formula and selling success to Benjamin Franklin. It was Franklin who inspired Bettger to change himself by selecting a trait that he wished to improve, writing it on a card with instructions on how to put it into practice, keeping the card in his pocket, and practicing the trait for several days.[19] In other words, Frank Bettger was reprogramming himself. Students have done this as an individual project in lieu of a term paper. Each selected those personality elements he or she felt needed improvement and turned in a project report with a self-analysis, a rationale for selecting each personality element, impressions of the responses of other people as the trait was practiced, and a project evaluation. Most reported that the assignment helped them become conscious of weaknesses in their personality programming, and many admitted that it helped them improve their relationships with other people. The important consideration is that this simple method is available for your use at any time. When you use it, be sure to practice just one or two personality factors at a time. Before long, you should be applying them unconsciously. Then you may count them as new assets for your image.

There are dozens of personality factors or elements recommended for practice in every book discussing the qualities of a good salesperson. The truth is the salesperson can benefit from almost every positive attribute in the dictionary. In the previous chapter, enthusiasm, attitudes, listening attributes, and other personality-related success theory elements were discussed. These success elements are primary and should be emphasized in any self-improvement project. There are other elements, however, that are also very important. Dale Carnegie, who wrote one of the simplest and most successful books on personality development ever written, emphasized just a few key elements.[20] Jack Lacy mentions a limited group of attributes that give the salesperson the "engaging, assuring, compelling, and dynamic" personality needed for selling.[21] The following self-improvement objectives have been selected from many sources and from dozens of elements:

- Call people by their names.
- Smile and be pleasant.
- Praise and compliment other people.

[19] Frank Bettger, "How I Raised Myself from Failure to Success in Selling," recording (Waco, Texas: Success Motivation Institute, 1962).

[20] Carnegie, *loc. cit.*

[21] Jack Lacy, *loc. cit.*

- Talk in terms of others' interests.
- Learn to be socially sensitive.
- Refrain from criticism.
- Watch your voice and appearance.
- Use humor carefully.
- Be sincere.
- Keep healthy.

Call People by Their Names

The most magic sound in the English language to any prospect is his or her name. Dr. Archie Dykes was promoted from Chancellor of the University of Tennessee at Martin to Chancellor at Knoxville, and within a few years, he became Chancellor at the University of Kansas at Lawrence. While at Martin, he made it a practice to know not only all of his faculty and staff by name but also hundreds of his students. He realized that knowing people by name expressed interest, reflected personal concern, and constituted the substance of courtesy. Customers like the personal touch. If you can remember the name of your prospects, their secretaries, and those to whom you have been introduced, and if you can pronounce the names correctly and say them in a friendly tone, you will help assure the acceptance of you and your product. Request a repeat if you did not hear the name clearly during the introduction, pronounce the name several times to yourself, use it in conversation as soon as it fits, and use association to help you remember the name. Not using the customer's name in the sales interview depersonalizes the presentation and creates an awkward atmosphere. Remembering it and using it is the mark of a thoughtful salesperson. Students who practiced learning names found it a fast way to initiate new friendships. Think of the prospect's name as a vital key to the sale, and you won't forget it.

Smile and Be Pleasant

A sincere and meaningful smile, used appropriately, helps prospects to identify with you, generates a pleasant atmosphere, and sets the stage for promoting positive buying emotions. A fake smile not supported by your mood or your other actions may convey insecurity, insincerity, nervousness, sarcasm, ridicule, or other negative attitudes. Compare the unnatural facial gesture made by a child who is told to smile for the camera with the smile resulting from inner happiness. Prospects should be able to infer from your smile that you identify with them, that you are happy and relaxed in their presence, and that you are honestly glad to be talking with them. Positive preinterview expectations can put sincerity in your smile or greeting, and the rest of the interview tone should be pleasant to support it. A genuine smile opens doors and closes sales. When smiling and being pleasant become a natural habit, you will feel happier through this self-suggestion and radiate a contagious optimism attractive to everyone you meet.

Praise and Compliment Other People

People like to receive recognition for the things they do well, and, even more so, they appreciate encouragement for things they are not sure they do well. A football player is confident about his skill on the field, but he may be uncertain about his acting ability. A young woman may be sure she is a good student but long for some sign to indicate that she is a good dancer. Compliment people on qualities they are uncertain about, and preface critical suggestions with a little praise.[22] Flattery is an insincere compliment. Look for something you can *sincerely* compliment before you praise someone. Speak well of other people in your prospect's presence. Everyone feels more comfortable talking to the person who sees the good in others rather than the bad. Safe practice is not to join the prospect in criticizing your competitor. Your prospect may be testing you to find out what kind of person you really are.

Talk in Terms of Others' Interests

You have to *think* in terms of others' interests before you can *talk* in terms of those interests. You have to use imagination to put yourself mentally in the prospect's place. Sales representatives who see the needs of others and can anticipate their wants can focus on the main buying motive and receive positive response. Salespersons tell prospects they will get the proper service, but do they indicate their concern by anticipating the prospect's need for a match, a pencil, or a writing pad? Does the salesperson realize the prospect's need for position in the firm, for esteem, for economy of operation? To practice thinking in terms of prospects' interests, think through their situations thoroughly, mentally ask yourself, "What would I want?" and offer your best solution to their needs. The smart salesperson looks and listens for signs and words indicating the prospect's desires.

[22] Paul P. Parker, "How to Use Tact and Skill in Handling People," recording (Waco, Texas: Success Motivation Institute, 1964).

Learn to Be Socially Sensitive

It is practical to learn to show social sensitivity. Increasing your social sensitivity requires practicing manners, improving your ability to converse with others without offending them, and learning to regard the resources of others as if they were your own. You may regard manners as superficial, but the prospect sees good manners as a sign of professionalism. All prospects appreciate salespeople with a knowledge of the social graces. Smoking without permission, discussing politics or other emotionally charged issues with prospects whose positions are unknown, interrupting a conversation, telling dirty stories, using profanity, or calling attention indirectly to any personal deficiency in the other person are bad manners. A significant part of social sensitivity is respect for the other person's resources. For example, when writing an order while using the prospect's unprotected desk for support, use a writing pad instead of a thin piece of paper. Keeping feet off the furniture is another example. Respect for another person's time is also essential. Purchasing agents frequently complain that salespeople take up too much executive time. Salespeople who will not end an interview when the business is accomplished are even less welcome than a party guest who will not take hints to go home. Another thing to watch is interrupting before the other person has finished talking. A good practice is to write letters of congratulation and gratitude.

Refrain from Criticism

If you are normal, you criticize others a lot more than you realize. Try for one day not to say anything critical about anyone and see just how much you do criticize others. Both engaging in criticism and not being critical are habits. Criticism is necessary for correction of society's ills and for reform, and it does give a common ground for conversation. If you can learn the habit of not being critical, however, your prospects will feel more secure in your presence. They will trust you with confidential information. Criticism is negative and unprofessional in most instances, and it does not promote a proper buying atmosphere.

Watch Your Voice and Appearance

Often you communicate as much by the tone of your voice, your gestures, and your appearance as you do by your words. The tone of your voice and your inflections radiate cues about your attitudes and motives. A confident voice inspires trust, a weak and faltering voice inspires doubt, and an angry or loud voice can increase interview conflict. Your voice is the rifle that fires your ammunition—words. Variation in the voice and rapidity of speech can spark enthusiasm and excitement, while monotone presentations generate little feeling or emotion. Make sure your prospect can hear you. Pronounce your words distinctly. Try to avoid speech mannerisms such as "you know" and "would you believe." Speak to a video recorder and review the replay to find out what you need to improve. Take speech courses and practice in front of a mirror.

Gestures may reveal more about you than your words. Your smile, what you do with your hands, your posture, your walk, how you sit, the expression on your face give a continual picture of your moods and thoughts. People who use gestures well are expressive. Salespeople are really actors, and their performances affect their paycheck. Do you show nervousness by fumbling with your hands, smoothing your hair, staring at the floor? Sit with your feet flat on the floor but not stiff. Do not slouch in the chair. Ask a friend to tell you about your mannerisms or to imitate you.

John T. Malloy is a wardrobe consultant to many of America's top corporate executives. He advises that if you are selling to businesspeople, you should wear clothes that are conservative yet do not place you above your prospect.[23] Small men and women should wear attention-getting devices such as stickpins or handkerchiefs. Large persons should not call attention to their size and should wear nonauthoritarian clothes of soft colors and textures. Dress as well as the people to whom you are selling and carry a good pen and pencil. Avoid the cheap kind.[24] Clean fingernails are especially important. Being clean and well groomed has an effect on your self-image. It gives you poise. Remember, prospects who do not know you are responding to clues in an effort to evaluate you. Your clothes and your appearance should make the prospect feel comfortable. Overdressing or underdressing is a mistake.

Use Humor Carefully

Good, clean humor can relax interview tension and create a friendly atmosphere. However, humor can be destructive to the object of the joke. It is usually permissible to make yourself the object of the joke, but don't embarrass prospects by indirectly pointing out their deficiencies, even if a long-established friendship is involved. You never know whether the prospect has relatives who are alcoholics, are in asylums, or are in the ethnic group in your joke. Dirty and sacrilegious stories are the mark of the unprofessional salesperson and are very offensive to many people. Knowing when to laugh and smile in the interview is important. Avoid nervous laughter when circumstances are serious. Having a good stock of

---

[23] John T. Malloy, "Clothes Make the Salesman—Never Wear Green," *Sales and Marketing Management,* 115, No. 10 (December 8, 1975), pp. 58–62.

[24] *Ibid.*

"I'll take it."

The Saturday Evening Post, © Vahan Shirvanian.

The salesperson's appearance can affect selling success.

inoffensive jokes is good practice *if you can tell them well.* If your friends will not laugh at them, chances are your prospects will not laugh either.

Be Sincere

Prospects like to buy from sales representatives who are honest and genuinely committed to serving them. Companies also like to promote salespeople who are committed to their work and to their company. Customers buy thousands of dollars' worth of merchandise on the sincerity of the salesperson's word. If you show any evidence of hypocrisy, the risk of dealing with you and your company increases. If you do not show loyalty to your own company and to other parties, the buyer cannot trust you. Suppose a customer admits to damaging a product in such a way as to void the guarantee. If you advise the customer to lie about the damage, or you say that you'll take care of it, and the customer knows you are not going to tell your own company the truth, you may lose that customer. You could lose your job too—a company *must* be able to trust you. Never tell your prospect a lie. You may have promised delivery on equipment only to find that the machine your prospect had planned to use will have to be delivered late. Tell prospects the truth, even if it makes them temporarily angry with you. They will respect you in the long run. Salespersons often purposely point out certain minor deficiencies in their product to establish sincerity. Salespeople even refuse to sell products that they feel will not suit a customer's needs. A reputation for sincerity and truthfulness in dealing with prospects makes it easier to close sales. The good word about you will get around. Some salespersons may fool a few people in the beginning, but in the long run, a bad reputation may close the door of opportunity for them permanently.

Keep Healthy

Health maintenance is essential to the salesperson desiring to stay on the job, endure travel, lift products, and project a confident voice and image. *Nation's Business* reported that more than 50,000 United States companies had installed physical fitness facilities for their employees by the mid-seventies at a total cost of about $2 billion per year. Over 300 of the facilities had employed full-time recreational directors.[25] Mental and physical health depends on attitude, knowledge, and a willingness to maintain good health habits. There is little question that despair, guilt, frustration, and anger can destroy personality and body and retard the healing process. Dr. Maxwell Maltz contends that rapid healers have one thing in common—they are all cheerful, optimistic, positive thinkers who have a zest for life and a real reason to get well.[26]

Health centers on diet, rest, and exercise. Many salespeople eat too much sugar, fat, salt, and starchy foods and not enough fruits, vegetables, and fiber foods. Some, instead of trying to lose weight by eating smaller servings, try out crash diets that can be harmful.

Good rest will enhance your ability to think, allow you to be calmer, and permit your body's systems to refresh themselves. A Harvard doctor contends that people are overweight because of lack of exercise and explains that exercise converts fatty tissue into beneficial muscle, strengthens the heart's collateral circulation, and reduces cholesterol levels in the

[25] "Staying Trim, Productive, and Alive," *Nation's Business,* 62 (December 1974), 26–28.
[26] Maltz, *op. cit.,* pp. 225–245.

blood.[27]   Kenneth Cooper, author of *The New Aerobics,* advocates such programmed activities as running, walking, cycling, and swimming on a regular basis.[28]   The salesperson can walk briskly, do push-ups, bent-leg sit-ups, and chair hangs even when on the road.   Health is a personal thing, and you should find out from your doctor what your correct weight should be and develop a good diet and exercise program.   Then do those things that will help you feel like doing an enthusiastic sales job.

OBSERVING AND REMEMBERING

The ability to notice important details, recall them, and use them strategically is such a necessary part of the persuasive sales personality that it deserves special consideration.   The salesperson's observations affect the quality of information stored, and memory influences the ability to recall and use strategic information.   The salesperson usually has little time exposure to the prospect and the prospect's office before beginning the presentation.   But the observant salesperson notices many important clues that can be used to customize the presentation, even in a brief interview.   Remembering names and recalling vital personal information is the essence of social sensitivity.   It indicates the personal interest the prospect expects of the professional salesperson.

Ideas for Observing

Our mind screens and filters information taken from our environment. In a book written for police officers and lawyers, Louis Basinger contends that the observer should know what to look for before experiencing the scene.[29]   The search for specific material should be systematic.   What you intend to observe should be verified, and immediate overlearning (see page 105) should be pursued to fix pertinent information in your mind. Most people spend too much time looking at the bottom right of a scene or fixating on an object in the middle.   The total scene should first be scanned, and then the observer should divide the scene into four quadrants and note the elements in each quadrant (see Figure 4.2).   The light should be behind you, if possible.[30]

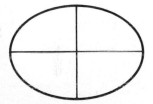

**Figure 4.2
Basinger's Scene-
Scanning Model**

Source: Louis F. Basinger, *The Techniques of Observation and Learning Retention* (Springfield, Ill.: Thomas, 1973), p. 24.

[27] "Personal Business," *Business Week,* January 5, 1974, p. 70.

[28] Kenneth M. Cooper, *The New Aerobics* (New York: Evans and Company, 1970).

[29] Louis F. Basinger, *The Techniques of Observation and Learning Retention* (Springfield, Ill.: Thomas, 1973), pp. 7–33.

[30] *ibid.*

It is very important for the salesperson to predetermine what to look for during exposure to the prospect and the prospect's place of business. Look for pictures on the office wall, trophies, or desk furnishings that might indicate interests, accomplishments, or affiliations of the prospect (see Photo 4.1). For example, you may be able to tell social associations from membership certificates, recreational interests from trophies or pictures, and artistic taste from other room furnishings. The prospect's dress, cleanliness, and greeting manner also give clues to his or her nature and inclination. The salesperson must learn to be a detective in regard to picking up clues from the buyer and the work environment.

Suggestions for a Better Memory

It is a good practice not to overrely on your memory. The ability to recall is affected by future information intake. New information can decrease the amount of older stored material that can be brought back

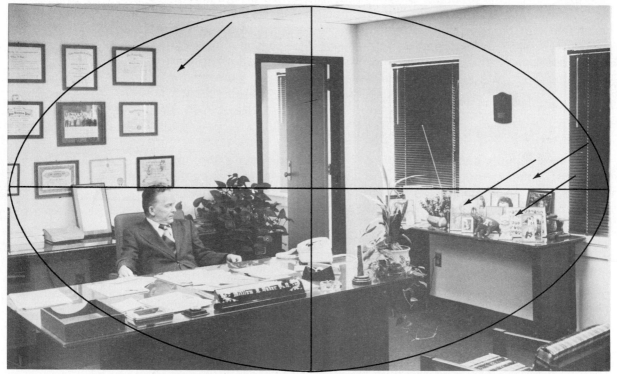

Photo 4.1 After scanning the whole scene, divide it into four parts and examine each part in detail. You can tell a great deal from this executive's office. The pictures of his family, the football, the Alabama elephant, and the degrees and pictures on the wall offer hints about some of his interests.

into the conscious mind. New salespeople or salespeople who have been moved to a new residence can become very frustrated trying to remember where everything is. Write down (do not abbreviate) all nonroutine activities and information on paper, and keep that paper in a customary place. Everyone has experienced losing memorandums written to themselves or forgetting the meaning of abbreviations used when making notes. It is good discipline to keep everything in a particular place. You will lose things that you leave out of their customary location. By doing these two things, you will free your mind for absorbing other, more important data.[31]

Memory practice shows little evidence of permanently strengthening the memory.[32] It is better to concentrate on *methods* of storing and maintaining information. It helps to "get into" a subject (focus your mind) for a few minutes before you attempt to memorize, particularly in the morning when you first get up. Fatigue, alcohol, loss of sleep, and old age are enemies of recall ability.[33] Vitamin B may help if you are vitamin deficient, and stimulants like tea and coffee may keep you alert in the short run.[34] However, good methods of storing and refreshing memory help you the most.

Four Essentials for Improved Recall

Four basic suggestions are made to salespeople wishing to improve the ability to remember:

- Be motivated and have the right attitudinal set to master the material.
- Respond and react fully to the material.
- Concentrate and give meaning to the material.
- Review the material at proper intervals.

Be Motivated and Have the Right Attitudinal Set to Master the Material. Approach whatever you wish to remember by setting your mind to learning the material and suggesting to yourself the importance of retaining it. Set definite learning goals for yourself. If the goals are set by someone else, your performance will not be as good. Intend to store the material in the memory instead of cramming and forgetting soon after the material is learned. Impress yourself with the benefits of storing the material. You

---

[31] Donald A. Laird and Eleanor C. Laird, *Techniques for Efficient Remembering* (New York: McGraw-Hill, 1960), pp. 10–17.

[32] *Ibid.*, p. 18.

[33] *Ibid.*, pp. 64–74.

[34] *Ibid.*, pp. 70–74.

will assimilate information that you enjoy learning quickly and retain it longer.[35]

Respond and React Fully to the Material. If you can get stimulated (not overmotivated) about the material you plan to learn, you can impress it on your mind more successfully. Material you see is retained better than material you hear, but you should involve as many of your senses as possible. Motorizing the information by saying it aloud involves your facial muscles and your hearing. Writing it down brings muscular activity into play. Repetition implants it in the mind.[36] If you speak the words into a tape recorder and play back the tape, you will hear it twice. Put the information on memory cards. Tell yourself to react emotionally and enthusiastically.

Concentrate and Give Meaning to the Material. You can fix your mind on the material by (1) classifying or grouping it; (2) visualizing it; and (3) associating it.[37] To focus your attention on the information, try to group it in as many ways as you can. This gives meaning to the information and helps you associate it with your current store of experience. Complex material and long numbers should be divided into groups, and objects or materials should be examined for similarities in space, time, or distance.[38] Incorporating the new information into a framework gives it meaning and significance. If you can store it *with existing knowledge,* it can be retained better.

Try to visualize everything you attempt to store in your memory. A vivid mental picture is like actually seeing the information. Make up a story about the material, no matter how imaginative, nonsensical, or fictitious, and memorize it in detail. Exaggerate the object to be learned visually, and put it into action or motion.[39] The story-visualization method is especially effective for disconnected words and numbers.

Associate (relate) the material in every possible way. Harry Lorayne and Jerry Lucas contend that all memory is based on association.[40] Always relate the new information to something you already know. Association is particularly recommended for remembering names and faces. Names are like nonsense symbols because we cannot connect them with any past experience. That is, we cannot remember them because we cannot

[35] *Ibid.,* pp. 27–98.

[36] *Ibid.*

[37] Basinger, *op. cit.,* pp. 36–43.

[38] *Ibid.*

[39] Victor Werner, "How to Remember Everything," *Retirement Living* (February 1973), 44–45.

[40] Harry Lorayne and Jerry Lucas, *The Memory Book* (New York: Stein and Day, 1974), p. 21.

associate them with anything familiar. When we meet new people, it is important to make sure we have heard the name correctly. It is perfectly permissible to ask for the name again, if we did not understand it the first time. We should immediately associate the name and the characteristics of the person. Physical, mental, and emotional characteristics are clues to remembering and associating.[41] Mr. Fox might have a long nose. Mr. Woodman may have a lumberjack build. Mr. Waverly may have curly hair. Mr. Strongham may be skinny and weak. Names like Gillette and Ford can be associated with advertised products. The names of some people can be associated with the name of a town. Visualize that person in the town. If you meet a Virginia Griffin and you know someone named Virginia and someone else named Griffin, form a mental picture of all three persons doing something together. Some names are particularly challenging. Mr. Kamzelski might be pictured as a can of Kam dog food skiing "zealously" down a mountain. Even foreign languages can be learned by this mental picturing and associational technique. If you can double associate the name, write it down, and say it over and over again in the mind—visualizing the silly associational picture you built in your imagination—you should not have any trouble with names and faces. You can also use association to remember positions and occupations of your prospects. Picture the person actively working at the job. Imagination is the key to memory, and it's fun and creative to use your imagination.

Review the Material at Proper Intervals. Forgetting occurs at a rapid rate, especially just after the material is learned. Overlearn the material before you store it. Overlearning is practicing the material beyond the point where you are first able to recall it correctly.[42] It is good practice to recall the material soon after you place it in storage for the first time, because if you wait too long to touch up the fading impression, it may leave for good. It is good to brush up early after the first storage, at bedtime, and about a week later.[43] Be sure you are brushing up correctly by checking the source, if possible. Distortion can be reduced by careful observation, by noticing gaps, and by frequent review and recitation.[44] If you find it difficult to recall, try to get into the same posture and mood and otherwise relive the situation you were in when you first learned the material. Try to think about the lost information intensely for a while and then rest. Return to it later with a renewed focus.[45] Your ability to recall vital names and information will directly affect your selling success.

[41] Werner, *op. cit.*, p. 44.

[42] Basinger, *op. cit.,* p. 45.

[43] Laird and Laird, *op. cit.*, pp. 107–115.

[44] Basinger, *op. cit.,* p. 50.

[45] Laird and Laird, *op. cit.*, pp. 137–147.

Although personality is strongly influenced during early childhood years, a widespread belief exists among psychologists and practitioners that personality can be improved by adults who have the motivation and technique. Self-image theory explains the importance of a healthy belief in one's self, and cybernetics encourages salespeople who want to improve their capabilities, and personalities, by furnishing them with an important model. In cybernetics, the mind is compared to a computer with a programming unit. Negative goals programmed into your computer (mind) will coordinate all the efforts of your mental apparatus to produce a *negative* result. Positive goals programmed into the control unit will coordinate all of your mental machinery to produce *positive* results. Since your mind, like the computer, is a goal-seeking mechanism, it is extremely important that you set definite goals and review them often. Synthetic experience, which is imagining (mentally picturing) that you are actively experiencing an interview situation or some other selling activity, can give you some of the benefits of field experience without the penalties. You can also avoid "hot doorknobs" (purpose tremor) by knowing your product and practicing under artificial conditions.

Another approach to personality development is to work on one trait at a time. An honest self-analysis should reveal some of your weaker personality traits, and you can improve your acceptability by focusing your attention on each weak attribute for a period of several days. Health maintenance is an extremely important personality asset and can be aided through a positive mental attitude, a balanced diet, proper rest, and sensible exercise. A good memory is also important to the selling personality. To improve your ability to recall, approach the material to be learned with the proper attitude, respond and react fully to it, concentrate and give meaning to the material, and review it at proper intervals. Mental visualization, association, and imagination play important roles in remembering information. Personality can make the difference in the sale.

REVIEW QUESTIONS

1. Explain all elements of the cybernetic model. How can it be used to improve personality and goal accomplishments?

2. How can a person reprogram?

3. What is synthetic experience?

4. What elements do you think should be included in social sensitivity?

5. How can you improve your appearance? Should salespersons wear leisure suits?

6. How does the text suggest you improve your ability to observe?

7. What would you attempt to observe in a prospect's office?

8. Give all suggestions that might help improve your ability to recall.

9. How would you remember the following names: John Smith, Ned Bigham, Albert Delmanski?

10. If you lost your keys, how would you try to remember where you left them?

11. What should a salesperson do to maintain health?

12. Outline a program to improve your personality based on the information in the chapter.

APPLICATION QUESTIONS

1. What traits mentioned in this chapter do you need to develop the most? Which ones do you feel you exhibit properly already?

2. Can you keep from being critical of anyone for half a day? Try it!

3. What do you think other people think of you; that is, what is their image of you?

4. Give an example of a joke that you feel would be appropriate to tell a business prospect.

INCIDENTS

4–1

Vice-president James Davenport and sales manager Tom Powell are discussing promoting either salesman Saul Abraham or Mike Kolb to zone sales manager.

James: Tom, Saul and Mike both have excellent sales records, but tell me how you see each of them and which one you recommend.

Tom: Well, Mike was outstanding in college, and he knows the technical side of the products better than Saul. Both of them have essentially the same selling records after six years with the company. Mike learns faster than Saul. I vote for Saul.

James: Why? I thought you just said that Mike was better . . .

Tom: I said he is better technically and can learn faster and that *is* important in our business. But Saul is a good listener, and he's good enough technically. I believe I can work better with Saul, and the other salesmen like him. We'll have less turnover of junior salesmen with Saul.

James: Well, I like them both, and they both seem to have good personalities. Mike had a 3.3 grade average in college, and Saul had a 3.0. Mike has outsold Saul by about 5 percent of quota. Are you saying that Saul is more cooperative?

Tom: Saul always thinks of the other fellow first and never says anything bad about anyone. He's better liked by the men, but they respect him, too. While he may not be quite as aggressive as Mike, I've never had a customer complaint on Saul. I've had four customers say they felt that Mike was a bit high pressure and arrogant. Mike is polite to us and respectful, I know, but he is *so* out for Mike. He's critical, too. I don't think he has the leadership qualities Saul has.

James: How do you think Mike would take it if we promote Saul over him?

Tom: Jim, he's ultra-ambitious and won't like it, but he'll mend. Saul is more level-tempered and just . . . well, more mature.

James: I can see what you are trying to say. I must confess I've always felt Saul was more of a team player—a company man. Mike is a driver and an excellently motivated individualist . . . I agree, in the zone position, it would be easier to teach Saul the technical side than it would be to try to change Mike's personality. Let's give Mike some additional territory, but let's give Saul the zone.

Tom: Right.

QUESTIONS

1. What do you think is more important for management, personality or high technical competence? Why?

2. Which man, Mike or Saul, is more achievement-motivated? Why?

3. Do you think Powell and Davenport looked at this situation logically?

4–2

Bill Mullins has worked for the Gulfside Chemical Company for twelve years. Until the last three years, he had always made over quota and was considered one of the best senior salespersons. Although his sales performance seems to slip a little more each year, he sold 90 percent of his quota last year. Everyone likes Bill. He's an extrovert with an excellent sense of humor, although sometimes his stories are a little off-color, and he uses profanity occasionally in talking to some customers. He has been depressed lately, because his wife left two months ago after eighteen years of marriage. The word is that Bill has been drinking heavily and that is why his wife left him. He was arrested for drunken driving last Tuesday at 4 P.M. and lost his license for at least a month. This morning he missed the eight o'clock sales meeting at the branch and came in at nine o'clock, looking a little "smashed." He was not quite drunk, but he was not quite sober either.

If you were the sales manager, how would you handle this situation? What would you say to Bill?
Do you think this is a common managerial and personal problem in personal selling?
If Bill keeps going in the same direction, what will be the eventual outcome?

4–3

Brad Brothers is an excellent student. He has an A average and spends a great deal of time studying. He is not very social and doesn't belong to any campus organizations. Although the university has winning teams, he seldom attends any basketball or football games. He likes other people but he has a tendency to talk about himself when he is with others. He really doesn't like to listen to what other people have to say. He has defended his self-image by telling himself that he is really much smarter than most of the other students and therefore doesn't have much in common with them. Most of his classmates respect his mind, but most prefer not to be around him because of the superior air he transmits. He doesn't seem to want to talk about the things that interest them. Brad is nice looking and keeps in fair shape by jogging around the track by himself. He is an introvert, but he is highly intelligent. Mary Lou Spencer is one of the few girls who has ever paid much attention to Brad. Because Brad met Mary Lou he wants to change. He realizes that he has been fooling himself and wants to be popular with people and accepted by Mary Lou. He is lonely and tired of doing everything by himself. He has decided that because he is good at computer programming and math that he would like to change his major to marketing and go into computer sales. At last he has realized his personality handicap and wants to do something about it.

Do you think Brad can improve his personality?
Based on what you have learned from this chapter, what would you advise him to do?

5 Communication and Persuasion

Every good sales representative must be able to communicate effectively. This involves much more than the competent use of words. Understanding theories of communication gives the salesperson access to new areas of thinking and practitioner experience. Communication entails nonverbal as well as verbal ways to put across the total sales message. It includes formulating persuasive strategy based on past experiences of successful communicators. To help you prepare for your role in persuasion, the following topics will be treated in this chapter:

- Communication ideas
- Nonverbal communication
- Persuasive strategies

COMMUNICATION IDEAS

Communications Involve a Common Basis

"Communications" comes from the Latin word "communis" meaning common. The more we have in common with other people, the better we communicate with them. A child may try to talk to a butterfly, but there are no common denominators for communication. Communicating with persons from a country with a different language and culture is also very difficult. We communicate best with people who are like us and who have shared common experiences with us. To the salesperson, this means that it is important to strive for maximum identification (emotional ties)

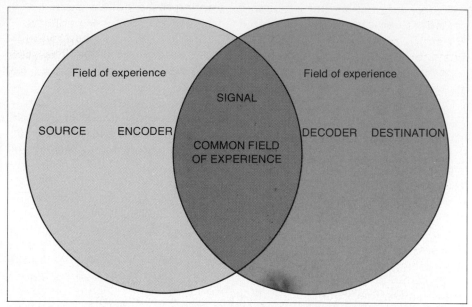

Field of experience

SIGNAL

SOURCE   ENCODER

COMMON FIELD
OF EXPERIENCE

Field of experience

DECODER   DESTINATION

Source: Wilbur Schramm, *The Process and Effects of Mass Communications*, (Urbana: University of Illinois Press, 1954), p. 6.

Figure 5.1   Schramm's Communication Diagram

with the prospect and to weave the conversation around agreeable interests. The communications model (see Figure 5.1) shows that communications take place only within shared fields (areas) of experience.[1] If there is little overlap, the transmission of exact meanings becomes a difficult challenge.

The Parts of Communication

The model also shows the elements of communication: "source, encoder, signal or message channel, decoder, and destination."[2] In the armed forces, it is necessary to encode and decode messages formally to keep the contents secret. In ordinary conversation, we encode and decode through words and nonverbal signals, although the sender and the encoder are usually the same person. When people say "Good morning," they are encoding. They do not really mean to comment on the quality of the day. They are saying, "I recognize you as a person, and I am acknowledging you pleasantly." The person decoding the message will determine ac-

[1] Wilbur Schramm, *The Process and Effects of Mass Communications,* (Urbana: University of Illinois Press, 1954), pp. 3–26.

[2] *Ibid.*

cordingly that the sender is simply attempting to be polite. Sales representatives particularly must be certain that their messages are interpreted correctly. Many English words have dozens of meanings, and potential exists for misunderstanding the exact intent of the message. The salesperson's choice of words, the phrasing, the way the words are said, and the gestures used must be correct.

Receivers consider the source of messages to determine how much attention they will give to the message and its content. Messages believed to be from a reliable and competent source are persuasive. This is why the prospect's impression of the salesperson is so important. The receiver always attempts to read the attitude and the motivation of the sender. The appearance of the sender (the salesperson) and the way in which the words are presented may convey more meaning to the receiver (the prospect) than the actual words. One reason why testimonials of satisfied customers are so effective is that the prospect believes that such seemingly unbiased sources have no monetary stake in the outcome. While prospects expect the sales representative to use every known device to influence sales, they usually believe that another customer is more sincere in evaluating the product.

The *signal* concerns the way the message is transmitted and the clarity of the communication. Face-to-face communications, which allow interpretation of nonverbal signals and more complete feedback, are usually persuasively superior to written messages or telephone conversations. Personal interviews allow more shared ideas and joint interpretations and reduce the chances of *noise*. *Noise* is any audible or other distraction that distorts the quality of the message.[3] The distraction may be so great that the message may not even be heard. Salespersons should minimize distractions during the interview by attempting to select a time and place as free as possible from interference. For example, it is bad practice to talk to the prospect in an atmosphere of distraction such as in a busy passageway. *Feedback,* or the response of the receiver to the message, is necessary to judge the effect of the message and to determine if the communication has been decoded properly. You should listen and adjust to *feedback*.

Four Good Rules for Communicating

There are four especially important rules for good communication.[4] First, the message must be planned and delivered in such a way as to

[3] Wilbur Schramm, "Information Theory and Mass Communication," *Journalism Quarterly* (Spring 1955) pp. 13–146.
[4] Wilbur Schramm, "The Process and Effects of Mass Communication," *loc. cit.*

attract the attention of the receiver. Not only should the message be loud or visible enough to be noticed, but it should contain some cue that will grab the receiver's interest. It should also reach the receiver when he or she is apt to be tuned in. Second, the message should incorporate words that relate to the common experience of the sender and the receiver. In planning the message, remember that it must harmonize with the receiver's point of view or it may be rejected or its meaning distorted. Third, the message should be designed to appeal to or arouse the personal needs of the receiver while suggesting a way to meet the needs. Prospects require action to fulfill their needs, and the action you wish them to take should be *specifically* suggested. The last rule is that the method of meeting needs should relate to group influences affecting the prospect at the time of the suggested action.

Communication May Have a Two-Step Flow Effect

Communication often flows from a source, through media, and to the opinion leaders, who influence the mass accepters of an idea.[5] Opinion leaders may be different for different products. Persons are usually leaders because they know most about the product, are socially well located, and/or are distinguished in a certain area. This suggests that you should first concentrate on opinion leaders and use their testimonies to influence later buyers. Many prospects are much easier to sell if they can be assured that respected leaders in their industry have endorsed the product. Positive word-of-mouth product evaluations are often the best promotion.

Two-Way Communication

Two-way communication promotes prospect participation and encourages adequate feedback. To promote persuasive two-way communication, use words your listener can understand, ask good questions, and listen carefully to what the person is saying. Inexperienced salespersons have a tendency to monopolize the interview and not give the prospect a chance to react. Questions should require more than just a simple yes or no answer; they should cause the prospect to think deeply about needs. You might ask, for example, "If you could have an automobile custom-made

[5] Elihu Katz, "The Two-Step Flow of Communication: An Up-tp-Date Report on an Hypothesis," *The Public Opinion Quarterly,* 21 (Spring 1957), 61–78.

for you, what kind of features would you like to see included?" or "How long does it take to do your entire payroll operation by hand?" Questions like these stimulate the prospect to review needs and give the sales representative a usable response. You may be tempted to plan and formulate strategy while the prospect is speaking, but if you do not listen carefully, you will miss valuable feedback and important clues as to how you should proceed. Everything the prospect says should be analyzed and considered as a basis of response.

Words Have Different Meanings

Words are symbols in which messages are encoded. Because words have different meanings to different people and suggest different mental images, it is almost impossible to transmit exact meanings by words alone. There are dozens of meanings for the word "round," and there are at least eight meanings for the word "frog," depending on the context in which the word is used.[6] The Eskimos have three words for "snow." The Greeks have three words for "love." And some tribes distinguish between all the different varieties of rice with a different word for each.[7] Children relive movies as they describe the vivid scenes, but the words mean little to the receiver who has not experienced the pictures or the music. Even small children have surprisingly large vocabularies, and the reason they are not able to communicate as well as adults is that they are self-centered senders, who expect listeners to understand without sharing the experience (frames of reference). Sales representatives need to be sensitive about using words within the experience of the prospect. Words also mean different things in different cultures. In England the hood of an automobile is a "bonnet," and in the Navy, the ceiling is the "overhead." To sailors, there is a difference between ships and boats. Some cultures have private meanings for hundreds of words. Such private meanings serve almost as passwords for acceptance into the culture or group and distinguish group members from outsiders. Scientific fields also have words forming private vocabularies.[8] Persons who have experienced similar educations and events can shorten conversations by using common terms and be well understood by their colleagues. But sales representa-

[6] S. I. Hayakawa, "How Words Change Our Lives," *The Saturday Evening Post,* December 27, 1958, p. 72.

[7] Stewart L. Tubbs and Sylvia Moss, *Human Communication* (New York: Random House, 1974), pp. 111–140.

[8] *Ibid.*

tives must use concrete terms or establish commonness by using the vocabulary of the field. In industrial or medical sales, professional salespersons must establish themselves by an appropriate vocabulary.

Denotation and Connotation. Words have both a denotative and a connotative meaning. *Denotation* indicates associations the word has for most people. *Connotation* refers to secondary associations that may differ among members of a language group. The word "cat," for example, usually denotes a four-footed domestic animal of rather mild disposition. To someone who has been bitten by a cat or to an animal trainer, the word has different secondary associations. You should watch words that may have severe negative connotations. People are also tempted to categorize and prejudge all "sailors," "salespeople," and "politicians." That is, they tend to stereotype all members of certain groups. You should be aware of the tendency to evaluate on one-word cues. Furnish more information if you feel the word might be misleading because it has a stereotyped image to the prospect.

Word Attributes. Word attributes may be concrete or abstract, active or passive, emotional or neutral, and holy or profane. Words may have racial or political overtones.[9] Concrete words convey more accurate meanings than abstract words like "beautiful" or "flexible." It is better to say, "This unit types 300 words per minute" than to say, "This unit types quickly." It is also better to use active verbs rather than passive verbs. "She bought that machine without seeing it" is better than "That machine was bought by someone who had not seen it." Some words like "communism," "death," and "home" have emotional content. A sign saying "Home for Sale" is better than a sign saying "House for Sale." The word "home" stirs positive emotions in most people, while the word "house" is a more neutral word. The use of profanity reflects on the sincerity and credence of the source and is offensive to most prospects. Sexual profanity will lower a salesperson's credibility even more than religious profanity.[10] Words like "Democrat" or "Republican" may be emotionally charged to many buyers, and slurs against a buyer's political party, however indirect, may promote a conflicting atmosphere. You should observe the political scene, in fact, to see how essential words can be. It is hard for politicians to be against bills entitled "Truth in Packaging," "Fair Employment," or "The Right to Work." Jimmy Carter created an uproar by his expression "ethnic purity," and other politicians have been career-damaged by using words carelessly.

[9] *Ibid.*

[10] *Ibid.*, p. 133.

Use Understandable Words. Your *signals* must be, above all, under-standable and prospect-oriented. Short sentences and short words are usually preferred in sales presentations. Your ability to use multisyllabic words may impress your prospect, but the words may either fail to communicate your basic selling message or make the prospect feel uneducated for not understanding you. Always use easily understood words in your messages.

Use "You" Not "I." In selling, it is far better to overuse the words "you" and "we" than it is to overuse pronouns like "I," "me," and "mine." Salespersons who overuse references to themselves indicate their self-centeredness rather than an orientation to the personality needs of others.

NONVERBAL COMMUNICATION

The potential for reading and sending nonverbal signals in the sales interview situation is exciting. More than two-thirds of the communication between a sales representative and a prospect can be nonverbal.[11] While prospects may hide truth and inner feelings with words, they may be revealing intent, attitudes, and emotions through body language. You may also be sending out nonverbal signals that prospects receive sub-consciously but which are the basis of their impression of you and your intentions. Every salesperson must learn to read and respond to cus-tomers' nonword signals and to increase their effectiveness through properly expressing this silent language.

The scientific stress on nonverbal communication is new. Because it is a largely unconscious language, which varies from culture to culture, great care must be taken in interpreting signals. Nonverbal cues are indications that should be read only in conjunction with other evidence or other nonverbal cues. People may cross their arms and still be interested and receptive; they may rub their nose because it itches, not to express doubt. Usually, nonverbal clues support the speaker's words, and when they do, they tend to verify what is said. When the nonverbal and the verbal messages conflict, it indicates that the whole truth is not being told. A woman prospect, for example, may say she is disinterested because she wants to bargain with you. However, you can tell by her expression and the way she handles the product that she is indeed interested.

A full coverage of nonverbal communication is beyond the scope of this text. This section is designed to help you become more aware of this

[11] William G. Savage, "Sure Listen; But Watch Their Gestures, Too," *Administrative Manage-ment,* 33, no. 8 (August 1972), 33.

iceberg existing below the surface of word communication, to give you some sources for further study (in the footnotes), and to acquaint you with certain signals that you might receive or use in selling the prospect.

The elements of nonverbal communication are:

- Space
- Body messages
- Touching
- Timing and voice characteristics

Space

The distances preferred by people who are communicating yield important clues to their personalities, their purposes, and the formality with which they plan to converse. While sweethearts may be less than a foot apart when talking to each other, impersonal business is usually conducted from a distance of between four and seven feet.[12] The sales interview should be conducted as close as four or five feet from the prospect and even closer, if the prospect is an outgoing extrovert or well known to the salesperson. Close distance promotes a more friendly and less formal interview climate. When too much distance separates the prospect and the salesperson, the salesperson may wonder why the prospect seems so psychologically distant and why good two-way communication is not taking place.

The average American has an imaginary *privacy bubble* that surrounds the body and extends out about two feet in every direction.[13] If you invade this personal space, the person will normally move back, stiffen, or become defensive in some other way. Introverts have a larger privacy bubble than extroverts. Mexicans demand less space and like to converse at closer intervals. Blacks have a larger personal space zone than whites.[14] Violent prisoners in jail for assault often have a personal space bubble many times larger than normal, and invading their personal space could be fatal.[15] Interrogators for the police are advised to interview suspects at close range with nothing (furniture) between questioner and suspect. The recommended procedure is to move even closer as the questioning progresses in order to break down the suspect's defenses by violating personal space.[16] Many excellent sales representatives enter the personal

[12] Edward T. Hall, *The Hidden Dimension* (New York: Doubleday, 1966), pp. 107–122.

[13] Julius Fast, *Body Language* (New York: Evans, 1970), pp. 28–63.

[14] Tubbs and Moss, *op. cit.,* p. 146.

[15] Fast, *op. cit.*

[16] *Ibid.*

space of indecisive and extroverted prospects by getting very close and maintaining good eye contact. *If handled correctly,* the silent pressure of being near is permissible with most prospects, improves attention and communication, and indicates friendliness and sincerity. Attempts to move closer to prospects depend on prospects' sensitivity to pressure and the selling situation. If the prospect indicates annoyance, you can move back a little. Introverts and prospects who wish to maintain a formal interview may resent attempts to move nearer as being "pushy," while others may interpret it as a sign that the salesperson is confident about the product. Certainly, if nothing else has worked on the prospect, this is a strategy that might be tried.

Space also indicates dominance. Persons of high rank or status tend to relax in close contact with subordinates, while lower-ranked persons tend to stiffen. Sales representatives that are ill-at-ease in close proximity to an important customer are conveying, "I haven't much confidence in myself or my product." The way the salesperson enters the prospect's office also indicates confidence and self-image. The quicker you enter the room, the greater your status will appear. The salesperson who lacks a confident self-image may stop at the door and talk to the seated executive

"Come all the way in, Ferguson. I want to have a little talk with you about self-confidence."

THE SATURDAY EVENING POST

Reprinted from *The Saturday Evening Post* © 1961 The Curtis Publishing Company.

Salespersons indicate much about their personalities by the way they enter the office.

across the room. If you stop half-way to the desk, you are indicating more confidence. If you stop in front of the desk, you are indicating that you feel you should have equal conversational status with the executive.[17] A failure to approach the executive sets an improper interview tone—one of subordination on the part of the salesperson—unless the executive is extremely high ranking.

Prospects, like other individuals, assume "ownership" of customary places in conference rooms, restaurants, and parking lots, just as you may feel that you have a priority on your customary classroom seat.[18] Moreover, if your prospect is sharing a table with you, he or she will subconsciously subdivide the table into two equal parts and assume ownership of the nearest half.[19] You can make other people uncomfortable by putting something of yours on "their side" of the table. The sales representative should respect these imaginary territorial boundaries.

We express liking for people by drawing closer to them, looking into their eyes, and taking positions near them. We say that people are "distant" when they attempt to avoid being close. When prospects try to avoid us or communicate with us through a more impersonal method than face-to-face interviewing, they may be signaling refusal attitudes instead of giving us a flat "no." People don't like to break bad news to us when we are in their presence, so they seek a more impersonal way to refuse our requests.[20] Special actions of avoidance, therefore, signal negative attitudes before the prospect has verbally committed to rejecting the offer, thereby giving the sales representative a chance to try a new tack before closing to a committed "no."

Body Messages

We send messages by means of body postures and positions, body movements, the face, and hands. We also consciously and subconsciously receive messages from prospective customers in the same way. While it is dangerous to be "clued in" and to react to one signal, signals in conjunction with words and a succession of consistent signals can give good indications about a prospect's thinking.

Postures and Positions. See Figure 5.2. Tense and rigid postures indicate anxiety, defensiveness, and/or unreceptivity. Perhaps the listener

[17] Albert Mehrabian, *Silent Messages* (Belmont, Calif.: Wadsworth, 1971), pp. 24–39.

[18] Fast, *op. cit.,* pp. 25–33.

[19] *Ibid.*

[20] Mehrabian, *op. cit.,* p. 11.

Defensiveness

Receptivity

Touching indicates interest

Close personal distance

Figure 5.2

is concerned that the interview is too long or that the product does not meet his or her needs. Perhaps the listener feels too much pressure. On the other hand, too much relaxation can show boredom and inattentiveness. The receptive prospect exhibits a semirelaxed posture, a slightly tilted head, and an open-armed, open-legged position.[21] Women unconsciously indicate receptivity and sincerity through the display of their open palms.[22] Prospects crossing their legs with their knee pointing toward you are indicating receptivity. If the knee points away from you, this implies orientation in another direction. Locked ankles and clenched hands reveal the holding back of strong feelings or emotions.[23] In tense interviews, as in the dentist's chair, people tend to sit with their ankles locked. The crossed-arm position, while sitting or standing, shows defensiveness and a lack of receptivity to your presentation. You might hand this prospect something, shift your position, or regain attention and receptivity in some other way. When people lean back in a chair using both hands to support the head from behind, they may be showing feelings of superiority. You may cater to these feelings by complimenting the customer or by showing respect in another way. A prospect who puts hands on hips may anticipate doing something.[24] Any change of position indicates a change of mind. The prospect may be trying to end the interview, may have reacted to something you just said, or may have decided to accept your offer if you ask for the order. Interestingly enough, people of the same opinion in a group tend to unconsciously assume the same body postures, especially if they are reacting to a speaker who has just expressed their point of view verbally.[25] If prospects agree with you, they may imitate your body position, which indicates a definite closing signal. Such opportunities should be met with at least a trial close.

Body Movements. Body movements send messages. Subconsciously we tend to get into the same rhythm with people with whom we converse. Gestures tend to move in similar patterns, like in music. This is part of the commonness that harmonizes face-to-face communications. Some sales representatives are better persuaders because of their basic body rhythms. Their individual movements aid their expression.[26] Their

[21] Gerard I. Nierenberg and Henry H. Calero, *How to Read a Person Like a Book* (New York: Pocket Books, 1973), pp. 1 ff.

[22] Flora Davis, *Inside Intuition: What We Know About Nonverbal Communication* (New York: McGraw-Hill, 1973), p. 16.

[23] Nierenberg and Calero, *op. cit.*

[24] *Ibid.*

[25] Fast, *op. cit.*, pp. 132–134.

[26] Davis, *op. cit.*, pp. 128–142.

head moves upward when they ask a question, and they tilt it slightly, moving closer to the prospect to show that they are listening with interest. The posture, rhythm, and tempo of their body conveys their alertness and enthusiasm.

As important as it is to send correct messages through actions, it is also necessary to interpret the prospect's motions accurately. For example, a male customer may want to hint to you that he is out of time or for some other reason wishes to end the interview. He may shift forward in the chair, move backwards, or get up and walk around.[27] If he is standing, he may walk away and back to you and start cleaning off his desk to tell you—without causing embarrassment—that your time is up, and he has other things to do. If you are perceptive, you should reinterest the prospect, conclude by closing, verbally acknowledge that you realize how valuable his time is, or make interview-ending signals. In a group-selling situation, the person who deliberately moves to a position different from the rest of the group may be attempting to assert superiority. The person whose body motions are imitated by others in the group may be telling you that he or she is the dominant person present and should be the focus of your selling efforts.[28] Variations in body movements and messages are almost endless. Many movements are not universal in meaning. The burden of learning geographical variations is up to each sales representative. Like the poker player, the salesperson must be adept at noticing every detailed movement that might reveal the intentions of the other "player" in the "game."

The Face. The face, particularly the area around the eyes, is a complex of small muscles capable of communicating hundreds of messages. Prospects use their faces to indicate approval, expectation, happiness, concern, or state of relaxation. The prospect may even try to use facial expression to prove disinterest in order to bargain. However, timing can indicate whether the prospect is sincere or not. Fortunately, you have learned to read faces fairly accurately, but you may need to be reminded of the potential for reading prospect emotions by observing facial expressions. The eye area is the most important. Magicians depend on the eyes of a subject to select the "right" card.[29] Eye expressions change when the right card (the card selected by the subject) appears, and the pupils enlarge with excitement. Similarly, salespersons can tell at what point their words have made an impression on the prospect. Good eye contact conveys interest and sincerity, while eye avoidance in our culture is

[27] Mehrabian, *op. cit.,* p. 3.

[28] Fast, *op. cit.,* p. 133.

[29] Davis, *op. cit.,* p. 80.

Everyone appreciates a sincere smile!

"Come now, where's that infectious little smile?"

THE SATURDAY EVENING POST

Reprinted from *The Saturday Evening Post*
© 1957 The Curtis Publishing Company.

associated with dishonesty and insincerity. We can smile with our eyes and convey many emotions by the positioning of our brows. We can catch the eye of our prospect to get attention, just as we can catch the eye of a waiter. While stares and glares are considered threatening, longer contact then usual indicates interest. Contact that is too long invades the privacy of the prospect and is considered bad manners in our culture.[30] Remember, the deadpan look is for comics and poker players, not for salespersons showing enthusiasm and attempting to generate interest.

Hands. Our hands help us communicate by allowing us to draw pictures in the air; to express size, shape, or direction; to command attention; and to convey dominance or acceptance. Prospects with tightly clasped or

[30] Tubbs and Moss, *op. cit.,* pp. 151–152.

fidgeting hands reveal tension. If they tap the desk or move a foot up and down, impatience or restlessness is indicated, and we have either lost absolute attention, or we are receiving a signal that the interview is taking too much time.[31] Prospects may cover their eyes to indicate embarrassment, cover their mouth to say something they don't want you to repeat, or hit their forehead to show forgetfulness. They may touch their nose to indicate that they don't fully believe what you are saying.[32] If they "steeple" their fingers (touch fingertip to fingertip), they may be signaling dominance or superiority. If they clench their fist, on the other hand, they may be strongly defensive and disagreeing mentally with what you are telling them.[33] If they stroke their chin, they may be evaluating (considering) what you are saying. Certainly, you can see that you must be very careful in making interpretations of hand movements, since any one of these signs can also mean something else. Again, these signals must be interpreted in context.

Touching

Touching indicates intimacy and should be done with sincerity. The handshake is of particular significance. The firm handshake indicates liking and friendliness, but the prolonged handshake (like prolonged eye contact) is too intimate in most situations. A limp, loose, or cold handshake shows a tendency toward uninvolvement, unfriendliness, and aloofness.[34] The first physical contact with the prospect is critical. Remember, closeness means liking, but too much or inappropriate closeness indicates insincerity—and touching is as close as you can get. While touching (putting your hand on the shoulder or on the back) may cause some prospects to drop their defensiveness, it may embarrass and offend others. Touching to get the prospect's attention is rude. The best rule is to confine touching to the handshake, except under unusual circumstances or with special friends who need consolation.

When prospects touch or handle the product, they may be signaling an intent to possess. Prospects usually convey true feelings about the product by the way they handle or try it. If they handle it carefully, they may feel that it is valuable; if they handle it roughly, they may feel that it is worth little or is durable. Prospects also form opinions about the product by the way the salesperson handles it. Aluminum-cookware

[31] Nierenberg and Calero, *op. cit.,* pp. 1 ff.

[32] *Ibid.*

[33] *Ibid.*

[34] Mehrabian, *op. cit.*, pp. 7–8.

salespersons will carefully pull their wares out of velveteen sacks to suggest that the quality of the utensils is like that of fine silver.

Timing and Voice Characteristics

Your timing and how you say what you say, like your body language, give clues to your attitudes, emotions, and thoughtfulness. Late appearances for engagements, neglect through inattention, and wasting prospects' time indicate that the sales representative is unreliable and discourteous. Needless to say, being late does not set a harmonious interview atmosphere. Your timing during conversations may be just as critical. Interrupting indicates an attempt to dominate, and few prospects appreciate being interrupted, especially when they have just begun speaking.[35] Long pauses before answering a question reveal the answer is not natural and may be falsified.[36] Long pauses in the middle of expressing an idea are especially bad in persuasive communications, because the prospect's mind is distracted from *what* is being said to *how* it is being said.

A good presentation voice should have proper tone, appropriate volume, and pleasing pitch.[37] The tone of your voice shows whether you have a positive or negative attitude toward the listener. It can reflect joy, sadness, apprehension, and fear. Apprehension may be interpreted by the prospect as dishonesty. Speakers who increase their pitch and speak faster than the normal 125 words per minute tend to seem more alive and dynamic. Sales representatives who talk too softly may lose the listener and may be thought of as shy or inhibited.[38] Talking too loud is also offensive and indicates a lack of manners and refinement as well as an attempt to be domineering. Pitch should be varied to produce interest; a monotone voice is boring to everyone. Lower pitch levels are more pleasing. While pitch level does not seem to affect the amount of information a prospect comprehends, it influences the attitude of the prospect toward the salesperson and the message. Voices differ, but through practice and interest, you can improve your voice and your acceptability.

PERSUASIVE STRATEGIES

A knowledge of general persuasive strategies should help you select and direct the specific selling methods that will be discussed later.

[35] Davis, *op. cit.*, p. 210.

[36] Tubbs and Moss, *op. cit.*, pp. 155–161.

[37] *Ibid.*

[38] *Ibid.*

The whole strategy of persuasion is to follow the train of thought of your prospects and not directly challenge or argue with them. Prospects cannot be expected to buy anything that is completely incompatible with their mental beliefs and attitudes. They won't buy unless they believe that by buying they will accomplish one or more specific goals. The more goals prospects see themselves accomplishing by purchasing your product, the more likely they are to buy it.[39] This is another reason why you should make sure that all the product's benefits and uses are explained in a complete presentation. The more clearly the prospect sees buying as accomplishing multiple goals, the more likely your recommendations will be accepted.[40] If your recommendations do not fit in with the prospect's thinking, your proposal will be rejected or altered, or the very structure of the prospect's thinking will be changed.[41] The salesperson should try to adjust the prospect's concept of the product to fit in with the prospects' attitudes, needs, and motives *without* rearranging basic thinking patterns. *The power of suggestion, selected strategic ideas,* and *propaganda techniques* as applied to persuasion should help you become more convincing.

The Power of Suggestion

Under hypnosis, people will do things they would not ordinarily do. As the chapter on personality mentioned, hypnotized people are able to do even more than they ordinarily would, because they are free from inhibiting restraints. Conscious suggestion has proven to be the basic tool in the salesperson's magic kit. Even hardened attitudes can be changed over time through repeated conscious suggestion. Hitler, who misguided millions of people, said that people would believe a lie if you told it often enough. Conscious suggestion is used in brainwashing. Yet it can also be used for good persuasive purposes. Repeated conscious suggestion is the basis for successful advertising campaigns and personal selling. Vividly suggest the benefits of using the product. Appeal to what you feel is the dominant buying motive. Be positive and precise in your suggestions. In closing, ask the prospect to take a specific action. After he or she buys, "suggest" other products. Sometimes, persuasive appeals have a delayed effect. All this does not mean that you should sound like a broken record. It does mean that by using variations in appealing to prospects' main motives, you can relax resistance and persuade them to

---

[39] Dorwin Cartwright, "Some Principles of Mass Persuasion," *Human Relations* (London: Plenum, 1949) pp. 253–263.

[40] *Ibid.*

[41] *Ibid.*

a definite course of action—buying your products to fulfill need goals. If you do not plant ideas leading to the purchase of your product, it is unlikely that you will reap many sales.

Ten Strategic Ideas

Many studies have been done to find out what general types of persuasive strategy should be used, with whom, and under what circumstances. The following ten suggestions were formulated from basic persuasion generalizations on opinion and attitude change, found in *Persuasion* by Marvin Karlins and Herbert Albeson, but paraphrased to fit the selling situation.[42]

1. *Attempt to promote harmony early in the interview by initially expressing views held by your prospect.* This is part of establishing rapport. You don't want to come on strong with anything that might promote conflict. Later on, when you present the challenge to change the prospect's mind, the close will be easier if you have gotten *agreement* on minor points and features first.

2. *Put your best selling points at the beginning or at the end of the presentation.* Those points made in the middle of the presentation stand the least chance of influencing a prospect or being remembered. When you are trying to organize your sales-presentation strategy, use some of your best selling points or features to gain attention at the very beginning. You should be aware that your very first words are especially important, because your prospect uses them in the process of deciding whether or not to give you time and attention. You also want to make a positive impact just before you attempt to ask for the order. So save a climatic closing feature for the close of your sales presentation.

3. *Appeal to as many of the prospect's senses as you can.* People understand products better if they can see them, touch them, hear them, taste them, or smell them. The sales representative should carry the actual product, samples, or pictures of the product into the meeting with the prospect for demonstration. The impression on the prospect's mind will be stronger because of the appeal to more senses. Few things are as persuasive as actually experiencing the product. New cars shine, smell clean and new, sound efficient, and respond easily to the prospect's steering commands. As prospects "experience the product" with their senses, you should use phrases like "Shines like glass, doesn't it?" to stimulate perception.

[42] Marvin Karlins and Herbert I. Ableson, *Persuasion,* 2nd ed. (New York: Springer Publishing, 1970), pp. 1 ff.

4. *Enlist the active participation of the prospect in the discussion or demonstration.* Several studies have shown that active participants are more persuadable than passive listeners. Getting prospects to participate is part of leading them to believe that they are making up their own mind rather than being sold. If the prospect can drive the car, operate the machine, or try on the clothes while you suggest the benefits of buying, you will have attention and be able to maintain interest. Ask questions to bring potential buyers into the discussion. One of the most important persuasion strategies is letting prospects think they made up their mind. No one likes to think of themselves as weak-willed enough to be ''sold.'' Have you ever heard anyone say, ''I was sold a new car''? No. A person would say, ''I bought a new car today.'' If you don't sell prospects on the particular sales call in which they participated, they will still remember the participation interview the most clearly. It doesn't take long for the effects of persuasive communication to wear off, unless the sales points are ingrained through participation.

5. *Balance your appeal in some cases by admitting to prospects one or more minor shortcomings in your offering.* To admit that your product is not perfect may enhance your believability as a communication source. It may also be good strategy if your prospects are intelligent, not in initial agreement, or when you think competition will tell them anyway before you get a chance to close the sale. Highly intelligent prospects like to hear both sides of an argument and are less susceptible to the ''card-stacking'' propaganda technique of citing a long string of plus features. If prospects don't know you very well, one of the most important things for them to determine is whether you are telling the truth about the product. Less intelligent individuals are more easily persuaded if you don't bring up any limiting features of the product. The decision to admit minor deficiencies depends on the situation. If you do, be sure to overbalance any weakness in your product with the weight of many product virtues. ''Yes, this typing unit is louder than we would like it to be, but having a removable typing unit will give you much more flexibility, and it will be easy to clean the typeface. The number printout is quieter than the competitions', and the numbers will be what you'll use most.''

6. *Use both emotional and factual appeals to change attitudes.* Studies show that information alone seldom changes attitudes, especially attitudes that are shared by the prospect's reference group. Prospects need the factual appeals to *justify* the change you propose mentally, and they need the emotional appeal *to want* to change. A fear appeal is a negative appeal and should be used with care and

only in certain circumstances. Studies indicate that a mild fear appeal is better than a strong fear appeal in persuasive situations where people will hear communications from the other side of the same issue. On the other hand, a strong fear appeal may be more persuasive in situations involving a threat to the prospect's family or when that strong appeal is backed by a highly creditable source and immediate action can be taken. Sales representatives often appeal to prospects' fear of losing the buying opportunity if they fail to act quickly. Stronger fear appeals are used by insurance company representatives and sales representatives for particular safety equipment. Humor is seldom an effective persuasive technique.

7. *In situations in which you are selling to a group of prospects, such as in a partnership, concentrate on the extroverts, the women, or the highly intelligent persons.* Evidence suggests that they are more persuadable and often may help you persuade the others. Introverts and the less intelligent are more difficult to persuade and usually less influential. The highly intelligent are more susceptible to logical, balanced arguments, and will usually listen to reasonable arguments with an open mind. However, they are influenced by authoritative sources. You can use high-powered testimonials from competent authorities to sway these prospects.

8. *Persuade, if possible, without directly opposing a prospect's reference group standards. And, whenever possible, make the message reinforce those influences.* Every individual relates to a group of people when decisions are made. The average person does not like to make decisions that are incompatible with his or her group's thinking. A member of a very conservative club, for example, would hesitate to buy loud, gaudy clothes or automobiles for fear of losing status and commonness with club members. Persons who identify strongly with particular groups resist the influence of appeals that conflict with group thinking. In this regard, opinions that prospects share with others are more difficult to change than those that they hold privately. It strengthens a prospect's loyalty to your product if you can get him or her to write a letter of endorsement or openly promote your product to others.

9. *Don't expect prospects to draw their own conclusions from the evidence you give. Conclude by giving a product-favoring interpretation of the facts and evidence.* Even intelligent persons may not favorably interpret the facts to your offering, and few people are insulted by a simple concluding statement, even when the interpretation is fairly obvious. If the audience is very suspicious or unreceptive, however, there is the possibility that they could interpret your conclusions as a propaganda ploy or an insult to their intelligence. But this interpretation is rare.

10. *If you feel that the prospect regards you as a highly creditable source, you might ask for a bigger order or a higher price than you are likely to get.* Part of the bargaining process is to take a position beyond what you expect. Politicians do it. Labor unions do it. Real estate salespersons do it. Real-estate sales representatives may ask $39,500 for a house that they would be willing to sell for $37,000. Prospects feel that they are getting a bargain. If the position is too extreme, however, the house will not be considered, and it may acquire the image of the house nobody wants. Studies on attitude change indicate that *polar position taking* by the persuader does have more change effect than taking positions close to that of the persuadee. It depends on the competitive situation. Polar position taking in a tightly competitive deal would probably be unwise.

Propaganda Techniques

To most people, the word "propaganda" has a negative connotation of unfair competitive influence or manipulation. Some propaganda techniques, however, are persuasive, usable, and acceptable in particular selling situations.[43] *Testimonials* involve open endorsement of the product by someone who is respected by prospects in the target market. It is one of the most persuasive techniques and should be considered in all selling efforts. A notebook with many testimonial letters from satisfied buyers is an impressive sales tool. *Name calling* is associating a competitive product with something undesirable by giving it a bad label. A salesperson may say in referring to a competitive machine that has a noise problem: "Make sure you don't get an accounting machine that sounds like a threshing machine. Noise is an important factor in an office." This technique should be used indirectly, if at all. The competitor should not be mentioned by name. *Card stacking* is giving one-sided arguments for a product. Most prospects expect salespersons to be biased in favor of their product, so they are seldom offended if a salesperson tells them only the good things about the offering. Card stacking is especially effective with less sophisticated prospects who won't hear the other side from competition.

The *bandwagon* technique is the suggestion that everybody's doing it (buying the product), so the prospect should too. This is a technique that is particularly useful in regard to clothes and automobiles, but it can also be used for products that are not quite as style-oriented. Persons who are strongly influenced by reference groups are more susceptible to this

---

[43] Propaganda techniques are from Alfred McClung Lee and Elizabeth Briant Lee, *The Fine Art of Propaganda* (New York: Harcourt, Brace, 1939), as treated in Steuart Henderson Britt, *Consumer Behavior and the Behavioral Sciences* (New York: Wiley, 1966), pp. 454–455.

appeal, while persons who pride themselves on being individualistic may be "turned off" by it. Most prospects don't want to be out of style or the last to adopt a better product, so this is usually a good appeal. *Association* is an effective propaganda technique that is usable in persuasive situations. The salesperson should always associate (relate) the product with pleasant scenes or events to promote positive emotional images. For instance, automobiles should be demonstrated and shown in conjunction with pleasant surroundings. Word pictures can be painted that encourage the prospect to associate the product with favorable settings. "You would feel comfortable in this suit in any luxury hotel," or "This car would be comfortable on a long-distance vacation." Positive mental images of the product are built by association.

SUMMARY

Effective communication requires a common field of experience between the message sender and the message receiver, transmission of the intended message to the receiver's senses, and proper encoding and decoding. Messages should attract attention, create interest, harmonize with the receiver's point of view, and relate to the receiver's reference-group influences. Good questions, careful listening, and adequate feedback enhance two-way communications. Words are encoding symbols and affect the reception of the message. Specific, understandable words with good connotation for the receiver are the building blocks of good sales presentations. Nonverbal communications include the use of space, body movement, body contact, physical appearance and arrangements, and vocal variations and silences. These convey intent, emotions, and attitudes. It is essential that the sales representative learn to read and use nonverbal language, which had been largely neglected in communications research until lately. Persuasive strategy features the use of the power of suggestion, ideas giving insight to interview planning, and propaganda techniques.

REVIEW QUESTIONS

1. We encode by means of word selection. Explain.

2. How buyers judge the sales representative's image affects how they accept the salesperson as a source of information. Explain.

3. Define "noise" and "feedback."

4. Make up three questions about your hypothetical product—an automobile—that are designed to establish two-way communication with your prospects and to cause them to think about their need for your product.

5. When should you use general terms in selling? When should you use specific terms?

6. What is the difference between connotation and denotation?

7. What kind of words should you avoid using in a sales situation?

8. When you use "I," "me," or "mine" too much in your conversation or letters, what impression does your prospect get? Why?

9. Are most communications between people verbal or nonverbal? Explain.

10. What are the pros and cons of getting physically close to the prospect in the interview?

11. What may be the meaning of the following "body messages":
    a. A person who sits in the middle of a bench
    b. A prospect who sits or stands with crossed arms
    c. A prospect who sits with locked ankles
    d. A prospect who changes position
    e. People in the same group who assume the same body position
    f. A woman who displays open palms to another person
    g. A prospect who taps a pencil or fingers on the desk

12. Explain all the messages a person's eyes and face can send that were mentioned in the chapter.

13. List at least six signals people may give with their hands.

14. What qualities should a good presentation voice have?

15. What can tone of voice convey? What can pitch convey? Volume?

16. What three reactions may your prospects have when your proposal runs counter to their thinking (cognitive structure)?

17. Explain the use of conscious suggestion in persuasion.

18. What are the ten strategic rules for persuasion?

19. Define each of the five propaganda techniques mentioned in the chapter. Which one do you think would be most useful to you in selling? Explain.

APPLICATION QUESTIONS

1. Explain Schramm's four rules for communicating. Can you suggest two more?

2. If you wanted to buy a car, whom would you ask for advice? Would you consider that person an opinion leader? Explain.

3. How do people react when you invade their privacy bubble? Try it on two people and record their responses.

4. What happens when you take someone else's customary chair at the dinner table or put your keys on their side of the table? Try it and see.

INCIDENTS

5-1

Roger Willis of Highlift Equipment Corporation sells industrial elevators. He is calling on Mike Polski, vice-president of Dutton Warehouses.

Roger: Mr. Polski, I'm Roger Willis of Highlift Equipment Corporation. I would like to discuss with you the incorporation of vertical elevators in your next warehouse expansion.

Mike: (*putting newspaper down on desk in front of him and offering hand*): Sit down, Roger. I was just reading about the campaign for the next presidential elections. What do you think of the Democrats and their platform?

Roger: I haven't had a chance to study it yet, Mr. Polski. I'm optimistic that the economy will pick up, however, no matter who wins. We seem to be in a time when business is thinking expansion. Is your company planning any new warehouses in the future?

Mike: Well, we may build a two story in about a year, but that's so far off. . . . We're just in the thinking-about-it stage. I'm not sure if Mr. Dutton is planning to go one story or two. It does depend on just how much space we think we will need six months from now. (*Still looking at morning newspaper.*) Say, look at these women at the Women's Conference. How do you feel about women in politics?

Roger: It depends on who the woman is, I guess. Some have made a very positive contribution, while others seem to have taken a short-range viewpoint. Mr. Polski (*pulls plans out of briefcase*), here are some warehouse plans that have enabled twice the storage capabilities of one story on the same amount of land with negligible loss in stock-movement efficiency. These buildings cost much less per square foot to build, even equipped with four vertical elevators. That would make a nice building, wouldn't it?

Mike: Yes. I would be glad to see what you have. (*Puts paper on a side table so he can look at the plans.*) Land space is expensive today, and I plan to recommend that we go two story on this one.

QUESTIONS

1. What was Roger's major communications problem in getting started on this interview?

2. Did he handle the politically charged questions correctly? Should he have been more open and stated his real views?

3. How did he regain attention and establish favorable two-way communication?

5–2

James Appleton, a vacuum cleaner salesman, is calling on Jane and Robert Smythe in their suburban home.

Robert Smythe: Yes?

James Appleton: Hello, I'm James Appleton, and I'm conducting a survey. May I come in?

Robert: Sure, what do you want to know?

James: We're interested in how many square feet of carpet you have in your house. Can you give me an estimate?

Robert: Say, are you a salesman? Wasn't that a vacuum cleaner you left on the porch?

James: Can I show you how it works? (*Sprinkles a bag of dirt on the rug.*)

Robert: What are you doing?

James: Don't worry, our vacuum cleaners are wonderful. I'll have it up in a jiffy.

Jane Smythe: What's going on in here? What is all that dirt doing on the carpet? I just shampooed it, and it is still damp.

Robert: You had better get that up, or I'm going to call a cop.

James: I'm trying. Something's wrong. It usually works.

Robert: Why didn't you ask me before you did that?

James: Have you got any shampoo?

Jane: Yes, here it is, and here's a brush. Get every bit of that up.

Robert: I see you have a Supervac. You know our vacuum played out on us last week.

James: There, it's almost clean. Can I show you how my great Supervac works?

Robert: I'd wash the whole thing with a toothbrush before I'd buy anything from you or your company. Get out of here fast before I change my mind and call the police. (*Reading Robert's body language, James makes a hasty exit.*)

Jane: Why did you tell him we needed a vacuum cleaner?

Robert: That's the only way I knew to get his goat since I couldn't hit him. Maybe he will think twice before he tries to con someone else.

James: (*outside to himself*) There must be a better way.

QUESTIONS

1. Tell James a better way to establish rapport and gain the prospect's attention.

2. In regard to communication theory, what do you think Jane and Robert think of the source of the communication and the pretense of conducting a survey to get in?

5–3

John Merino sells agricultural chemicals to farmers. His main line consists of herbicides (weed- and grass-killing chemicals) and insecticides. The herbicides are mostly premerge (mixed with the soil during planting to prevent weed and grass growth), and the insecticides are sold later in the growing season after the crop comes up and is threatened with insect infestation. John has an excellent education and has a tendency to express himself in big words. He feels that this gives him a professional image. He also likes to wear fashionable suits when calling on customers.

John's sales manager went with him on a call because John is behind on quota. John was dressed in a fashionable Ivy League suit and wore highly polished black shoes. The sales manager heard John use these two sentences during the course of the conversation with a farmer:

"On this particular premerge compound, photodecomposition will occur unless incorporated."
"This compound is subject to microbial breakdown when applied to the soil and may be antagonistic with preapplied compounds."

The farmer replied at the end of John's presentation that he would consider the chemicals and would call if he needed any of John's products. John's sales manager reviewed the interview with John and told him that the farmer probably didn't understand all of the interview. He also suggested that John wear clothes more suitable to field interviews. John agreed that perhaps farmers would not identify with him unless he spoke in simpler terms. He also decided that he should dress in more appropriate clothing.

John didn't shave the next morning and wore some faded jeans and a tattered jacket. He left his sports car at home and borrowed an older compact model. This time John talked in as simple words as he could and even tried to imitate the particular dialect that was used in that part of the state. He tried to talk "country." When he finished, the farmer spoke to him with perfect diction and without the slightest trace of a country accent (the farmer knew he was being talked "down to"):

> "Mr. Merino, I'm going to be honest with you. If your chemicals are so good, why haven't your sales been good enough to keep you in clothes and a good truck? I need another hand here on the farm, and it doesn't matter whether you can talk well or not. Would you be interested in a steady-paying job?"

What communication mistakes did John make with the first farmer? With the second farmer?

If John's sales manager had been present for the second interview, what do you think he would have said to John?

Why is it important to establish identification (a commonness) with your prospects?

5–4

The Hampton Corporation makes a full line of aquatic equipment for divers and wants to expand its operations by going international and selling to aquatic interests in Spain. Several alternatives have been suggested as to how to do this. One corporate vice-president recommended that American sales representatives, who already know the product, be taught Spanish and transferred to Spain under a bonus agreement. A member of the board of directors recommended hiring Puerto Rican or Mexican-American citizens and training them in product knowledge for the job. The corporation president wants to hire Spanish nationals and train them in the United States.

In terms of what you know about communications theory, make your recommendations as to which of the three alternatives you would select and fully support your decision.

6 Understanding the Buyer

Before selling strategy can be properly devised, the salesperson must know *how* to identify and classify prospects, *why* prospects might want to buy the product, *how* prospects make their decisions, and *who* influences them. Thus, it is important to know how to measure your market and how to identify personality differences in prospective buyers. *Why* the prospect wants to buy the product is the cornerstone of strategy. If a salesperson wants to use a customized appeal during the interview, some premise (estimate) of buyer motivation must be made. Sales experts stress the idea of focusing the interview on *one* dominant buying motive. This requires being able to identify dominant buying motives first. Identification is made easier by learning to recognize the usual motives that prompt people to purchase. The quality of your persuasive appeals and your strategic timing depend on *how* buyers make their decisions. In order to make the best possible estimate of how prospects think, you should understand buyer decision theory. Accordingly, this chapter is offered to give you a better understanding of the basic areas essential to selling strategy. They are:

- Buyer identification
- Buyer motivation
- Buyer decision theories and models

139

BUYER IDENTIFICATION

Who Is the Prospect?

There are really three prospects who must be considered in every selling strategy: the prospective user, the prospective decider, and the prospective buyer. Often, the decider *is* the user and the buying agent, and this simplifies focusing persuasive effort. In some businesses, however, the production engineer must decide when the production worker needs new equipment. The engineer sends a requisition to the purchasing agent to procure a new machine. In a case like this, the sales representative would need to consider all three persons in strategic planning. When several persons influence the purchase, it would be naïve not to consider each of them.

Market Identification

The sales representative identifies the market in terms of certain buyer characteristics. Prospects may be described in terms of income, geographic location, education, occupation, age, sex, race, and many other easily determined attributes. U.S. censuses give this kind of socioeconomic information about most localities. Your company should also be able to furnish you with profiles (identifying characteristics) of the kinds of customers who have traditionally bought the products you are selling. Sometimes, however, distinguishing characteristics are not as measurable and noticeable. In that case you must look for behavioral characteristics such as club memberships, hobbies, interests, life-styles, and philosophies that distinguish buyers from nonprospects. If you sell industrial products, you will be interested in the characteristics of the *firms* that might use your product.

Buyers Are Different

Although your best prospects will have much in common in terms of age, income, education, and other measurable characteristics, you will encounter many different personality types among your customers. The strategies that might work for you with an extroverted prospect may be completely wrong for an introvert. Even more challenging is the prospect who seems to change moods from visit to visit. Some of the personality differences you may encounter are discussed below.

Introverts and Extroverts

Introverts are usually rather quiet, studious people who may be suspicious of salespersons. Usually, they are very analytical and want complete information about the offering, but if they think you are wasting their time, they may terminate the interview without notice. They often prefer rational appeals over emotional appeals and are not heavily influenced by the salesperson's personality. They listen well, but it is difficult to elicit feedback from them. They are sensitive buyers and easily take offense at statements that conflict with their basic attitudes and beliefs. It is harder to establish two-way conversations with introverts, since they pride themselves on their independence of thought and individuality.[1] Most introverts are formal and like to talk to the salesperson at a comfortable distance. You should not violate their imaginary personal space bubble or fail to respect their "territories" (see Chapter 5). They prefer not to be "sold" but to feel they have made up their own minds about purchasing the product. They prefer a businesslike interview.

Extroverts, on the other hand, like to talk, care little for formality, and react to a sales representative's personality when considering the buying proposal. They are people oriented and will avoid causing unpleasantness or hurting the salesperson's feelings. Like the introvert, they like to be listened to when talking, but they may get off the subject of the business at hand.[2] Extroverts are more social-minded and less analytical than introverts. They may be interested in testimonials and appeals that emphasize others are buying the product. They like to laugh and joke, and you may move closer to them and be more animated in your nonverbal communication. They are susceptible to emotional appeals and may be impulsive deciders. Most people are combinations of the two types, but you must decide in *what ways* each prospect is an introvert or extrovert.

Other Prospect Profiles

Joseph W. Thompson classifies prospects into ten different types and suggests a strategy for handling each type (see Figure 6.1). Knowing how to vary selling strategy to fit the prospect is one of the basic differences between the experienced salesperson and the rookie. And experience can be gained more rapidly if the salesperson considers types and matches the strategy with the type.

[1] Carlton A. Pederson and Milburn D. Wright, *Selling Principles and Methods,* 6th ed. (Homewood, Ill.: Irwin, 1976), pp. 84–85.

[2] *Ibid.*

Figure 6.1 Prospect Classes and Strategy

Classification:	General Strategy:
1. The silent prospect	1. To get a response, ask questions and be more personal than usual.
2. The procrastinator	2. Summarize benefits he will lose if he doesn't act. Be positive, self-assured and dramatic but not overpowering. Suggest that he has the power and ability to make decisions. Use showmanship to overcome indecision.
3. The "glad hander," talkative or over-enthusiastic type	3. Salesman must lead prospect back into the sale. This person sells you, but doesn't seem to buy. Say, "By the way, that reminds me, etc." Keep on the track—be brief.
4. Slow or methodical type	4. He appears to weigh every word, so slow down and amplify on details. Adjust your tempo to his.
5. Pugilistic, chip-on-shoulder or argumentative type	5. Usually insincere and tries salesman's patience. He is a difficult type to deal with but sincerity and respect on the salesman's part create respect.
6. Over-cautious or timid type	6. Take it slow and easy. Reassure on every point. Use logic, but make it simple.
7. Ego-involved or opinionated type	7. Give him rope by flattering his ego and catering to his whims. Listen attentively. Take the cash and let the credit go.
8. Skeptical or suspicious type	8. Acknowledge his background, stay with facts, be conservative in statements.
9. The grouch	9. Ask questions to ascertain real problems. Listen and let him tell his story.
10. Impulsive, changeable, fast type	10. Be rapid, speed up, concentrate only on important points, omit details when possible.

Source: Joseph W. Thompson, "A Strategy of Selling," in Steven J. Shaw and Joseph W. Thompson (eds.) *Salesmanship* (New York: Holt, Rinehart and Winston, 1966), pp. 13–25.

Transactional Analysis

Transactional analysis is one of the newer and more sophisticated guides that can be used for typing prospects and devising selling strategy. Its basic concept is simple enough to understand and can be used as a model for improving communications. An *ego state* is a condition of mind, a consistent mental reference state that influences the behavior of both the prospect and the salesperson. It is a set or system of feelings that prompts certain consistent patterns of behavior.[3] Each person has three ego states that determine that person's mental attitudes, communication messages, and actions. They are the *parent*, the *child*, and the *adult*. One of these ego states is dominant at a particular time and influences the person's words and actions. However, the person may change from one ego state to another during the course of an interview. Since each person is a combination of three ego states, six ego states are represented when two people communicate. Many combinations can take place.[4] Transactional analysis is a conscious attempt to identify the ego state of another person in order to formulate a suitable strategy before responding to that ego state. Voice tones, gestures, vocabularies, speech rates, and facial expressions all give clues to the ego state prompting them.[5]

The Parent Ego State. When people are acting in the parent ego state, they behave the way their parents seemed to act towards them when they were children. Someone acting from the parent ego state is judgmental, authoritative, dominant, arbitrary, and demonstrates a superior attitude. They may be hardworking and rule abiding but closed-minded, critical, and outmoded in respect to living and thinking in the present.[6] Such a reference state is indicated by accusing voice tones and dominant types of body language (the pointing finger).[7] The prospect who won't listen, attempts to dominate the salesperson, and is highly critical is probably acting from the parent ego state. The salesperson who is high-pressure and unyielding is also acting from this state. The parent ego state reflects the idea that the *parent* is right, and the person to whom the parent talks is the *child* who must "shape up" and yield to superior authority.

---

[3] Eric Berne, *Transactional Analysis in Psychotherapy* (New York: Grove Press, 1961), pp. 17–22.

[4] Dudley Bennett, "Transactional Analysis in Management," *Personnel,* 52, no. 1 (January–February 1975), 34–36.

[5] *Ibid.,* p. 36.

[6] *Ibid.,* pp. 37–39.

[7] *Ibid.,* pp. 34–43.

The Child Ego State. The child ego state (not related to age) is reflected in defensive behavior. Every person has the *child* inside somewhere who responds and acts in reference to behavior patterns learned in preschool years. Eric Berne, the father of transactional analysis, feels that to the person, the child is perhaps the most valuable ego state.[8] While a person is in the child ego state, he or she is more creative and innovative. Because the child is more submissive and humble (at times the child can also be rebellious), the child is more adjusting and is better liked. The person may, however, communicate and act out of emotions and fantasies and distort reality.[9] People avoiding problems and practicing escapism are usually acting in the child ego state. They are receptive, apologetic, and feel they should adjust and change. Persuasive service salespersons are often dominated by their child ego states and project a friendly, helpful attitude that allows their prospects to enjoy the dominant role.[10]

The Adult Ego State. Persons acting out of the adult ego state are realistic and rational. Problems are faced squarely, and the person functions much like a computer using mathematics and probability in decision making. All alternatives are considered in an orderly, unemotional manner. The emphasis is on the present, and the approach to any situation is scientific and thorough. Indicative of this ego state are nods, open-minded listening, and a willingness to exchange information without emotional involvement.[11] A fair, businesslike attitude indicates the adult ego state. The highly professional innovative sales representative would act out of this reference. The sales representative would be friendly but realistic and "fact-minded." Customers accept this kind of salesperson as a great source of help (see Figure 6.2).[12]

Life Positions and Communication. A person in the dominant *parent* ego state transacts from an "I'm O.K.—you're not O.K." life position. The *child* may, from a yielding nature, transact from a "You're O.K.—I'm not O.K." position. The *adult* ego state transacts from the "I'm O.K.—you're O.K." position. When two people can communicate and transact from an adult to adult reference, emotions and power relationships (status) do not hinder their communications.[13] The salesperson may attempt to switch

[8] Eric Berne, *What Do You Say After You Say Hello?* (New York: Grove Press, 1971), pp. 12–20.

[9] Bennett, *loc cit.*

[10] *Ibid.*

[11] *Ibid.*

[12] *Ibid.*

[13] Heinz Weihrich, "MBO: Appraisal with Transactional Analysis," *Personnel Journal,* 55, no. 4 (April 1976), 173–175.

Figure 6.2 Transactional Analysis, Ego States and Situations

When people are acting out of this ego state, they talk and behave in reference to their concept of parental behavior, formed when they were children. Persons acting out of this state tend to be authoritative, dominant, judgmental, arbitrary, protective, critical, rule abiding, outmoded in thinking, and superior in attitude.

Persons acting out of the adult ego state tend to be realistic, scientific, unemotional, rational, fact-minded, and they emphasize the present. Such people are likely to have fair, businesslike attitudes and a willingness to exchange information without emotional involvement.

When persons act out of this ego state they imitate patterns of behavior learned in preschool years. The *"child"* is creative, imaginative, submissive, humble, emotional, sometimes unrealistic, and sometimes rebellious.

In this exchange, a critical, authoritative supervisor or prospect may converse with a submissive and humble employee or salesperson. The *child* may resent the superiority exhibited by the *superior*. The *child* will probably reserve hostility and withhold information from such a supervisor or prospect that would indicate his or her true feelings. Such conversations rarely uncover the real facts.

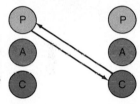

In this exchange, two rational persons are talking productively, unemotionally, and realistically. They are likely to transmit accurate information and get to the root of a problem. This is a desirable transaction from both sides.

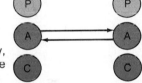

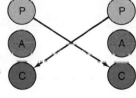

This exchange is likely to wind up in heated words or a fight. Both authoritative ego states are clashing and neither is submissive or yielding. Such cross communications can be highly unproductive.

Sources: Based on information from Dudley Bennett, "Transactional Analysis in Management," *Personnel*, 52, no. 1 (January/February 1975), 34–36; and Heinz Weihrich, "MBO Appraisal with Transactional Analysis," *Personnel Journal*, 55, no. 4 (April 1976), 173–175.

The adult should be dominant in the innovative salesperson, because high-level buyers prefer to communicate on a rational, factual basis. The engaging personality and the imagination of the child are needed for likability and creativity. The critical and nurturing parent should be suppressed for most sales situations.

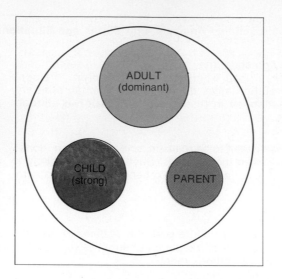

Figure 6.3   A Good Ego State Composition for the Innovative Salesperson

the prospect's ego state to the more responsive child or try to approach the more rational adult ego state to justify a product. The salesperson may adjust and listen to authoritative *parent* prospects and let them talk themselves into the sale. The basic strategy is to determine the prospect's present ego state and either *cater to or attempt to switch it* to suit the interview strategy. Miscommunications often take place when the salesperson makes a statement from the adult ego state, and the prospect answers from the parent or child ego state. Just being aware of the barrier to profitable two-way conversation suggests the remedy: Lead the interview to the proper ego-state interaction. A good sales personality ego-state profile is reflected in Figure 6.3.

BUYER MOTIVATION

In order to direct persuasive appeals, some premise, scientific or intuitive, must be used to identify buyer motivation. Familiarization with motivational classes and theory should result in a more realistic assessment of dominant prospect-activating forces. A motive is an inner tension that causes the prospect to act. If there is no problem (or disequilibrium), there is no motive. Often, a prospect is unaware of a problem or need. The salesperson should be able to translate an unrecognized need into an action-producing want. First, the sales representative must estimate potential buying motives and identify the most dominant one. Motives are based on needs. Salespersons must question, observe, and recognize what needs prospects *should* have, based on their circumstances. Salespeople must form an initial premise and then try to get prospects to reveal their specific motive(s). Often, the situation is complicated because there are several motives, and buyers are hesitant to reveal real motives, particularly if the motives affect their image. Also, sometimes buyers are unaware of their drives. If salespersons are unable to uncover much about the buyer's motives or about the selling situation, they must rely on past experience and standard appeals. They must assume usual motives exist for wanting the product. However, such a salesperson is at a competitive disadvantage. The sales representative can better assess motivation by learning more about:

- The kinds of motives
- Maslow's dynamic theory
- Allport's ideas
- Sociological influences

The Kinds of Motives

Freud was a pioneer in motivational theory. To Freud, the *id* was the originator of strong drives and urges, and the sex motive or the wish to return to the security of the prenatal state was the underlying drive. Advertising strategists and occasionally salespersons are accused of overstressing the sex motive. Freud's explanation proved to be too simple, and later writers recognized the urge for power and the need to be accepted by others as being just as important. Today, scores of motives are recognized and classified. Classifications that are particularly useful to the salesperson are: emotional, rational, and patronage motives. Some motives may fit into more than one classification, and in such cases, the motive is included where it is most likely to occur.

Emotional Buying Motives. Buyers prefer to appear rational and scientific in their decisions, and they hesitate to admit that they bought a car to be envied or esteemed. Nevertheless, most buyers are persuaded through direct or indirect appeal to emotions. The manager may buy the computer because he wants to point with *pride* to the fact that the company now has a data-processing system. Love, hate, fear, the urge to be esteemed, the need for power, the need to be accepted and liked, the desire for achievement, the need for recreation and pleasure, and the need for bodily comfort create the strong tensions and disequilibriums that ultimately move consumers and business prospects to action. Most persons are not highly rational computers when it comes to buying decisions. But they do feel they must *justify* their purchases to themselves or to others in terms of rational reasons for buying.

Rational Buying Motives. Rational or economic buying motives include such reasons as resale potential, dependability, flexibility, durability, efficiency, reciprocity (you buy from me; I'll buy from you; and we'll both profit), cost savings or earning potentials, economy in use, and uniformity of finished product. The main motive for industrial buyers may be advancing their position in the firm. Many industrial buyers who can fully justify a purchase for the firm's benefit will not buy unless they see the purchase as beneficial to themselves or without risk to their careers. I remember a man who managed an office for a chain of theaters. He did not buy a bookkeeping machine, because he thought it would replace two of his employees and he would have less people to supervise. While economic buying motives are widely accepted as the force behind purchasing industrial goods, there are usually emotional motives somewhere behind the economic ones. For example, the retailer wants to make more money so he can take that recreational trip to California. Emotional motives are more direct and usually stronger than economic motives. You should look for the underlying emotional motive when you make a sale.

Patronage Motives. A special set of motives explains why people buy from you rather than from your competitor. People like *variety and selection* and will patronize stores and salespersons affording them ample choice. *Price* is one of the strongest patronage motives. If you can convince prospects that your price is less for the same quality, they will usually buy from you. A reputation for *quality* helps reduce the buyer's risks. The *service* given with the product is another patronage motive. With some products such as computers, the software (service) is almost as important as the hardware. *Location and convenience* are also important. People do not like to inconvenience themselves, and many would rather pay $10 more per night to stay in a motel on the waterfront than walk across the street to a motel 300 feet from the water. The *personality of the salesperson* is stressed throughout this book as a very important reason for buying from a particular firm. The firm's *reputation* is another strong patronage motive. What other people think about a firm matters a great deal in selecting a buying source.

Maslow's Dynamic Theory

A. H. Maslow's *Dynamic Theory* not only classifies motives (see Figure 6.4) but also explains their interactions. Maslow recognizes five motive

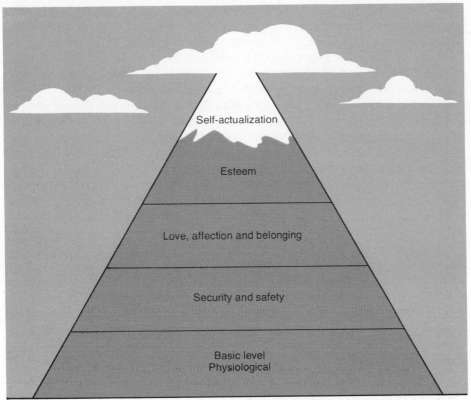

Maslow stated that there were five levels of need from basic needs to more social needs. Self-actualization needs may be hard to define and are never really satisfied. When a person satisfies lower-level needs, he or she is released to recognize higher-level needs.

Source: A. H. Maslow, "A Theory of Human Motivation," *Psychological Review*, 50(1943), 370–396.

Figure 6.4   Maslow's Motivational Theory

levels. He writes that satisfying one motive frees a person to recognize that he or she has other needs. In other words, that person is released from a lower level of need to satisfy a higher level of need.[14] Maslow's basic level of need comprises the *physiological needs* or body needs (for food, water, and so on). These needs cease to exist as active determinants of behavior, once they have been satisfied.

After the basic level of need has been satisfied, *safety needs* emerge. When a person's security is threatened, he or she develops tension and becomes motivated. Because most American safety needs are met through laws, there is little daily threat to citizens in this country. Safety needs do become important, however, in times of emergency.[15]

[14] A. H. Maslow, "A Theory of Human Motivation," *Psychological Review,* 50 (1943), 370–376.
[15] *Ibid.*

Assuming that *physiological* and *safety* needs are satisfied, *love, affection, and belonging needs* then emerge. The satisfaction-release-motivation cycle repeats itself. The person feels the absence of sweethearts, spouses, children, or friends. This level of need in our society is strong and is often at the root of severe psychological maladjustments and pathologies. The love need is both a giving and receiving need.[16]

All people have a need for a good self-image and want to feel strong, adequate, and confident. The *esteem need* is a desire for prestige and reputation. Satisfying this need leads to feelings of self-confidence, worthiness, and a stable, high-level self-image. Not being able to satisfy this need leads to inferiority complexes and damages self-image.[17] Many things people buy are related to the esteem need—new and expensive cars, extravagant houses, and fashions. With many of the other levels satisfied, the esteem need level can lead to strong buying motivations.

If all of the other need levels are satisfied, the need for *self-actualization* will surface. This is the need to reach one's full potential—physically, mentally, or spiritually.[18] Alexander the Great is reported to have cried when he had no more worlds to conquer. When people extend their horizons, they always find new potentials for personality development. If you notice television advertisements for food, you will see that the appeal is more often aimed at self-fulfillment for women in their role as creative homemaker than it is to basic hunger. Also notice magazine advertising appeals in relation to this theory.

The five motivation levels do not appear in the same order for all people. Most religions urge, in fact, that believers reverse the natural order and put spiritual self-actualization first. Sales representatives should recognize that in our wealthy society, they must appeal to the three higher levels of need in most cases. In less-developed societies, safety and physiological needs might gain more response, but in America the more social needs (love, esteem, self-actualization) will probably continue to receive major emphasis.

Allport's Ideas

Gordon W. Allport wrote that if an action is done habitually it becomes a motive.[19] This explains why a laborer works at a skill long after it is no longer required, why businesspeople work themselves into ill health long after economic security has been reached, and why people loyally buy

[16] *Ibid.*

[17] *Ibid.*

[18] *Ibid.*

[19] Gordon W. Allport, "The Functional Autonomy of Motives," *American Journal of Psychology*, 50 (1937), 141–156.

products, even after something better has come onto the market. Allport also recognizes the need to finish tasks. Incomplete work results in tension and a negatively motivated state.[20]

Allport contends that direct methods are better than indirect methods to ascertain motives. He strongly believes that you can take what most normal people say about their motives on face value; unless admitting the motive reflects negatively against their self-image.[21] People have a tendency to hide motives that might reveal them as vain or self-centered. However, in an indirect way, the salesperson can appeal to those motives that prospects do not want identified.

Sociological Influences

Sociological theories explain that motives stem from a person's relationships with groups. These theories corroborate the need to belong and to be esteemed. People engage in *role playing* and take their identification group into consideration before buying products. Social class also influences what products and stores people patronize. People buy products that are culturally compatible with their social system ideals or norms. Appealing to the person's *desire to identify* with a group can lead to the sale. When people are "role playing," they will be motivated to buy the clothes, automobiles, or other symbols identified with that role. The "benevolent employer role" may lead a person to buy industrial safety equipment or work improvements. The "good mother role" may lead a mother to buy encyclopedias or educational toys for her children. People also like to dress like members of their group or like a group to which they aspire. A shriner, for example, might be motivated to buy a motorcycle or an antique car to fit into his group better. It has been shown that women seldom patronize department stores that are out of their social class (up or down). It is also true that prospects are influenced by how much they identify with the salesperson. The need to belong, to be accepted, and to be esteemed by one's reference groups and aspiration groups (groups to which one would like to belong) explains many sales.

DECISION THEORIES AND MODELS

Knowing *why* prospects buy is not enough. You also need to understand theories about *how* people buy. Learning theory and self-image matching

---

[20] *Ibid.*

[21] Gordon W. Allport, "The Trend in Motivational Theory," *American Journal of Orthopsychiatry,* 23 (1953), 107–119.

theory will be examined to explain the influences, timing, and processes of consumer decision making.

Howard's Learning Model

John Howard sees customers as *learning* to buy products, and his theory is compatible with Allport's emphasis on habit. As Figure 6.5 shows, consumer decision making is divided into three stages: extensive problem solving, limited problem solving, and automatic response behavior.[22] *Extensive problem solving* is the most important stage, because buyers recognize a problem in this stage and search for a solution. Certain personality traits, prices, time pressures, financial statuses, social and organizational settings, social classes, and cultures influence prospects' searching behavior. Internal variables or personality variables also influence actions of buyers. Internal variables might be mental attitudes (predispositions), strength of motivation, and how a product is seen and understood.[23] The salesperson's job is to furnish information and assurances that influence the buyer's mental machinery. External variables, such as time pressure and reference-group influences, should be identified and taken into account in selling strategy. It is during the first stage of *extensive problem solving behavior* that the buyer will seek information to solve his or her problem and is most susceptible to selling appeals. The salesperson may place buyers in this receptive stage by proving that they do have a problem with their old product.

Each time the buyer makes a purchase and the product yields satisfaction, the buyer learns that the product satisfies his or her needs, and the tendency to buy again is increased. After a few purchases, less search and mental activity will be necessary, and the buyer enters the *limited problem-solving stage.*[24] The buyer still considers the purchase briefly and is still open to consideration of alternative products, but a purchasing habit is beginning to take shape. The salesperson must show buyers a definite relative advantage to get them to change products. In the final stage, *automatic response behavior,* the habit is complete. The probability of repeat purchase is very high, and the buyer believes that the problem has been solved. It will take strong sales appeals to make a loyal customer switch. During this stage, buyers will not consider alternatives unless

[22] John A. Howard, *Marketing Management,* revised ed. (Homewood, Ill.: Irwin, 1963), pp. 33–113.

[23] *Ibid.*

[24] *Ibid.*

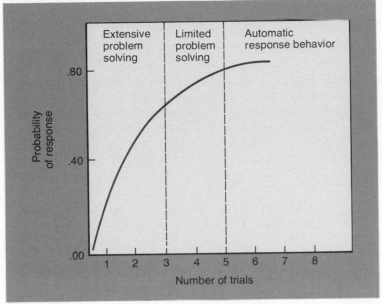

Source: John A. Howard, *Marketing Management,*
rev. ed. (Homewood, Ill.: Irwin, 1963), p. 36.

Figure 6.5   John Howard's Learning Model

forced to do so, or unless they find a problem with the old product because
of additional information or because the product ceases to satisfy.

Howard's learning theory explains why new products without a definite
relative advantage over existing products have such a difficult time in the
market. It also explains why the salesperson who encounters a consumer
in ARB (Automatic Response Behavior) for a competitive product must
use strong persuasive methods to change the buyer's mind. The theory
underlines the importance of establishing habitual buying behavior in the
prospect for both the product and the company. It suggests that a full-
line strategy is helpful in serving all of the prospect's needs. It shows the
need for customer cultivation. It indicates the need for a more informative
risk-reducing strategy if the prospect is "open" in the *extensive problem
solving stage.* A harder impact strategy, perhaps with more emotional
appeal, will be necessary to help buyers overreach the threshold of
resistance and change from the competitive product when they are in the
automatic response behavior stage. New products without a strong
relative advantage are likely to fail because purchasing habits are so
ingrained.

Kotler's Explanations and Models

Philip Kotler reviews five explanations of why people buy: *Marshall's Economic Model, Pavlov's Learning Model, Freud's Theory, Veblen's Concept,* and *Hobbes' Model.*[25] Each theory offers insights into buyer decision behavior. Alfred Marshall saw the buyer as a rational, calculating individual determined to get maximum satisfaction from money. The *Marshall Economic Model* emphasizes the buyer's tendency to compare your product and competitive products in regard to relative prices. The buyer will attempt to select the offering that yields the greatest satisfaction (utility) for the money. The *Pavlovian Model,* like Howard's, emphasizes the customer as a learner. This theory stresses the importance of strong reinforcement (satisfaction from using), strong motivational drives, and the necessity of cues (the weaker stimuli that influence how, when, and where the prospect responds).[26] It also stresses the tendency for the buyer to "forget" because of failure to use the product for a long period of time. *Freudian theory,* with its emphasis on sex, indicates that people buy things because of subconscious influences.[27] Many research approaches attempt to probe deep into the subconscious and determine subconscious motives, in order to obtain direction for selling appeals. However, it is unwise for the salesperson without adequate psychological training to attempt to determine unconscious motives.

Thorstein Veblen wrote that most consumption is motivated by prestige seeking. Buyers decide to consume conspicuously with reference to their social classes, reference groups, and family pressures.[28] Thomas Hobbes postulated that the buyer is guided by group and individual goals. Buyers think both of what the purchase means for their company and how it will affect personal goals.

Kotler offers a model (Figure 6.6) of the buyer's decision-making process.[29] The model is oversimplified since it does not explain what goes on inside the buyer's psyche. But, salespeople can take their pick from theories about motivation discussed earlier. The model does organize and show as a process the working together of influences, information channels, mental digestion, and buying responses. The model also gives the sales representative some idea about sequence and the various fac-

[25] Philip Kotler, "Behavioral Models For Analyzing Buyers," *The Journal of Marketing,* 29, no. 4 (October 1965), 37–45.

[26] *Ibid.*

[27] *Ibid.*

[28] *Ibid.*

[29] *Ibid.*

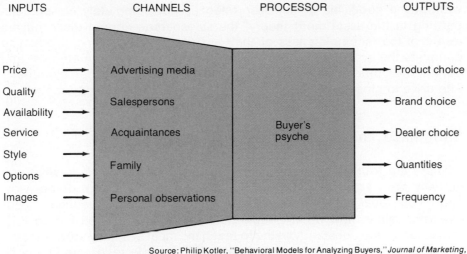

| INPUTS | CHANNELS | PROCESSOR | OUTPUTS |

INPUTS

Price

Quality

Availability

Service

Style

Options

Images

CHANNELS

Advertising media

Salespersons

Acquaintances

Family

Personal observations

PROCESSOR

Buyer's psyche

OUTPUTS

Product choice

Brand choice

Dealer choice

Quantities

Frequency

Source: Philip Kotler, "Behavioral Models for Analyzing Buyers," *Journal of Marketing,* 29, no. 4 (October 1965), 37–45.

Figure 6.6 Kotler's Model of Buyer Decision Making

tors involved in a buying decision. Consumer decision making is complex, and it involves many influences that must be considered when devising effective selling strategies.

Alderson's Assortment Theory

Alderson sees the buyer as primarily engaged in a process he calls assorting. An *assortment* is a system of goods used for a particular purpose. For example, to play golf a person needs a golf course, golf clubs, and golf balls. An assortment without the golf balls would be useless. It could not be labeled as *closed*. Closure results from acquiring the needed golf balls. The assortment would then have *potency,* or the power to satisfy.[30] Alderson explained that buyers are seeking closure of assortments and potency of assortments. These complete systems of goods are accumulated to accomplish a certain task or satisfy a need. An *out* condition—being out of a good—opens up the assortment again and provides the motive to buy.[31] A sense of incompleteness may develop when a new good comes into the market, and the buyer recognizes that

[30] Wroe Alderson, *Marketing Behavior and Executive Action* (Homewood, Ill.: Irwin, 1957), pp. 195–214.

[31] *Ibid.*

without the good, his or her assortment is not completely closed. According to the assortment theory, the salesperson should make buyers aware of the incompleteness of their assortment and offer a product to complete the group. "You have everything you need for an efficient and confidential office, Mr. Bennington, *except* an Acme paper shredder." The drive to close a product group can be a dominant buying motive.

Self-Image Theory

There are four components to self-image. Your *real self* is what you actually are. Your *reference-group self* is how you think others view you. Your *ideal self* is how you would like to think of yourself. Your *apparent self* is how other people actually view you[32] (see Figure 6.7). Since people are constantly trying to reach the ideal self, they are interested in appeals directed toward their ideal self.[33] People reflect an image by the clothes they wear, the automobile they drive, the house they own, and the decorations, implements, and ornaments they use. Nearly every purchase that is visible affects personal status. Through careful buying, the prospect tries to bring the real self closer to the ideal self. Under this concept, then, the prospect buys to project an image. The man who sees himself as the life of the party or the big man on campus buys the red sports car to buttress his extrovert image. The woman who sees herself as a sophisticate would never shop at a lower-class dress shop. She buys stylish goods that she may not be able to afford. The couple who want to establish themselves in an upper-middle-class neighborhood buy the station wagon instead of the pickup truck they really need.

When people believe that a suit or a car or a house is incompatible with their self-image, they probably won't buy. The risk of losing image can be a strong and real objection. Are you an image buyer? Are some automobiles so completely at odds with your image that you would not even consider them as alternatives? Would you feel out of character in certain clothes? Would salespersons who insist that you consider certain items be wasting their time? What many prospects do is generalize about a certain product—to them it has a definite image (as does a firm). Buyers then examine the product image and compare it to their ideal self-image. If the product reflects those qualities the person desires to project, the person may have strong drives to purchase. Through suggestion, the salesperson can influence the delicate mental process of product-image formation. "That dress really brings out your eyes," or "This car is perfect for the traveling executive." Some products have little image dimension,

[32] C. Glen Walters, *Consumer Behavior* 3rd ed. (Homewood, Ill.: Irwin, 1978), pp. 181–188.

[33] *Ibid.*

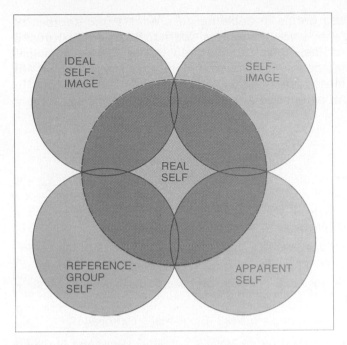

Source: C. Glen Walters, *Consumer Behavior; Theory and Practice*, rev. ed. (Homewood, III.: Irwin, 1974), p. 87.

Figure 6.7   Buyer Images

but most visible products, consumer and industrial, may be at least partially viewed as an extension of personality. Salespersons project image in how they handle and show a product. They must be aware that the prospect is constantly determining if that product "is really me."

SUMMARY

In professional selling it is important to be aware of the socioeconomic and behavioral dimensions of target customers. Salespersons should know that customers differ widely in characteristics and temperament. Thus, selling strategy must be directed toward fitting specific needs. Extroverts may be outgoing and friendly, while introverts may be cold and rational. Transactional analysis concerns the conversational reference of the bargainer and suggests interview strategies. Customer motivation is complex, but classifications of motives and theories based on research give important clues as to what motives to expect in particular situations. People are highly influenced by other people and refer to reference groups and social class norms in deciding on products and sources of goods. John Howard shows how customers "learn to buy." Philip Kotler's model shows many of the influences involved in the buying decision. Alderson explains that people buy to complete useful *assortments* of goods which they "close" for maximum use potential. People buy in reference to their ideal self-image and the image they would like others to have of them.

REVIEW QUESTIONS

1. List and describe the prospect types suggested by Thompson.

2. According to transactional analysis, outline the characteristics of the parent, the child, and the adult ego states.

3. What is meant by life positions, and with what life position is each ego state likely to be associated?

4. What are typical rational buying motives? Emotional? Patronage?

5. What are the two basic elements of Maslow's theory? What are the need levels? Would need levels in an underdeveloped country be different from those in the United States? Explain.

6. Give examples other than the ones given in the text of products people buy when they role play.

7. Explain the elements in Howard's theory. What does it mean to the salesperson? For the new product promoter?

8. How do customers behave in extensive problem solving, and what influences them to buy a particular product?

9. Explain the five theories of what might take place in the mind of the buyer in regard to buyer's psyche.

10. What are the elements in Alderson's assortment theory? Do you feel that this is a less realistic theory of how buyers buy than the economic theory explanation? Why?

APPLICATION QUESTIONS

1. Give what you feel might be the socioeconomic and behavioral characteristics of the typical customer for: a compact car, a luxury car, a fifty-thousand-dollar house, and life insurance.

2. Draw a diagram like Figure 6.3 to analyze your own personality.

3. When you buy a car, are you a self-image buyer? What is your self-image in regard to buying clothes?

6–1

J. N. Hinson, sales manager, has called Ted Carr into his office to discuss Ted's above-average expenses.

J. N.: (*Pointing his index finger at Ted and talking in a loud, accusing voice*): How did you possibly manage to spend $20 per day on meals and average $40 per night on motel rooms? You know the company guidelines, Carr.

Ted: (*Humbly*): I'm sorry, Mr. Hinson. Things were high in Norfolk; there was a convention in town. Things like that always seem to happen to me.

J. N.: This isn't the first time your expenses have been too high. What do I have to do to impress on you to go easy? Fire you?

Ted: But sir, I did get a large order from Dedmon Supply. I thought it would be O.K. to celebrate a little, so I stayed in a nice motel.

J. N.: I see you only made ten calls in Norfolk. What did you do, go to the beach?

Ted: Oh, no sir.

J. N.: How did you waste the time then? Selling is hard work. How did you get the order?

Ted: That's what took the time. I listened to Mr. Dedmon's problems for two hours and spent most of the day at his warehouse. I think he will reorder from us.

J. N.: You waste so much time and expense money. I don't see how you made quota last year. What am I going to do with you, Carr?

Ted: I'll watch it from now on, Mr. Hinson.

J. N.: We have to make money, you know. I want you to read up on the company guidelines for expenses. Next time I'm going to cut your expense claim.

Ted: Yes sir.

QUESTIONS

1. In terms of transactional analysis, from what ego state was J. N. acting? Ted?

2. What are the probable life positions of Ted and J. N.?

3. Did J. N. handle the situation correctly? Explain.

6–2

Greg Lynnson sells raw material steel in various shapes and qualities to manufacturers. He is calling on a new purchasing agent, Paul Mason, whose company manufactures tools of many kinds. Greg has been kept waiting for twenty minutes, although he was on time for the appointment.

Greg: How do you do, Mr. Mason. I'm Greg Lynnson with Durable Steel Corporation. I would like to review with you your needs for steel input as raw material for your manufacturing processes. (*Paul Mason does not extend his hand, nor does he return Greg's warm smile. He replies coldly . . .*)

Mason: You may sit over there if you wish. This is the flu season you know. We already have a two-months' supply of steel on hand, and we are likely to use that same supplier again.

Greg: (*Taking the appointed seat about six feet away from Mason*): Thank you, sir. As you know, we are a leader in raw material steel because of our service and our prices. We will even ship steel by air to customers in a tight situation and pay half the freight. Our prices are competitive, even though our delivery service is faster to you because we have warehouses located within 50 miles of your plant. That's something our competition can't match. We feel that our tonnage is of better quality and that our stock is easier to handle. It comes in more shapes and sizes than other suppliers' in this area. For how long of a period do you usually order?

Mason: It varies.

Greg: We have found that a six-months' supply is good for customers who use average amounts. May I ask how much steel you usually use during a six-month period.

Mason: You may ask, but our production output is not common knowledge, and I intend to keep it that way. I'm sure your prices and service are no better than our supplier's.

Greg: Yes sir, it is true that prices are similar in this industry, but steel, especially alloy steel, may become scarce again. Many companies are buying from more than one source to assure themselves a supply should steel suddenly become scarce. We would like to prove ourselves to you by being one of your suppliers . . .

Mason: I could care less what other suppliers are doing, Mr. Lynnson. I feel that we can get better discounts by dealing with one supplier, and I feel that is sound logic.

Greg: Have you ever considered staggering your orders? If you order from one supplier for one order and another the next time, you would be buying in the same quantities and getting your full discount. You would have the healthy situation of two suppliers should either one not be able to fill your needs at any time.

Mason: Well ... that sounds plausible. Leave your price list here, Mr. Lynnson, and I will consider it.

QUESTIONS

1. Would you classify Mason as an introvert or an extrovert based on the answers he gave Greg?

2. Do you think that Greg handled the situation correctly?

3. What is the best way to handle customers who give you a cold reception?

6–3

Kimmons and Company is adding a document copier to their line of photographic equipment. It will be sold to executive offices at a price slightly below competition. Up to this time, sales representatives with high school educations have been recruited and taught stimulus-response (memorized sales presentations) to sell a simple line of cameras and associated equipment to retail dealers. The copier will not be handled by dealers and will be sold directly to offices. You are the sales manager, and you have ten sales representatives working for you. Seven have been with the firm less than three years. The president of the firm has called you in to discuss marketing the new copier. It is as good as any on the market, but it does not have the established reputation behind it as do the copiers of other competitive firms. He wants to know what kind of prospects you plan to visit, if additonal salespersons will be needed, and what strategy you plan to follow in reaching the new market. He also wants your advice as to what types of appeals should be made to persuade prospects in the new market.

What is your advice?

7 The Selling Environments

To meet selling opportunities fully, you must understand, estimate, and be responsive to many changing environmental influences that affect sales and the selling situation. If you sell for a company or if you manage a selling company, you need to know how the company as a system or team works, what can go wrong with it, and how it can be kept healthy. You must also understand how your customers' firm environment influences their motivations. The firm system for which you work *is* your *internal environment*. It requires adjustments on your part and sets restrictions on your operations.

Other environments are usually less controllable than your company environment. Normally, *competitive-environment* pressures that affect your chances of making sales change as time passes. This requires continued attention on your part. Customers will revise their attitudes toward your products (the fashion cycle), and rapid changes in the American *culture* may open and close doors to selling opportunities. *Business cycles,* too, can greatly influence the demand for your products. You should be aware of how consumer income changes, price changes, and advertising changes affect sales. You should also know how your actions as a sales representative can keep you or your company out of *legal* trouble. In this chapter environmental situations that influence your opportunity to sell will be examined. They are:

- The firm-system environment
- The competitive environment
- The business environment
- The sociocultural environment
- The legal environment

163

THE FIRM-SYSTEM ENVIRONMENT

The company for which you work is a behavioral system—a group of people working together toward a common goal.[1] Such a group can be thought of as a complete team unit with characteristics, tendencies, and illnesses similar to those of an individual. Just as a football or basketball team behaves as a coordinated unit to win, so must the firm system. You must understand the nature of the firm-system team, to make good decisions as a salesperson.

System Characteristics

According to Wroe Alderson, every economic behavioral system (whether the firm is a corporation or a partnership) has four dominant characteristics (see Figure 7.1). They are:

- A power unit
- A communications structure
- A system of inputs and outputs
- A system of internal and external adjustments.[2]

The *power unit* is composed of one or more persons who form the system's brains and who direct and coordinate all operations. The board of directors, the president, and the managers are part of this power unit. They plan, direct personnel, and see that plans to meet the firm's objectives are carried out. The power unit may be thought of as a team's "coaching staff," and it is expected to see the overall situation and to make sure everyone is working together to win. The power unit sets territories, quotas, and rules of operation for each salesperson.

The firm also has *communications structures* through which all system members receive plans and instructions from the power unit and through which feedback on how goals are being met is transmitted back to the power unit. Whenever a group works together toward a goal, there is a need for coordination. Coordination, in turn, is accomplished through good communication.[3] On a good selling team everyone knows "the signals." Each salesperson on the selling team should be set to receive and interpret signals from management as well as transmit information from the field to supervisors.

[1] Wroe Alderson, *Marketing Behavior and Executive Action* (Homewood: Irwin, 1957), pp. 35–97.

[2] *Ibid.*

[3] *Ibid.*

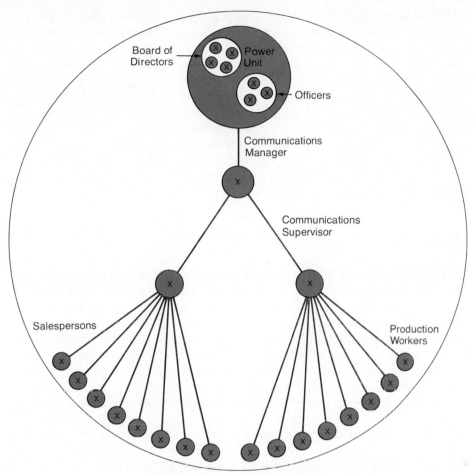

Source: Based on Wroe Alderson's behavioral system in Wroe Alderson, *Marketing Behavior and Executive Action* (Homewood, Ill.: Irwin, 1957), pp. 35–97.

Figure 7.1   Model of the Aldersonian Behavioral System

The firm is a *system of inputs and outputs.* Just as fuel input for an engine yields the power to move as output; personnel, money, materials, machinery, and methods become a firm's input, and the outputs are products, sales, and profits. The quality and availability of inputs vitally affect the results.[4]

The firm also is characterized by a *system of internal and external adjustments.*[5] To survive and grow, a company must adjust internally to

[4] *Ibid.*

[5] *Ibid.*

changes in its environment. If a new competitor, for example, offers a product at a lower price with a strong relative advantage over your product, important adjustments must be made in your product offering, or you will eventually lose your customers. Government regulations, consumer attitudes, and business conditions change quickly. Actually, there are dozens of rapidly changing factors in the selling environment, to which the firm and the salesperson must adjust. The ability to adjust, or "plasticity," as Alderson calls it, is essential to a healthy company system.[6] When a system (or a salesperson) becomes unyielding and unresponsive, it cannot adjust to changing selling situations. Just as the home team must adjust when an opposing football team changes its defensive tactics, the salesperson must adjust or suffer a competitive disadvantage.

System Tendencies

The firm system is able to attract and hold its members, because each member who belongs has an increased expectation of gain from belonging. You probably entered the system as a salesperson because you felt that joining the company team would benefit you more than working alone. This expectation of gain from belonging is the organization's "structural glue," because it holds it together.[7] Nearly every decision made by the power unit strengthens or weakens the "glue" and unity of the system. This is why managers must take into consideration the secondary effects of every directive (order) on the cohesiveness of the firm team. You went with XYZ Company, because you thought the opportunity to advance and make a better living would be increased. Suppose you find that the XYZ Company manager promotes only his lodge brothers. Your expectation of gain is weakened, and your loyalty to the firm may also be weakened. You may even leave the team system. The entire system can become more vulnerable because of managerial decisions that block paths of advancement to members and thus diminish the opportunities gained from belonging.

Firms have a tendency to stay in business and persist even after their original purpose is accomplished.[8] The March of Dimes retained its organization after polio was conquered and directed its resources toward fighting birth defects. A carriage company going into the manufacture of automobile bodies illustrates this tendency to shift purposes to survive after the old purpose is no longer relevant in the light of a changing environment.

[6] *Ibid.*

[7] *Ibid.*

[8] *Ibid.*

A firm also has the tendency to develop pathologies or sicknesses just as a person develops illnesses.[9] Some typical corporate illnesses will be analyzed in another section of this chapter. Since you must live in your firm's system, you as a salesperson should be aware of such maladjustments. A weakness in a customer's firm may point to problems that can be solved by buying your product. You may be able to affect the health of both your work environment system and your customer's company system.

System Functions

The team system performs certain functions to enhance the gains from belonging. The system is expected to *create a surplus,* or an excess for reserve, to assure its survival and growth. In a corporation this is known as *earned surplus* and can be used to take advantage of special opportunities or provide security for team members. The system's power unit is responsible for *rationing* (dividing) the gain of the system among system members. If the surplus is not divided fairly, the expectations of gain from belonging will diminish for the members and many are likely to drop out and seek a fairer system. The system also provides security for members by protecting against competition and loss of market.[10] This defensive function can be supported by financial strength, research, and aggressive selling.

Power and Communications Structure Operations

Two structural operations—the power group and the communications network—are critical to system accomplishments. But, according to Alderson, the power group has a tendency to act in such a way as to promote their power to act. Managers constantly strive to maintain and advance themselves. This explains many of their actions. Most firm members, in fact, are concerned about their position in the firm and will seek to advance their standing. Some members will even attempt to weaken the position of other firm members in order to promote themselves. They are engaging in positional behavior.[11] *Positional behavior* explains why you must not trust fellow sales representatives with information that could hurt your position in the firm. Don't criticize people in the power structure, for example, or tell your fellow sales representatives

[9] *Ibid.*

[10] *Ibid.*

[11] *Ibid.*

about a selling mistake you just made—unless you want it to get back to your superior. People in competition with you within the firm have a motive for making you look bad so they can advance. Positional behavior explains why a group of firm members at the same level may promote the weakest and not the strongest member in selections or evaluations. It explains why sales managers may resent and suppress "star" salespersons who are threats to their position. It also explains why prospects will not buy industrial equipment that either replaces personnel in their "empire" or poses a threat to their own positions. You can understand the positional behavior of office managers who oppose the purchase of a computer that they feel may lead to the loss of their jobs. You should be constantly aware of positional motivation when selling to buyers.

Power is maintained through persuasive communication rather than through coercion in a free-enterprise system. The same persuasive techniques you learned as a sales representative will serve you as a manager or as one of the power structure members. The power unit members use *power symbols* to maintain their power image.[12] Special dress, a big office, the diamond tie tack, and titles are designed to emphasize high position and the necessity for subordinate members to conform to directives and instructions. The firm itself in its trademarks, buildings, and image personnel has symbols that reflect its market power. Such symbolism is highly valued.

System Pathologies

As mentioned earlier, the firm has pathologies or illnesses that can occur because of weaknesses in the power unit, the communications structure, the inputs, or because of a lack of adjustment to changing situations.[13] Power unit leaders sometimes become obsessed with their personal power and begin to disregard the needs of other system members. Often, leaders neglect to listen to information coming up the channel. Sometimes leaders are over- or underconfident and occasionally expect too much of subordinates. Members of the power unit may also be torn between conflicting loyalties, such as loyalty to the firm and loyalty to themselves and others. Sometimes there are simply too many members in the power unit, and this can lead to indecision, conflict, and wasted executive resources.

The communications structure may contain both authorized and unauthorized systems. The unauthorized system, or grapevine, may distort information or leak confidential information. Bad news, even bad news

[12] *Ibid.*
[13] *Ibid.*

that requires action, sometimes doesn't flow up the channel. Often power unit members substitute idealism for information and formulate unrealistic plans and orders based on theory instead of analyzed information.[14] Because of the lack of feedback, power unit members may be cut off from reality.

A potentially serious sickness exists for many firms in the 1980s, as input resources, particularly energy, become increasingly scarce. High energy costs and high labor costs can drive up the cost of production, and sales representatives may find their products overpriced in comparison with the prices of foreign goods. Scarce inputs may reduce supplies to the point where you might have to allocate among customers at least temporarily. Input changes, therefore, also affect the sales situation in addition to the lack of adjustment to system environments.

System Remedies

Understanding how the system operates is the first step toward *preventive maintenance* of a healthy system. Preventive maintenance involves the practice of anticipating and correcting potential problems before they develop. *Maintaining growth* promotes system health by providing advancement opportunities for members and thereby strengthening the "structural glue." Good *feedback* mechanisms (communication systems and listening managers) built into the system help detect problems in early stages. *Realism* instead of idealism for power structure members fosters system health. The *power principle* itself, or "acting in such a way as to promote the power to act," encourages the capacity to adjust to changing conditions.[15] Other remedies are suggested by the nature of the individual pathology.

Application of the Model

The Aldersonian behavioral system model can be used to understand your company and your customer's company. The model not only specifies the system parts that must be kept healthy (communications, power, inputs, and adjustments), but it also provides insight into the motivations involved in corporate buying situations. Each firm operates the four subsystems differently. In some firms communications are formal, while in other firms salespersons must observe carefully to receive needed information from management. In some firms communications are im-

[14] *Ibid.*
[15] *Ibid.*

plied, and management expectations must be anticipated since they are never communicated verbally. The concept of *positional behavior* that reveals purchasing motivations and team member rivalries should aid the new salesperson in adjusting to the corporate world. Many times you will not be in a position to correct pathologies or system deficiencies, but understanding them will help you to predict and react to your company environment.

THE COMPETITIVE ENVIRONMENT

In 1977 imports rose some 21 percent over 1976 (see Figure 7.2), increasing the foreign share of the domestic United States market considerably. Electronics, automobiles, toys, sporting goods, clothing, shoes, office machines, cameras, tape recorders, sewing machines, and a host of other consumer products from abroad are seriously threatening the sales of American industries.[16] Since foreign competition is based on a considerably lower labor cost, domestic salespersons find it increasingly hard to justify their products with competing foreign products. As more and more *American* products pour into the marketplace, competition among American manufacturers is also increasing. Customers have a greater variety from which to select, and your customers will have more exposure to competitive sales representatives. It has already been mentioned that increasing competition should be expected in the last part of the growth stage of the product life cycle, because many new firms are entering to take advantage of profit opportunities. Few salespersons sell products that are so advantageous, different, or protected that competition isn't a major environmental consideration. In normal selling situations, there are changes in the product line each year, designed to keep the company up with or ahead of rivals. But, it is a lucky sales representative who doesn't feel the pressure of increased competition.

Competition is generally greatest in highly populated city areas. Sales personnel in competitive companies may change, making a great difference in the selling potential of your product. If you suddenly find yourself against a "star" competitive salesperson, you will have to improve your selling methods or personality to stay even.

The sales representative must look at future as well as present competition and develop specific strategies to outwit rivals. If your company emphasizes research and stays one step ahead of other firms in developing new products and features, your chances of success are better. In selling, as in most sports, relative strength determines who wins in close rivalries.

[16] "International Commerce Report," *Commerce America* U.S. Government Printing Office (U.S. Department of Commerce), 2, no. 11 (November 21, 1977) 18–21.

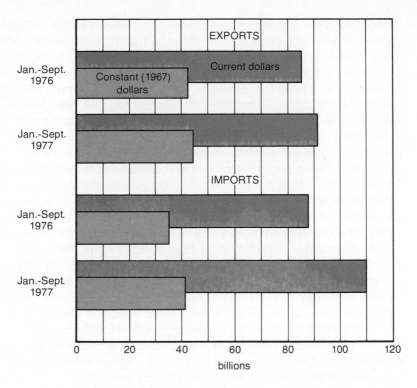

Source: "International Commerce Report," *Commerce America*, U.S. Government
Printing Office (U.S. Department of Commerce), 2, no. 11 (November 21, 1977), 18.

Figure 7.2   Competition from Imports

THE BUSINESS ENVIRONMENT

Product Sales' Sensitivity to Business Conditions

Most products are affected by business cycles and economic conditions. The sale of automobiles, appliances, and other durables is highly
responsive to changes in the personal incomes of consumers. Purchasing
durable products can generally be put off when consumer discretionary
incomes are low. When real personal income is rising and discretionary
income (income that does not have to be spent on necessities) rises with
it, consumers usually buy more new cars and other types of durables.
Security sales are dependent on the outlook for economic prosperity and
on speculation about interest rates. Money is often taken out of the stock
market and invested in bonds and mortages when interest rates are

high. The housing market and the myriad of dependent industries associated with it suffer when interest rates rise to high levels. High interest rates can increase consumer monthly house payments significantly.

Durable industrial equipment is even more sensitive to cycles. It may be very responsive to changes in consumer demand for the buying industry's products. Suppose a firm needs ten minicomputers to operate, and suppose the firm normally replaces a depreciated machine each year. If this firm has a 10 percent increase in business, it will buy two more machines—one as a replacement and one to take care of additional business. The equipment sales representative, therefore, has twice the sales potential that he or she had the previous year. Suppose, on the other hand, that business decreases 10 percent. The company would then put aside the depreciated machine and would not need to replace it. The other nine machines would be sufficient for operations. The salesperson would have zero potential with this company for that year, and, if that condition were multiplied throughout the territory, he or she would have a bad selling year irrespective of efforts. During a recession companies have a tendency to repair existing equipment or rent rather than commit additional investment. Fortunately, most products are not as sensitive as industrial equipment to the business cycle. However, most products *are* affected to some extent. Used equipment, repair services, and cheaper consumer goods that can substitute for higher priced goods may even enjoy increased sales during recessionary periods.

Inflationary Influences

A high rate of inflation also influences buying decisions, for several reasons. The cost of holding big inventories is high. When the price level is increasing rapidly, it pays to buy more stock for inventory and hold it instead of buying it later at a much higher price. Buying in anticipation of a price increase is always an important closing appeal, and the salesperson may use the inflationary situation to load customers with a larger inventory. Once inventory levels are high, however, replacement sales are again dependent on customer purchases. Purchases may be down during inflation because of a loss in spending power. If inflation and taxes rise faster than income, the consumer will have less to spend for items other than necessities. Necessities are less responsive to income changes. So, while inflation may create an opportunity to sell in the short run because of buyer desire to hold goods instead of money, it can decrease selling opportunity in the long run because commercial customers may sell off their stock when faced with uncertainty.

The Effect of Economic Cycles on Sales

Every salesperson should have at least an elementary understanding of economic cycles, since cycles do affect selling potential. Some economists see long-run (or kondratiff) cycles that indicate a serious depression about every fifty years as significant. The depression occurs because of an overexpansion of debt. The burden of debt becomes great, incomes are not able to service it, and the economic structure collapses in a wave of repossessions and pessimism. Albert Summers contends that while we are approaching the end of the fifty-year cycle (indicating a possible depression), our staggering debt is mostly governmental rather than private. Under these circumstances, the debt may produce inflation rather than depression.[17]

Inflationary cycles can be caused by excess government spending, deficits, high labor costs (the wage-price inflationary spiral), or higher raw material costs. The recession in the early seventies was accompanied by rising prices from higher energy costs. A certain amount of inflation is built in by cost-of-living wage increases that, in turn, increase the cost of manufactured goods. This causes prices to go even higher and leads to further increased wage demands by workers. A wage-price spiral results. Government deficit spending may supply additional purchasing power without increasing the amount of goods available. Consumers then drive prices higher by chasing the same amount of goods with more money. The higher prices for energy and raw materials from developing countries with monopoly control increase the price of goods and decrease the real income of consumers in importing countries. Rising prices, however, always give the buyer a reason for buying now—prices will be higher in the future.

Business Cycles

Business cycles concern prices, output, and employment and vary in intensity and duration. The cycle is characterized by four stages—prosperity, recession, depression, and recovery. It may last two years or as many as ten years. In the prosperity or expansion stage, everything is on the upswing—employment, production, prices, wages, and spending by consumers and corporations. Many companies are making business investments, and new salespeople are hired to serve the enlarging market. Inventories build up, excess capacity disappears, banks lend freely,

[17] Albert Summers, "Cycles for All Occasions," *Conference Board Record,* 13, no. 4 (April 1976), 8–12.

savings increase, few businesses fail, the stock market rises, and a spirit of optimism prevails. Near the end of the prosperity phase, the rate of investment may fall. Some businesses find that they have overexpanded. The mood changes to pessimism as prices begin to fall on the stock market, more business failures are evident, banks restrict their lending, business firms become afraid to invest or borrow, and consumers become uncertain. Firms allow their inventories to get low and restrict buying. Sometimes government spending takes up the slack in private business spending, but most products become harder to sell. In recession and depression, few salespersons fare as well as in times of prosperity, but recession usually leads to recovery, and the upswing cycle starts again. All cycles are part of a dynamic environment to which sales representatives must adjust.

Technological Changes

Technological changes in the economy also affect product sales. Computerization, transportation, and communication advancements may promote or retard the market climate for your offering. Transistorization and the resulting inexpensive pocket calculator have profoundly affected the office-machines industry. Consider the effects of the home computer that can be bought for less than $1,000. Every technological innovation has repercussions throughout the economy, and important innovations stimulate the prosperity part of the business cycle while causing readjustments in product offerings.

Selling in Scarcity

In the early seventies many petroleum-based products became scarce, along with certain critical raw materials for hundreds of American industries. As during World War II, some sales representatives had to face an unusual situation when they were not able to supply the needs of even their best customers. They were required to coordinate elaborate allocation programs. Steel, aluminum, plastics, and synthetic fibers used by so many firms in fabricating hundreds of industrial and consumer products were suddenly in short supply. Salespersons found themselves working just as hard during these temporary shortages, attempting to allocate (ration) fairly, discourage bribery, ignore threats, and maintain goodwill by steering customers to surpluses from other firms' stock and sometimes even to competitors.[18] Special care was taken to keep purchasing agents

[18] Michael B. Rothfeld, "A New Kind of Challenge for Salesmen," *Fortune,* 39, no. 4 (April 1974), 156–162.

informed of any changes in allocation procedure, and many salespersons used the situation as an opportunity to extract more information about customers' future plans and programs.[19] Given the scarcity of certain raw materials and the political instabilities and monopolistic tendencies of foreign suppliers, the situation may reoccur. Salespersons will have to be prepared to switch their thinking to accommodate temporary shortages that may occur more frequently than they do now.

THE SOCIOCULTURAL ENVIRONMENT

Because markets are composed of people with money (or credit) and inclinations toward certain products, the trends of the sociocultural environment have considerable effect on selling opportunities. Population and income trends, education and occupational changes, spending behavior developments, fashion cycles, and a myriad of cultural influences constantly modify the selling situation. An analysis of these cultural-change directions provides a basis for estimating your selling opportunity and buying motivations.

Population Trends

The rate of population growth in the United States has slowed considerably because of a declining birthrate (see Figure 7.3, p. 176). More people are living alone than ever before. There is even discussion of a future stationary population or a zero-growth situation. While lives have been extended because of medical advances, the low birthrate trend could diminish the market for children's products. However, even though the birthrate was low during the Depression, it was high just after World War II. Babies born in the late forties and early fifties formed a "baby boom," creating markets and crowding school facilities. Those postwar children are now swelling the labor force, and the women in this group are of childbearing age. Although the birthrate is low now, a greater number of children should be born during the next few years. The large base of childbearing women, many of whom have delayed having children because of career commitments, are beginning to start families. While families will be smaller, there will be more "higher order" births (first and second children). Since last children in large families get hand-me-downs that have already been purchased, the market for children's and infant's products should continue to grow with the prospect of more "higher

[19] *Ibid.*

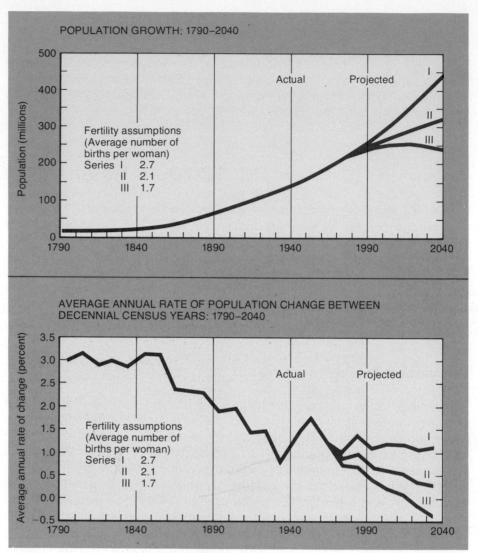

POPULATION GROWTH: 1790–2040

Actual   Projected

I

II

III

Fertility assumptions
(Average number of
births per woman)
Series I   2.7
       II   2.1
       III   1.7

Population (millions)

AVERAGE ANNUAL RATE OF POPULATION CHANGE BETWEEN
DECENNIAL CENSUS YEARS: 1790–2040

Actual   Projected

Average annual rate of change (percent)

Fertility assumptions
(Average number of
births per woman)
Series I   2.7
       II   2.1
       III   1.7

I

II

III

Source: *Social Indicators 1976,* U.S. Government Printing Office (U.S. Department of
Commerce), Office of Federal Statistical Policy and Standards, Bureau of Census, p. 4.

Figure 7.3   Population Estimates

order'' births.   The demand for houses, apartments, and associated
products—furniture, textiles, lawn mowers, do-it-yourself home improvements, paint, construction materials, construction equipment, house trail-
ers, land, and air conditioners—should be strong in the early eighties.
The mid-seventies recession with high prices and high interest rates may
simply have temporarily suppressed the pent-up demand for living

space. With about 20 percent of the population moving each year, affluent home owners will continue remodeling houses to meet their new self-images. This will support the home decorating market.[20] The suburban movement, with its emphasis on back-yard living, the countermovement to the central city high rises, and the population shift from the Northeast to the South and West will continue to influence the types of products purchased. Shifts to sunshine areas may stimulate the purchases of sportswear, recreational equipment, and air conditioners.

Income Trends

With the recession of the mid-seventies apparently over, the long-run trend toward increased real family incomes should resume. By 1980 about half, or 30 million, U.S. families should make over $15,000 per year.[21] (See Figure 7.4, p. 178.) The baby-boom young adults are now productive in the labor force, and there are more working women increasing the output of the nation's goods and services. Productivity will continue to rise with better technology.[22] Increasing energy costs and raw material costs (from monopolies in supplying countries) could dampen the prospects of increased discretionary income (income left after buying necessities like food, clothing, and shelter). Better technology and the discovery of new, less expensive energy sources, on the other hand, could accelerate income growth. Greater discretionary incomes allow people to spend more for luxuries, services, durables, and investments. Ethnic groups, particularly blacks and Spanish-speaking Americans sharing in the increased affluence, are buying more middle-class products. If incomes do become much higher—as many forecasters predict—it will be natural to expect better markets for the above-mentioned product classes.

Spending Trends

The purchase of durable goods, particularly cars, has significantly increased since 1976. The shift to services (intangibles, such as haircuts, rentals, and repairs), which spurted during the fifties, has slowed down.[23] However, this shift should continue in the 1980s, if affluence

[20] *Wall Street Journal,* March 13, 1973, p. 20.

[21] Fabian Linden, "Family Income—1985," *Conference Board Record,* 13 (May 1976), 25.

[22] Fabian Linden, "The Arithmetic of Affluence," *Conference Board Record,* 12 (September 1975), 13–16.

[23] Fabian Linden, "The Business of Consumer Services," *Conference Board Record,* 12 (April 1975), 13.

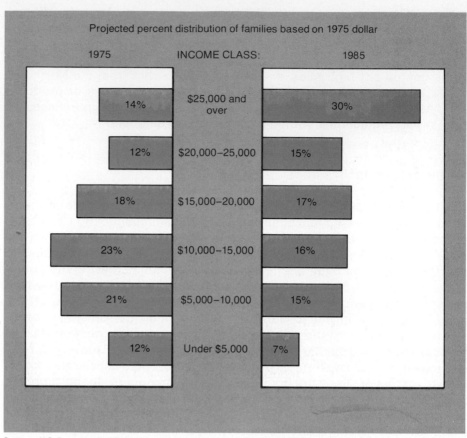

Projected percent distribution of families based on 1975 dollar

1975	INCOME CLASS:	1985
14%	$25,000 and over	30%
12%	$20,000–25,000	15%
18%	$15,000–20,000	17%
23%	$10,000–15,000	16%
21%	$5,000–10,000	15%
12%	Under $5,000	7%

Sources: U.S. Department of Commerce. Fabian Linden, "Family Income—1985," *Conference Board Record*, 13 (May 1976), 25.

Figure 7.4 The Changing Income Pyramid

increases. Sporting equipment, home appliances, health foods, pets and pet care, accessories, do-it-yourself products, and leisure-recreational offerings show continuing promise if present spending trends continue. People will also be able to afford better medical care.

Education Trends

The population is becoming more educated, with a larger percentage of young people finishing high school and college. In 1975, over 25 percent of the population had some college training.[24] The educated buyer is a more thoughtful, deliberate buyer. This suggests a more professional selling strategy. The educated buyer also buys a different mix of products.

Style and Fashion

The normal fashion cycle is *distinctiveness*—when only a few distinguished people are using the product; *emulation*—when the product is popular in the middle socioeconomic groups; and *economic emulation*—when all economic groups have accepted the innovation and it appears in bargain basements.[25] The fashion cycle was accelerated during the sixties, and wardrobes became rapidly style-obsolete. Style obsolescence stimulates buying, because people become dissatisfied with serviceable but out-of-fashion items and rebuy. However, many became disenchanted playing the fashion game. Today, many middle- and lower-class people are still wearing old styles and are no longer accepting the new styles as quickly. It is also becoming more acceptable in some circles not to conform to fashion pressures. Nevertheless, when old clothes *wear out*, new purchases do reflect existing fashions.

Cultural Changes

Cultural changes include many trends, but *other-directedness*, consumerism, feminism, life simplification, youth orientation, leisure spending, reference-group influences, self-service acceptance, security consciousness, and changing moral and work attitudes are among the most important. David Riesman contends that society has become more *other-directed*. Once people were tradition-directed and followed traditional ways of doing things and buying products. People next became *inner-directed* or independent in their decisions. Now, people are other-directed and prone to consider the social pressures and the buying influences of their reference groups.[26] People are deeply concerned about what their peer groups think of them. If this is true, the value of testimonials in selling is greater.

Consumerism involves the increasing tendency of consumers to question suppliers and to pressure for restrictions on and regulations for selling

---

[24] George H. Brown, ''America's New Demographic Profile,'' *Conference Board Record*, 12 (October 1975), 53–56.

[25] Jerome McCarthy, *Basic Marketing,* 6th ed. (Homewood, Ill.: Irwin, 1978), p. 246.

[26] David Riesman, *The Lonely Crowd* (New Haven: Yale University Press, 1961), pp. 1 ff.

activities. Books such as Rachel Carson's *The Silent Spring,* Ralph Nader's *Unsafe at Any Speed,* and Vance Packard's *Hidden Persuaders* have encouraged the consumer movement. It has succeeded in obtaining influence in the legislative and executive branches of government and in passing important laws affecting marketing.[27] Automobile safety legislation, labeling acts, packaging legislation, and a host of other regulations have resulted from this movement. The sales representative should realize that new activism by consumers will continue to influence market decision making. Much of the new legislation has helped the ethical salesperson and company provide safer and more acceptable products. Technological advances, more educated consumers, and a growing distrust of corporate supplier motives will probably perpetuate the trend unless sellers adopt the marketing concept in greater number.

Feminism has fostered products associated with the feminist image such as certain cigarettes, emancipated clothes, little cigars, and certain perfumes. An increasing number of products are being designed to release the housewife from household chores. Blenders, disposals, dryers, compactors, dishwashers, and self-cleaning ovens are part of a trend toward simplified housekeeping. More and more food is being prepared outside of the home. People in today's markets are demanding instant satisfaction by purchasing such products as Polaroid cameras and fast-food services. Even older people want to be included in buying products catering to a *youth image*, especially with regard to clothes. More leisure time has encouraged booms in motel rooms, campers, tennis rackets, bicycles, health club memberships, boats, and a host of other leisure-recreational products. With the prospect of a decreased work week and earlier retirements for some, the trend should continue and bolster the sales of recreational products.

Young people are shifting their buying decision orientations away from the family and toward other reference groups. Parental influence in buying has declined because of the working mother and the influence of television. Products that were not previously advertised on the air are now being promoted on television. A change in moral standards has occurred, and certain magazines, movies, and home furnishings that were not acceptable in the 1950s are now on the market.

THE LEGAL ENVIRONMENT

Trends point to even more laws restricting the operation and decisions of salespersons. As the population grows and improved transportation

[27] Philip Kotler, "What Consumerism Means for Marketers," *Harvard Business Review,* 50, no. 3 (May-June 1972), 48–57.

and communications facilities develop, people will interact more and tend to get in each other's way, providing cause for more regulation. In addition, social and legal trends, such as more liberal legislative bodies, environmentalism, and feminism, will promote new laws affecting sales. This section is not designed to afford sales representatives proficiency in any legal area but rather to make them conscious of legal pitfalls and complexities. If you are unaware of important restrictions, you could get yourself and your company into serious trouble. This section will offer an overview of:

- The law of contract and agency
- The law of warranty
- Fraud
- Laws affecting pricing decisions
- Laws relating to competition
- Green River Ordinances

The Law of Contract and Agency

A contract (see Figure 7.5, p. 182) is an agreement that binds you and your company to perform what you promised. A valid contract involves an offer, an acceptance of the offer, *consideration* (money, written promises, or goods given to show intent to enter the contract), parties with the capacity to contract, and a legal objective.[28] If you as a salesperson can legally obligate your company, you must exercise care in entering legal contracts.

An offer does not become a contract until the opposite party accepts the terms of the offer. An offer can generally be withdrawn at any time before acceptance.[29]

A request for bids is simply an invitation to make an offer.[30] If buyers propose terms different from those stated in the offer, they are making a counteroffer (not a contract). A valid offer must state what the person making the offer promises and asks in return. Once a valid offer is accepted, the contract must be performed or the buyer (offeree) can sue for damages. It is important that your data be correct and that your proposal offer be profitable for your company before you tender an offer to a buyer.

[28] John W. Wyatt and Madie B. Wyatt, *Business Law*, 5th ed. (New York: McGraw-Hill, 1975), p. 36.

[29] *Ibid.*, p. 43.

[30] Michael P. Litka, *Business Law* (New York: Harcourt, Brace & World, 1970), p. 86.

PURCHASE ORDER — FOR JOHN DEERE AGRICULTURAL EQUIPMENT

C18986

☐ NEW ☐ USED ☐ DEMONSTRATOR | ☐ TIME SALE | ☐ CASH SALE

PURCHASER'S NAME AND ADDRESS (First Signer)

	INITIALS	DATE OF ORDER			ORDER NO.
Last Name, then initials		BRANCH		DEALER ACCT. NO.	TO BE DELIVERED ON OR ABOUT
Street or R.F.D.		DEALER NAME AND ADDRESS			
Town, State and Zip	STATE ZIP CODE				

PURCHASER'S NAME AND ADDRESS (Second Signer)

	INITIALS	
Last Name, then initials		
Street or R.F.D.		PURCHASER'S SOCIAL SEC. NO. (First Signer)
Town, State and Zip	STATE ZIP CODE	COUNTY OF FIRST SIGNER

I (we), the undersigned, hereby order from you the Equipment described below, to be delivered as shown above. This order is subject to your ability to obtain such Equipment from the manufacturer and you shall be under no liability if delivery of the Equipment is delayed or prevented due to labor disturbances, transportation difficulties, or for any reason beyond your control. The price shown below is subject to your receipt of the Equipment prior to any change in price by the manufacturer. It is also subject to any new or increased taxes imposed upon the sale of the Equipment after the date of this order.

INVOICE No.	INVOICE DATE	INVOICE AMOUNT	QTY.	EQUIPMENT (Give Model, Size & Description)	SERIAL No.	DEL'D CASH PRICE

I (we), offer to sell, transfer, and convey the following item(s) at or prior to the time of delivery of the above Equipment, as a "trade-in" to be applied against the cash price. Such item(s) shall be free and clear of all security agreements, liens, and encumbrances at the time of transfer to you. The following is a description and the price to be allowed for each item.

| | SALES TAX | |
| | 1. TOT. CASH PRICE | |

A. TOTAL AMOUNT OWED	QTY.	DESCRIPTION OF TRADE-IN	SERIAL No.	AMOUNT
B. OUT-OF-POCKET EXPENSE				
C. TOTAL (A plus B)				
D. NOTE AND CASH RECEIVED				
E. MAX FLOOR PLAN ALLOWABLE (C less D)				

2. TOT. TRADE-IN ALLOWANCE	
3. CASH WITH ORDER	
4. TOTAL (ITEMS 2 & 3)	
5. BALANCE DUE (ITEM 1 LESS ITEM 4)	

The Warranty on the reverse side is a part of this contract and the following applies where permitted by law: Neither seller, John Deere Company, nor the manufacturer makes any other representations or warranties, express or implied (AND EXPRESSLY DISCLAIMS THE IMPLIED WARRANTIES OF MERCHANTABILITY AND FITNESS) or has any obligations to the Purchaser except as provided on the reverse side.

I (we), promise to pay the balance due (line 5) shown above in cash, or to execute a Time Sale Agreement (Retail Installment Contract) for the purchase price of the Equipment, plus additional charges shown thereon, on or before delivery of the Equipment ordered herein. Despite physical delivery of the Equipment, title shall remain in the seller until one of the foregoing is accomplished.

Purchaser's Signature _____

Accepted by _____
(Authorized Signature for Seller)

Purchaser's Signature _____

Date Accepted _____   Salesman _____

DC-770-STOCK 9-77 PRINTED IN U.S.A.

DEALER'S COPY

Source: John Deere Company, Moline, Illinois.

Figure 7.5 The Sales Contract

Acceptance must be made freely and not under threat or duress (undue influence).[31] The giving of money or products is substantial evidence of intent to enter a contract. Evidence of unfair dealing may be cause for the courts to set aside the contract or render it unenforceable.

A buyer must have the capacity to contract, and under most circumstances, the buyer must be a bona fide agent of the corporation to contract legally. Infants, insane persons, drunks, aliens, and corporations may not have full capacity to contract in certain circumstances.[32] Many kinds of contracts with minors can be voided at the minor's election, although the adult is fully bound. Most sales representatives are not agents and have the power to solicit only written offers (called orders) from customers. The written orders must be signed by the branch manager or some other authority before it becomes obligatory.[33] Such *orders* may contain a clause stating that the salesperson cannot make statements that are binding and point to the terms of the written agreement as the legal obligation of both parties. Branch managers, for example, can look at the terms of the agreement and determine before they sign it if the trade-in would be unprofitable. By handling the offer and acceptance this way, the company is not bound by the statements (promises) the salesperson made while soliciting the order. The written contract itself becomes the binding document. If the salesperson has made false and misleading statements, however, the buyer can usually have the contract declared void by legal authority.

Salespersons owe certain obligations to their companies. They are legally bound to be loyal, and they should never reveal confidential information that might hurt the company. They should not sell to themselves (buy their company's goods) without making full disclosure of all the facts. They must always represent the seller in a transaction, since it is illegal to represent both buyer and seller. They must not mix the company's property with their own without a strict accounting.[34]

The Law of Warranty

Sellers must use "due care" in designing, manufacturing, preparing, inspecting, or selling goods. The buyer can sue for damages due to negligence, if the buyer is injured because of a defective product. Unless effectively disclaimed, every product has an implied warranty for mer-

---

[31] *Ibid.*, p. 153.

[32] Ronald A. Anderson and Walter A. Kumpf, *Business Law*, 6th ed. (Cincinnati: Southwestern Publishing, 1975), pp. 199–207.

[33] *Ibid.*, pp. 842–843.

[34] *Ibid.*, pp. 817–819.

chantability and, sometimes, an implied warranty of fitness for a particular purpose.[35] If the buyer inspects the merchandise or is asked to inspect the merchandise and declines to do so, the implied warranty does not pertain to defects the inspection should show up. Statements in the contract like "as is" or "with all faults" may exempt the seller from implied warranties.[36] The product must be adequately packaged and conform to its label—statements in the label are express warranties. False or misleading statements beyond the normal exaggeration of benefits, or puffing of wares, to induce buyers to purchase usually mean that buyers can void the contract if they so desire.

Fraud

Fraud is the misrepresentation of an important fact that is knowingly and deceitfully made to try to make someone else rely and act on that fact to their detriment. And the person who relies on the wrong statement must be harmed in some way (usually economically). Merely stating an opinion about a product is not fraud. But making a positive statement, with no information as a basis and knowing it is probably wrong, *is* fraud.[37] Salespersons must be sure to have a good basis for their product claims and should not make careless statements about what the product can accomplish if they are uncertain about the promised capability. Because salespersons are also subject to a buyer's fraudulent statements and can be defrauded themselves, salespersons should get promises to buy (contracts) in writing.

Laws Affecting Pricing Decisions

The Sherman Antitrust Act of 1890 was passed to protect the public from monopoly practices that would hinder competition. The courts soon determined that a combination that sought to fix prices adversely affected competition. The Clayton Act, an amendment to the Sherman Act, contained provisions that were codified to restrain businesspeople from circumventing the Sherman Act by engaging in such practices as exclusive dealing contracts and tying agreements that substantially affected competition. Section 2 of the Clayton Act made price discrimination illegal under certain conditions. Price discrimination is a monopolistic practice that entails supplying certain buyers at one price and other buyers at another price.

[35] Wyatt and Wyatt, *op. cit.*, pp. 198–208.

[36] *Ibid.*

[37] Anderson and Kumpf, *op. cit.,* pp. 220–224.

The Robinson-Patman Act, like the Clayton Act, was an amendment to the Sherman Act designed to close loopholes in the law. The Act specifically forbids price discrimination in interstate commerce where the effect of such discrimination may tend to lessen competition or create a monopoly in any line of commerce. It did allow differentials or quantity discounts based on differences in manufacturing or marketing costs for selling in larger quantity. However, the burden of proving cost savings was on the seller. It also allowed differences for different quality goods, and prices could be lowered in an area to meet competition in good faith. Other provisions of the law called for advertising allowances and services to be made on a proportionately equal basis to customers. Dummy brokerage houses set up by buyers to disguise actual price concessions were outlawed. The Federal Trade Commission, set up in 1914 as a companion law to the Clayton Act, was responsible for enforcing the Robinson-Patman Act. Violators were subject to triple damages from private damage suits. The actual enforcement of the Sherman Act has varied, but in 1962 corporate executives of certain electrical equipment companies went to jail for conspiring to fix prices. Since that time, more sales representatives have been trained in this legal area.

Laws Relating to Competition

The Federal Trade Commission under Section 5 of the FTC Act was given broad powers to oppose unfair methods of competition in commerce and unfair or deceptive acts and practices. Usually, the Commission holds trade practice conferences by inviting firms in a particular industry to Washington where leaders in that industry decide which practices should be disallowed. The FTC usually orders the company to "cease and desist" the malpractice, but if the company persists, the case can go to the court system. If a competitor is injured because your corporation or you as an agent acted wrongfully against a firm or issued misleading statements hurting the firm's business, that firm can sue your company (see Figure 7.6).

Green River Ordinances

Municipal ordinances have been passed in certain metropolitan areas restricting salespersons from calling on customers door-to-door, because of the resistance to door-to-door solicitors by local merchants and certain consumers. The first legislation of this kind stipulating that door-to-door soliciting without prior permission of the householder was illegal was

Figure 7.6   Procter & Gamble's Personnel Guidelines for Legal Constraints/Antitrust Laws*

Procter & Gamble's business is conducted throughout the world under conditions of intense competition. The Company has always been and remains committed to the concept of fair and vigorous competition as the mechanism most conducive to economic and social progress. Our performance demonstrates that, as a company, we thrive on such competition. In general, the laws of antitrust and trade regulation codify a philosophy to which the Company fully subscribes.

We try at all times to conduct our business in accordance with the letter and the spirit of the law of each of the nations in which we operate. It is each manager's duty to conduct the business falling within his or her area of responsibility in a lawful manner, and each is held accountable for doing so. This specifically includes the laws of antitrust and trade regulation.

While generally these laws are not extensive, their meaning is not always clear. In addition, several sets of antitrust laws may have applicability to the same transaction. Accordingly, while the legal principles of antitrust reflect Procter & Gamble's philosophy of full and fair competition, it is recommended and expected that each manager make full use of Procter & Gamble legal advisers with regard to the interpretation and application of these laws.

In applying these principles, the following should guide your actions in the United States and abroad:

1. The Company's basic policy is for its employees to have no contacts with our competitors. This enables us to maintain our full independence and freedom to act. Any business activity on your part which puts you into contact with competitors, whether at meetings, in telephone calls or by correspondence must be an authorized exception to the Company policy concurred in by your manager and the Legal Division.

2. The Company offers its products for sale to its customers at a price which it unilaterally determines to be appropriate. All competing customers are offered our products on the same price basis. Plans concerning prices and the terms or conditions of sale of our goods may never be discussed with competitors.

3. Accurate information about conditions in the market is essential to effective competition. The Company obtains available information about the market, including the activities of competitors, from trade and other public sources. The Company will not permit competitive information to be obtained through bribery, fraud, theft or coercion.

Government personnel, particularly in foreign countries, may ask or require your discussion or meeting with representatives of competitors. Before undertaking such discussions or meetings, you should secure concurrence of your manager and the Legal Division.

Source: *Procter & Gamble—Your Personal Responsibility.* Courtesy of The Procter & Gamble Company.

* This brief summary statement is intended to synthesize much more detailed guidelines, which exist throughout the company.

passed in Green River, Wyoming in 1933.[38] The laws are not so widespread in the United States that they pose a serious threat to the national distribution of products and selling efforts by this method, but salespersons should investigate any restrictions in their area.

SUMMARY

The internal working environment for the salesperson is the firm, which can be viewed as an organized team or system. Belonging to the system affects the motivations and decisions of people in the system. System members are usually motivated to maintain or better their position in the organization, and this may conflict with deciding what is best for the organization itself. Systems can have illnesses, especially in the communications and power structure that need to be anticipated and corrected.

Competition, foreign and domestic, is increasingly affecting the selling situation. Some products are especially sensitive to economic conditions and business cycles. The salesperson should use knowledge about economic conditions in strategic planning and in personal appraisal of selling opportunities. Great changes are also occurring in the sociocultural environment. The increases anticipated in real personal incomes, spending behavior shifts, population changes, consumer education, and consumerism (and attendant trends) continually shift selling opportunities.

The legal environment always conditions the salesperson's decisions and opportunities. Sales representatives should be aware of all actions that might jeopardize the firm. They should understand legal obligations to the company and that products sold are under warranty. They should know about laws regarding prices, fraud, and advertising. It should be understood that the law is complex and requires study and that in many instances a lawyer's services are valuable. Knowledge of sales affecting environments permits more realistic strategic planning.

REVIEW QUESTIONS

1. What holds the firm together and is considered the "structural glue"?

2. What are the tendencies and functions of the firm system?

[38] Theodore N. Beckman, William R. Davidson, and W. Wayne Talarzyk, *Marketing*, 9th ed. (New York: Ronald Press, 1973), p. 247.

3. What is *positional behavior*, and how might it affect buying decisions?

4. What things can go wrong with the firm system, and how can these pathologies be prevented and corrected?

5. In what ways is the competitive environment changing?

6. Explain why durable industrial equipment is sensitive to business cycles.

7. How does inflation affect selling strategy?

8. Identify and explain economic cycles.

9. What do sales representatives do in periods of scarcity when they cannot supply their customers with the products they want?

10. List the important population trends that affect selling opportunity.

11. What is the outlook for future incomes, and how will this affect the demand for durables, luxuries, services, and necessities?

12. In what ways has American culture changed? How will this affect the demand for particular goods?

13. What does a valid contract involve?

14. Do most sales representatives make an offer to the prospect? Explain your answer.

15. Who might not have the capacity to enter into a contract?

16. What two implied warranties does every product carry?

17. What kinds of statements might exempt the seller from implied warranties?

18. What conditions are necessary for fraud?

19. How do the Robinson-Patman Act and the Federal Trade Commission Act affect selling?

APPLICATION QUESTIONS

1. Compare the firm to an athletic team in as many respects as you can.

2. Explain four different examples of how a salesperson might practice *positional behavior* in a corporation.

7–1

Ralph Hudgins sells steel cable, but he has only one roll left that is marked 12,000 pounds strength. His sales manager has told him that this particular roll was rejected by another customer because it has a defective section. Hudgins has been led to believe that the cable is weaker because of the defective section. He is calling on John Kilgore, a cable prospect . . .

Ralph: Mr. Kilgore, I'm Ralph Hudgins with the Atlas Cable Company. I noticed that the cable you have on your cranes looks rusty. Have you considered replacing it to insure the safety of your workers?

John: The cable we are now using *is* a few years old, but I believe it is still strong enough for our purposes.

Ralph: Yes sir, it *may* be, but then it may *not* be. With our cable you would be sure, because it tests 12,000 pounds tensile strength. It would be fine for lifting the scrap vehicles you have to lift.

John: Well, we have been lifting some heavy scrap lately. Some of those trucks weigh 8,000 pounds. Do you have any of that strong cable in stock now?

Ralph: You're in luck. We have a roll in stock that is 12,000 pound test. It should be enough for several of your cranes, and it's only $435.

John: That sounds O.K. and you're probably right, Ralph, you can't be too safe. Can you deliver it tomorrow?

(A week later on the telephone)

John: Mr. Hudgins, I have bad news. We rerigged our cranes with your cable, and it broke this morning, crushing an operating vehicle. The cable failed to hold a 7,000-pound scrap truck, and the load narrowly missed killing our foreman. You told me that it was guaranteed to hoist 12,000 pounds. I'm afraid your company will have to pay for the truck cab and engine that is almost a total loss.

Ralph: That's terrible. I don't have any idea what could have gone wrong. The cable spool said 12,000 pounds, didn't it?

John: Well, our lawyer will be over to call on your manager shortly.

QUESTION

1. Evaluate this conversation in regard to the laws of warranty, fraud, and agency. From what you know, do you think Ralph is in trouble?

7–2

Salesman Max Relker, who represents the Fastwater Pump Company, is interviewing industrialist John Whitcombe.

Max: Mr. Whitcombe, I know you called up about a Fastwater pump, but I can get one for you cheaper if you can wait a month.

John: What do you mean?

Max: Well, Fastwater is on the verge of bankruptcy, and there is a possibility that you might have trouble getting your pumps repaired in the future. I plan to quit Fastwater next week and go with Austin Wells. I believe their pumps are better, and they are more stable financially than Fastwater.

John: Do they have better prices?

Max: I can get an Austin Wells pump for you for 10 percent less with a better warranty, two years instead of one year. You will have to promise you won't tell anyone about the price, however. We don't give the same price concession to everybody. You can't lose if you will just wait a week or two.

John: Max, we've been dealing with Fastwater for fifteen years, and they have always given us good service in the past. Are you sure they are in danger of going down the drain?

Max: Well, that's what I picked up through the grapevine.

John: We can wait, of course.

Max: Good, I'll see you in a few weeks.

John: (*After Max has gone*) Mrs. Jackson, will you please get my old friend Hal Fastwater on the phone. I have a few things to tell him.

QUESTION

1. Is Max in possible legal trouble? He already secretly owns a fourth interest in Austin Wells.

7–3

Ted Armstrong has been head of the Armstrong Chemical Company for three months. Already he has instituted a bonus plan based on evaluations of employees by their fellow employees (or peers on the same level) and by subordinates. Mr. Armstrong believes that subordinates and fellow workers are in contact with the employee to be evaluated more than supervisors. Therefore they are in a better position to evaluate performance. Mr. Armstrong has made two supervisory appointments so far. He has replaced a retired manager with one of his lodge brothers and replaced a fired employee (fired one year before retirement because of a poor sales performance for a six-month period) with another lodge brother. Armstrong has been advised that the firm needs a computer, and he has put the office manager in charge of evaluating the purchase of the computer.

Evaluate Armstrong's leadership in regard to the behavioral system and especially in regard to the "structural glue" and *positional behavior.*

7–4

Gladys Beason is a sales representative for Monrovia Plastics, a corporation supplying basic raw materials for many manufacturing industries. John Heiston has always been one of Gladys' best accounts. His corporation, the Wellsafe Toy Company, has always paid its bills on time and has averaged ordering over $200,000 worth of raw materials each year for the last five years. Gladys has always wanted to sell to William Toone of S. V. Specialties, who has the potential to purchase over $400,000 worth each year. Mr. Toone has been a hard prospect, but Gladys has considered him a challenge since the word is that he doesn't like to buy from a woman. This year for the second time Monrovia Plastics has found itself in short supply and unable to accommodate all of its customers. Sales representatives, in fact, have been put on notice to allocate existing supplies carefully and to ration among their best accounts. Gladys thought that she would take a chance and try to get Mr. Toone to become a regular buyer. She allowed him to buy $50,000 worth and he snapped up the offer immediately. Because of that sale, she was only able to allow Mr. Heiston of Wellsafe half of the amount that he wanted. He found out at the State Purchasing Agents' Convention that Gladys had made the sale to Toone. Gladys now finds that both accounts are hostile to her and that John Heiston is especially upset. The scarcity situation shows no signs of getting better for at least two months.

Under the circumstances, did Gladys act ethically in selling to Toone?
What should she have done?
What should she do now?
What other selling problems arise in scarcity situations?

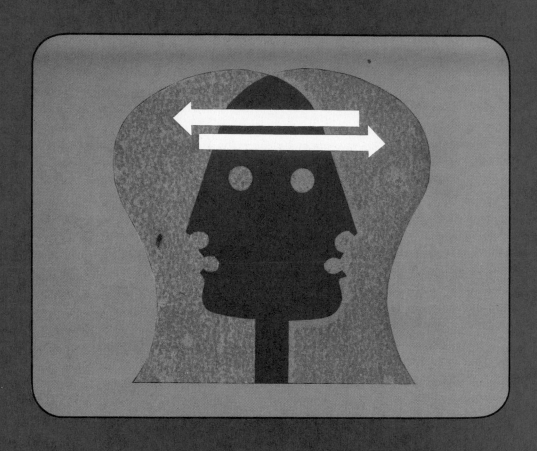

Selling Techniques

Part I emphasized the personal preparation of the sales representative and the important areas of development and understanding basic to success in selling. Part II examines specific practical procedures and focuses on the interaction of the salesperson and prospective buyers—the interview. Successful sales representatives build on the experiences of others and select from a broad range of tested methods and techniques to reach their goals. Consider the competitive advantage of the sales representative who understands the better procedures used by the professionals in the field over the representative who insists on learning by trial and error alone. There are many psychologically sound ways to meet the challenges of recurring selling situations. This part is designed to broaden your consideration of methods and techniques for use in tactical situations, by affording you proven and effective alternatives for accomplishing prospecting, planning, and interviewing.

8 Prospecting and Preapproaching

The prospect is the target—the objective—of all personal selling effort. Careless prospecting and poor techniques are like fishing in a well. Yet, thousands of salespersons will start the workday with little idea of whom they are going to visit. Since prospect selection is critical to most selling situations and responsible for a large portion of selling successes (and failures), a knowledge of techniques and information sources is a necessary first step in building selling plans. If you call on enough of the right type of prospects and ask each one to buy, you will sell, even if your presentation is deficient. On the other hand, you may have the best personality and presentation in the industry, waste it on nonprospects, and come up empty.

Once you have found someone whom you feel might be willing to buy your product, you are still not ready to make the sales call. You must first thoroughly investigate that prospect and customize your approach. In this chapter we will look into the following prospecting areas leading up to planning and routing.

- Understanding prospecting terms
- Qualifying the prospect
- When prospecting is especially important
- Prospecting methods and techniques
- Additional prospect sources
- Ideas for better prospecting
- Preapproaching

Learning how to "peck" on the right doors is the theme of this chapter.

UNDERSTANDING PROSPECTING TERMS

A *prospect* is a person or firm who needs or wants your product and has the ability to buy. A *lead* is a person or firm that has not yet been qualified and put into the prospect category. A *referral* is a lead that has been given to you by someone else—usually another customer. A *hot prospect* is someone who is considered ready to buy and deserves immediate attention.

QUALIFYING THE PROSPECT

Examining leads or referrals to determine if they might be potential buyers is known as *qualifying.* The lead or referral can become a prospect if he or she has a need or desire for the product, has the financial ability to buy, is qualified or eligible to buy, and has the authority to buy.[1] Experience as a sales representative shows you that sometimes people buy when they apparently have little need for the product but *want* the product anyway. For example, a man bought a multithousand-dollar payroll accounting machine, although he only had two people on his payroll. Another man, who wanted fancier, more expensive equipment for an accounts receivable service, insisted that if the salesperson did not show him a more elaborate posting machine, he would call a competitor.

[1] Carlton A. Pederson and Milburn D. Wright, *Selling Principles and Methods,* 6th ed. (Homewood, Ill.: Irwin, 1976), p. 217.

He bought the machine but failed to pay for it. After he tried the machine, he found it had *too much capacity* and was *too expensive* to operate. However, the key to looking for and qualifying prospects is finding need. Some people buy things they don't need simply because they want them and have the money, but these people are rare.

The person or firm must also have the ability to buy—the enabling factors of credit, money, or assets that can be turned into money. Usually people or firms without ready cash or the equivalent can buy on credit, rent, or make some other financial arrangement if they sincerely *need* the product. Claiming lack of funds to buy is more often an excuse rather than a real objection. However, if products are forced on a lead who *really* doesn't have the money, a lot of time is wasted, and the goods may have to be repossessed with unhappiness resulting for everyone.

A lead may not have the eligibility to buy or the authority to buy. Life insurance salespersons know that many unhealthy people who would like to buy life insurance at regular rates cannot pass the required medical examination and are, therefore, ineligible. Some drug items are only available to physicians and pharmacists. The sale of explosives, chemicals, and guns may be restricted. Sometimes only specific groups of individuals, such as students in university apartments, are eligible to rent particular real estate. In dealing with corporate executives or employees, the sales representative must be sure that the person representing the firm has the *authority* to buy. The purchasing agent usually has this authority, while a production worker may give an "O.K." but may not be an authorized agent of the firm. Most industrial sales representatives have experienced wasting hours talking to some official-looking corporate executive without the authority to buy and without even a moderate influence on the purchasing decision.

When you have subjected the lead to all four criteria: (1) need, (2) ability, (3) eligibility, and (4) authority, you can *qualify* and declare him, her, or the firm a prospect. The prospect, however, still may not be *your* prospect. The prospect may be a designated account for another sales representative in your company or may not be in your geographical territory. The prospective firm may purchase centrally from an office in another state. If the prospect is not in your jurisdiction, you still have an obligation to turn in the name to your sales manager or to your employer.

WHEN PROSPECTING IS ESPECIALLY IMPORTANT

The importance of prospecting varies widely from firm to firm. Some individual sales representatives have markets so limited that there is little question of the identity of their prospects. Some salespersons, in fact, have less than ten special accounts and are precluded from selling to anyone else. If you were selling a product that could be used only by battery-making firms, you could eliminate all other firms and easily identify your prospects. On the other hand, when there are numerous customer types and the characteristics of a typical customer are not easily obtainable—no obvious, identifying characteristics—prospecting may be critical to your success. Prospecting for life insurance, investments, and office equipment is complex and involves the expenditure of a great deal of time and effort.

Most firms have ideas from experience in the market as to who will buy their products. That is, from an analysis of past sales records, they can give their sales representatives a rough profile of the kinds of people who normally buy. Even if the product is new, the firm should have built it to fit specific target markets and, consequently, should be able to describe the characteristics of individuals in those markets. Prospecting is likely to be of special importance (1) if many firms or most people can use your product; (2) if there are broad target market definitions; (3) if market identifying consumer characteristics are not readily apparent; or (4) if you sell long-lasting products to former customers. Under these conditions your potential from good prospecting methods is high and your success may be determined by your prospecting skill.

PROSPECTING METHODS AND TECHNIQUES

There are several systematic ways to locate and qualify prospects. The plan or combination of plans that should be followed depends on the sales representative and the product. Most salespersons should use all of the techniques over time, unless they find that one certain method is so productive that the others are not necessary. The prospecting methods are:

- The center-of-influence method
- The spotter method
- The endless-chain method
- The observation method
- The advertising- or telephone-lead method
- The cold-canvass method

The Center-of-Influence Method

Sales representatives who have influential people—accountants, law-yers, doctors, teachers, city officials—helping them find prospects have a better chance of locating buyers. Some sales representatives make it a point to look up influential acquaintances and use them as *centers* of prospect information. Such people often belong to several clubs or organizations and come into daily contact with many people. A young man enrolled and took courses in medical school simply to gain centers of influence for his insurance business. Denby Brandon, general agent for Pan American Insurance Company in Memphis, hosted a local television show that helped him gain contacts for his insurance business. Sales-persons join country clubs, civic organizations, fraternal orders, and other groups to become closely acquainted with influential people. Prominent socialites, ministers, businessmen and businesswomen who interact with many people, supervisors, coaches, and noncompetitive sales represen-tatives are among those with respected occupations who know many people. They all can be used as *centers of influence.*

The best approach to a center of influence is low-key but honest. The sales representative can explain the product without pressure and assure the center of its quality and benefits. If the center buys from the low-key sales presentation and the product genuinely fits his or her needs, it is an ideal situation. If the product does not fit, the center can still recommend you or your product. Because of their interactions with people and their knowledge about the needs of others, centers can furnish valuable leads and may even be persuaded to go on a sales call and introduce you. Long-term cultivation of centers is important. The sales representative should thank these unpaid business partners, take them out to dinner, and treat them as valuable customers. When centers give leads in *confidence,* this confidence must be respected. The center's name should not be used.

The Spotter Method

Spotters, bird dogs, or *sales associates* are different terms for people who look out for prospects for salespersons (see Photo 8.1, p. 200). Spotters are sometimes paid directly for leads or prospects that result in a sale. They are generally used for information and are not expected to be important centers of influence. Route drivers, gossips, repair people, police officers, taxi drivers, salespersons for other products, bookkeepers, meter readers, retail clerks, inspectors, managers, barbers, bus drivers, secretaries, junior sales representatives, customers—people who get around and hear information about other people—make good spotters.

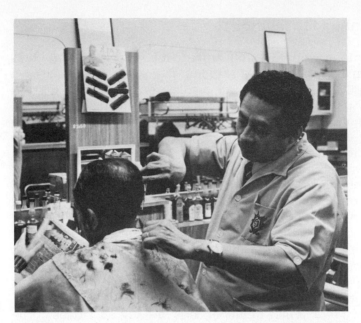

Photo 8.1

Barbers and others who come in contact with many people are good spotters and can help the sales representative find prospects.

Joe Girard, reportedly the most successful automobile sales representative in the country for years, promises his customers money for bringing in other prospects who buy. This not only furnishes Mr. Girard with a steady stream of prospects, but it also gives prospects another important reason for buying.[2] If people can earn a little by referring qualified prospects to you, and if you can earn a lot more by selling to those prospects, everyone gains but your competitors. But in some localities paying spotters is illegal, so check state and local laws.

Junior sales representatives are special types of spotters. They can use various prospecting methods to identify good prospects and allow senior sales representatives to close the sale. This is a productive way for new sales representatives to learn this basic step, and it allows the more experienced sales representative to come in and close the sale, thus reducing the risk of losing the sale for the company.

The Endless-Chain Method

Referred prospects from satisfied buyers are often *hot leads,* especially

[2] "Autos Joe," *Newsweek,* July 2, 1973, pp. 62–64.

if you have a note of introduction from the buyer, or better still, a signed letter praising your product. (See Figure 8.1.) A buyer is thought of by prospects as an impartial source of information. Actually, a new buyer has a psychological stake in praising your product. The sales manager of the Quality Stamp Company (trading stamps) equipped each sales representative with a notebook filled with copies of letters from satisfied customers. New accounts were hard to get, but these letters of testimony

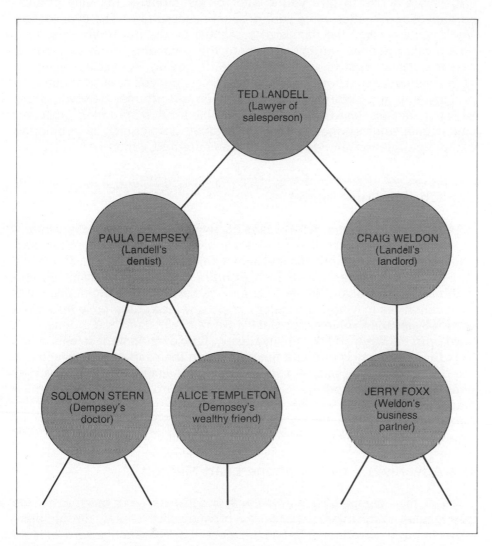

Figure 8.1 Endless Chain for a Securities Salesperson

from prominent leaders in such retail operations as gasoline service stations, cleaners, and clothing shops created immediate interest and helped close many deals. Using well-known merchants as buying examples, even without testimonial letters, is like magic in interesting others. Most merchants cannot afford to dismiss an offer, without consideration, that has already been accepted by their successful business acquaintances. Intangibles, encyclopedias, pots and pans, and books are also sold by referrals and name dropping.

If buyers refuse to give you a letter of testimony at the time of sale, perhaps they will after using your product successfully. The chances are when you are given the names of prospects by the buyer, you may also obtain other needed information about the prospects, such as income, personal characteristics, and motivations for buying. A special advantage of this method is that you not only have names, but you also have qualified prospects to see. Word-of-mouth will soon get around, however, if the salesperson fails to satisfy referral customers. A disgruntled customer can negate endless-chain efforts in a small community by promoting counterinformation embarrassing to contacts and centers of influence.

The Observation Method

The salesperson can find prospects through organized observation. Insurance sales representatives look through local newspapers for marriage, birth, and death notices that signal an opportunity to sell. Marriages and births indicate an acceptance of more financial responsibility, and death reminds people that life insurance is necessary. Automobile sales representatives may notice accident reports. Since automobile insurance pays for damaged vehicles, prospects with heavily damaged automobiles have both the need and the ability to pay. Office equipment salespersons look for new construction and fire damage in their territories. Machines are durable but they seldom survive fires, and, again, the insurance may enable the prospect to buy. Sometimes overheard conversations furnish leads. Salespersons should always listen for leads in clubrooms, trade fairs, and other places where prospects may gather.

The Advertising- or Telephone-Lead Method

Direct mail campaigns, newspapers, magazines, and bulletin boards may create enough interest that certain prospects will contact the company either to buy the product or to find out more about it. Such advertisements can be indirect when readers are promised a free memo book or some other type of premium for responding. One company has found it highly

Photo 8.2

This tragic fire destroyed many valuable products that must be replaced. Businesses that are unfortunate victims of fires must begin again by buying new products to replace those burned up or ruined by the fire. This business may be a prospect with a need for your product. Many salespersons loan demonstration equipment to help disaster victims.

profitable to sell health insurance through newspaper advertisements. Real-estate brokers make heavy use of the classified section in newspapers. Many calls to all kinds of businesses are prompted by ads in the Yellow Pages. Direct mail with return postage guaranteed works for products that are bought fairly often. Trade magazines are also a good way to reach the buyers in a particular industry. Purchasing agents who have an interest in the product for their firm may respond. When prospects return an inquiry from any advertised source, they have qualified themselves by showing a genuine interest. Most inquirers know they are extending an open invitation for a salesperson to call on them promptly. Some sales representatives even use plastic signs on their vehicles to invite inquiries.

The telephone is a more direct and personal method of securing leads and qualifying prospects. Telephone calls require little time and little expense and are particularly appropriate when there are too many leads to qualify through personal visits. Securing an appointment by telephone is one way to qualify prospects, because leads who grant appointments are either interested in the offering or have little sales resistance. (See Figure 8.2 for procedures.) Another advantage to the telephone is that a sales representative's secretary or spotter can make the calls to assure that valuable personal interview time is spent with genuine prospects. What a difference this can make in sales volume!

The Cold-Canvass Method

The cold-canvass method can be productive and is especially helpful if none of the other methods prove fruitful. It involves calling on every door that might have a use for the product. It works best in regard to products that nearly everyone may need—encyclopedias, Bibles, automobiles, typewriters, pocket calculators, vacuum cleaners, home appliances, and other durables. Calling cold for insurance and investments doesn't work as well, because these products require a more sophisticated approach in order to maintain image.

Sometimes, instead of calling at every door, sales representatives pattern their canvassing. An office equipment sales representative may select particular professional people from the phone book or an air-conditioning salesperson may call only on homes without central air conditioning—

Cold canvassing may not be the best way to prospect, but it frequently uncovers a potential customer with a need.

Reprinted from *The Saturday Evening Post* © 1962 The Curtis Publishing Company.

Figure 8.2   Precall Planning for Telephone Prospecting

I. Establish criteria for qualifying prospects
  A. size of prospect's business
  B. type of business
  C. financial condition
  D. facilities

II. Develop a list of prospects
  A. use the criteria established above to develop the list

III. Prepare an opening statement
  A. identify yourself and your firm
  B. establish rapport to reduce negative reaction to the call
  C. make an interest-creating statement or comment that will focus the prospect's attention on your product or service
  D. example:
     "Good morning, Mr. Banning. I'm Paul Rafferty of Handy Household Products. I just heard that Banning Housewares has added another branch in Center City. Congratulations. I'm calling because I know you'll want to see a demonstration of the fantastic new floor finish we've developed that's actually tougher than wax."
  E. to establish rapport
     1. make a friendly remark
     2. mention something you and the prospect have in common
     3. tactfully acknowledge that he or she is probably busy
     4. say something to stimulate pride
  F. put yourself in your prospect's shoes in creating the interest-creating comment

IV. Prepare fact-finding questions
  A. searching questions that demand a detailed response
  B. questions that begin with *who, what, where, why,* and *how.*
  C. fact-finding questions to help you determine if the potential customer is a valid prospect
  D. example:
     "What type of truck tires do you stock?"

V. Prepare a sales message
  A. stress benefits over features
  B. use a sales vocabulary

VI. Prepare your request for an appointment
  A the request should include a lead-in
     "I would like to meet with you to show you in detail how our Model X-5 can increase your sales volume."
  B. the request for an appointment should be based on several product benefits, not just one
  C. in requesting the appointment with an actual question, give your prospect a choice:
     "Would ten o'clock Wednesday morning or three o'clock Friday afternoon be better for you?"

Source: Phone-Power Self-Instruction Kit, Courtesy of Bell Telephone Company, Memphis, Tennessee.

suspects who by observation should be better prospects. Door-to-door salesworkers frequently ask about prospects in a neighborhood. Aluminum cookware sales representatives, for example, might ask where single, young working women under the age of thirty-five live, since they are more likely to buy an expensive set of new cooking utensils. After finding primary prospects, the sales representative may go into an endless-chain plan.

For some products, the cold-canvassing method is best, because it covers all bases and depends on selling percentages. You may have less competition with prospects identified by this method. Only a few seconds need to be spent at places that obviously do not have any potential. The cold canvasser who visits and tarries too long with nonprospects is violating the very spirit of cold canvassing. If the place canvassed contains no prospects and the occupants do not recommend any, leave gracefully but immediately.

ADDITIONAL PROSPECT SOURCES

Internal Records

In addition to regular prospecting techniques, there are many specific sources of names and information that can yield good returns. A fruitful and inexpensive source of prospects is internal records kept by the sales representative's company. Credit departments keep customer and purchase records and can furnish vital qualifying information.

Service Personnel

Coordination with service department repair personnel is important for industrial equipment, automobiles, office equipment, and other products that require servicing. Service personnel either visit customer facilities or repair equipment in the branch service center. In either case, they are in an excellent position to recommend new equipment to prospects and inform salespeople when products need replacing. Often, these service personnel sell operating supplies. The sales representative can help them in return for vital information concerning major replacements. A close rapport with repair personnel can be like having a partner in the business.

You should not depend on the firm to keep all of the records. You need to keep your own records, especially if you sell durables to a limited number of customers. You should have a file for each customer, and if your product is expensive and big, perhaps a file for each product. Your files should give you an idea when equipment will need replacing. Other important internal sources are your sales manager and your fellow sales representatives. A company should be a team where everyone works to win sales.

Use of Directories or Lists

The Yellow Pages telephone directory is a good source for prospects, since it classifies business firms and professional persons (listing them in alphabetical order and furnishing addresses and phone numbers). Other important directories are the Thomas Register, Dun and Bradstreet directories, College Placement Annual, and Fortune's directories. You can also go to the trade association representing your target customers and get good information. Chambers of commerce and Welcome Wagon personnel in your territory can supply you with a list of old and new firms and help you qualify prospects. You must be careful to maintain good relations with these sources at all times. Some individuals (list brokers) sell lists for a living. Here, you must balance the cost with possible gains.

Group or Party Plans

Some products are sold by party plans. Women's clubs are anxious to raise money for various projects and may agree to listen to the salesperson's presentation for a reasonable "donation." Demonstrations of products before large groups of prospects is ideal because of time economies and because word-of-mouth interaction can stimulate interest. Almost everyone is familiar with plasticware parties, where the hostess is rewarded for letting the sales representative demonstrate to friends and acquaintances in the hostess' home. Salespersons for soap and other home products operate the same way. If you can arrange to show your product before large groups of prospects, you should do well regardless of what you sell.

Fairs and Exhibits

Sales representatives may consider exhibiting at fairs or trade conferences as a public relations duty done for the firm. Important prospects can be gained this way. An office-machine corporation set up equipment demonstrations for schools of business at colleges and universities in an effort to reach future businessmen and businesswomen even before these businesspeople were in a position to buy the product. The wise salesperson might talk to these types of students (many of whom have parents in business in the territory), and secure present leads by asking the right questions. Some office-machine companies have schools to train machine operators. Not only can they supply personnel for firms who might hesitate to buy the equipment without someone to operate it, but these graduates are important prospect-generating sources and influencing pressures for years.

Contests

Contests can be another angle in prospecting strategy. Those registering for prizes are at least showing interest in the product, especially if the product itself is the contest prize. The contest rules usually require the prospect to make a statement about the product or consider the product benefits in some way. Therefore, prospects have to sell themselves to make a good entry or sample the product (buy it to be able to turn in labels).

Other Sales Representatives

Fellow sales representatives and competitive salespersons can help you find buyers. In your search for prospects, you will uncover potential customers who are in your fellow salespersons' territories. Your colleagues will also uncover leads in your territory. Cooperation means more sales for everyone. Sometimes, competitive sales representatives can't supply a customer with the needed product. They may refer the customer to you, if you have good relations with them and help them in similar situations. All kinds of salespersons make good spotters, because they know the value of good prospects. Some sales representatives even hire full-time employees whose sole responsibility is to spot prospects.

IDEAS FOR BETTER PROSPECTING

Although we have looked at the main methods and sources of prospects, there are several ideas or principles that can make you a better prospector.

Classify Prospects

An important concept is to group potential buyers. New business can come from present customers, old customers who haven't bought lately, lost customers, and new prospects.[3] *Old customers* who haven't bought lately certainly deserve attention. Be sure you know why you haven't had a recent order from them. Are they buying from a competitor? Have you something new to offer them that you didn't have the last time you called? Have you just neglected them? *Present customers* are even more important. They are probably your best prospects for new business. You can increase your sales by selling more to current customers who see you most often. Are you sure they know about your whole line? *Lost customers* need to be found. Even though the person has bought from a competitor doesn't mean he or she is not a prospect. That competitive product may be giving so much trouble that your lost customer may acknowledge the mistake and start buying your product again. Prospects prejudiced against your company because of a misunderstanding with the salesperson who had the territory before you can be brought back to the company's products by attention and diplomacy. *New prospects,* however, are the building blocks of the business. This means you should never be satisfied by just calling on present customers. Sales representatives who cut the lunch hour short to do a little canvassing or make just a few more canvass calls at the end of the selling day usually get more orders than those who do not. Always keep the number of prospects up, because running out of prospects is like running out of opportunity (see Figure 8.3, p. 210).

Be Mentally Set

Cybernetics also works in prospecting. Sales representatives should program themselves to be continually alert and listen for prospect information. You should be actively discovering new ways to find prospects all of the time. Prospects for most products can be anywhere. This mental set should motivate you to ask many people many questions and may lead to more sales.

Know Whom You Are Going to Call On Before You Leave the Office

It is a good idea to make a prospect list for the week, subject to change, before you go to work on Monday. This should give you both purpose

---

[3]Charles B. Roth, *How to Find and Qualify Prospects and Get Interviews* (Englewood Cliffs, N. J.: Prentice-Hall, 1960), pp. 56–57.

Figure 8.3   Prospecting Methods and Source Summary Table

METHODS	STRATEGIES
Center of Influence	Persuade influential and/or important people (those who interact often with prospects and customers) to help you prospect.
Spotters	Persuade people who are not centers of influence, but who are in a position to gain information about other people, to help you prospect.
Endless Chain	Ask everyone you interview for the names of potential buyers.
Observation	Be alert for various changes and events in your territory that might affect your sales, by watching, reading, or listening.
Advertising or Telephone	Use these communication aids to prospect directly and inexpensively.
Cold Canvass	Knock on every door in a prospecting area to uncover potential buyers.
Internal Records	Gather information from company records that may point you to prospects.
Service Personnel	Work closely with repair persons and other personnel who visit customers and who may tell you when customers need to buy again.
Directories or Lists	Gather information from these sources that may help you contact prospects.
Group or Party Plans	Use this plan to allow many types of people to witness the product at once, saving time and causing word-of-mouth interaction.
Fairs and Exhibits	Demonstrate the product when interested people gather and get names and addresses for interviews.
Contests	Use contests to find out who is interested in your product.
Other Sales Representatives	Swap information with other sales representatives (colleagues and competitors) who can find prospects for you.

and motivation. Each night review the possibilities in your territory and know whom you are going to call on the next morning before you go to bed. Revise this list the next morning before you go out to sell.

Keep a Customer Record Book

Remember that everyone forgets. You will forget important facts about the prospect unless you keep a book with the names and pertinent information about all of your better customers. Jot down in your *prospect book* everything about customers that might help you sell them on future calls (see Figure 8.4).

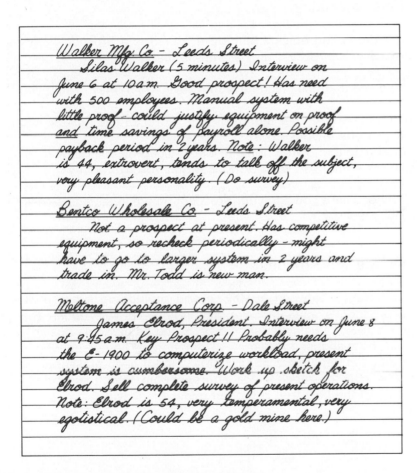

Walker Mfg. Co - Leeds Street
Silas Walker (5 minutes) Interview on June 6 at 10 a.m. Good prospect! Has need with 500 employees. Manual system with little proof - could justify equipment on proof and time savings of payroll alone. Possible payback period in 2 years. Note: Walker is 44, extrovert, tends to talk off the subject, very pleasant personality. (Do survey)

Bentco Wholesale Co. - Leeds Street
Not a prospect at present. Has competitive equipment, so recheck periodically - might have to go to larger system in 2 years and trade in. Mr. Todd is new man.

Meltone Acceptance Corp. - Dale Street
James Elrod, President. Interview on June 8 at 9:45 a.m. Key Prospect !! Probably needs the E-1900 to computerize workload, present system is cumbersome. Work up sketch for Elrod. Sell complete survey of present operations. Note: Elrod is 54, very temperamental, very egotistical. (Could be a gold mine here.)

Figure 8.4 Prospect Book Scratch Notes

Set Up the Customer for the Next Sale When the Order Is Signed

While installing bookkeeping machines, a successful office machines sales representative would remind new buyers that the machine should be traded in at a specific time. He or she would suggest that if business increased at the present rate, there would be a need for a new posting machine in so many months, or that with the present rate of tax credit for new investments, the customer's corporation should keep equipment as modern as possible and trade it in every three years. Prospects primed during a previous sale are already set up for the next closing effort.

Use Questions to Qualify

The right questions can quickly tell you if a lead is a prospect. Ask prospects directly or indirectly if they are in the market:

- If you could see that this machine would save you money, would you buy it?
- If you could make $100 per month on this merchandise rack, would you let us put one in your store?
- Would you be able to own a home in the $40,000–50,000 range?
- What features would you want on a boat that you would buy?

Qualifying questions save you and your prospect time and set a business-like tone to the interview.

Do Not Prejudge the Prospect

There is a difference between qualifying and prejudging a prospect. Sometimes a prospect's appearance might indicate poverty when the exact opposite is true. Qualifying should be based as much as possible on facts and not on response to sketchy information. The person who is a prospect and doesn't appear to be probably has not been pressured by competition and may be much more approachable than the obvious prospect. Some of the best fruit is hidden under the leaves.

PREAPPROACHING

After you have qualified a prospect and determined that the person is a potential buyer, you still may not be ready to make the presentation.

The preapproach involves all the necessary preparations that must be completed before you visit the target prospect. To call on a prospect "cold," with no knowledge of needs, problems, personality, or peculiarities indicates an intent to treat all potential buyers alike and an unwillingness to make adjustments to individual personalities and needs. When sales representatives approach with vital information about prospects and their specific problems, they flatter the prospect by their interest. The prospect is likely to respond favorably to such a "professional." Preknowledge of the buyer allows customization of strategy. Thus, preapproaching involves:

- Strategic information about the buyer and firm
- Obtaining preapproach information from competent sources
- Insuring a good reception

Strategic Information About the Buyer and Firm

Personal Information.   Practically everything you can find out about the buyer can be used strategically. This type of information is so important in certain industries that some sales managers urge their sales representatives to make a fact-finding call on the buyer, or someone else in the firm, before attempting to persuade them. You should know the potential buyer's full name, whether he or she wishes to be addressed formally by title or informally, the person's position and authority in the company in regard to buying your product, the potential buyer's education and technical competence to communicate, and the person's social affiliations. Perhaps you can use testimonies of other customers who belong to the same club or lodge. Knowing the prospect's activities and hobbies helps establish commonness and rapport. You should also know about the person's politics and philosophies to avoid offending. All people are interested in their family, and buying behavior often reflects this interest. You should know specifically what people do during the work day to approach them under the best circumstances and at the right time. Certainly, you should know individuals' needs for your product and their financial conditions. You should also find out how each individual prospect treats sales representatives, how each likes to be approached, how each likes to buy, what times each likes to be visited, how each usually pays for purchases, and who influences his or her decisions.

Personality Traits.   The prospect's personality traits are also important to strategy. Is the person an introvert or an extrovert? Are there personality needs, such as the need to dominate or the need to feed the ego? Is he or she susceptible to flattery? Does the prospect drive a hard bargain? Is the person truthful? Does this prospect have any peculiarities in dealing with sales representatives? A certain man had the reputation of being argumentative and overbearing with sales representatives. If the salesperson argued back, the prospect would interpret it as "believing in the product." Armed with this information, the sales representative made an exception to the rule of never arguing with the prospect and answered him forcefully. The man bought.

The Total Buying Situation. When sales representatives consider a corporation or a business firm as the potential buyer, they must gather information about the total buying situation. The company name and location are essential for research and routing and must be determined. The purpose of the business and the product assortment it sells give clues to needs. Usually, the volume of business also affects the firm's purchasing potential. The way the firm is organized indicates approach strategy. Who in the firm initiates purchases of your type of product? Who uses the product? Who else influences acquisitions? Does the purchasing agent have sole authority, or does the decision to buy rest with engineering or accounting? The firm's financial capabilities should be determined relative to financing the purchase. The credit position and the liquid assets of the firm determine its ability to pay and indicate whether the sales representative should press for rental or extended terms for high-dollar items. The vocabulary used in the trade should be known to give the salesperson an insider's image.

The Firm's Problems. The firm's problems are the focal point of selling strategy. Problems that can be alleviated or solved by one of your products constitute selling opportunities. Sometimes a question session is necessary before the real problems are uncovered. It is also helpful to review all previous contacts with the firm if you have them in your internal records.

Obtaining Preapproach Information from Competent Sources

General Sources. The sources of preapproach information are for the most part the same as the sources already mentioned for identifying and qualifying prospects. Preapproaching, however, involves deeper research and indicates more detailed questioning of sources who know more than just names and possible needs. *Chambers of commerce personnel* may surprise you with their knowledge about operations of important area businesses. *Trade association secretaries* often keep clippings with details about successes and problems of industry firms. Certainly, *employees of the prospective firm* may be in a position to tell you a great deal about who really makes buying decisions and how they are made. *Secretaries of prospective buyers* may be more open in revealing strategic facts than you might suppose. They are also in an excellent position to know about buyer's problems and competitive activity. Analysis of *credit ratings* and annual reports reveal financial strength and buying-power information. Again, *a diary* of past dealings with specific customers will prove valuable in aggregating preapproach data. Government records should never be overlooked.

The Preliminary Call. System sales representatives may call on prospects to gain preapproach information for proposals before making a sales call aimed at the signed order. Prospects themselves are usually the best sources of information about themselves. In these cases, the salesperson must first sell the operations survey or fact-finding interview, because asking for executive time is like asking for money. Some executive prospects resist such surveys, feeling that they may disrupt normal activities, constitute a threat to the firm's right to privacy, or create an obligation to purchase. Most potential buyers, however, realize that a sales representative selling industrial systems or accounting equipment is unable to analyze their problems and serve their needs without detailed operational information. If prospective buying executives decide that the sales representative is professional and may be able to suggest possible improvements without threatening the executive's position in the firm, they normally will permit the necessary information gathering. It is best to get permission from an authoritative executive to make needs surveys, if you wish to contact the right employees and avoid suspicion.

Insuring a Good Reception

Preapproach activity includes mentally preparing the prospect for the call. The more positive information prospects know about your company and your products before the call, the more receptive they will be to your presentation. Direct mail letters, with advertising explaining product benefits or even a personal letter, may be sent ahead to pave the way for your interview. Buyers often need time to consider the merits of offerings and may resist the closing appeals of sales representatives who call without sending information ahead to start the deliberating process. Thorough planning of the time and setting of the call is relevant to receptivity.

SUMMARY

This chapter has introduced specific techniques for selling. Prospecting is a vital early step in the selling process. For many sales representatives, separating good prospects from poor ones through determining needs and the ability to buy is critical to efficient selling strategy. Salespersons with products whose prospective buyers are hardest to identify have a greater opportunity to use tested prospecting methods.

Prospects can be found by using the center-of-influence method, the spotter method, the endless-chain method, the observation method, the advertising- or telephone-lead method, and/or the cold-canvass method. Other sources of names and information about prospects include internal company records, sales representatives' prospect records, lists and directories, fairs and exhibits, party plans, contests, and other salespersons. Sales representatives should remember that they can sell more by reactivating old customers, selling more products to current customers, affording tactful attention to lost customers, and actively searching for new buyers. Good prospecting also involves being mentally set to look for prospects, planning calls from prospect lists, keeping a diary about customers' habits and purchases, preparing the buyer for becoming a prospect again, asking questions frequently, and not prejudging whether or not a prospect is qualified.

Preapproach information is necessary before detailed plans for visiting the prospect can be formulated. Such knowledge permits the customization of selling strategy. It is important to know about the prospect's personality, interests, and special needs. Often, it is good strategy to make a special visit to the prospect's place of business and survey problems in detail before attempting to make a selling approach. Preapproach information can be obtained from chambers of commerce, trade associations, employees of the prospect's firm, credit ratings, financial statements, and other sales representatives. Advertising or personal letters may be sent ahead to prepare the prospect for the actual approach.

REVIEW QUESTIONS

1. Define:
   a. Lead
   b. Referral
   c. Prospect

2. What criteria do you use to qualify a lead?

3. Is a person who doesn't have any cash a poor prospect? Explain.

4. Under what circumstances can a prospect for your company's product not be your prospect? What should you do about such a prospect?

5. When is prospecting of special importance?

6. How does the endless-chain prospecting method work?

7. Explain how observation might help the sales representative for:
   a. Insurance
   b. Real estate
   c. Typewriters
   d. Air conditioners

8. For what two reasons should you consider leads who grant you an interview over the telephone good prospects?

9. Make up two good rules for cold canvassers to follow.

10. Where would you look in the firm for information about prospects?

11. Name six different sources for prospect lists.

12. How does a party plan work?

13. How might a sales representative make fruitful use of the time spent in demonstrating at fairs and exhibits?

14. Do you feel that contests are a good way to uncover prospects? Why or why not?

15. How can good relationships with company and competitive salespersons pay benefits in more prospects?

16. From what four types of prospects can new business come?

17. Give six ideas for better prospecting.

18. What information should you know about the prospective buyer before you attempt a persuasive sales call? What should you know about the firm?

19. What are good sources of preapproach information?

APPLICATION QUESTIONS

1. Characterize a person who might be a good center of influence, and give seven good examples of occupations or roles that centers of influence might have.

2. Give ten examples of people who might make good spotters.

3. Write an advertisement that might help you discover prospects.

INCIDENTS

8-1

Jerry Markham and Hubert Abraham are drinking coffee at a shop near the branch. It is 9 A.M. Monday morning. Both sell document copying machines.

Jerry: Wonder where I ought to go today. I need a bigger territory. What do you have on tap, Hubert?

Hubert: Well, here's my list. My first stop is the library, just half a mile up the street. I have an appointment with Mr. Bender—I'm going to show him this copier that can make transparencies from a master. Then I'm going to North Central Community College and see what their buying plans are. Then, well, there are four more professionals I need to see today.

Jerry: You sound pretty organized, Hubert. But I've been to my schools and my libraries and my banks. I need a bigger territory.

Hubert: Have you tried the savings and loans lately? I got a nice order from Jacob Lumber Company last week. How about the architects and engineers? In September an accounting firm bought a "Big Boy" worth $1,050 in commissions. Have you ever tried looking in the Yellow Pages for some of these professionals? Some of them operate out of their homes or small unmarked offices, you know.

Jerry: Well, I try to ask accountants and physicians if they have other professional friends when I'm calling on them, but I haven't gone to the phone book yet. I guess I'd better do something like that today. It may be better than driving the streets.

Hubert: Have you ever tried your small insurance companies? You can never tell when they get enough volume to be in the market. Say, Jerry, I noticed that Davidson Real Estate Company burned down last week. I'll bet that copier you sold them last year burned up and they will need a new one, even in their temporary office. Why don't you try there right now!

Jerry: That sounds like a good idea. You know, I think I need to do more planning. I sure don't like these Monday mornings when you have to think over coffee. Thanks for the tip. Hey, it's five after nine.

Hubert: Yeah, I'd better go too. It will take me about five minutes to get there and I like to hit it on the dot. Good luck, Jerry.

QUESTIONS

1. In what respects are Hubert's prospecting ideas and attitudes better than Jerry's?

2. If you were Jerry's sales manager, what prospecting advice would you give him?

8–2

Gary White sells securities for a national brokerage firm. One of Gary's biggest assets in the business is Dr. Edwin Basalt, a general practitioner, who has recommended Gary's services to over twenty-five other doctors. Gary has even been able to establish other centers of influence in the medical community as a result of Dr. Basalt's support. Just a week ago, Gary heard something that greatly upset him. He heard from Dr. Blanton, another customer, that Dr. Basalt had told him that he was going to use another broker. Gary knew that the stock market as a whole had gone down in the last few weeks, but he had told Dr. Basalt that he expected it to go down and had advised him to sell some of his more speculative issues. Then he remembered that Basalt had bought a stock against his recommendation. He looked it up to make sure, and there it was. Basalt had purchased 1,000 shares of Alacon at $79.50 a share, and it had gone down to $33. Gary remembered cautioning him against buying the stock but wrote it up anyway when Basalt insisted.

Dr. Basalt was pretty cold over the phone but agreed to see Gary for just a minute or two. Gary was very polite as usual but asked Dr. Basalt directly about the Alacon deal. Basalt answered that the loss on the Alacon deal was only part of it. He said that there were two other stocks that he wanted to buy that went up even in the face of the bearish market, and he would have made $20,000 on those two stocks if he had trusted his own inclinations and bought them when he wanted to. He finished his explanation with this sentence: "I don't know Gary; I like you, but you don't seem to give good advice anymore."

How should Gary handle this situation?

9 Planning and Approaching

Sales managers and trainers agree that sales representatives who consistently produce high sales volume are the better organizers and planners. Good planning will help you by:

- Assuring that you assign priorities to your scarce time
- Furnishing organization to coordinate your efforts
- Reminding you to accomplish what you need to do to reach your goal
- Providing you with standards to help you measure your progress

Planning is especially important after preapproach information is assembled and before you contact the prospect. The most productive of all nonselling time can be the time you spend organizing and interpreting prospect information and translating this data into a persuasive strategy. Planning, however, must begin before this. This chapter will treat planning from the setting up of yearly goals through the selection of approach methods. It will cover:

- Planning by objectives
- Planning aids
- Routing
- Considerations in the approach
- Approach methods

PLANNING BY OBJECTIVES

You should *plan by objectives* if you work on your own or your firm does not have a *management by objectives* program. The first step in all constructive planning is to establish goals to direct your efforts. Goals should be written, precisely stated, and provide obtainable targets. In many organizations, the sales manager holds a yearly Management by Objectives (MBO) conference with each sales representative, to decide on goals. These objectives should reflect more than yearly and monthly sales quotas. They should contain detailed subobjectives, such as the number of calls and demonstrations agreed upon as necessary for that sales representative to reach those sales quotas (see Figure 9.1). A performance review method should also be devised. The review method provides feedback on the salesperson's progress in successfully accomplishing the subobjectives.[1] It should reveal whether or not salespersons have averaged the four daily demonstrations to which they committed themselves to reach their sales goal. (MBO will be discussed further in Chapter 16.) If the firm you select does not practice *management by objectives*, you will do well to set overall, detailed goals for yourself. Set up a self-appraisal method to show your failure or success in meeting your own standards. Then you can tell if you have made the number of presentations, prospecting calls, and demonstrations you planned to make. Such a program should motivate you to do and sell more.

Goal setting is normally based on a review of past experience. After sales representatives submit their daily sales reports with details about their calls and other activities, computers can analyze the data. They can organize information about characteristics of the better customers and the conditions under which they buy. This report can then become the basis for setting new personal planning priorities. Typically, about 80 percent of sales comes from about 20 percent of the customers in a given territory. Other useful past information, which would help you set new standards might be:

- The average number of sales calls you have made each day
- The number of calls on both existing and potential accounts
- The average time spent on each call and traveling to each call
- The time spent waiting
- The total nonselling time spent each day
- The presentations made
- The cost and the profitability per call[2]

---

[1] Donald W. Jackson, Jr. and Ramon J. Aldag, "Managing the Sales Force by Objectives," *MSU Business Topics* (Spring 1974), p. 56.

[2] Robert F. Vizza, "Managing Time & Territories for Maximum Success," *Sales Management*, 107, no. 4 (August 1, 1971), 30–32.

Figure 9.1 MBO Planning Card

SALES YEAR 1980

MBO CARD FOR John Rankin

INTERVIEW DATE 3   JANUARY 1980

TIME AND LENGTH OF INTERVIEW 8:30 am   TO 9:15 am

TERRITORY DESCRIPTION: Between the parkways
from the river east

PLANNED GOALS		ACTUAL
TOTAL $ SALES	$ 240,000	$
PRODUCT I	120,000	
PRODUCT II	70,000	
PRODUCT III	50,000	
TOTAL UNIT SALES	87	
PRODUCT I	50	
PRODUCT II	20	
PRODUCT III	17	

DEMONSTRATIONS (PER WEEK)

PRODUCT I	9	(AVG.)
PRODUCT II	3	(AVG.)
PRODUCT III	3	(AVG.)

INTERVIEWS (PER WEEK)	30	(AVG.)
COLLECTION CALLS (PER WEEK)	7	(AVG.)
INTERVIEWS PER SALE		
** PERCENT QUOTA	%	

After you have examined your past accomplishments you should specify new goals. Use such details as an increase in the sales volume by a specific dollar amount, unit amount, or percentage. You may decide to increase the number of daily calls, the orders you get per call, or the average order size. You may reduce the average cost per call by a specific amount. You might also decide to generate a certain number of new accounts or make a set number of cold-canvass calls each week.[3] Each new plan gives you a clearer idea of what you can do to reach your goals and make more profit. Records also indicate practices that should be discontinued. If the analysis of past records indicates that more than two call-backs on insurance prospects are unprofitable, future call scheduling should exclude the third call-back and allow a more effective use of time.

A good overall objective should be stated in monetary terms and should require action from the prospect. It is also important to set dates to accomplish specifically stated goals that are fixed only after a prospect's company operations, prospect dissatisfactions, and competitors are identified.[4]

Daily planning should be easier if general objective goals are specified. The first step in deciding on the specifics of the daily plan should be a mental review of daily subgoals aimed at reaching yearly and monthly targets. A good procedure for selecting daily plan details is to write down each night all activities that should be done the next day. Assign priorities to the activities, and start the selling day with priority one and the determination to see it through to completion.[5] Reviewing the plan for the next day the night before programs the subconscious and promotes motivation and direction. It also allows review the next morning, when the mind is fresh to reaffirm priorities. With definite goals set, there is little danger that productive selling time will be spent in the coffee shop frantically trying to decide where to start the day. The priority list should be adhered to rigidly unless an emergency situation develops, or common sense dictates a change. This type of programming should keep you from the human tendency to neglect important items and become side tracked into spending too much time on the unimportant.

PLANNING AIDS

Certain reports, files, and schedules can make planning easier and should be used if they are practical and fit your needs. *Call reports* that

[3] Jackson and Aldag, *op. cit.,* p. 55.

[4] Robert A. Else, "Selling by Measurable Objectives," *Sales Management,* 110, no. 10 (May 14, 1973), 22–24.

[5] Vizza, *op. cit.,* p. 32

analyze opportunity and set new objectives have already been mentioned. Almost 70 percent of the firms that use call reports require the salesperson to include every call made.[6] It should be advised that call reports of this sort should be filled out carefully, while you still remember the details. A *time and duty analysis form,* which divides the salesperson's working day into half-hour periods, allows specific activities for many days to be recorded. The detail contained in these forms and their accuracy are more important than specific form design.

Planning forms that help the sales representative schedule activities vary from firm to firm. Modification of two types of planning forms (shown in Table 9.1), customized to accommodate the needs of the particular sales

TABLE 9.1
MAJOR-ACCOUNT SALES PLAN

XYZ CO.
FIRM NAME
CENTER CITY
CITY

SALES ENGINEER SAM DOAKS

Major Objectives	Measurable Attainable Realistic	Date to Accomplish	Persons Affecting Decision(s)	Accomplish Objective	Date to Accomplish
1. Assure continued purchase of product "B" by convincing purchasing agent of the superiority of our paint.		10/1	John Jones, Purchasing Agent	1. Convince Jones to come to our plant for a visit— make appointment.	9/15
				2. Conduct tour of plant and demonstrate paint finish.	10/1
2. Obtain an initial order for product "C" of at least $5,000.		11/15	John Smith, Plant Engineer	1. Make appointment with John Smith to find current supplier and find out decision maker.	9/5
			Jim Brown, Maintenance Superintendent	2. Determine whether moisture or aging is most important problem to Smith.	9/5
			John Jones, Purchasing Agent	3. Get appointment for demonstration of product "C" to Smith, Brown, & Jones.	9/15
				4. Hold presentation and ask for order.	10/1

Source: Robert A. Else, "Selling by Measurable Objectives," *Sales Management,* 110, no. 10 (May 14, 1973), 24.

[6] *Ibid.*

TABLE 9.1a TERRITORY SALES PLAN

SALES ENGINEER SAM DOAKS

Account Name	Sales History ($000)			Estimates Available ($000)	Number of Sales Calls Allocated Per Year	Planned Sales (or Available Sales) by Product Line ($000)				
	1969	1970	1971			Prod. A	Prod. B	Prod. C	Prod. D	Prod. E
XYZ Co.	100	110	90	250	48	10	25	25	75	25
ABC Co.	75	75	90	300	48	25	50	25	10	5
EEG Co.	40	50	60	175	24	10	10	40	20	10
GFF Co.	20	30	50	150	24	10	20	—	10	30
FFH Co.	10	10	25	100	18	30	—	25	—	—
HGG Co.	0	0	30	100	18	—	10	30	—	40
JKL Co.	0	0	0	80	18	25	—	—	10	40
KGG Co.	0	10	20	75	12	—	10	10	20	30
MNO Co.	0	5	12	60	12	20	20	20	20	—
QEC Co.	0	0	10	60	12	—	10	—	40	—
ZZZ Co.	10	8	9	50	12	2	5	5	20	5

Note: Since product-line goals should have stretch, they should not be added either horizontally or vertically.

Source: Robert A. Else, "Selling by Measurable Objectives," *Sales Management*, 110, no. 10 (May 14, 1973), 24.

firm, can be helpful. Note the detailed information in the major account sales plan. Specific objectives as well as the date for accomplishment are stated on the completed card.[7] Also indicated are the people who can exert major influence on the purchase and a step-by-step strategic plan to achieve results. The territorial sales plan listing major accounts, their potential, calls allocated per year, and the product mix to be pushed are also included on a planning card. Each card indicates how scheduling can be made easier through the use of proper objectives that are specifically tailored to the needs of sales representatives and a particular company. If your company is without such forms, designing them for your own use would help you in your planning.

ROUTING

Minimizing traveling time and automobile expense must be considered in planning a sequence of calls. You must also consider the importance of the call and the ideal time to approach each customer or prospect. Although you may have an excellent idea of territorial distances in your mind, you should secure maps of your territory from service stations, chambers of commerce, or city halls and plot your route on the map with dots and numbers. The first planned stop, for example, might be indicated by a "1," and "2" might designate the next planned call. (See Figure 9.2.) You might then consider the distances involved along with other reasons for call sequence and change the originally planned routing. You should also mark alternative calls in case certain stops don't require the amount of time planned for them.

The kind of routing plan used depends on the distribution of prospects, their accessibility, how often you call on prospects, distances covered, and prospect availability.[8] Several different patterns are available, depending on these factors. A circular plan may be used, when customers are distributed uniformly throughout the territory, are accessible, and call frequency is about the same for most accounts. A clover-leaf pattern is indicated when accounts are bunched up in certain parts of the coverage area. A hub point may be used for each bunch and calls are made in loops around this hub. When call frequency is important, sales representatives may start at a far point in the territory and work their way back home. They may skip some customers along the route and call on those who should be given attention on that particular day. If business is scattered, the sales representative may make a straight reference line

[7] Else, *op. cit.,* p. 24.

[8] W. J. Crissy and Robert W. Kaplan, *Salesmanship* (New York: Wiley, 1969), pp. 168–169.

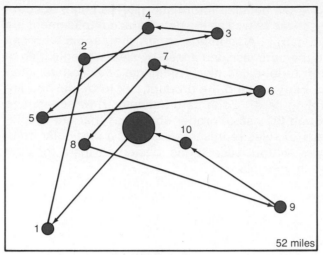

Unplanned

52 miles

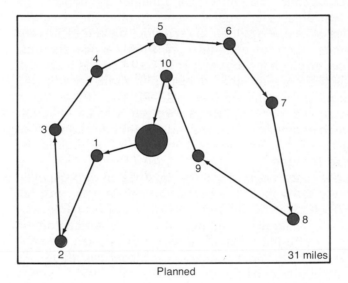

Planned

31 miles

Figure 9.2 Routing, Planned Versus Unplanned

through each cluster of businesses, changing direction for each cluster group.[9]   The important factors to remember in routing are to use the map, consider all elements affecting the sequence of calls, and consider both distance and timing.   Be flexible and provide for alternative calls, but don't go out into the territory without a plan.

[9] *Ibid.*

After a planned route is tentatively scheduled, sales representatives must call for appointments (if they plan to ask for the interview in this way), spend time waiting in offices, get past the buffers or barriers to see the right persons, and follow good preinterview methods. Included in this section are the following preinterview considerations:

- The interview as a separate sale
- Cultivating assistants
- Insisting on seeing the right person
- Gracious waiting
- Knowing when "no" may not mean "no"
- Remembering your goals in approaching

The Interview As a Separate Sale

Every sale is really two sales. You must first sell the interview to be able to tell your story. If you have already called the prospect and have an interview scheduled, you will probably announce your arrival, tell the secretary of your appointment, and patiently wait until you are asked into the prospect's office. If you are calling without an appointment, you must first sell the secretary or other *buffer* on the importance of granting you an interview with the prospective executive. In this case, the barrier or buffer will "size you up," and it is usually more important for you to sell yourself in this situation than it is to try to sell your product. If you are shut out at this point because of your personality, whatever great advantages the prospect might have derived from using your product won't be communicated and won't make any difference.

Cultivating Assistants

You never know who can help you get the order. It is good to be nice to everyone from the assistant janitor on up. To make a sale it is essential to get as many people as possible working for you with access to prospects in the firm. Nearly all corporate prospects are surrounded by *barrier* or *buffer* personnel (see Photo 9.1). For all important prospects there is at least one secretary, and for most top corporate officials there are executive buffers. The person with the power to say yes usually depends on the advice of these buffers. They are there to protect a most valuable resource—time. Buffers separate sales representatives who might have

Photo 9.1

It is important to make a good impression on the buffer who protects the prospect's time by screening salespersons.

something to offer from sales representatives who probably will waste the superior's time. In dealing with buffers, there is a difference between acting professional and acting "superior" to subordinates who can get you in and help you get the business. The buffer's concept of your attitude is critical. Your dress, your body language, your voice, and other clues will be read to determine if you are worthy of the boss' attention. Charles Roth advises that sales representatives develop magic phrases like: "This is a courtesy call," or "I would consider it a great personal favor, if you could secure an interview with Mr. Jones for me."[10] If you can make the buffer feel justified by allowing you in, you can usually get in. You should not appear impatient or ill at ease.

[10] Charles B. Roth, *How to Find and Qualify Prospects and Get Interviews* (Englewood Cliffs, N.J.: Prentice-Hall, 1960), pp. 90–100.

If you can't get an appointment or you can't get sufficient time to make a good presentation, it is best to come back later. If the answer is "no," but a "put-off no" rather than an "honest no," you might ask the secretary to let you speak to the prospect on the house phone and try to sell an interview that way.[11]

Insist on Seeing the Right Person

While sales representatives should be courteous to subordinates and sell their way into seeing the prospect, it is extremely important to eventually interview the actual person with the power to make the decision. Sales representatives have a tendency to sell to employees at lower levels. They feel more comfortable with them and hope that the persuasive information will filter up to the level where the decision will be made. The problem is that the employees who will be presenting your case to higher-level executives will not be as motivated or as persuasive as you are. In addition, the product will not be presented in its best light to the decider; and there is no chance for you to answer the vital questions raised by the real prospective buyer. It is far better for the representative to overcome timidity and see the right person. Key executives are people, too, and often they are more understanding and considerate than lower-level employees. One of the reasons they are in a high position is because they are able to understand and communicate better than the average person.

Gracious Waiting

Waiting time should be productive time. Remember that while you are waiting, you are still selling the buffer. You might convince the secretary that you are important by using this time to open your valise and review material and plans pertinent to your profession. If you must read a magazine or a newspaper, be sure to read a professional journal or a financial journal rather than a crossword puzzle. If you waste time while waiting, the secretary will think your time is not valuable and that you are not on a level with the boss, who is a busy person. Many sales representatives have a cut-off time on waiting, a preset time in minutes. They have found from experience that some offices will let you wait as long as you will sit there and even forget you. Some prospects will let you wait just to convey that they are important and hard to see. Wait patiently to your limit, and then explain to the secretary that you must go and will return at a more opportune time. It is permissible in some cases to say: "I have another appointment in a few minutes. Will you check and see if Ms.

[11] *Ibid.,* pp. 101–111.

Gray will be free in a little while?'' Or you might say, ''Could I speak to Mr. Smith on the company phone before I leave, to find out when it will be convenient for him to see me?''

Knowing When ''No'' May Not Mean ''No''

When you are refused an interview, it may be because the person is actually busy, or it may be a ''no'' to discourage sales representatives with little conviction about their product from taking up the prospect's time. The salesperson should have a few rebuttal phrases for the perpetual ''no'' of people who use ''no'' to shield their time. You should give a reason for seeing the prospect. ''Tell Mr. Jordan we have a price increase that will go into effect on the first of next month, and he can save 15 percent by ordering now, if he is interested.'' Or ''I want to show Mr. Jordan a new product which he has never seen before that can speed up his production line 10 percent.'' Certainly, when the sales representative has spent a great deal of time in fruitless waiting on several occasions, it is time to try a new strategy. Try to reach prospects on the phone or soften them up with several letters, if they merit this kind of attention. When *you* have trouble gaining access to a prospect, you can expect that your competitors will have the same problem. You may find the hard-to-see prospect a superior prospect, if you can make the first sale—getting in to tell your story.

Try to maintain a good image while waiting.

"Look—I said he was out!"

Reprinted from *The Saturday Evening Post* © 1960 The Curtis Publishing Company.

Remembering Your Goals in Approaching

You have only a short time to get the prospect's interest and attention. Like the buffer, prospects are probably judging your position to see if it is worth their time before listening to your entire presentation. Your goals should be to whet curiosity, make prospects want to listen, establish rapport, and reduce any disharmony that might exist. You must quickly establish that you are there to help and not to waste time or push products that are not needed.

APPROACH METHODS

To many prospects, time is as valuable as money. Therefore, it is not surprising that prospects concentrate maximum attention on your opening to determine whether or not to give you a full hearing. Their first mental impressions of you and your offering are all-important. Their receptivity, for the rest of the interview, depends on those first few moments when they are scanning your appearance, your attitude, your offering, and responding to a few important clues. If they decide, "Maybe this salesperson can benefit me, so I'll listen," you have accomplished the primary objective of the opening. If they decide, "I really don't need what this person has and my time is going to be wasted," it is difficult to get them to change their minds. The first few words from the sales representative set the whole tone of the interview and are of vital importance. If sales representatives appear poised, gain immediate interest and attention, and reduce conflict, their first impression will lead to a better presentation. If, on the other hand, awkwardness, embarrassment, and conflict characterize the initial confrontation, they will have difficulty reestablishing harmony and compatibility. Experience with more than one opening permits the salesperson to adjust remarks to fit the situation on entering the prospect's office or home. It is good practice to have several alternative openings and to use the one that best fits the circumstances. Because every product and every prospect is different, it is difficult to devise opening words for all situations. The following methods, however, have been used to advantage in many situations.

The Self-Introduction Approach

Once invited, the salesperson should enter the prospect's office or home unhurriedly, but not casually, and stand facing the prospect. A genuine smile is always in order at this point to relax the atmosphere and dispel tension. Do not enter in a hurried, anticipatory fashion as if you are on the attack. Let your body language convey a good image. Remember, while you are sizing up the prospect, the prospect is making many judgments about you from the clues you are signalling about yourself. Once these impressions are formed—and they are often formed in a few seconds—it is difficult to change them. Do not stop short of the prospect's immediate presence unless you have a reason. In an office, come to the front of the desk facing the prospect. To stop at the door or midway into the room indicates that you feel subordinate or that you are hesitant about the worth of your offering. It is best to establish two-way communication as an equal. Staying too far away is a body language way of apologizing for being there. You might then say in a poised manner: "How do you do, Mr. Jones. I'm James Scott, representing the Acme Corporation." The handshake should not be forced, since a few prospects have an aversion to shaking hands. If the prospect extends his or her hand, the shake should be brief and firm but never discomfortingly hard or "weasely" soft. It helps to look the prospect in the eyes but not to stare continually. Glance away naturally and occasionally.

It is controversial at this point whether or not you should hand the prospect your card. Giving the card at the beginning assures that the prospect can call you by name, and this can make the conversation more cordial. Most prospects are so busy sizing you up they miss or forget your name. Some sales representatives find it better not to use cards at all, and others extend it only at the end of the interview. In most sales situations, card or not, it is common courtesy to tell the prospect who you are and what company you represent. Any other opening may seem evasive and unprofessional. All this is really preliminary to your real opening remarks, so what you say next is especially critical to the success of the interview.

The Mutual Acquaintance or Reference Approach

Using the name of another customer or a friend is one way to start and make the prospect feel obligated to listen. It can also stimulate interest, especially if the prospect respects the judgment of the referenced person and that person just bought from you under similar circumstances. You might say, "Ms. Johnson bought a copier from us this week, and she indicated that you might be interested in information about copiers," or "Mr. Talbert of Artist's Piano Company in this area bought one of our payroll machines last month. Your larger payroll certainly would indicate even greater costs savings from a machine system." If you reference the names of several customers who have recently bought, you will usually find that this is a compelling opening, especially if those customers are competitors of your prospect. You also might begin by handing the prospect several testimonial letters signed by new customers in the same business or with the same circumstantial needs and simply say, "Many people in your business are switching to this promotion. Read what some of them say about what it has meant in their businesses."

Never drop a name unless you want that person to be contacted, because in many instances the prospect *will* contact that person before buying. If you are using other people's names to gain interviews, remember that you are representing those persons as well as yourself and your firm. If they are customers, you may lose them if you stretch the truth about your relationship or what they said about your product. If you are merely name dropping so that you will be extended courtesy by the prospect, the prospect may listen but resent the obligation to listen and discredit your selling points. Make sure the person whose letter you have or whose name you mention will back you up.

The Question Approach

Questions require responses from prospects, indicate your interest in their problems, and lead prospects to concentrate on the need problem rather than on the possible loss of time from the interview. Questions allow the prospect to participate early and establish two-way communication from the very beginning. You might think of the question approach as securing a hold on the prospect's mind. There is a habit-promoted compulsion to respond to questions, because we have been taught since childhood that it is courteous to consider a question and answer.

A broad range of opening questions is available in any selling situation. The challenge is to find the question that best secures attention and interest and the willingness to listen with an open mind. One kind of question that might be asked is a *qualifying or commitment-inducing question.* "If I could show you how this machine could pay for itself within two years, would you buy it?" or "If you could get 10 percent interest on a government-guaranteed certificate, would you invest $10,000 today?" or "Suppose we could find you a car that is comfortable, safe, handles well, and gives you over 40 miles to the gallon. Would you invest $4,000 in it?" This type of opening question requires thoughtful consideration on the part of prospects and usually they will qualify themselves. Occasionally, the prospective buyer *will* say yes, and all you have to do is prove that you can deliver your side of the bargain. Very often you will get the interest and two-way involvement you need to maintain prospect attention for the rest of the interview. The commitment question is excellent for separating the "lookers" from the "buyers," and it facilitates the close.

The *benefit* question is usually a leading question designed to stimulate a mental commitment. "Mr. Smith, you would need a compact that would accommodate a tall man, wouldn't you?" "You would insist on a car that would hold up for at least 100,000 miles under normal driving conditions, wouldn't you?" "Wouldn't you want a policy that would give you cash in times of emergency?" "Do you realize that this wasted space in your store could mean $500 a year more profits for you at the end of the year?" This is a favorite approach with advertisers as well as salespersons and is a much-used headline in advertising copy.

An *image* question suggests a mental picture and is another way to make the prospect think. "How long would it take you to get out of this house in case of fire?" "If you suddenly get sick and are out for four months, what income are you and your family to live on?" "Will you have enough at retirement to maintain your standard of living in the face of 10 percent inflation?" "How are you presently planning for the expenses of Jerry's college education five years from now?" "Can you imagine how much fun it would be to own your own outboard?" Questions like these can get prospects to see themselves using the product in ideal situations.

Questions can also whet *curiosity*. "Have you ever seen a television projector that can throw a picture on the wall as big as life?" "How could you cook a hamburger, in a motel, in less than two minutes, without a stove, and not upset the management?" "Can a flashlight work without batteries?" Curiosity-inducing questions grab the prospect's attention. If you can switch into the rest of the presentation without making this approach appear deceitful, you should have a good audience.

Spend time devising and field testing good opening questions tailored to your prospect. Ask questions that stimulate your prospect to think about needs and focus attention on your offering. Don't ask questions that will lead to the ending of the interview or suggest unpleasant circumstances. "How are you doing, Mr. James?" may lead Mr. James to think that because he is not doing well, your offering should not be considered. "Do you like cars with fuel injection?" Suppose the answer is "no" and that's the only kind of car you have? Some questions stimulate thoughtful response, and these should be preferred. Definitive questions are usually better than general questions. Ask questions that suggest a positive and known response. Just as questions in advertising persuade people to read the rest of the copy, they can serve the same purpose of cementing attention in the personal interview.

The Statement or Benefit Approach

An opening statement is like the headline of an advertisement. It must attract attention. It can be a statement of the primary benefit of the product. It should be an important reason for listening and should make the prospect's risk of not listening greater than the risk of listening. The statement can be news to the prospect—something new, vital, and different that he or she has not heard before. It should pave the way for the rest of the interview and be the cornerstone of the persuasive appeal. Most prospects have a dominant buying motive. The opening statement should appeal to that motive if at all possible, and the entire presentation should be built around it.

No matter what statement you use, how you say it can make as much difference as what you say. If your opening statement sounds practiced and unnatural, it may appear to be a gimmick and lose its effect. Like every approach, the statement should cement the prospect's attention and stimulate thought about needs. Ask yourself these questions about your opening statement. Will it get undivided attention? Can I lead into the other selling points naturally from it? Will it establish harmony or disharmony as the tone of the interview? Will it make the prospect think in terms of solving needs with my product? Examples of opening statements are:

- Prices on all of our models are going up next week, but you can buy at a 10 percent savings this week.
- Mr. Baker, with your present accounts-receivable load, every day you continue to use a manual system you are losing $25.
- I want to serve you by doing an analysis of your materials-handling procedure at no cost or obligation on your part.
- You will get a higher return on this bond issue with less risk than on any we have had to offer in the last ten years.
- I challenge you to find any chemical that will clean your equipment better or more safely than Acme.
- Your secretary can save an hour a day with this typewriter.
- The government's new accelerated depreciation plan goes into effect on January 1, which means that they will, in effect, pay more than 40 percent of the cost of modernizing your equipment.

The Praise Approach

This approach must be done carefully, or it will be considered "flattery in bad taste" by your prospect. The salesperson is expected to use flattery in persuasion, and a subtle, flattering opening may be acceptable in establishing communications. However, flattery often shuts off the opportunity to use a more effective approach. The person may easily decide that if all the sales representative can do is offer flattery, the benefits of the offering must be weak.

On the other hand, a deserved compliment is a positive personal approach and may set a good interview tone and foster appreciation of the salesperson's sense of courtesy. Some prospects are so thirsty for a kind word, that even obvious flattery is perceived as a natural attempt to be pleasant. A compliment which is not directed at the prospect's personal attributes is usually safer and less pointed. A pleasantly expressed appreciation of the prospect's secretary or home-office environment indirectly reflects the prospect's good judgment and taste and doesn't cause embarrassment or promote a defensive attitude. You might please the prospect by quoting a compliment that someone else has paid him or her—it is always gratifying to discover that other people speak well of you in your absence. Below are some examples of praise openings:

- You are certainly fortunate to have a secretary as thoughtful as Mrs. Ashley.
- Where did you find such a beautiful chair?
- Your company has always been the innovator in the industry. This advanced fork-lift truck should help continue that tradition of being the first to furnish your employees with the best work equipment.
- Congratulations on your promotion to branch manager, Mr. Owen. It will be a pleasure to serve you in regard to your paper supplies.
- I see that you've modernized your office beautifully. Whoever decorated it certainly did an outstanding job.
- You must be very proud of your son for winning that scholarship to law school for next year. I'm sure he learned a great deal by working here with you each summer.

The Free Gift or Sample Approach

Gifts or free samples may appear to the prospect as an attempt to buy interview time. But the prospect may be willing to accept and hear your story. Many door-to-door sales representatives find greater receptivity by offering a small brush or cosmetic sample as a goodwill gesture. A professional salesperson selling an intangible or industrial equipment may offer an invitation to lunch or a golf game in the same spirit. Or, he or she may volunteer to give advice or free consulting work that might be regarded as a "sample" of professional services. Leaving small equipment or appliances for a trial period might also be thought of as a method of letting prospective buyers "sample" items too expensive to give. The sample should be in keeping with the product image and the level of selling.

Showing or giving the prospect a sample can quickly draw attention to the offering by bringing in the other important senses besides hearing—sight, taste, touch, and/or smell. Something tangible is introduced in the interview and it can serve as a focus for two-way conversation. Offering samples may reinforce your product claims, since you are obviously willing to let the prospect try and use the product before buying. In a sense, you are challenging the buyer with the implication that surely if it is used, it will be appreciated. An immediate problem is that buyers may want to try it later and put off buying until they have a private chance to evaluate. Other prospects may take the sample and dismiss the salesperson before the interview is really started. For this reason, the free gift may be promised in the opening and given at the completion of the interview. Below are examples of this approach:

■ The computer salesperson unfolds and explains a printout with a completed management report customized for the prospect.
■ The candy sales representative hands the grocer a candy bar, saying, "Taste this, and you will know why this new bar is capturing the market."
■ The pump salesperson hands the prospect a paperweight model of a new pump to focus discussion on an industrial need.
■ The perfume salesclerk sprays mist on the prospect's wrist, saying, "Doesn't it have a delightful fragrance?"

The Product or Ingredient Approach

What can you do when the product is large and indivisible and too valuable to give away or leave on trial? An office-machine salesperson may carry a hundred-pound bookkeeping machine into a hardware store programmed to demonstrate an accounts-receivable operation. "Mr. Taylor, you have a large accounts-receivable burden, and I want you to see how efficient a machine operation can be." This direct approach is honest, it creates interest, and it usually results in the demonstration of the equipment. Not many prospects will make you carry that load back without at least looking at it, and most will clear off a place for you to put it down. Shoe salespersons may use a cut-away shoe to show premium construction. The tire sales representative may show you the cross section of the tire, revealing the protective steel belts. A real-estate sales representative may show you an ear of corn grown on a farm and open it for visible proof of its high fertility.

Some salespeople like to hand the product to prospects and let them open the conversation or hand the product and ask a question about it. Usually, the prospect will ask a question that makes it quite natural to start an invited interview. Quite often, time pressures will be forgotten, and the prospect, with curiosity aroused, will allow you to explain operations or benefits. Auto sales representatives, office-equipment sales representatives, food sales representatives, clothing sales representatives, and many others agree that it is good practice to get prospect and product together from the beginning. If there *is* interest, it will soon be shown, and if there is no interest, you have at least qualified the prospect.

The Gimmick Approach

When all other approaches seem to fail, sales representatives may turn to unusual ways of getting the prospect's attention. Some salespersons, for example, have silently lighted a dollar bill with a match to emphasize dramatically how the prospect is losing money by not buying the proposed product. Other sales representatives have simply walked past the buffer by pretending to be an employee of the firm. Encyclopedia representatives have wrongfully approached prospects under the guise of "doing a survey," only to twist into a full-blown sales presentation after the prospect

Your approach should be designed to capture the prospect's attention. Will this sales representative have trouble getting into the rest of his presentation?

"You're probably thinking, 'A burglar—and I have no insurance!'"

© Orlando Busino 1962.

answers the qualifying questions. Salespersons have also entered homes on the pretense of using the phone or needing a glass of water and worked into a sales presentation. Others have begun by offering a set of books free to prospects on the pretense of using them to "advertise the books in their area." A particular shoe salesman claimed he always opened by showing a prospect an unattractive pair of shoes and remarking, "These shoes just don't seem to fit your image." The third pair of shoes he would show would be the ones he expected the prospect to buy. His rationale for this strategy was "People don't buy the first pair of shoes you show them, anyway." Naturally, gimmicks like these are a long way from the spirit of professional selling and can create anger in the prospect. They can make it hard to lead into the sales speech and promote a conflicting type of atmosphere. It is easy to see how the image of salespersons and their firms might be hurt in the long run if certain gimmick approaches are used. Some salespersons use them only as a last resort, and most of them should not be used at all.

Other Approaches

The shock, the service, or the opinion approach might fit a particular situation.[12] In the shock approach, information can be advanced or a scene dramatized to shock the prospect into seeing need. A salesperson may set a cloth sample on fire that burns quickly and say, "You wouldn't want your customers' children to wear sleepwear made of this kind of material, would you? Our line of pajamas is completely flameproof." The opinion approach is an indirect compliment that draws the prospect into conversation. "Mr. Smith, I would like you to examine this automobile and give me your honest opinion about it." The service approach simply promises a service benefit to the buyer and is, therefore, a specialized benefit approach.

Bad and Good Approaches

Bad approaches cause the prospect to think negatively and make it easy to say no. Remember never to mispronounce the prospect's name, provoke an argument, talk about sex, religion, or politics, open with a dirty joke, indicate that you intend to waste the prospect's time, use vague

[12] Alan Reid, *Modern Applied Salesmanship,* 2nd ed. (Pacific Palisades, Ca.: Goodyear, 1975), pp. 204–208.

generalizations instead of specifics, or create conflict of any kind. It is best to use an approach that is proven, rivets attention and interest, promotes identification of the prospect with the salesperson, and leads naturally into the rest of the interview.

SUMMARY

Planning is necessary before approaching a prospect to set up a persuasive hearing for your presentation. Well-defined, specific objectives should be devised ahead of time to direct planning and provide controls for sales efforts. It is important to determine the prospects you plan to visit and the route you plan to take before you go out into your territory. Call reports, time and duty analyses, account sales plans, and computer-generated data on customers can greatly facilitate planning. Routing may be accomplished by a circular plan, a clover-leaf pattern, a skipping pattern, or a cluster pattern. A map with plotted call locations should be analyzed before finalization of routing to evaluate time and distance considerations.

The approach should be considered a separate sales situation, and buffers protecting the prospect should be treated as important individuals. Everyone in the prospect's firm should be treated courteously. Waiting time should be used to help you build an effective image, you should make sure the right person is seen, and you should know how long to wait and how to interpret the various "no's." The first ten seconds of exposure to the prospect are critical, because impressions are being formed that are hard to change. Unhurried and poised body language and carefully selected first words are essential. Salespersons must set the tone of the interview by establishing themselves as considerate, service-oriented persons with something to offer.

The sales representative should have several methods of approaching and select the best one to fit the situation. The reference approach is excellent with prospects who are extroverts and are susceptible to strong reference-group pressures. The question approach establishes two-way conversation and involves the prospect immediately. The benefit approach can hit the dominant buying motive with the very first words. The praise approach, if not giving the appearance of flattery, can soothe the prospective buyer's ego. The free-sample approach can buy the salesperson interview time. The product approach can focus attention on the product offering immediately. Ethical gimmick approaches might be used in difficult cases. The approach selected for the situation should create immediate interest, be different, cause the prospect to forget that you have just interrupted him or her from another purpose, and lead naturally into the rest of the interview.

REVIEW QUESTIONS

1. What are the benefits of planning?

2. What features are involved in planning by objectives?

3. What are the criteria for good objectives?

4. What types of information can be gained from an analysis of past reports that can be used as a basis for planning?

5. What specific goals can a salesperson use to increase profitability?

6. Name three good daily planning procedures.

7. Name and describe the reports and forms that a salesperson can use to good advantage in planning.

8. What factors determine the kind of routing plan used?

9. Name and describe four patterns that might be used in routing.

10. List important considerations in getting past the buffer.

11. Why do salespersons visit with lower level personnel when they should be interviewing higher echelon people with the power to buy?

12. What are the goals of a salesperson in the approach?

13. Describe the elements in a good approach.

14. Describe and evaluate the reference approach.

15. What are the benefits of the question approach? What kinds of questions might be asked?

16. What are the hazards of the praise approach? How may they be overcome?

17. Describe the ways salespersons can "buy" interview time with free gifts or samples.

18. Evaluate the product or ingredient approach in the light of approach objectives.

1. Make up five good rules for interview waiting.

2. The first five seconds after the prospect views the salesperson are critical. Why? What can the salesperson do in terms of body language to make a favorable impression on the prospect in the first five seconds?

3. Give three examples other than the examples in the text of a good benefit statement approach.

4. Explain several gimmicks that sales representatives have used to start interviews.

INCIDENTS

9–1

Bert Brewer is calling on John King, who is a prospect for a life insurance policy.

Bert: Mr. King, I'm Bert Brewer with Nordic Insurance Company. (*Hands him a calling card.*) I want to congratulate you on your recent marriage. Mr. Langdon Humphries (the bride's uncle) said you might be interested in financial planning through life insurance.

John: Bert, I'm glad to meet you, but my wife and I are just getting our apartment furnished, and we can't afford an insurance policy right now.

Bert: I know how tight things are when you first get married. I've only been married for two years myself. I just wanted to meet you and Mrs. King and answer some of the questions you might have about financial planning, so when you feel able to make a move toward protection, you will consider Nordic.

John: Well, if you're sure you understand that we're not in the market for insurance just yet with all we have to buy, I guess we can talk for just a minute or two. Nancy, we have company who knows your uncle.

(*Nancy enters the living room.*)

Bert: Hello, Mrs. King. Your uncle, Mr. Humphries, is one of my Nordic policy holders. You must be his favorite niece; he talks about you a lot every time I see him. You know, one of the things you and Mr. King need to think about when you establish a home is financial security for the future. Might I sit down with you for a minute and simply explain some factors that might have a significant bearing on your financial future?

Nancy: Well, if you are a friend of Uncle Lang's, sure. We can talk for a minute, but we need furniture right now and not insurance.

Bert: I sure understand that. Do you (to John) have any life insurance protection at all?

John: Why would we need any just now? We don't have any children and Nancy is a schoolteacher . . . but to answer your question, we don't.

Bert: Most married couples wind up with children, and if the husband is not insurable when the children are young and something happens to him, then the wife is left with a difficult burden. The monthly premiums for insurance also grow more expensive with each "insurance birthday." That is, if you take it out this year, the premiums would be less than if you waited until next year. We have plans, for example, that recognize the money needs of young marrieds and defer much of the premium cost until you get on your feet. Let me show you the details of this term policy that guarantees your future insurability for additional amounts. . . .

QUESTIONS

1. What type of approach did Bert use on John? on Nancy?

2. Was it a good tactic in this situation to use Uncle Langdon's name?

3. What do you think of Bert's approach tactics?

4. How would *you* have approached John and Nancy?

9-2

The following letter was written by a "Legion of Honor" senior salesperson with the Burroughs Corporation.[13] Evaluate the letter in respect to planning. Write a shorter letter along the same lines, using a different product.

Mr. R. K. Weisinger, Branch Manager
Burroughs Corporation
231 Monroe Avenue
Memphis, Tennessee

Dear Keith:

As you requested, I am listing a few ideas regarding the work plan I use in working my territories.

[13] Reproduced with the permission of the Burroughs Corporation.

When I first came with Burroughs several years ago, Mr. F. T. Miller was District Sales Manager. I remember two things he told me. One was that things never looked better for Burroughs men; the other was that to be successful in this business you should plan your work and work your plan. He was right about the first, because things have been getting better most of the time since then and still will, particularly if we each help a little. I know he was right about the second, too, because it has been told to me by every manager and supervisor since then.

They were all right. It is the answer to success. However, though everyone recommended it, and Burroughs gave me a territory and a quota and opportunity, no one gave me a plan. In working a territory, however, I have found that there are so many variables in the different ones, that it would be hard for the Company to devise one that would work for everyone. It is probably better, with some help, for a man to develop his own. I have talked to other salesmen about it, and many seemed to have only the plan to close a few deals for big equipment, get rid of a debit balance, and draw some big commissions. Occasionally, this works out, but most men with that plan have some lean years and many lean months and a lot of disappointments. They frequently find themselves rushing around on the last day of the month or the last week of the year trying to close something to salvage the record. And that is selling at its very toughest.

Most Burroughs men have developed their own plan of working their particular territory. Most of them are very good and well suited to the problems they face. Doing the same thing, I have found some things that work well for me in my territory, and I am giving them to you for what they may be worth.

I have found that a *Big Plan,* which is not composed of hundreds of little plans, which you carry out every day, is almost worse than no plan at all. My Big Plan is to get just as large production and commissions as I possibly can from my territory. If it goes no further then that, it is merely hoping. But I break it down to make it reasonable. If I intend to sell $100,000 a year, for instance, I figure it will take me $8,500, and then I see it will take about $2,200 per week to sell that much monthly. Then I try to sell as much of it before noon on Monday as I can. Never wait until the last of the week or the last of the month to reach your goal. To help do this, I set as a small goal to have no shut-out weeks, even if I have to work late Saturday to close the deal; but it is a lot more comforting when you start a deal on Monday. Selling is sort of like fishing; the first one is the hardest. Then they frequently come in bunches. So try to get an order as close to the first of the year as you can, and the first day of the week, and the first day of the current month. When you do, the period is generally going to be good.

The first step in planning is to analyze your territory. Work it for what is in it. If the best part of it is bank business, apply a good bit of your time proportionately to working that line. If manufacturing, or government, or retail or wholesale, figure it out and do the same thing. Work it all, but do not get so carried away on any machine, application, or business that you neglect your better prospects. It is tough to lose any business, but do not lose the easy business. That's like a pitcher walking another pitcher.

Most territories are seasonal to a degree. I know from experience that I generally get more business in my territory in January, February, and March, than any other three-month period. Be sure you build up good live prospects to the point that they are ready to close when the seasonal pickup comes. It is usually too late to start on them when buying time comes. Likewise, if we have a list of "hot prospects" when we have a price increase, which we have from time to time, it's easy to close the "hot ones" then. But, if he has not been convinced he is a prospect, it is useless to try to make a prospect of him because of a price increase. The mention of it might even serve to make him mad. Most of us are pretty happy when we have a month in which we close a lot of orders, sort of despondent when we have not; but the time to be despondent, even if we are closing some orders then, is when we are not initiating and building up a good number of live prospects; because that always means some lean times two or three months from now. If you want to keep having good months, don't get too satisfied because you are getting some orders. You must build prospects at the same time.

I find it most valuable to have a complete list of all Burroughs users in the territory and the machines they use and try to keep it up-to-date. I figure everyone with a machine three or four years old is a prospect for replacement. Be sure to give them a proposal and a chance to buy. The deals you get when the machines are this age are always easier than they would be if they were eight or ten years old, and there is very little danger of losing them to competition. I often canvass out of my users' list, and generally look it over before I make a call on any customer.

Consider the serviceman in your plan. He can be the best sales aid you have. Most servicemen know they are now in Marketing, but it is up to us to show them they are appreciated and just how valuable they are in the operation. I try to talk to the ones that work the territory I do daily when possible, look over their calls, and see that they have information and literature on any new machines we are trying to sell. I discuss the prospects I am working on with them, and the equipment we are proposing. That way they will know the situation when they call on the customer, and we can work to the same end on the deal. If they have customer trouble or any machine trouble on which I can help, through my contact or knowledge of the particular machine application, I make it a point to go with them or help in any way I can to the exclusion of anything else at that time. I have found it always pays to do this. There is no business in which cooperation between sales and service is as necessary or as effective as in ours.

Sell supplies on your calls where possible, and try to turn them over to the Service Representative. He gets a thrill out of sending in orders, too. We don't get a commission on it, but it is most valuable in promoting selling that does pay us a commission.

It does several things:

(1) Keeps us in a selling mood. Nothing helps like getting orders. After you take a supply order or two in the morning, you are in a much better frame of mind to close a machine deal later in the day. Try it.

(2) It helps the serviceman. He needs the sales for his record, and he can return the help many times over.

(3) Someone is going to get the business and our company needs it just as badly as any competition. If a competitor is in there on any basis. we are that much weaker.

(4) Better customer contact. It takes little time to ask for supply orders, and any sale you make to the customer makes the next sale that much easier no matter what it is for.

We can call on only a limited number of people daily, but we can sit down for a few minutes at night or on the weekend and drop a short note with some pertinent information to at least a half-dozen customers. They are usually prepared and softened up from this by the time you call. I have had many sales materialize a year or two later from a short note to the customer about an application. Whenever I make a bookkeeping installation in a town, I always write a few other similar businesses in that town or nearby towns, tell them of the installation, suggest they might like to visit it, and send them a picture of the machine. Enthusiasm about a new machine is usually at its peak at this time. It helps to have other people know about it. You can tell a few of them in a short time this way.

I make it a point to never call on anyone without giving them a proposal to buy something before I leave. It can be very informal, just a pencilled offer to trade on the back of a piece of literature. Be sure you let them know you are there to sell them something they need. They will appreciate your effort even if they have to say "no" that time.

We must sell large machines to build up satisfactory volume, and these should and do take time. But, if you have a full-line territory, plan to sell the full line. That is the gravy that provides the money to pay the expenses, so that all the rest of your commission is clear. The nice part about it is that it takes so little time to do it. Just remember in the back of your mind all the machines you have, look around on all calls and installations, give them proposals to trade, keep a list of people wanting used machines. If you are looking for them, you can stumble over two or three small machine prospects weekly, without canvassing for them at all. I figure that every full-line salesman should sell at least 100 units per year, and that should be a minimum goal in your planning. If you sell 150% of quota on 125 units, you and your territory are a lot better off than if you sold 150% on just 75 units. Because you have created users, users create other users for both big and little machines. If you don't sell your share in the territory, somebody is going to do it. And, when they do, your territory will be just that much weaker for you and Burroughs.

248

Selling Techniques

Plan to work the hot machines while they are hot. When we get something like the Microtwin was a few years ago, or our Proof Machine and "E" are now, clearly better than most competition in its range, make a point to see everyone that is a likely prospect just as quickly as you can. Tell them about it, give them a proposal, and try to close the deal. These are the easy ones. Don't wait to call until competition sells them, because they will be sure trying to beat us to it. Remember such machines won't stay hot long, because they will sure try to catch up or get an order before we do.

There are a few other general rules I have for myself. One is, if I'm trying to close a deal and think I have a chance to do so that day, I don't leave it for any reason, no matter what comes up, until I get an answer. Deals can cool off mighty fast overnight. When you get the order, they slow up thinking about objections. Since they have already bought, they start thinking how they can justify their purchase—and forget any objections they may have had to buying. But, if I am merely attending to details or looking for business or just working up a deal and hear about someone interested in buying, even if it is just an 8 07 01, across town or in the next county, I always drop whatever I'm doing and go at once to get the order. I have learned from bitter experience that whenever you hear of someone who is ready to buy, if you wait until you are working up that way the next week or even the next day, he will have just bought something else shortly before you arrive.

When you are making an installation, make it as good as if you intended to have the same territory until you were 65, but remember, this is not lost sales time, providing you use it right. I try to lay the groundwork for trading each bookkeeping machine while I am installing it, by taking time to discuss depreciation plans, cost after taxes, advantages of replacement in four or five years to stay up to date, etc. You can make the next sale easy for yourself or the salesman following you in this way. You are closer to the customer on the installation than at any other time. Use this time to build his goodwill, observe other equipment needs he has, and clinch his future business for yourself and Burroughs. Don't skimp on installation time. It is the best selling time we have.

Plan to use your time preparing layouts and proposals not as lost time, but as valuable sales time. When you draw a layout, don't just think about crossfooters, registers, carriage movement, etc., but who else in your territory can use the same or a variation of it. You can think up prospects this way, and most sales of large equipment have to be made in your mind before you can make them to the customer. You'll find some of them do not even know they are prospects until you go around and tell them. I have closed deals to customers by simply showing them a layout just completed for a similar type business. Most of them do not completely understand it, but it is impressive to them and creates respect for us and our equipment. It can help make detail time into valuable sales time.

Don't fall into the mistake of shying away from a customer because he is having a lot of trouble with his equipment, even if it is relatively new. Frequently, this is the best time to ask for an order for additional equipment. When it is down, he can easily see just how much it means to him and how necessary it is. Also he is being called on by our servicemen, zone service supervisors, and sometimes even managers. The whole magnitude of the Burroughs organization and what we are geared to do for him is spread out before him, as is the machine they are working on.

At such a time he knows what his machine means to him and what lengths we will go to in order to take care of him. He may be sort of upset sometime; but, if he needs more equipment, try to get the order at this point. At least do not be afraid to ask for it. After it is fixed, he'll just remember his trouble, and he may be looking around at something else.

There is one thing I can tell you, which I believe would be certain to increase the average sales of anyone from the top man in Burroughs to the newest junior. It is this:

Remember you are a salesman all day long. When you are going to and from work, when you are driving between calls, when you are talking to other men in the business, when you are drinking coffee or having lunch, drawing layouts, making proposals, installing equipment, you are still a salesman. Consider everything you do in relation to getting an order signed by some customer. If you spend your time this way, you will find there are plenty of potential sales you have completely overlooked. We are not technicians, systems designers, students, or goodwill men, except to the degree these things help us get orders.

Remember, we are salesmen: that is what we are paid for, and it pays to remember!!!!

The above are a few of what I call my small plans or methods I use in operating my territory. For me, they have always helped in making my big plan for a good year come true. I hope some of them may help you.

Your friend,

Phil Williams
Sales Representative

Planning Letter Outline

The important ideas in Phil Williams' planning letter can be summarized as follows:

1. Planning begins with a realistic, but optimistic, attitude.
2. "Plan your work and work your plan" is a good selling motto which is endorsed by many managers.

3. Sales planning is largely an individual responsibility. It is almost impossible for a company to provide a uniform plan for all salespersons, because of the large number of variables involved.

4. Plans that are not sufficiently detailed may lead to disappointing results.

5. It is important, for motivational reasons, to start accomplishing goals as soon as possible. Break your major plan down into subobjectives and concentrate on accomplishing each of them.

6. The first step in planning is territorial analysis. Consider the actual opportunities in each separate part of your territory.

7. Plan for the element of seasonality in your territory.

8. Use price increases to sell prospects who are ready to buy.

9. Build up a good reserve of prospects. Review user records to help you develop your list.

10. Help the service representative get orders for supplies and he or she will help you find prospects.

11. Drop a short note to at least a half dozen customers each week. They will be more receptive when you call on them later.

12. Never call on anyone without giving a proposal to buy before you leave.

13. Sell the full line to make quota.

14. Make sure all prospects know about those products with a strong advantage over the competition.

15. Give hot prospects immediate attention even if the monetary value of their order is small.

16. Give excellent customer service, and lay the groundwork for the next sale during this sale.

17. Do not shy away from customers who are having problems with the product. This is the very time you need to maintain goodwill.

18. Remember that a sales representative is a sales representative all day long.

10 The Presentation

The *approach* should attract the prospect's attention and set the tone of the interview, while the *presentation* should be the main persuasive effort and must be designed to produce most of the "change of mind" that permits the sale. Before you attempt to detail interview plans, it would be helpful for you to learn what purposes you might accomplish through the presentation, understand the different types of presentations, know when each can best be used, and know each presentation's strengths and weaknesses. Also, you can make a good presentation under adverse circumstances if you are familiar with techniques that can solve interview problems. The presentation must meet the main acid test—it must produce orders from prospects. This chapter is designed to help you plan a better presentation by giving you information on the following topics:

- The objectives of the sales presentation
- The alternative types of presentations
- Techniques in solving presentation problems

THE OBJECTIVES OF THE SALES PRESENTATION

Every presentation is an attempt to sell an interview, a product, a service, or an idea. To do this, a complete presentation should be planned that includes both logical and emotional points. It should anticipate prospect questions and objections, handle competition, and explain prices. The goals reflected in the definition of selling—leading people to buy, furnishing information and assurances, and promoting harmony—can be used as a basis for initiating and reviewing interview plans. In order for you to gain a full perspective of what is involved in setting interview goals, you should understand three areas: (1) the basic strategies used in sales presentations; (2) the five important prospect decisions you want the prospect to make during the presentation; (3) the ways you can reduce the prospect's risks of buying and thus get the order. The methods you can use to customize presentations are developed throughout this chapter.

Basic Strategies Used in Sales Presentations

You may select from several general persuasive strategies that serve as guides in planning the interview: *Stimulus-Response Strategy, Formula Strategy, Want-Satisfaction Strategy, Problem-Solution Strategy, Depth-Selling Strategy, Group-Selling Strategy,* and *Team-Selling Strategy.*[1,2] Each strategy suggests an overall purpose for the presentation as well as subobjectives to help accomplish that purpose. The strategy or strategies selected should depend on such factors as the selling situation, the skill of the salesperson, the nature of the product, and the intelligence of the prospect.

Stimulus-Response Strategy. In this method, a series of selling points (stimuli) are arranged to lead the prospect to a favorable reaction (see Figure 10.1). Stimulus response does not necessarily demand the use of leading questions, but the strategy may take that form. For example, as you demonstrate particular features to the prospect, you might say: "You would want that feature on any equipment you buy, wouldn't you?" After a series of leading questions like this to gain agreement from the prospect, you might continue: "You would want this equipment delivered next week then?" The suggested answer is "yes." Stimulus-response strategy can be applied by new and inexperienced sales representatives and relies on using tested magic phrases with customers. The prospect learns to say "yes," and a series of acceptances leads up to the sale. There is little prospect participation in this strategy, however, except for agreement responses; and the listener may react negatively to not being treated as an individual with distinct needs.[3] Also, this kind of presentation can be memorized, and it may sound artificial. The strategy is best used in

---

[1] Joseph W. Thompson, "A Strategy of Selling" in Steven J. Shaw and Joseph W. Thompson (eds.), *Salesmanship* (Chicago: Holt, Rinehart and Winston, 1966), pp. 13–25.

[2] Thomas F. Stroh, *Salesmanship* (Homewood, Ill.: Irwin, 1966), pp. 161–242.

[3] *Ibid.*

Figure 10.1 Stimulus-Response Series

This car has beautiful lines, hasn't it?

Look at this spacious trunk. It would be nice to get all of the family suitcases and clothes back here on trips, wouldn't it?

This car has five more cubic feet of space inside, too, than most mid-sized models, plenty of leg room and extra good vision out of the front windshield. That's important for tall men like you, isn't it, Mr. Burnett?

This stainproof leatherette upholstery will keep looking like new even when the children's shoe dirt has been cleaned off. That would be nice, wouldn't it?

This is a safe car. The special power brakes stop 15 feet faster than the average car at 60 miles an hour, and there is special steel bracing in case of collision. It sure is important to be safe in an automobile, isn't it?

This car has a diesel engine with fewer moving parts, should require less repair, and is designed to last 50 percent longer than standard engines. That's important in buying an automobile, isn't it?

The diesel with fuel injection will *average* 27 miles per gallon with 32 on the road and run on less expensive fuel. That will mean big savings, won't it?

This car is equipped with air bags that could save lives. What could be more important than to walk away from a head-on collision? You'd want that kind of safety, wouldn't you, Mr. Burnett?

With this car you can have your comfort and good fuel economy, too, at a reasonable price. This is the answer for today's family, isn't it?

This beautiful gas-saving diesel is the car you want, isn't it, Mr. Burnett?

situations where interview time is short, and the salesperson confronts the prospect infrequently or only once. The professional sales representative dealing with high-level prospects should use stimulus-response only as a part of the interview and possibly in conjunction with an explanation of feature benefits just before the close. In this case, two-way communication interaction with the prospect should be planned earlier in the interview.

Formula Strategy. Formula strategy is associated with industrial selling, multiline selling, or complex product selling, where memorization of the sales talk is impractical because of the variation in products or the sophisticated level of selling required.[4] This strategy allows more customization and more participation than stimulus-response programming but still stresses the product rather than customer needs. The formula most often advocated is based on the anticipated mental steps of the prospect in making the decision: *A*ttention, *I*nterest, *D*esire, *C*onviction, and *A*ction (AIDCA). In following the formula, the salesperson can concentrate strategic efforts on one objective at a time and lead the prospect smoothly from one step to another on through to action. That is, attention is translated into interest, interest into desire, desire into conviction, and conviction into action.[5]

The approach's attention-getting objective is stressed in the opening moments of the interview. The transition from attention to interest is critical and depends, in part, on the approach used and its relation to the rest of the presentation. For example, you can get attention by blowing a trumpet on entering the office. But unless you can relate this action to what you are selling, you may evoke little positive interest. Interest is built when prospects can apply what you have to offer them to their needs and problems and can visualize themselves using the product successfully. If no need connection is made in a very short period of time, the prospect may shift attention to find a way to get rid of you tactfully. Actually, interest may depend on disturbing the satisfaction of the prospect. If the prospect feels there is no problem, there is no reason why there should be any interest in your product. *Desire* must be built by translating product features into those benefits that meet the needs of your particular prospect. *Conviction* is reached when the buyer decides that the benefits in terms of satisfaction outweigh the sacrifice that must be made in terms of money. Logic and an emotional appeal may have carried the prospect this far, but a mental threshold must be crossed before an order is finalized, and this depends on good closing techniques (Chapter 13). Unless the salesperson is careful, the attempt may make prospects feel that they are being controlled, and they may react negatively to the pressure. Good two-way communication may be hard to establish. The

[4] *Ibid.*

[5] Thompson, *loc. cit.*

strategy does allow salespersons flexibility, but it requires a thinking persuader who can adjust for product and prospect differences.[6]

Want-Satisfaction Strategy. The want-satisfaction strategy is prospect-oriented and requires a skilled salesperson. Basically, the objectives are to find the prospect's dominant need or needs, translate need into a "want" by accentuating the need and causing the prospect to visualize it as much as possible, and finally satisfy the want in terms of the salesperson's offerings. The emphasis is to get prospects to talk about their needs through thoughtful questions.[7] Next, listen carefully, suppressing all premature tendencies to talk about your product. Finally, present the product as satisfying the particular want. Questions should be designed to cause the prospect to think analytically about personal needs. "Yes" and "no" answers reveal little. Questions that cause your listener to imagine and explain are preferred to questions that can be answered in a few words. In this strategy, sales representatives are taking on the role of the prospect's psychologist. They must be discerning, patient listeners and not interrupt or prevent prospects from revealing their inner personalities. This strategy fits in well with the concept of "leading" a prospect to buy. When the needs are revealed, the sales representative must get the prospect to see them as "wants." You must keep relating product features that fit the want pattern to the dominant buying motive, by a subtle matching process. Prospects must feel that they are in control, even though you are actually doing the controlling.

This strategy may take a great deal of time to develop and is usually used in conjunction with important deals involving expensive merchandise or services. When done by an inexperienced salesperson, it may appear awkward and obvious. It requires practice and experience. Misuse of this strategy may prevent promotion of some important benefits and cause an overstress of buying motives that may turn out to be not dominant after all. However, it does require a customer interview and provides good interaction between the salesperson and the prospect.

Problem-Solution Strategy. A problem-solution strategy goes beyond the want-satisfaction approach in respect to professionalism and consumer orientation, because it may be necessary to present the prospect with several solutions.[8] Determining the problem can require considerable time and effort. Careful research might have to be done. A detailed written proposal containing the problem analysis and solution often

[6] Stroh, *op. cit.*, pp. 185–204.

[7] *Ibid.*

[8] *Ibid.*, p. 217.

requires expertise. In a sense, the professional salesperson is selling his or her consulting expertise in an effort to find the prospect's real needs. He or she must project the anticipated results of using several product solutions and let the prospect decide. This strategy is used in technical fields, where repeat sales are cultivated, and long-range goodwill is important. It may be regarded as an exhaustive effort to reduce prospect risk and instill confidence by using problem-solving techniques to analyze business needs. It works best with technical business products and complex intangible offerings with strong relative advantages over comparable offerings. The salesperson using this strategy can build reputation but must be technically competent to analyze the problems involved.

Depth-Selling Strategy. Depth selling attempts to combine the other four methods and profit from all of their advantages. It is a flexible, customized approach, utilizing each of the other strategies in parts of the presentation. A saleswoman, for example, may begin an interview with want-satisfaction questions and listen attentively to learn about the prospect and establish prospect confidence. She may analyze the prospect's problems in depth and propose alternatives, some of which do not even mention her own product offering. She may explain her own offering in terms of benefits, asking stimulus-response questions to get the prospect to agree about the different features of her offering. Finally, she might suggest that the prospect accept the alternative involving her product. All of these techniques may be accomplished within the framework of the AIDCA formula.[9] Certainly, a buyer can be led to interest by careful questions and proposals and to desire and conviction by a stimulus-response presentation. Depth selling, therefore, presents itself as a customized strategic mix of the best of the other four plans. It requires an intelligent, prospect-perceptive salesperson.

Group-Selling Strategy. Most sales representatives will find it necessary to sell to a group of individuals rather than to just one person (see Photo 10.1).[10] In this case, each member of the buying group may be interested in separate aspects of the offering and have different buying motives. The machine operator may be interested in the ease of operation, the engineering executive may be interested in the machine's efficiency, and the firm president may respond to profit possibilities. Proper questioning techniques are important in group buying situations to find the need as each member sees it. A complete and honest presentation of all offering benefits should characterize the meeting and cover the range of prospect thinking. The salesperson should be careful to determine the effects of

[9] *Ibid.,* pp. 228–229.
[10] *Ibid.,* pp. 242–255.

product purchase on each buying team participant and use both logical
and emotional appeals to bring out prospective benefits for each. When
talking to a group, salespersons have the same problem as politicians—
they must not gain the approval of some in the group at the expense of
losing the support of others.

Team-Selling Strategy. In team selling, when the salesperson visits
prospects with the sales manager and/or a company technician, the team
leader should "carry" the interview. The other members should be passive
participants reinforcing the leader in body language and affirmations but
not be outspoken or detract from the leader's role as spokesperson. It is
hazardous to plan team selling where participants representing the company want equal time. If one team member is a technical representative
or product expert, his or her role should be to answer technical questions
about the product when asked to explain complicated operations. Sometimes, it is permissible for the nonleading member to take over and attempt

to close the sale, if it is evident that the presentation leader has failed in this regard. However, prospects who feel outnumbered can build up resistance and become negative unless active-passive roles are maintained by the sales team.

The sales representative can set strategic interview objectives by using any one or combinations of these basic selling strategies. It is important to consider the specific needs of the selling situation when planning strategies. (See Table 10.1 for a summary of the basic strategies used for presentations.)

Five Important Prospect Decisions

Your prospect must make five decisions, if you are to come out of the presentation with an order. Your objectives must be: (1) to help buyers realize *needs*; (2) to help them see that *your product* is the best solution for their needs; (3) to help them understand that your *service* will be adequate; (4) to help convince them that the benefits received will outweigh the *price* paid; and (5) to help them feel that they should *buy now*.[11] When the sales representative approaches, the buyer may be completely satisfied in the *need* area. In most cases, then, the salesperson must disturb this satisfaction to get the prospect's interest. Dissatisfaction with the status quo can be brought about by communicating the benefits of having the product and/or the disadvantages of not buying it. Enthusiasm is vital here, to help the listener visualize the use of the product or service in the best possible light.

After the need is realized, a clear case must be given to satisfy the motive with *your product* offering rather than in some other way. The relative advantages of the proposed offering should be stressed in direct application to the buyer's expressed need. At this point, the prospect may want your product but may not be fully assured that your service offering will satisfy the need in the exact manner that you have promised. You must assure, through risk-reducing techniques, that the product will be delivered as promised and is fully backed by you and your company. A desire for the product is meaningful only if the *price* can be justified and if the prospect feels it can be afforded. An explanation of the various ways to buy the product (straight, installment, rental, delayed billing, and so on) or expressing the price in relation to the benefits received over the entire expected life of the product often helps the listener clear this hurdle. Finally, the prospect must have a clear reason for buying *now*

[11] Allen L. Reid, *Modern Applied Salesmanship,* 2nd ed. (Pacific Palisades, Ca.: Goodyear, 1975), pp. 220–221.

TABLE 10.1 SUMMARY TABLE OF BASIC STRATEGIES

Strategy	Explanation	Advantage
Stimulus-Response	A series of positive leading statements or questions.	Customer gets in the habit of saying yes and may respond positively to the close.
Formula	Salesperson leads prospect through the mental states of buying (attention, interest, desire, conviction, and action).	Prospect can be led to action one step at a time, and prospect is led to participate in interview.
Need-Satisfaction	Find real needs and translate them into wants. Cause prospect to see the need through questions or image-producing words.	Salesperson can listen and respond to the prospect. "Leads" prospect to buy. Salesperson learns motivation.
Problem-Solution	Involves thorough research of prospect's problem and determining supported solutions.	Reduces prospect's risk and can be highly convincing.
Depth Selling	Utilizes a combination of the above four methods.	A customized mix of the best elements of all of the strategies. Can realize all of the advantages but requires skill.
Group Selling	Sell all the features. Try to avoid intragroup conflicts and promote harmony. Learn and cater to the needs of each interest group.	Group selling conserves time.

Based on information from Thomas F. Stroh, *Salesmanship* (Homewood, Ill.: Irwin, 1966), pp. 161–256.

instead of later. Immediate benefit enjoyment, future price rises, or a limited time offer are ways to convince a prospect that something can be lost from putting the decision off. The salesperson must always be prepared to give the prospect a reason for prompt action, since the buying mood can be lost and never regained. Never forget to ask for the order, since the prospect can make all five decisions and still not buy because of your reluctance to take the initiative.

Reducing Prospect Risk—A Major Strategy

A buyer who makes a decision mistake has more to lose than money. Not only is vital time lost, but bad buying decisions reflect negatively on the decider, and the respect of others, self-image, and even position can be damaged. All positive actions that give assurance and reduce risks help eliminate this important barrier to buying. The prospect must believe the information for it to be effective. Plus, it is difficult to resist proposals logically when the risk has been reduced to almost zero. In the paragraphs below ways are suggested to reassure the prospect that giving you the order will not be an uncorrectable mistake.

Sell Features and Benefits Completely. It is natural to emphasize those positive benefits that seem to fit the buyer's needs exactly, but you should also include product attributes that establish the worth of the offering, even if they aren't directly relevant to known needs of the particular prospect. The prospect may not presently need the total machine capacity, but needs do change. If the prospect wants to sell or trade the equipment later, its total capabilities would be meaningful in convincing a secondary buyer. Durability, seller reputation, and styling can slow obsolescence and allow the future conversion of the product into money.

Maintain Source Confidence. The prospect must believe what you say, and he or she is constantly judging you as a source of information. If you make hard-to-believe product claims at the beginning of an interview, even if they are true, the prospect may discount the rest of the presentation or become defensive. If you make conservative claims at the beginning and build up believably, stronger claims can be made once you have gained the prospect's confidence.[12] All hard-to-believe claims should be backed up with good evidence. Prospects become very suspicious of sales representatives who do not stand behind their employers or their company in an effort to take sides with the listener. Such conduct by agents is unethical, and few prospects want to buy from a source who is not loyal to the firm represented.

Prospect Involvement. Perhaps nothing is more convincing than letting the prospect inspect, handle, operate the product, and experience the benefits firsthand. Prospects may watch you demonstrate the operation of a camera, for example, and attribute the resulting clear picture to your special expertise. When they see the good picture *they made* after you allowed them to adjust the lens, they believe that they can make good

[12] Frederic A. Russel, Frank H. Beach, and Richard H. Buskirk, *Textbook of Salesmanship,* 10th ed. (New York: McGraw-Hill, 1978), p. 226.

pictures with the product. Automobile sales representatives know that the prospect must feel the new car respond to his or her control, and they encourage the prospective buyer to drive it. When the prospect touches the product or takes an active part in the presentation, it is easier to instill the feeling of ownership, prospect image, and product image. All three become welded together, with greater buyer confidence resulting.

Records and Statistics. Specific and detailed data from records and statistics can be compelling. The Environmental Protection Agency gasoline mileage ratings may have been obtained under ideal conditions by test drivers, but the printed results usually have a convincing effect on buyers interested in fuel economy. Especially risk reducing is information obtained from supposedly unbiased sources such as governments, consumer interest magazines, and trade associations. Even sales statistics compiled by your own company are convincing, though not as convincing as statistics from independent sources. Quality-control standards and product-testing results to assure that the product meets certain requirements can be cited to good advantage.

Testimonials. It is the nature of buyers to want assurances from other buyers before they sign the order. If you can furnish the prospect with written or oral testimony from a satisfied user, you have given an important assurance. Few people want to be the first buyer, and most prospects welcome the testimony of reliable persons who have purchased the product under similar conditions and found it satisfactory. The findings of recognized experts may also remove the risk barrier. If written testimonials are not available, the salesperson may offer to phone a satisfied customer and let the prospect talk to him or her. The sales representative can mention the names of previous buyers to the prospect but should be sure that the experiences of all of these previous users were good, because the prospect may accept the challenge and check it out. A reassuring experience for the prospect is to accompany the salesperson on a visit to see the product being used by a satisfied buyer.

Factory Tours. The outward appearance of many products fails to reflect the workmanship and premium materials that constitute the finished form. The quality of workmanship, the care and orderliness of manufacture, and the inclusion of high-grade materials can be witnessed by an arranged visit to the plant. Such visits are productive only when positive quality image is projected by manufacturing conditions. Visits should be prearranged with production personnel to prevent embarrassment, in case the manufacturing operation isn't proceeding as usual or observation by outsiders would disrupt operations.

WARRANTY

JOHN DEERE AGRICULTURAL EQUIPMENT

EQUIPMENT WARRANTY— 12 MONTHS—HOURS UNLIMITED

All parts of John Deere equipment, except tires, tubes, radios, and batteries, will be repaired or replaced, as John Deere elects, without charge for parts or labor, if a defect appears and is reported to a John Deere dealer within 12 months from the date of delivery to the original purchaser, regardless of the number of hours of use.

*EXTENDED ENGINE WARRANTY—24 MONTHS/ 1500 HOURS

The rocker arm cover, cylinder head, engine block, crankcase pan, and timing gear cover of the engine and the parts fully enclosed within these units will be repaired or replaced, as John Deere elects, without charge for parts or labor, if a defect appears and is reported to a John Deere dealer within 24 months from the date of delivery to the original purchaser, provided that the equipment has not been used for more than a total of 1500 hours.

**EXTENDED POWER TRAIN WARRANTY— AGRICULTURAL TRACTORS—24 MONTHS/ 1500 HOURS

The clutch housing, transmission case, torque divider housing, differential housing, final drive housings, and parts fully enclosed within these housings, including the drive axles, will be repaired or replaced, as John Deere elects, without charge for parts or labor, if a defect appears and is reported to a John Deere dealer within 24 months after the date of delivery of the tractor to the original purchaser, provided the tractor has not been used more than a total of 1500 hours.

PARTS REPLACED DURING WARRANTY

Genuine John Deere parts or authorized remanufactured assemblies that are furnished under this Agricultural Equipment Warranty and installed by an authorized John Deere dealer or by a John Deere Service Center will be repaired or replaced, as John Deere elects, without charge for parts or labor, if a defect in materials or workmanship appears and is reported to a John Deere dealer within 90 days from the date of installation of such parts or authorized remanufactured assemblies or before the expiration of the applicable original warranty period, whichever is later.

*This extended engine warranty applies only to John Deere-built engines.
**This extended power train warranty applies to tractors with PTO horsepower of 90 and above.

EXHIBIT #3
SECTION 50

Source: Courtesy of John Deere Company, Moline, Illinois.
Note: This figure highlights the terms of the express John Deere company warranty, which appears on the back of the John Deere purchase order.

Figure 10.2

Warranties and Guarantees. Some warranties are implied by law, but most products and services carry written guarantees that furnish full assurance that the company will stand behind the product and that defective products will be replaced. A warranty stated in writing and certified by the selling firm carries much more weight than a verbal promise by the salesperson (see Figure 10.2). The equipment buyer, for example, is interested in the continuity of operations. The breakdown of products could stop assembly line operations and cost important employee time. Assurances that service is quickly available to minimize downtime is particularly important in cases like this. Money-back guarantees can assure that the product has the quality to merit that kind of backing. Guarantees or "service forever" or double-your-money-back on expensive items may indicate that the price is much higher to reflect an unusual guarantee. Being able to have the company correct any product problems encountered is usually fair enough to the buyer. After all, a buyer wants to buy the product, not the guarantee.

Trial. If a prospect has mental reservations about the suitability of a product and the order is difficult to close, you may be able to offer a trial at no obligation. Many people feel morally obligated to keep the product if they take it on trial and it lives up to its stated performance. Others simply feel it is not theirs until they pay for it or feel like they are borrowing it from the salesperson's company. If something happens to it, they feel that they must pay for it. Others may be delighted that there is an expressed understanding that the product is on trial and can be returned without question.

ALTERNATIVE PRESENTATIONS

There are basically five different types of presentations with respect to the amount of control the company has over the interview and with respect to the salesperson's flexibility. The *automated presentation* is essentially the company message through audio-visuals. The salesperson stands by to answer questions and provides the human touch in closing.[13] The *memorized* or *canned presentation* also rigidly reflects the company's message. However, it is the way the presentation is given and the salesperson's nonverbal communications that make it effective or ineffective. The *organized presentation,* structured by the company but expressed by the salesperson, is a good marriage of salesperson and company

[13] Marvin A. Jolson, "Should the Sales Presentation be 'Fresh' or 'Canned'," *Business Horizons* (October 1973), pp. 81–87.

input. The *survey-proposal presentation,* used heavily in systems selling, and the completely unstructured presentation, or the *unplanned interview,* are largely the contribution of the salesperson with little company participation except backup. Each of these plans represents an important alternative that should be considered in light of the product to be sold, the customer, and the salesperson's ability. Accordingly, each will be examined with regard to when to use it, accompanying strategic purposes, and advantages and disadvantages.

The Automated Presentation

This procedure requires that the sales representative make the contact and sell the audio-visual or visual presentation to the prospect (see Photo 10.2). Suppose, for example, that the presentation is a movie showing an earth-moving machine in action, performing to the limit of its capabilities to impress the prospect. The film would probably be in color, have music in the background, and use a pleasing voice to explain the benefits. Between operations, the film might show prominent buyers and have them give a testimony about the economic savings associated with ownership of the equipment. The action, the testimonies, and the music set a mood and maintain the prospect's attention. The prospect can't really muster sales resistance against the film's contents, since the film is not a living object. All points are presented in a minimum amount of time clearly, concisely, and emotionally (music arouses emotions). There are usually no interruptions. Objections are anticipated, and most prospects' questions are answered in the narration. The equipment is shown in its best light, since the film can be edited and mistakes eliminated. At the end of the presentation, the sales representative is available to answer questions and ask for the order. The salesperson can ask such questions as: "That equipment can really move the earth, can't it?" or "Would you like us to demonstrate one on your location?" or "Can we put your order in for delivery this Monday?"

There are several problems with fully automated presentations. During the presentation, there is little prospect-salesperson interaction, and the mood of the presentation is broken when the film is over. It is difficult to establish two-way communication again, and the close may seem unnatural. Another problem is customizing the application shown in the film or flip chart to the prospect. It may closely coincide with the prospect's application, or the prospect may be able to say, "Well, it looked all right for them but, after all, their operation is not like mine. It might not work that well for me." If there are problems with the presentation, if the film breaks, or the electricity goes off, or there is an interruption, the mood is

Photo 10.2

Salesperson making an automated sales presentation.

broken, and it may be hard to reestablish interest. This type of presentation may also not enhance the self-image of sales representatives. They might resent their reduced role in the sale, begin to lean on the device, and not develop their persuasive qualities as they might in a more participatory presentation.[14] It is perhaps best used in cases where the application shown coincides with the prospect's application, with products that are difficult to demonstrate, when the sales force is inexperienced, or when other methods have been tried and failed.

The Memorized Presentation

The memorized or canned presentation is similar in company input to the automated presentation, except that the salesperson expresses the predetermined message, and there is no real break in continuity (like when the film is over). Inexperienced sales representatives learn the right words and tested selling phrases this way. They are able to give the prospect a complete account of benefits with high hopes that the right response chord will be struck somewhere in the recitation. This method is most popular with low-dollar items and in cases where it is important to tell a complete account in a short amount of time and where there is little

[14] *Ibid.*

intention of revisiting the prospect or buyer. This method is based mainly on stimulus-response strategy or conditioning the prospect for favorable response by overbalancing the scale with benefits. Again, questions and objections are anticipated in this well-ordered and well-conceived scientific "masterpiece" by company sales experts. An alternative to complete rote memorization is having the salesperson memorize the key selling phrases and the sequence but allowing some deviation in wording. A new sales representative could learn the presentation by heart and then be allowed to change it slightly to incorporate his or her own expressions and personality. The NCR Corporation (formerly National Cash Register) is the classic example of the successful use of the canned presentation (see Chapter 11, NCR Primer). Most door-to-door sales representatives essentially use a memorized talk.

Marvin Jolson explains that while many sales managers feel that standardization makes presentations less effective, a study he conducted indicated that the reverse may be true. In research comparing a memorized presentation with an outlined presentation, matched groups of respondents were used. Jolson found that the group exposed to the memorized sales talk indicated more willingness to purchase, more interest in learning more about the proposal, and less expression of intention not to buy than those exposed to the outline.[15] The memorized presentation was judged more high pressure but more exciting. His conclusion was that salesperson flexibility was not as necessary in persuasion as was previously supposed.[16]

The canned presentation can't be used in all selling situations. It would be hard for the full-line sales representative selling dozens of products to memorize that many sales presentations verbatim. It would not be feasible for repeat-call salespersons to give the same sales talk every time they visited a customer. While inexperienced salespersons are more likely to use this kind of company-controlled presentation, they are probably less skilled in delivering the intended message. What is said is important, but how it is said is also critical. It takes skill to use someone else's words and supply the proper inflections, tonality, and nonverbal gestures. The memorized speech seems to be weak in sincerity and conviction. It can easily appear to be artificial and impersonal. It may not seem to treat prospects as individuals at all or allow their participation and involvement. It contrasts with strategies that call for good two-way communication or questioning and listening techniques. The prospect may, indeed, feel insulted by being treated impersonally and may react negatively. This type of presentation tends to ignore the peculiar problems and motivations of

[15] Marvin A. Jolson, "The Underestimated Potential of the Canned Sales Presentation," *Journal of Marketing* 39, no. 1 (January 1975), 75–78.

[16] *Ibid.*

the prospect and tries to hit on everything without emphasizing anything. It can, however, be thorough, accurate, and impressive when used correctly.

The Organized Presentation

The organized or outlined presentation is a favorite with sales managers. In a comparative study of the major types of sales presentations, sales executives ranked the organized presentation first in saving prospect time, completeness, persuading the prospect, anticipating objections, making sales training easier, increasing the sales representative's confidence, and facilitating sales supervision.[17] They also reported that it was the most often used of all the alternative methods. In this presentation method, the sales representative follows a company outline or checklist of points that should be covered. The company may also sequence the points. The use of visuals is optional, but visuals seldom make up the entire presentation. Salespersons are free to cover the features and benefits using their own words, and this should make the interview less awkward and more reflective of their sales personalities. The relative freedom allows the sales representative to establish rapport and encourage more prospect interaction. The prospect can interrupt, and there is less difficulty in reestablishing the pattern and continuity of the presentation. There is more opportunity to use the organized presentation in connection with the problem-solution, formula, or need-satisfaction strategies. The method seems to have just the right blend of company control and presentation flexibility for most firms.

The effectiveness of the organized presentation again largely depends on the competence of the salesperson. Salespersons who are free to express benefits in their own words may express themselves awkwardly and incorrectly and not use the magic words that were so carefully included in the canned sales talk by the company sales executives. In any organized presentation, the salesperson may overexpand some minor or unimportant points and fail to stress benefits and information important to the prospect. The freedom to emphasize certain benefits over others means that the wrong emphases may be made. With so many advantages and so few disadvantages, however, this method should be fully considered as a favored alternative.[18]

[17] Jolson, "Should the Sales Presentation be 'Fresh' or 'Canned'," *op. cit.*

[18] See Carlton A. Pederson and Milburn D. Wright, *Selling Principles and Methods,* 6th Ed, (Homewood, Ill: Irwin, 1976) pp. 253–263, for good presentation type evaluations.

The Survey-Proposal Presentation

This presentation has the structure of the problem-solution strategy, requires a professional inquiry into the prospect's problem, and usually takes two visits to implement. Accounting-systems sales representatives, industrial sales representatives, life-insurance sales representatives, and other sales representatives who must investigate prospect problems before proposing a specific solution must first sell prospective clients on the need for investigating their problems thoroughly. The prospect should appreciate that the solution of complex system problems involves detailed inquiry and study. After the problem is studied and analyzed, the salesperson builds a solution and shows how various hardware (products) or financial components fit together into a solution system. This proposal may take long hours and is usually presented in written as well as oral form, complete with prices and justification. The salesperson is implying that he or she is an expert consultant. Prospects are usually impressed by the professionalism of this approach and feel obligated to give real consideration to the proposal in view of the obvious amount of time required to produce the written solution. The effect of seeing a complex problem solution justified on paper lends assurance to the undecided prospect. The mood is usually rational, and the salesperson tries to establish the adult-adult transactional analysis relationship. The proposal can be used by the prospect to justify and convince other members of the buying team of the merits of purchase. This option features the extreme of customization and adaptation to prospect needs. Equipment may be programmed (set) to show the exact application to the buyer's problem solution. Prospects usually feel obligated to justify any refusals they might make.

This option depends heavily on the professionalism and expertise of the salesperson making the problem survey and the proposal. Usually, a great deal of technical knowledge is necessary, and the sales representative must exude confidence by his or her personality. The main disadvantage is that it takes time to make good proposals, and if the prospect doesn't buy, the time is lost. Proposal deals may be very competitive, because of the large unit prices involved and the time elapsing between survey and proposal.

Unplanned Interviews

Many senior sales representatives seem to work without any planned structure. The truth is that they have made so many presentations and have so much interview experience that they unconsciously follow a pattern and use many of the same expressions in each selling situation.

This kind of presentation in the hands of a skilled professional can be very successful. In the first place, it has the unity of a particular strategy, and at the same time it has the freedom for instantaneous adjustment to the prospect's needs. Good questions and listening can establish a congenial salesperson-prospect interaction, and the selling personality can be expressed without restriction.

Following an unconscious pattern takes a maximum of experience and product knowledge. Beginning salespersons should use more structure, and even senior sales representatives will make important omissions this way, leaving out benefits that can stimulate prospects to buy. It can result in overconfidence without justification, mediocrity instead of the realization of full selling potential, laxity in preinterview investigation, and eventually bad morale and low professional growth. An experienced professional following this nonmethod should remember to keep learning. All salespersons should pattern in their minds a general strategic approach based on their knowledge of the selling situation.

TECHNIQUES IN SOLVING PRESENTATION PROBLEMS

Two interview problems—answering objections and closing—will be treated in a later chapter. However, there are other important situations that merit careful handling: interruptions, competition, prospect inattention, prospect anger, and time limitations.

Interruptions

Interruptions are any disruptions to the continuity or tone of the presentation. An excited employee may demand the buyer's immediate attention, the secretary may bring in coffee, a telephone call may take several minutes, or prospects may excuse themselves to attend to another business matter for a period of time. Disruptions may be anticipated and prevented. If the meeting place is too busy to hold the prospect's attention, the salesperson may request a quieter meeting place. You might say, "Can we talk where I might explain this to you without outside interruption? Mr. Miller, this application is vital to your business, and I know you will want to give it your undivided attention."

When interruptions do occur, the main problem is regaining attention. There are several ways to do this. If the interruption occurred while the salesperson was talking, it is usually a good practice to state the point or points made just before the interruption. When the customer was speaking, the salesperson can remind the prospect of the general nature of what he or she was saying at the time of the interruption. Repetition of selling points made before the interruption simply serves to reemphasize those points and shouldn't be offensive in view of the distraction. In fact, all of the previous points might be reviewed to reestablish continuity. You might ask the prospect a question to encourage him or her to get the benefits back in mind again. The mental effort necessary to answer will help prospects forget the interruption and reestablish their train of thought back on the offering. You might say, "Of the features we talked about, fast operation and improved capacity, which do you think would be more important to you?" Sometimes handing the prospect an object or brochure connected with the product will help refocus attention.[19] You might take out a pencil and prepare a sketch during the interruption, move closer after the interruption, and go over the sketch with the prospect at a close—personal distance.[20] If the product is present, you might point out and explain a particular product feature. If the interruption is long, you might reestablish communications by a bit of small talk before getting back to the business at hand.

It is best not to refer to the break in the presentation as an "interruption" or "disruption." It is usually safe to say nothing at all about it. You might acknowledge it with a smile and a statement commenting on the nature of the pleasantness of the break, such as, "Miss James was certainly thoughtful to bring us this good coffee," or "I met Mr. Latimer earlier this morning. He seems to be a conscientious young man" (in case Mr. Latimer came in and left). During the interruption, you should be careful to afford your prospects the privacy they desire by directing your attention to your own papers or offering to leave the room if the conversation appears to be a private one. If the prospect is so disturbed by the nature of the interruption or, through body language, shows a desire to end the interview, you may want to come back when it is easier to establish enthusiasm and mood again. Interruptions can improve buyer mood if the news is good, or they can seriously disturb your buyer's receptive mood if the news is bad or if the buyer's presence is needed elsewhere. Try to be understanding and sensitive to needs in this situation.

Competition

Competition was discussed previously, but it is best to review how it can relate to an interview. Even if competition is not indicated, it is still the best practice to stress the particular advantages of your product that

[19]Reid, *op. cit.*, pp. 230–231.
[20]*Ibid.*

competition can't match. If competition can match all of your features and benefits, then you must convince your prospect that you are in a better position to serve by selling your abilities and attitudes. Even when you feel that competitive salespersons will be talking to your prospect, it is best to make your comparisons without ever identifying the name of a competitive firm. If your prospect brings up competitive company names and specific competitive equipment or asks you point blank why you feel that your product is superior in offering, you might say, "That is a good machine, Mr. Steele, and a good company, but our machine is constructed with a rust-resistant plating and produces 20 percent more units per hour than any machine on the market. You would want to have those advantages in the equipment you buy, wouldn't you?" You still haven't mentioned competition directly. Be sure that your claim is true. Since competition is an ever-present threat, it is important that you cover all your offering's benefits completely and treat competition fairly and without harsh criticisms. If the competitive offering has a serious defect in terms of serving your prospect's needs, point it out indirectly by a statement like, "Be sure to check any equipment you consider for copying speed. While our machine takes only three seconds to copy, some machines take seven seconds. Our faster capability can save you hundreds of dollars in employee time over the life of the equipment."

Prospect Inattention

You should be able to tell by the prospect's body language if he or she is inattentive or defensive. If prospects start to give attention to other things while you are talking, do something to bring them back. Smile, draw your chair closer, or ask a question. To answer a question, prospects have to think and talk about the subject at hand. It is rare for people to be disinterested in what *they* are saying. The other methods mentioned for handling interruptions also apply, since this is an interruption of the prospect's train of thought. Never let a prospect throw you "off image" by inattention or any other failure to be courteous to you. Cater to ego needs and make this prospective buyer feel important and respected.

Prospect Anger

When prospects show anger toward you or your company, the best strategy is to let them talk it out of their systems. Let them confess *your* sins. In fact, ask questions to find out exactly what is wrong and listen, listen, listen. Not every sales situation you will have is going to be pleasant, and you must keep in mind that the salesperson who can handle the hard customers is the real professional. The person who is angry or prejudiced needs a psychologist. So be one by being especially attentive, understanding, and quiet until the prospect or customer finishes. Know that this prospect needs to explain the problem (or your problem) emotionally, and when the verbal tirade is over, you might seriously suggest a reasonable remedy. He or she will appreciate your maturity in this and may even become ashamed at the loss of control and seek to make amends by being especially reasonable.

Time Limitations

While some prospects enjoy talking to sales representatives, for most prospects, time is money. If conserving time is not important to them, then it should be to you. Respect the prospect's time. Tell the whole story, do a thorough job, listen carefully to what your customer has to say, but don't misuse time by taking too long to "establish rapport" or by getting off on unimportant conversational topics. It is important to talk about the prospect's personal interests if he or she wants, but don't talk too long about yours. Try to determine if you will have time to make an effective presentation and remember that only you can decide whether to make an abbreviated presentation or return at a more opportune time. If you can shorten the interview without losing the essence, it may be even more effective than a longer meeting. But the appearance of "hurry" in an interview can ruin the mood. If prospects are definitely telling you by nonverbal communication that your time is up, you might ask if they have pressing business, try to close the sale based on the points already made, or request another interview. Purchasing agents and corporate executives report that salespeople who waste valuable time are inviting closed doors in the future.

SUMMARY

A basic selling strategy should be reflected in the presentation, which is the main persuasive effort made to secure the sales order. Stimulus-response strategy, formula strategy, problem-solution strategy, want-satisfaction strategy, depth-selling strategy, group-selling strategy, or combinations of these are alternatives. The presentation should help the prospect realize need, see that your product is the best solution to that need, feel that your price is fair in relationship to the benefits received, believe that your service will be adequate, and understand the advantages of buying now. To reduce the prospect's risk, sell features and benefits completely, maintain confidence in yourself as a source, involve them in the demonstration, show them records and statistics, furnish them with testimonials, take them on plant tours, inform them about warranties and guarantees, and/or let them try the product without obligation.

The four basic presentation types differ in respect to salesperson flexibility and company control of the sales effort. The automated presentation explains the product's benefits completely but allows little interaction between the salesperson and the prospect and may not reflect the individual prospect's exact needs. The memorized presentation is convenient for new sales representatives but relatively inflexible and may seem artificial to the prospect. The organized presentation is recommended by most sales managers because of its flexibility and because it allows prospect interaction. The survey-proposal type is strategically and psychologically sound for high-level systems selling.

Four problems basic to most presentations are interruptions, the handling of competition, prospect inattention, and prospect anger. After interruptions, review previous selling points, get nearer to the prospect, hand him or her something, or point out a particular product feature to regain attention. Stress your product's particular advantages, even if competition is not brought up by the prospect, but, in your comparisons, don't mention competition by name or harshly criticize. Your main method to diminish anger is to listen to prospects attentively as they air complaints. Always respect the prospect's time.

REVIEW QUESTIONS

1. What are the major purposes of the sales presentation?

2. What are the advantages and disadvantages of the stimulus-response sales strategy? When is it used?

3. Explain briefly how each of the objectives of the common formula strategy, AIDCA, might be accomplished.

4. What is the role of questioning and listening technique in the want-satisfaction strategy? What are its disadvantages?

5. How does the problem-solution strategy differ from the want-satisfaction strategy?

6. Explain how strategies are effectively combined in depth selling.

7. How does the strategy of selling to a group differ from selling to an individual? What problems are encountered?

8. What is the role of each participant in team selling?

9. The prospect must make five decisions if the salesperson is to leave the interview with a signed order. What are they?

10. How, specifically, can the salesperson reduce the risks of buying for the prospect?

11. Evaluate the automated presentation and explain when it may be used to best advantage.

12. What are the advantages and disadvantages of the memorized presentation?

13. What support does Marvin Jolson's study give to the effectiveness of the memorized presentation?

14. Why is the organized presentation most popular with sales managers and probably the most widely used presentation structure?

15. When is the survey-proposal presentation likely to be used? Explain the steps in accomplishing this kind of presentation.

16. List the positive points of unplanned interviews.

17. What are the ideas the text offers for handling interruptions?

18. In what situation should you vigorously criticize competition by name?

19. How can you tell when a prospect is not paying attention to your presentation?

APPLICATION QUESTIONS

1. Make up an organized (outline) presentation for a product of your choice.

2. Your customer, Mr. Jones, is angry because delivery of your last merchandise was late. Advise how you might cool him off and prepare him for a presentation designed to sell him a new lot of merchandise.

3. Write several rules for handling interview time.

INCIDENTS

10-1

Ted Darby has made calls on the mayor and three aldermen in the city of Nellburg and interested them in a copying machine for City Hall. A competitive salesperson, Barry Lindy, has also seen and made presentations to these four men. Equipment that is needed by the town is bought after the representatives of at least two competitive companies make formal presentations before the whole group at a called meeting. Ted has been selected to make his presentation first.

Ted: Mayor Needham, John, Bill, and Sam. It is now 8 P.M., and I know all of you have been working hard and have had a long day. The sales representative who will follow me is one of the top salespeople with the BTL Corporation, and it will probably take him at least an hour to persuade you to buy his machine. We have a copying machine like the one I am offering in Bettsburg, Leesville, and in over half the other cities this size within a hundred-mile radius of Nellburg. Our equipment is fully guaranteed to make copies like this (*shows sample*) at the rate of one every three seconds, and the price to municipalities is $4,787.50, after the 10 percent governmental discount. Do you have any questions about this offer? (*waits*) I sure would appreciate your business.

Mayor: Thank you, Ted, we appreciate your concern for our time. Most of us have seen the machine you have at Bettsburg. Tell Mr. Lindy to come in.

Barry: Gentlemen, I want you to see a color film of this excellent equipment that will take about an hour. After that, I will explain some of the technical details of the COPIER 3000. Please hold your questions until after the film. (*Shows the film and talks about copier for twenty more minutes.*)

Mayor: I'm sorry to interrupt you, Mr. Lindy, but could you please wrap up your presentation. It's getting late. (*Lindy summarizes and leaves.*)

Mayor: Please raise your hand if you want to vote for Ted Darby's machine ... The ayes have it. Please tell Mr. Darby he has the order, Mrs. Sedbury.

QUESTIONS

1. What was the primary need of this buying group?

2. Did they really care about the technical properties of the equipment?

3. Assuming they considered the machines equal in price and capabilities, why did they give Ted the order?

10–2

Andrew Nail has completely memorized his sales presentation for Feelright Tennis Supplies, which he sells to sporting goods store retailers. Andrew is now approaching Nathan Schwab Sporting Goods Store with his line....

Andrew: Mr. Schwab, I'm Andrew Nail with Feelright Tennis Supplies. Here is our Rightshot Racket, the top of our line. This racket is carefully balanced so that shots hit next to the wood will have almost as much power as shots hit in the center of the racket. Notice that it is laminated with eleven layers of the finest wood. It is made just like a fine musical instrument, but it is so tough that it will endure concrete court scrapes and other punishments that tennis rackets have to stand these days. The five layers of varnish are like a hard plastic coating. This one is strung with top-grade gut. Notice the center, right under the racket head. The open space there cuts down on air resistance and allows the racket to address the ball harder and with more power. This model comes in five different hand sizes, but we have grips, leather and plastic, that will help fit the hard-to-fit. You can see why customers go for this racket.

Schwab: But, sir . . .

Andrew: (Interrupting) The best thing about this racket is its profitability for you. This racket is being advertised next month on spot announcements on national television during the prespring tennis tournaments. Our total campaign also includes the sports pages of the newspaper in Taylorsville. We have point-of-purchase cards that tie in with the national theme . . .

Schwab: But, Mr. Nail . . .

Andrew: (Interrupting again) . . . and with all this we are offering a special to retailers, like yourself, who are willing to adopt the whole line of racket frames, stringing materials, grips, presses, covers, shoes, and balls. Regularly, these frames which sell for $29.50 would cost you only $17, but during this special promotion they are only $15 in lots of 50, if you agree to display the whole line. That's a very good markup, isn't it?

Schwab: Just a . . .

Andrew: (Continuing with his presentation) That's not all, Mr. Schwab. If you buy 100 frames, we give you as a promotion a color slide series showing the proper grips and playing stances in tennis. Users tell us they are more valuable to them than professional lessons. You can promise this lesson series with the sale of each racket and increase your racket sales by double. With all these special deals, you could really make money by handling our tennis equipment. We can give you delivery in early February, just in time for the start of the new season. You can win with this package, Mr. Schwab.

Schwab: I've been trying to tell you. I'm just watching the store for two hours. You have the wrong Mr. Schwab ... you want to see my brother. I'm Sam Schwab, and I'm a retired jeweler. I don't know anything about tennis rackets, at least not until now. Let me tell you something if I might, young man. I have been selling for fifty years. You have to do more listening than you do talking if you really want to sell to retailers. If you come back in a couple of hours and give all that rigmarole talk to Nathan, he might not be too receptive.

QUESTIONS

1. What mistakes did Andrew make in his presentation?

2. What do you think of Mr. Schwab's appraisal of the situation?

10-3

Andrew Nail, who sells Feelright Tennis Supplies, is approaching the Nathan Schwab Sporting Goods Store for the second time in the same day. Earlier, Andrew had given a complete memorized presentation to Sam Schwab (Nathan's brother) only to learn that Sam was just minding the store and had no authority to buy.

Andrew: Mr. Schwab, I'm Andrew Nail with Feelright Tennis Supplies. I came by earlier today and talked to your brother, who said I should see you.

Nathan: (*Smiling*) Yes, Sam told me about you.

Andrew: We have a special for dealers who will accept our line and stock a minimum number of frames, such as this Rightshot Powerhitter. (*Hands racket to Nathan*) That's a well designed racket, isn't it?

Nathan: This is a well made racket, but we already carry the Trueplay brand, and I certainly think that one line of rackets is enough ... as you can see, I don't have much time ...

Andrew: Here is a letter from one of our dealers (*hands him the letter*) who carried both our line and a competitive line last year. He started out with a minimum order, Mr. Schwab, and as you can see, he plans to stock 250 frames in preparation for the new season. In fact, he states that our racket outsold the competitive brand by a 2:1 margin, which grossed him an additional $5,000, in the single month of May. That's not bad for a medium-sized store, is it?

Nathan: He certainly does seem to believe in your racket, but we just don't have room in our store to carry two lines of tennis supplies.

Andrew: Well, I see you have a large display of bicycles. One dealer found that by displaying fewer bicycles, he had plenty of room for the frame display rack. I noticed that you are within ten blocks of the Garden Park Courts, which means that demand is strong enough to support a variety; and I'm sure that your customers would appreciate a choice of brands.

Nathan: Well . . . maybe.

Andrew: Also, Rightshot plans an extensive national advertising campaign to coincide with the beginning of the new season. We can tie you in with their national theme, which should increase your yearly sales of tennis supplies considerably. With this advertising, plus Feelright's special offer, is there any reason why you wouldn't give us a try, Mr. Schwab?

Nathan: Wait a minute now . . . what is this *special* that you're talking about?

Andrew: If you are willing to display our whole line of racket frames, presses, covers, shoes, balls, stringing material, and grips, then our $29.50 list price for frames would cost *you* only $15 each, instead of $19 each—provided you order in 50-unit lots. If you buy 100 frames, then we will give you a color slide series showing the proper grips and stance. These lesson slide series have been proven to stimulate sales, especially since this helps beginning players. Do many of your customers request lesson material?

Nathan: Yes. A lot of the young kids do; probably because they can't afford the pro fees. But still, there is just too much risk involved in being stuck with $1,500 worth of inventory if it doesn't sell . . .

Andrew: We will pick up the frames that you don't sell at the end of the season and refund you $15 for each frame if you just display them through the entire season. You can't lose on a lead-pipe cinch like that, Mr. Schwab. How much would you estimate your cost to be if you took this special deal?

Nathan: Well, let's see . . . I would perhaps lose a few bike sales and the interest on the money invested in inventory . . . Not really too much, Andrew. However, I want something in writing saying that you will pick them up if they are not sold by the end of the season.

Andrew: Fine. How many would you like to order?

Nathan: One-hundred racket frames and a minimum of the accessories.

QUESTIONS

1. What advantages does this participative, less structured interview have over the memorized (canned) presentation?

2. The preceding incident (10-2) contains many more sales points than this incident. Considering this and assuming Andrew was talking to the right prospect in incident 10-2, which presentation do you feel is more convincing?

3. Explain the role of questions in this sales presentation strategy. Which one of Andrew's questions do you feel is the most effective? Why?

4. Point out statements by Andrew that reduced Nathan's risks of buying. Comment on the effectiveness of these statements.

10–4

Sylvia Lowenstein sells name brands of women's clothing mainly to dress shops and department stores in New England. One of her best accounts is a medium-sized department store in Connecticut, and she feels she has an excellent line to offer the buyer, Mr. Haas. Mr. Haas is an introvert but has been courteous in the past. Sylvia is quite apprehensive about the interview this time, however, because of an unfortunate experience Mr. Haas had when he received part of the last order from her. It seems that the ladies' dresses reached the selling floor with a label stating: Made Especially for Morgan's Discount House. The mixup caused Mr. Haas considerable embarrassment, since his store caters to upper-middle-class trade. He, in fact, cancelled part of the same order for ladies' coats that had not been shipped with the dresses. Of course, it was not Sylvia's fault that the manufacturer had shipped the dresses to the department store with the wrong label. Sylvia knows that Mr. Haas is still upset about the embarrassing dresses and has decided to visit him, leaving her samples in the car, and let him sound off at her and get it out of his system. To her surprise, Mr. Haas' secretary gives her almost immediate access to Mr. Haas. Mr. Haas this time simply glares at her, takes out his pocket watch, lays it on the table, and says: "Young lady, you have ten minutes to present your line." Sylvia can tell that he plans to say no more until the interview is over.

How should this interview problem be handled?

II Communication Aids

Communication tools such as visual aids, the telephone, advertising, and the product itself can be used effectively to increase selling potential. Having the prospect experience the product, through participation in a demonstration, often provides the positive impression required to lead him or her across the buying threshold—to overcome the resistance to change and part with money. Visuals include films, portfolios, samples, models, presentation boards and posters, sales manuals, tables, charts, and graphs, all of which can help convince your customers about the benefits of buying. The telephone can be an exciting communications tool in the hands of a trained salesperson. It can speed and facilitate every phase of selling, including prospecting, appointment making, and complete presentations. Advertising pieces and campaigns can also be effective in selling. When you finish this chapter, you should know more about how communication devices can be used to persuade prospects. Some of the areas to be covered are:

- The advantages of aids and selling devices
- The effective demonstration
- The use of visual devices to sell
- The telephone as a selling tool
- Advertising and the sales representative

283

THE ADVANTAGES OF AIDS AND SELLING DEVICES

Aids Promote Two-Way Communication

You will sell more if you know how to use selling aids and dramatization devices properly. Products or selling aids can be focal points for sales strategy, since they encourage natural discussion between the sales representative and the prospect. Your prospect will be encouraged to ask questions about the product's features, and seeing the product or visual in front of you will aid you in remembering its particular benefits. Aids provide a structure for a natural presentation, by stimulating good two-way conversation and keeping interest focused on the product.

Aids Save Time

When you are able to show a product's features in a demonstration or visual, you can not only offer a simple and unified presentation, but you can also save the time of both you and your prospect. The many descriptive words required to help the prospect visualize product features will not be necessary, since the prospect can see and/or feel the model. Thus, you will be able to use the valuable interview time you saved in other important ways.

Aids Appeal to Many Senses

Perhaps the most important advantage of using communication aids other than the telephone is that they appeal to senses other than hearing. Seeing ordinarily makes a stronger impression than hearing; and touching, smelling, and tasting add to a total understanding of the product offering. The insurance sales representative can introduce sight through diagrams and models. The food sales representative can use all of the senses, including taste and smell, to stimulate buying emotion and the desire for ownership.

Aids Get Attention

Using a multisense approach through dramatization aids commands the prospect's attention and interest. The buyer feels more a participant and less a mere listener when allowed to judge the merits of the offering firsthand. While buyers may resist your words and discount you as a prejudicial source, they are much less likely to mistrust their own judgment. The communication aids you use allow them to feel and visualize the offering. They can become a part of it. Touching a product often imparts a feeling of ownership that cannot be induced by a verbal appeal.

Aids Cause the Prospect to Remember When Situations Change

Communication devices make prospects remember your demonstration, and if the impressions are favorable, the predisposition to buy will be strengthened. Even if you are not able to close the sale during the interview, a demonstration or a dramatization device may work in the prospect's mind long after the presentation is over. Demonstration aids, therefore, continue to convince and prompt buying action in the future.

Aids Persuade the Prospect

If "seeing is believing," then "sensing is convincing." It is one thing to hear that the car responds easily to command, but it is much more impressive to feel the response by taking the wheel and driving it. Prospects want to know *how* the product will work for them, and while they may believe the testimony of others, they *know* when they experience it for themselves.

THE EFFECTIVE DEMONSTRATION

Most companies have detailed records proving that sales representatives who demonstrate products excel in getting orders. Words can never be as effective as seeing a product being used under favorable circumstances. Part of every salesperson's detailed goals should be to make a certain number of demonstrations every week, if the product is one that can be shown to advantage. Even life insurance can be demonstrated through charts and graphs. While a good demonstration convinces the prospect, a weak or poor demonstration has the opposite effect. In a department store, a salesperson was trying to demonstrate a cookie gun that would "shoot" a shaped wad of cookie dough onto a piece of waxed paper in preparation for cooking. The dough was too thick, and after depositing three or four misshaped cookie mounds, the gun jammed. The

"Now you're probably asking yourself, 'Is it shockproof?'"

© Orlando Busino 1962.

Demonstrations can create a big impression.

disposition to buy was weakened by the ineffective demonstration, and the prospect's conclusion was "If the expert can't do it, I'll probably have trouble, too." In order to give more effective demonstrations, consider the following suggestions.

Determine if the Demonstration Is Really Necessary

If you already have the prospect sold, which really was the case with the cookie gun, it is not necessary to give a demonstration. Things can go wrong even during simple demonstrations, and seeing a product malfunction leaves a lasting negative impression. Prospects draw conclusions from incomplete evidence. On the other hand, demonstrations do offer superior attention-getting benefits and can be highly convincing. They are definitely worthwhile in nearly every presentation, except in situations where the deal can obviously be closed without it. The main fault of most sales representatives is not demonstrating enough.

Plan and Organize the Demonstration

The demonstration should fit naturally into the presentation, and there should be smooth transitions from interview to demonstration back to interview. The speed of the demonstration should be coordinated with the prospect's experience. If the prospect already understands the product's application, the demonstration can move more quickly. If the application is technical and new, it is better to move slowly and make sure that every feature and benefit is understood completely. Avoid the temptation of assuming that the prospect should know beforehand as much as you do. Arrange to explain features in the best sequential order, and make the demonstration the proper length. If you have little time, stress those features that have a strong differential advantage over competition. Don't hesitate to make sure that the prospect understands. Throw out a few questions to gauge response and go over points that may not be clearly understood. Be particularly careful to plan and control all prospect participation. Never let prospects attempt anything they probably can't do. Set up an easy but effective operation or function with the product that can be easily accomplished. It is hoped that product and prospect image will blend with the prospect's greater familiarity with the product.

Set the Environment

Demonstrations should be given in environments that have a minimum number of interruptions and distractions. Demonstrations of complex equipment can best be given at the branch office or at a customer's installation where there is no traffic or noise. The demonstration room or setting should be impressive, and in some instances low background music is appropriate to help set the mood. The furniture should be arranged so that when prospects are seated, they can see the entire operation and can talk to all present without furniture blocking conversation. Everything should be in keeping with the image you wish to convey of the firm and of the product.

Check Out the Materials

Equipment to be demonstrated should be thoroughly checked by maintenance personnel, and all software such as forms, charts, and visuals should be reviewed for accuracy and completeness. Malfunctioning equipment can be the death of a sale—it is hard to overcome demonstration mistakes of any kind. All equipment should be thoroughly cleaned and operated in the demonstration room to make sure it is at optimum operational levels. It should be programmed or adjusted, if possible, to the customer's application. Demonstration materials should be in place, and they should be in the sequence in which they will be used. Fumbling for forms and materials leaves a bad impression. Once the materials are inspected and set, make sure no one disturbs them before the demonstration. If you plan to demonstrate equipment in the prospect's office, make sure you have the proper extension cords and plug-ins. If you plan to show the prospect another customer's application at the customer's place of business, everything must be thoroughly prearranged. Get your customer's best operator to operate the equipment or operate it yourself. If possible, you should visit the customer's installation before you take the prospect there.

Practice

Master the operation of any equipment and review the exposition of any charts or software. A musical genius who could have been a concert pianist made a fortune demonstrating pianos instead. He made the prospect feel that anyone could do it. You must do the same thing. Go over the entire presentation thoroughly before you attempt to show it to the prospect. You can make the hard parts look easy through your mastery of the product, but let your prospect attempt only the easy operations. Prospects do not expect to be able to master the complicated parts of an operation immediately, but if it looks easy when you do it, they will believe it can be learned.

Use the Right Words

Good descriptive words and comparisons reinforce the demonstration. Consider these suggestive words to accompany a showing of the product:

- It is hard to believe that the machine could do all that in just seven seconds, isn't it?
- Did you notice how smoothly this car glided over those rough railroad tracks? It was almost as if we were on a cushion of air, wasn't it?
- Look at the clarity and detail in this instant picture—you snapped the shutter less than two minutes ago.
- Have you ever tasted anything as refreshing as that?
- Look at the spaciousness of this room. You would never feel cramped in here, would you?
- It is as silent as a candle. Can you hear it?

Handle Mistakes Properly

Few demonstrations of complex operations are completed without any mistakes, and even in the simplest operations, malfunctions and errors can occur. Suppose, for example, an error is made in demonstrating a cash register. Instead of calling attention to the error, use the error to demonstrate the error-correcting procedures available with the equipment. Sometimes errors go unnoticed by prospects. Like a good entertainer, you might simply go on with the show if the mistake is small and unimportant. Sometimes demonstrators make errors purposely to illustrate a point or to test the prospect's attention or understanding. Be realistic, however; if the product doesn't work and you can't get it to work, the malfunction will be extremely difficult to explain away. Make sure that

Always be ready to give good answers when problems arise in the demonstration.

you know what to do when the product does malfunction and do it quickly. Suggest how easy the product is to fix when the "infrequent" malfunction does occur. Remember, also, that prospects are concerned that you might deliver the demonstrated equipment to them which they regard as slightly used. You might explain that the product they will get is still in the package, or offer them the demonstration equipment at a reduced price.

Use Showmanship

Showmanship, usually associated with a product demonstration, is the use of any dramatic method to impress a point. The salesperson who smashes a fist down on the keyboard of an office machine, who purposely drops a watch on the concrete floor, or who jumps up and down on a suitcase is using showmanship to say that the product is durable. The sales representative who holds up the jewelry against a dark background, who puts the color-coordinated tie and socks against the newly purchased suit without saying a word, or pours water in a glass while a car is going over a rough road is using showmanship—silent language to make impressive points about the product.

THE USE OF VISUAL DEVICES TO SELL

While seeing the product being used in its intended role is reassuring to prospects, there are many other visuals that can be used to dramatize a presentation and stir buying emotions. Some of these will be examined.

Film

As mentioned before, fully programmed films with sound can cover all a product's feature benefits in a vivid and convincing way. A film can include music to set a buying mood, can offer testimonials, and can minimize distracting influences on the prospect. Since visuals are carefully edited, there is no danger of product malfunction during the presentation. It is very embarrassing, however, when the film breaks or the start of the film is lost because the showing equipment is not properly set up and focused. If audio-visuals are used at the sales branch, the film should be prerun in part and ready to show. If projectors are to be set up at the customer's location, it should be remembered that the salesperson's professionalism is being judged by the way he or she handles the video equipment.

Easily portable equipment that is not as bulky as the big screen and projector arrangement is available. It allows more control (replays) and permits discussion by the salesperson and the prospect during the showing. There is less awkwardness changing from this type of visual into the closing, since the visual does not contrast so markedly with the straight presentation. Also, the break from film to two-way conversation is easier with this type of visual (see Figure 11.1, p. 292).

Transparency Portfolios

The inner composition of complicated products like pumps and industrial machinery can be illustrated by transparency overlays that successively reveal the interior makeup of the product. An understanding of these qualities would be impossible otherwise, since disassembly might be impractical because of the size of the product and the time required to remove the outer parts.

The usual transparency portfolio for selling less-complicated tangibles or intangibles consists of such items as properly sequenced feature-benefit illustrations, supporting statistical tables and charts, and testimonial letters from satisfied users. Such presentation aids may be furnished by the company, or salespersons can construct their own illustrative portfolio from advertisements and customer letters. It is very effective for prospects to review the testimonies of buyers they know and respect, and portfolio entries in loose-leaf binders can be augmented and deleted easily. The salesperson also has an excuse to move closer to the prospect and converse at close personal distance. This can make the interview mood seem less formal and more friendly.

Samples and Models

Products such as rugs, upholstery materials, food, heavy equipment, and pharmaceuticals can sometimes be presented through samples and models. Large lots of raw materials can be presented by small testable samples. The virtues of nonportable products can be embodied in simplified models that show the relative advantages without clouding the presentation with too many complex details. Legally, samples should be taken from the lots of merchandise they represent. Prospects who hesitate to buy a rug until they see how it fits the image and decor of their home are reassured and experience a temporary feeling of possession when

Figure 11.1

they actually observe the texture and color of the sample in their home setting. The industrial buyer is constantly reminded of the need for a huge water pump by playing with the toy working model that serves as a paperweight on the desk. Again, it is up to the salesperson to make the prospect experience the virtues of these samples and models as they are shown. Salespersons who bring in heavy loads of bulky samples may put the buyer on the defensive, but in most cases, they are being direct in nonverbally communicating that they are there to serve and sell.

Presentation Boards and Posters

An effective way to emphasize the main points of any presentation is to use a felt board and sandpaper-backed cutouts that seem to stick to the felt like magic. The cutouts are easy to prepare, and different colors can be used to indicate different groups of points. The features could be shown in orange on the right side of the board, and the benefits could be shown in green on the other side. Almost any rough type of texture will stick on a felt board wherever it is placed. The cutout stick-ons can guide and furnish an outline for the sales presentation. Felt boards are usually used for group presentations.

Posters featuring pictures of the product, successive steps in operations, or multiple uses for an offering can dramatize the worth of a product, much the same as a cleverly devised advertisement. They reinforce the verbal presentation. Such posters show care and preparation and save time by illustrating the worth of the offering quickly. This is an inexpensive way of having the prospect visualize the benefits and brings in the additional sense of sight to maintain attention.

Sales Manuals

Sales manuals contain technical information about the product and sometimes detailed diagrams of component parts. Seeing the information about the product in authoritative print may have a reassuring effect on prospects that is much stronger than merely telling them about the offering. Some people have a tendency to believe more of what they see (including printed words) than what they hear from a sales representative. These manuals also help the multiproduct and complex-product sales representative by furnishing a quick reference for prospect questions. No one can understand all there is to know about certain products and product lines, and having the information at hand to show the prospect is good common sense.

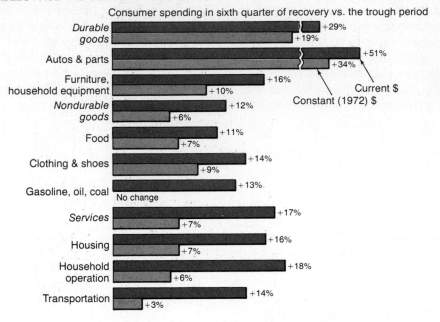

Figure 11.2

This graph could be used by a durable goods salesperson to help persuade a durable goods buyer to maintain heavier stocks of merchandise and therefore buy a larger amount.

Tables, Charts, Graphs, and Maps

Each of these visual devices can make it easier to explain a benefit to a prospect and save interview time (see Figure 11.2). The simpler and less complicated the device, the more effective it will probably be. Each table, chart, or graph used should have an explanatory title and be easy to understand. Even if the visual is self-contained and explained in the title, the salesperson should explain it verbally to the prospect and use questions to be sure the prospect understands. Many prospects will not take the time to study data that appears complex, and a visual aid that is not understood is more of a hindrance than a benefit. Many prospects will put away anything the sales representative has given them and not look at it again. If you don't go over material with a prospect, you may waste it. Nearly all visuals are expensive, and the salesperson has an ethical obligation to the company to use them wisely.

THE TELEPHONE AS A SELLING TOOL

Demonstrations using showmanship and visual aids are usually used in the presentation to dramatize selling points, but the telephone is a communications tool that can be used in every phase of the selling process. It can even take the place of an in-person sales call. If visual circuit phones come into widespread use, allowing those conversing to see each other while talking, a new era of selling will be ushered in. In the meantime, more and more firms are discovering the potentials of the standard telephone. The telephone is a fast method of contacting the buyer and an inexpensive way to have two-way communication with customers. A St. Louis company that sells 3,000 products (pipes, casing, and pumps for energy exploration) contacted 20,000 customers by phone, using thirty-five sales representatives. Sales increased from $50 million in 1971 to $180 million in 1974. Instead of making eight visits per day, the sales representatives were able to interview from sixty to seventy buyers on the phone.[1] In a program called "Tellsell," the Bell and Howell management pulled their entire sales force out of their territories two or three times a year, usually before a price increase or at the end of a promotion, and had them phone dealers from their homes.[2] Sales departments throughout the country are increasingly using the phone for making appointments and for follow-ups. Many are also installing inbound WATS (Wide-Area Telephone Service) lines and increasing customer-service departments by adding inside salespersons who know how to make inquiries.[3] American Hospital Supply and Inland Steel are among the many firms that have successfully used WATS lines.

Advantages

The reason so many firms are rediscovering the telephone is that it has inherent advantages. The telephone reaches prospects at distant ends

[1] "Valley: Calling by Moonlight," *Sales Management,* March 3, 1975, pp. 16, 23.

[2] John H. Rosenheim, "Telephone Selling's Finest Hour," *Sales Management,* 112, no. 2 (January 21, 1974), 30.

[3] *Ibid.*

of the territory immediately. Busy and important buyers who would not allow you a personal interview will tolerate a brief interruption to talk to you long-distance or locally. Prospects who are ready to buy can be contacted immediately and asked to wait until they see *your* product. Local calls cost little, and long-distance calls are relatively inexpensive in comparison to the money tied up in time and travel. Seven to eight times more prospects can be contacted by telephone than can be personally interviewed even in a city territory. Telephone selling is especially good for standard products like raw materials and intangibles that can't be seen anyway. It is used most often in making appointments, in prospecting, and in follow-ups after delivery, but telephone selling can also be used for closing sales.

Disadvantages

On the other side, every telephone call is an interruption. Some products that have to be seen to be appreciated do not lend themselves to telephone selling. Plus, the enthusiasm of in-person communication is missed, and it is easy to say "no" over the phone. There are more misunderstandings over the phone, and interview length is limited. Since neither sales representatives nor prospects can use gestures or other visible actions to communicate, excitement and emotion are harder to generate.

Procedures

Telephone selling is a practiced art. John Rosenheim recommends that: plans be made in advance about exactly which accounts will be called and how frequently; objectives be set for each call as well as for the total effort; direct mail be used to follow up and confirm what was agreed upon during the call; each person be trained in telephone technique; and results be evaluated and procedures redirected if necessary. He also recommends that each person's voice be audited for pitch, volume, and rate of speech (rate should be 160 words per minute). Plans for each call should be outlined on paper with the opening written down word for word. Role playing should be practiced on extension phones and, if possible, critiqued. Prices, terms, and schedules should be restated to emphasize accuracy and avoid misunderstanding.[4] Care should be taken in letting

[4] *Ibid.*

Figure 11.3   A Step-by-Step Procedure for Opening New Accounts over the Telephone

I. Build a list of potential customers
   a. The Yellow Pages
   b. Trade journals
   c. Membership lists of trade associations
   d. The local chamber of commerce

II. Determine each prospect's ability to pay
   a. Financial condition
   b. Credit rating
     1. Dun and Bradstreet
     2. Local credit-rating bureaus
     3. Your own credit department

III. Set specific objectives for your call
   a. The clearer the target, the easier the aim
   b. Prepare fact-finding questions to ask. Do prospects currently use the product? Do they have a need for the product?
   c. Sell a limited order over the telephone. Have objective to get prospect on the books.

IV. Prepare your sales message
   a. Stress benefits over features
   b. Use a sales vocabulary
     1. Expressive adjectives
     2. Dynamic words, like rugged, power, speed
     3. Personal words, like you, me, I, we
     4. Picture phrases

V. Prepare an opening statement
   a. Identify yourself and your firm
   b. Establish rapport
   c. Make an interest-creating comment
   d. Fact-find to qualify the prospect

VI. Deliver the sales message
   a. Stress benefits over features
   b. Use a sales vocabulary

VII. Overcome objections
   a. Prepare prospect for your answer
   b. Answer the objection
   c. Stress the product benefit

VIII. Close the sale
   a. Start out with an open-ended question or a forced-choice question

IX. The sales wrap-up
   a. Confirm the order
   b. Arrange for the next call
   c. Express your thanks

Source: Phone-Power Self-Instruction Text: *Opening New Accounts*, Courtesy of Bell Telephone Company, Memphis, Tennessee.

the phone ring for just so long, since even if prospects answer a long ring, they probably have been interrupted from some important business, and they may be unreceptive. Certainly, good telephone manners preclude calling during late-night or early-morning hours. Begin to develop a phone personality by evaluating others you hear speak on the phone. Listen to the excitement in the voices of people like Howard Cosell, Billy Graham, or other broadcast media personalities, and be aware of telephone manners. Telephone visual selling may be the wave of the future, and you might want to be part of it. At least, consider the present phone a very important sales tool (see Figure 11.3).

ADVERTISING AND THE SALES REPRESENTATIVE

Advertising, like the telephone, is another valuable communications tool that can be used to create attention, interest, desire—and sometimes action. While advertising alone may inform and condition the prospect for the sale, a salesperson is needed to listen, evaluate, interpret, respond to the prospect, and close the sale. You can ask for an order forcefully, expecting an immediate answer. In advertising you can't perform such human functions. There are, therefore, many products that can't be sold in quantity through advertising alone. However, advertising closely coordinated with personal selling can produce maximum impact and make the selling process easier. You should have, therefore, a good understanding of this selling aid. You should know:

- How advertising can help you present a unified message, acquire prospects, sell your offering, acquire a consulting image, and find words for your presentation.
- Your responsibility in coordinating point-of-purchase materials.
- How to use direct mail and newspaper advertising.

Present a Unified Message

Advertising conditions prospects to buy by getting them to think positively about the product. Few prospects buy important items on the first call unless advertising has "softened them up" before the additional appeals of the salesperson. You may mention the positive benefits of the offering, using the same magic words and phrases as the advertising copy. Repetition of buying appeals used in advertising provide a unified company image and increase believability. Repeated positive suggestion is a primary persuasive strategy and advertising suggestion. Prospects may also be reminded that the advertisement appeared in *Good Housekeeping* or some other medium that has a reputational stake in its featured advertisements. If you *don't* support advertising claims in talking to prospects, you may raise questions in their minds that may hamper closing efforts.

Acquire Prospects

Advertising furnishes leads for sales representatives. People who send in coupons or who phone in with questions after being exposed to advertisements are usually interested prospects who should be contacted as soon as possible and given further persuasive information.

Sell Advertising in Your Offering

The wholesale dealer or retailer may like your product but may be much more interested in whether or not *customers* like your product. The dealer sales representative doesn't sell tangible goods as much as the ability to move stock off the shelves and through the cash register lane. The dealer wants profits. Dealers know that a good advertising campaign can improve their ability to sell the merchandise, can increase the flow of customers through their stores, and give them ideas about how to talk to their customers about the product.[5] Through knowledge of company advertising, sales representatives can sell the campaign and its benefits just as they would sell tangible product features. To be able to do this effectively, sales representatives must understand the purposes of the campaign, the media where the consumer advertising will appear, and the projected effects on consumer sales. Samples of the copy for printed media (such as magazines and newspapers) or "story boards" for television give visible assurances that the dealer will be supported in merchandising the product. Often cooperative arrangements can be worked out with dealers whereby the product is advertised in association with the dealer's name and costs are shared. The creative work and materials for such advertisements are usually furnished by the sales representative's company.

Acquire a Consulting Image

Many professional salespeople are expected to aid dealer customers with overall advertising decisions by offering help with dealer advertising problems. Salespersons who answer dealer questions should be knowledgeable about media and other alternatives. They should not only study advertising from company sources, but they should also solicit information from experienced customers in other parts of their territory. Salespersons who talk to many dealers are in a good position to accumulate and distribute operational information about advertising alternatives and thereby improve their effectiveness and enhance their professional image.

Find Words for Your Presentation

Large corporations pay thousands of dollars for expertise in developing advertising appeals. Often the words and themes used in advertising appeals express product benefits clearly, concisely, and vividly. The

[5] Carlton A. Pederson and Milburn D. Wright, *Selling: Principles and Methods,* 6th ed. (Homewood, Ill.: Irwin, 1976), pp. 173–175.

competitive advantages of the product are brought out in positive statements whose truths are under the watchful eyes of governmental agencies. These selling phrases should be considered by the salesperson for use in the sales presentation. Saying it face-to-face to the customer reinforces suggestions and words from advertisements in selling proposals. (Selling proposals are written, and pictorial explanations show how product benefits fit the prospect's special needs and how the product can be bought.) Most companies have hand-distributed folders or direct-mail pieces showing pictures of the product being used under favorable circumstances together with feature-benefit explanations. Such information left during calls reminds the prospects between visits and is available at their convenience.

Handle Point-of-Purchase Materials

Sales representatives selling to retailers and other dealers are expected to be proficient in setting up point-of-purchase materials and other type displays. These materials for in-store use are expensive, but if they are set up properly, the results will be more dealer sales and, consequently, bigger orders for the salesperson. Dealers who associate no expense with the materials, however, are prone to waste them or use them improperly. The salesperson should sell the dealer on the importance of putting displays up and leaving them up.[6] All too often, point-of-purchase materials are taken down by the next competitive salesperson visiting the dealer and thrown away. Dealer salespersons must also know where the product should be shelved and displayed to attract maximum customer attention. Aisle-end displays and eye-level shelving can sometimes produce over twice the sales of poorer in-store locations. Displays near the cash register or in center-of-aisle gondolas are desirable. Stocking meat, milk, bread, or whatever product category you sell at the beginning of a display—in regard to in-store normal traffic flow—may give you a decided competitive advantage. The main competition in retail stores, in fact, is the rivalry for display advantage.

Newspapers and Direct Mail

Newspapers cover all kinds of people in local geographical areas. Real estate, automobile, and other sales representatives whose products can be used by most people find classified ads important in prospecting.

[6] John S. Wright, Daniel S. Warner, Willis L. Winter, Jr., and Sherilyn K. Zeigler, *Advertising,* 4th ed. (New York: McGraw-Hill, 1977), pp. 310–314.

Direct mail can be used to find prospects, but it can also help cultivate customers. Because it can be initiated and controlled by the salesperson and because nearly every salesperson can use it advantageously, direct mail merits separate consideration. A business-machine corporation, for example, once provided a brochure explaining how doctors could use bookkeeping machine applications to solve their accounting problems. Since it was difficult to arrange personal interviews with doctors, all branch salespersons participated in a direct-mail campaign. It took only a few minutes to look in the Yellow Pages, select a doctor in each territory, and mail them the advertisement with a return postcard included. The mailout was a success, and sales were made with a minimum investment of time and money. Direct mail is a rifle shot to the prospect that can be used whenever you want to use it.

Customers like attention, but personal calls are expensive. They appreciate the salesperson who is interested enough to think about them between calls. Whenever the company furnishes brochures or you find any kind of information that might be of direct interest to your customers, write a short note, include the new material, address the envelope, and put it in the mail. This may take you ten minutes. Sending out special mailing pieces assures that the next call you make won't be completely cold, and your customer may surprise you by contacting *you* and requesting a visit.

SUMMARY

Communication aids such as the visible product, audio-visuals, the telephone, and advertising make the selling process easier and clarify the sales presentation for the prospect. The effective demonstration is an effective interview tool, but care should be exercised in using it. Thorough planning will help avoid irreversible mistakes. Good showmanship assures that the interview will maintain attention and will be long remembered. Films, transparency portfolios, samples, posters, sales manuals, charts, maps, and graphs make it easier for prospects to visualize benefits and save time in selling.

The telephone and advertising are being increasingly used to contact potential buyers rapidly and inexpensively, especially buyers who are hard to reach any other way. Contacting by telephone takes up less time and saves traveling costs, but the art of telephone selling requires special techniques and practice. Advertising is especially useful in prospecting, as a selling feature of the product offering to dealers, and in paving the way for the presentation. Direct mail, newspaper ads, and ads in other media can cost even less per contact than the telephone. The salesperson has an obligation to the firm to sell the advertising campaign and coordinate advertising materials for maximum effect.

REVIEW QUESTIONS

1. Why is it important for salespeople to use communication aids effectively?

2. What are some important rules to follow in making good demonstrations?

3. To what extent should the prospect be allowed to participate in the demonstration? How can this participation be controlled?

4. What can you do if you make a mistake demonstrating or the product does not operate correctly?

5. Give several examples of "showmanship" in selling.

6. What are the advantages and disadvantages of film presentations?

7. Under what circumstances is a felt board a good aid to use?

8. What do transparency portfolios usually contain?

9. How are sales manuals used as aids?

10. What are the advantages and disadvantages of using the telephone in the selling process?

11. List five good rules for using the telephone effectively.

12. List ways advertising can help the salesperson.

13. How does the salesperson sell advertising as part of the product offering to the dealer prospect?

14. What are the salesperson's responsibilities in regard to point-of-purchase materials?

15. Explain how the sales representative can use newspapers and direct mail to advantage.

APPLICATION QUESTIONS

1. Explain the preparations you should make before demonstrating such office equipment as a photocopy machine.

2. Find three ads in a magazine or newspaper and underline words and expressions that might be used by a salesperson in the presentation.

11–1

Ed Ingram sells fire-alarm systems and extinguishers for the home and has decided to pick out names from the phone book at random instead of going door-to-door, because it's raining out. Mr. Carter answers after four rings.

Carter: Hello.

Ed: Is this Mr. Gary Carter?

Carter: Yes, who is it?

Ed: I'm Ed Ingram. Mr. Carter, if your house caught fire tonight while you were asleep, what would happen?

Carter: Are you a salesman or something?

Ed: Yes, I represent Fire Safe Alarms and Extinguishers. Would you have any warning if your house caught fire while you were asleep?

Carter: My dog would bark and wake me up, and I would either go out the door or the window, depending on where the fire was. We haven't had a fire yet. Of course I would try to put it out if I could.

Ed: What if the fire were electrical and you couldn't put it out with water. Do you have an extinguisher?

Carter: No, I would throw soda on it or try to smother it. Look, if I wanted an extinguisher, I would have bought one from the discount store.

Ed: Our extinguishers are reliable and easy to use and can save you valuable seconds in case of a fire. Can I come by and show you one tomorrow?

Carter: Look, you woke me up . . . I'm on the night shift, and I need to get back to sleep. I've lived a long time and never needed a fire extinguisher.

Ed: I'm sorry I woke you. Sometimes fires happen while you sleep and the fumes and smoke get you before you can get out. Many lives have been saved by our smoke alarm. It warns you early—even before your dog would realize that the house was on fire. It's ionized and very sensitive and even lets you know when the batteries have to be replaced. Really, Mr.

Carter, it could save your life or your family's life. Insurance companies will even give you a discount on your house insurance if you buy two, and I can show you where to put them in your home.

Carter: Look, I can get those at the discount store too, and right now I'm tired and can't afford your products. I'm sure that kind of alarm would be expensive.

Ed: Only $42.50 each and no home can afford to be without them.

Carter: I'm going back to sleep—goodbye. Don't try to call back because I'm taking the phone off the hook.

QUESTION

1. Evaluate Ed Ingram's telephone procedures. What did he do right and what in your opinion could he have done better?

11–2

Marie Montesi sells real estate for the Brandon Agency. She has just learned from one of her sales associates that the Gilbert Pickards have recently moved to the city and are temporarily living at the Oak Terrace Apartments until they can find a house. Mr. Pickard is a manager for a battery manufacturing company, and they have two children, a boy twelve and a girl seven. Nancy Pickard is answering the phone . . .

Nancy: Hello.

Marie: May I speak to Mrs. Pickard, please?

Nancy: This is Nancy Pickard.

Marie: Mrs. Pickard, welcome to Centerville. I'm Marie Montesi with the Brandon Real Estate Agency. I understand from a friend of mine who lives in Oak Terrace that you and Mr. Pickard are considering a new home. We have some exciting listings now and I want to serve you if I can by showing you some of our homes.

Nancy: Well, Mrs. Montesi, we have just come to Centerville from Chicago. Buying a home in a new city is a big step for us. We felt that we needed to rent for a while and take our time and find what we really wanted after studying the situation for a few months.

Marie: You are very wise in being cautious about considering a new home. What generally are you looking for?

Nancy: We want a home in the $75,000–$90,000 range in the suburbs near good schools that won't be too far from Gilbert's work at the Storebest Battery factory. We want a four-bedroom with dining room and a large den, preferably on a wooded lot. It must be in a good neighborhood. But, as I say, we are not in a hurry.

Marie: We have three excellent homes that fit that description. The one on Pine Grove Road is a classic two-story that has lots of room for a family of four and beautiful trees in the yard. The other two are in Grandwood Subdivision just two blocks from the best elementary–junior high school in town! I would love to show all three of these fine homes to you. It is unusual for us to have such a good offering in executive-type homes. It would only take a few hours, and it would help give you an idea about real estate in Centerville.

Nancy: You understand that we will probably look a long time before we settle on a home. We want our children to grow up in a good environment.

Marie: Two of these homes are in Grandwood Subdivision, one of the finest subdivisions in Centerville. Could I show them to you this Saturday at one o'clock?

Nancy: Just a minute . . . (*to Gilbert*) Gilbert, there are some homes I would like to see this Saturday afternoon. Would you like to come with me or do you want to watch football? (*to Marie*) We'll go. Where can we meet you?

Marie: I'll meet you at your apartment, then, at one o'clock Saturday. I know you both will love these beautiful homes.

QUESTIONS

1. Evaluate Marie's telephone procedures. Can you find any mistakes in her methods?

2. What, in your opinion, was her best line. Why?

11–3

John H. Patterson, the founder of the National Cash Register Company, now the NCR Corporation, was one of the first, if not *the* first, industrialist in America to standardize the sales presentation and demonstrations of his sales representatives. *Every* salesperson had to learn the *Primer* and repeat it exactly as it was written. It was written by compositing the best selling procedures of the best salesperson in the company.[7] It is a historical classic and one of the first and most successful memorized sales demonstrations ever devised. Pages of the *Primer* are included below for your analysis.

Identify the good selling principles used in this planned demonstration and evaluate it in the light of today's selling problems.

Could this demonstration with slight modifications to reflect new machine features be used to sell cash registers in the 1980s as it was in the 1920s?

[7] Samuel Crowther, *John H. Patterson* (Garden City, N.Y.: Garden City Publishing Company, 1926; Copyright 1923, Doubleday, Page and Company), pp. 103–155.

Figure 11.4

The National Cash Register Primer

January, 1916

Preface.

The man who sells a cash register should understand the fundamentals.

This book gives the fundamentals in simple form.

It is a textbook, the object of which is to assist the salesman by simplifying the demonstration.

The part printed in black applies fundamentally to any register we make, and is the foundation for all demonstrations. Salesmen will of course, in demonstrating the 400, 500, and other classes, bring out all of the additional advantages of those registers, explaining their value to the merchant.

It is published at the request of many members of the Selling Force.

It is the same Primer, in substance, that was used twenty-five years ago, and if it is rewritten twenty-five years hence, it will still be the same.

It is not obligatory on you to learn the Primer verbatim.

If you **do** learn it verbatim, you can either learn that printed in black only, making yourself **familiar** with what is printed in red, or commit it all to memory.

How to Learn the Primer.

The object of a cash register is to prevent mistakes in all transactions that occur between clerks and customers.

Mistakes occur in—
1. Cash sales.
2. Credit sales.
3. Money received on account.
4. Money paid out.
5. Making change.

Before studying this Primer, study the No. 300 with the color system and detail-strip.

The fundamental principles are the same in all registers.

While learning, never try to recite any part of the Primer without having a register before you, or a vivid image of one in your mind, so that you may describe something that you see and avoid the folly of trying to memorize lines and passages of "dead words."

Fix in mind the **idea** for which each sentence stands before attempting to speak it.

Always repeat **aloud**, and say the Primer to **somebody** (present or imagined).

3

Demonstration of the Register.

This,* Mr. Merchant, is a National Cash Register of the most approved pattern.

To appreciate what a help it would be to you, we must see what things you do in your store of which you keep a record.

I think the ordinary daily transactions with your customers may be arranged in five classes, thus:

1. You sell goods for cash.
2. You sell goods on credit.
3. You receive cash on account.
4. You pay out cash.
5. You change a coin or bill.

Am I right?

Now, sir, this register* makes the entries.

The indication* of the transaction shows through this glass.*

The amount* of the last recorded transaction is always visible, and the records are made by pressing the keys.

*Point out what is referred to.

4

When you sell for cash, these* black cash keys make the record.

When you sell on credit, this* red "Charge" key makes the record.

When you receive cash on account, this* yellow "Received on Account" key makes the record.

When you pay out cash, this* blue "Paid Out" key makes the record.

When you change a coin or bill, this* orange "No Sale" key makes the record.

When one or more keys* are pressed, six results are accomplished at the same time:

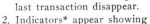

1. The indicators* showing the last transaction disappear.
2. Indicators* appear showing a new transaction.

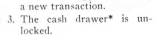

3. The cash drawer* is unlocked.
4. A spring throws it* open.
5. A bell* is rung to show that a registration has been made.

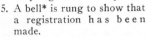

6. The proper entry is made inside.

*Point out what is referred to.

5

Cash Sales.

Cash sales are taken care of in this way:

Suppose you sell something for $1.00.*

Carry the dollar* to the register, press the "$1" key, put the dollar into the cash drawer, and shut the drawer.

You see that you have locked up the money in a safe place, and have made a record of the transaction at the same time. The indicator shows everybody in the store what has been done.

Now let us register different amounts.

Here the salesman will register various amounts, explaining to the merchant as he proceeds, about as follows:

Take 50 cents.* Press the "50-cent" key, put the cash into the drawer, and shut the drawer; 75 cents, 4 cents, 60 cents, 2 cents.

You see, Mr. Merchant, how very simple this is. Press the key, drop the cash* into the open drawer, and shut the drawer.

More than one key may be required in some cases.

You have, for example, $1.25.

*Show it.

6

Press the "$1" key and the "25-cent" key at the same time.

Suppose your next sale is 73 cents and the customer hands you $1.00.

Press the "70-cent" key and the "3-cent" key, put the $1.00 into the drawer, take out 27 cents change, shut the drawer, and hand the 27 cents to the customer.

You see that each cash sale is quickly registered and indicated when it occurs, with very little chance of mistake.

Now, I will show you how the register takes care of credit sales.

Credit Sales.

One of the greatest sources of loss in retail stores is the failure to charge goods sold on credit.

Clerks put up the goods and deliver them all right, but forget to make the proper entries.

Customers, as a rule, keep no account of such purchases, and so, in nineteen cases out

7

of twenty, these uncharged sales are never heard of again.

I believe that you, sir, like every other merchant who uses the ordinary system, will admit that you lose considerable money in this way, won't you?

You know, of course, why these losses occur.

A customer orders a number of articles, which you put up and deliver to him.

Then you intend to make a memorandum of the sale, but before this is done you are interrupted, and forget one or more of the items; or it may be that the whole transaction slips your mind.

In that case the customer gets the goods and you get nothing.

The trouble is that you trust to your memory instead of making a record on the spot.

Just here the National Cash Register is a friend in need.

It stops this drain on your profits by taking as good care of your credit sales as it does of your cash.

We provide each salesman with a dupli-

8

cating "Charge" book like this,* which he carries in his pocket.

When a customer orders goods on credit (for example, to the amount of $5) the clerk pulls out his book, inserts name and date, and sets down the items.

Then he writes "Charge" on the slip and tears it out, like this.*

The memorandum, as you see, is in duplicate, a copy having been made by the carbon sheet.

He tears the slip in two, does up the original entry with the goods, and keeps the duplicate.

Now he is in no danger of forgetting the items, for he has a written statement of the whole transaction; and, having waited on the customer, he takes this to the register, presses the red "Charge" key and the "$5" key and puts the slip into the cash drawer where it is safe.

You readily see, Mr. Merchant, how this way of handling credit sales prevents losses.

*Show it and read.

9

Two written statements of the items and prices are made in the presence of the customer before the goods are delivered—he takes one and the clerk the other.

The customer carries his home and the clerk makes a record of his in the register as soon as possible and **puts it into the cash drawer.**

Cash on Account.

If so many mistakes are made in handling credit sales in the usual way, there is also danger that cash received on account will be put into the drawer without being credited.

If a National Cash Register be used such a mistake is impossible.

When cash is received on account (say $2), fill out a "Received on Account" slip,* press the yellow "Received on Account" key and the "$2" key, put the cash and slip into the drawer, and shut the drawer.

*Show it and read.

10

Cash Paid Out.

When cash (say 50 cents) is paid out for any purpose fill out a "Paid Out" slip, press the blue "Paid Out" key and the "50-cent" key, put the slip into the drawer, pay out the cash, and shut the drawer.

Money Changing.

When a coin or bill is changed press the orange "No Sale" key and make the change.

The Argument.

You remember that we divided the ordinary transactions with your customers into five classes.

Now, I have shown you that the National Cash Register takes care of each and all of them in the same way.

Whether you sell for cash, sell on credit, receive cash on account, pay out cash, or change a coin or bill, you go straight to the register and record what you have done by pressing the keys.

A clerk won't be likely to forget this, for

11

 in each case he has something in his hand which he must deposit in the drawer to complete the transaction.

With the cash sale, he has the cash in hand.

With a credit sale, the "Charge" slip.

With cash received on account, the "Received on Account" slip and the cash.

With the cash paid out, the "Paid Out" slip.

With a coin or bill to be changed, the coin or bill.

Every clerk must go to the **same place** to complete **every** transaction, so he forms a habit of doing this without fail.

As soon as a key is pressed a record of the transaction is made inside the register, the fact is announced by the ringing of the bell, and the kind of record is shown by the indicators.

Our system of recording transactions and taking care of receipts in a store like yours, Mr. Merchant, is simple to understand, easy to learn, quick to operate, safe from chances of mistake, and always ready for use.

12

308
Selling Techniques

Balancing the Register.

The total amount of cash registered and the number of slips of each kind deposited in the cash drawer are recorded on the adding wheels of the register.

To get a cash balance at the end of a day's business, we need not look into the drawer, but raise the lid of the register and enter in a statement book, like this,* the amount shown by the adding wheels.

Salesman then balances the register, using Statement Book, and explaining, as he goes, about as follows:

Looking here I find the amount recorded ($6.89).

This is the total amount of the cash taken in during the day.

On these adding wheels* I find recorded one "charge," one "received on account," and one "paid out" slip, which are also to be entered in their proper spaces.

Now, I have entered a record of the day's business in this Statement Book.*

———

*Show it.

13

In the drawer I find one "charge," one "received on account," and one "paid out" slip, corresponding to the record taken from the adding wheels.

From the total amount of cash taken in during the day ($6.89) deduct the 50 cents paid out, and the balance ($6.39) is the amount of money now in the drawer.

Let us count it.

You see there is just $6.39.

When balancing the register lay aside the "charge," "received on account," and "paid out" slips, so that a proper record may be made of them on the books.

The duplicating "charge" slip, by the way, has a special advantage which I have not explained.

The original, sent with the goods, is an itemized bill which the customer can examine at his leisure.

The amounts from the duplicate can be posted directly to the ledger, which saves bookkeeping.

Having now this written statement of the day's business which can be preserved, the last thing to do is to reset the register to zero, ready for the next day's business.

14

This is done by simply turning this key* to the right until you hear a very distinct "click," or until it stops.

On this strip of paper is printed, in the order in which it occurred, the amount and kind of each transaction made during the day, so that you can tell the amount of each transaction, as well as the total amount of all money taken in.

1. 00
. 50
. 75
. 04
. 60
. 02
1. 25
. 73
5. 00C
2. 00R
. 50P
0. 00

This is a total-adding cash register.

All the wheels of the counter now show zero.

I press the "1-cent" key* and one cent is registered.

Press the "9-cent" key* and nine cents are added to the one cent, making ten cents.

Press the "90-cent" key* and it shows a dollar.

Press the "$9" key* and the register shows ten dollars.

You see that each time a key is pressed the amount represented by that key is added

———

*Show it.

15

---

to the amount already shown on the counter, so at the close of a day's business the total amount of money taken in is shown; also printed in detail on the detail-strip, making this a perfect total-adding and detail-printing cash register.

When a color key is pressed the wheel corresponding adds one to the number previously shown by it, so that at the close of a day's business you know the number of slips of each kind that should be in the drawer.

This is an abridgment of the original primer.

16

12 Answering Objections

Two problems, which might also be regarded as opportunities, are so important to the success of the interview that they require special attention: (1) meeting the sales resistance prospective buyers express in the form of objections and (2) leading the potential purchaser over the buying threshold. The first of these problem/opportunities, answering objections, is the subject of this chapter, and the second, closing the sale, will be discussed in the following chapter.

The challenge of answering objections and meeting the sales resistance of buyers can best be met by understanding the buyer-psychology involved, the sales attitude required, and the standard tested methods that have been used to advantage by practicing sales representatives. Indeed, in many instances, customer resistance denotes interest and may often be read as a closing signal. Closing can seldom be accomplished before prospect questions are satisfied. Answering objections will be treated under the following headings:

- The significance and psychology of objections
- Considerations in handling objections
- Alternative ways to handle objections
- Examples of handling common objections

THE SIGNIFICANCE AND PSYCHOLOGY OF OBJECTIONS

Experienced sales representatives welcome objections, because they realize that in many instances the buyer is expressing interest, participating in the interview, and furnishing valuable feedback. Disinterested prospects, prospects who are afraid of the sales situation, prospects who resent the sales representative for some reason, or prospects who feel the salesperson's presentation is an implied challenge to their judgment may throw up a wall of resistance. However, even in this type of situation, prospects are throwing out ropes that the skillful sales representative can grab to get the prospects interested.

Objections May Be Questions in Disguise

In the selling situation, the interested prospect uses objections as a way of asking indirect questions and, in effect, bargaining at the same time. Many prospects feel that asking direct questions will make them seem an easy mark, weaken their bargaining position, or encourage the salesperson to shade the truth about the product. On the other hand, prospects can use objections to get assurances without obligation. They feel risks are reduced by indirectly asking for information without overencouraging the sales representative. The prospect may say, for example: "They say that this model gives mechanical trouble," rather than ask, "Does this car require much maintenance?" The question form is not used, because the prospect feels that it would encourage the salesperson to respond with a biased opinion or an untruth. The salesperson would probably say that the car doesn't require much maintenance at all. By asking for information indirectly through an objection, the prospect has put the burden on the salesperson to furnish supported information and prove convincingly that the car doesn't require abnormal maintenance.

Answering Objections Removes Barriers to the Sale

Indeed, objections are so important to the interview that the professional sales representative is most afraid of the quiet prospects, who hold questions in their minds and give few clues about their inward resistances. Good sales representatives usually encourage prospects to air their objections in order to find out what barriers stand in the way of the sale.

Objections Are Made for Many Reasons

There are other reasons besides seeking information, attempting to bargain, and trying to terminate the interview that prompt prospects to raise objections. The prospect may not honestly have the time to hear the sales story that particular day. The prospect may not have the money to buy the product, and not wanting to admit this openly, may raise a false objection with little relevance to the real reason for objecting. The prospect may be afraid to make a decision and try to hide this through resistance. This type of resistance can mislead even the experienced salesperson, but in the game of bargaining, buyers as well as salespersons often unconsciously relax their standards of honesty.

The prospect may feel that there is no need for the product or that there is no hurry to buy. For example, Professor James has access to university libraries and may not feel the need for an encyclopedia set for his own use; or the career woman may be convinced that she should keep her old car at least until spring. If there really is an honest lack of money or need, it saves everyone's time if the prospect is qualified early. It must be remembered, however, that most buyers resist buying until they are convinced that the satisfactions to be gained from the product overbalance the money sacrifice necessary to obtain it. Prospects also object because of the risk involved in changing products and because it is natural to resist change. People who have found their needs satisfied for long periods of time by a comparable competitive product naturally can be expected to contest suggestions that they try an unfamiliar and unproven product even if it "may" be better than the one they habitually use. Other prospects object to defend their egos, enhance their self-images, or just because they enjoy putting the salesperson in a bad light. Some have simply developed the habit of objecting.

An Objection May Be an Excuse

Many writers explain that it is an important strategy to find out whether objections are a *real reason* or an *excuse*. Edwin Greif indicates that when prospects say they are too busy, can't afford the product, are not interested, want to think it over, or want to talk it over with someone else, they are probably making an excuse or stalling.[1] The prospect with more specific objections, on the other hand, may be giving a valid reason. A real objection is a barrier to the sale and must be answered satisfactorily.

[1] Edwin C. Greif, *Personal Salesmanship* (Reston, Va.: Reston Publishing, 1974), pp. 245–249.

An excuse should be examined to find why it was used. Excuses can be met by countering the objection with more risk-reducing benefits. A real objection that cannot be answered satisfactorily or overbalanced may become an impasse, which makes it difficult to close the sale.

CONSIDERATIONS IN HANDLING OBJECTIONS

There are several important ideas that will help the sales representative in answering objections: maintaining the proper attitude and interview tone, anticipating and forestalling objections, programming and timing objections, and clarifying objections.

Attitude

An important goal stated in the definition of selling is to reduce the conflict-of-interest situation and create harmony in the interview. Accordingly, sales representatives must have a positive service attitude throughout the presentation and especially when handling resistances and objections. They must always use tact to protect the ego and enhance the self-image of the prospect. There may be a temptation to become a little combative when the prospect raises difficult objections that are aimed at testing the temperament of the salesperson. Your attitude will help you control your body language and the tone of your voice and keep command of the interview. Objections may be designed to test your personality, but consider that the prospect is watching how you play the game of selling; so keep your composure. You may have a sure-fire answer that could put prospects in their place and show them how unnecessary it was to even bring up the issue, but that kind of answer will lose the sale.

Remember always to respect the feelings of prospects and never say anything that would lead to contention or put them in a more opposing position. It is good practice to assure prospects that their objection was a logical and well-conceived observation and compliment them on their intelligence for thinking of it. Sometimes a hesitation before answering will convey to the prospect that they brought up a thoughtful consideration, and the tactic may also help you avoid the combative position. If prospects

"I warn you—I won't be back."

THE SATURDAY EVENING POST

Reprinted from *The Saturday Evening Post* © 1960 The Curtis Publishing Company.

Even when prospects object in a dramatic way, the salesperson should try to maintain interview tone.

see that you can take their resistances, that you won't break your shield of goodwill, and that you are able to maintain a helpful rather than a superior attitude, they will respect you for it.

Interview Tone

Since objections are conflict points, every effort should be made to minimize their effect on interview tone. Answer the objection thoroughly, but don't dwell on it or make it overly important. Be concise and move to more positive interview points, unless you can turn the objection into a big buying reason. If, on the other hand, you overlook the fact that the prospect has even made the objection and proceed without acknowledging it, you are engaging in a risky practice. Prospects may feel that you have not been attentive to needs or that you don't have the answer. They may stop listening to you and let their minds dwell on the unanswered obstacles. Prospects may believe that a weakness in your product offering has been found.

Anticipating and Forestalling Objections

Experience in selling the product will give you a good idea of the kinds of objections that will arise. If you are reasonably sure that the prospect will sooner or later raise a particular objection, you can forestall it by answering it before it is made; or you can be prepared with the best answer available to the objection when it *is* made. Forestalling objections prevents prospects from committing themselves in opposition. Once committed, it is human nature to defend a position. Knowing, for example, that the prospect will question the safety of the smaller car, you can point to the fact that many accidents can be avoided altogether because of the superior maneuverability; or you can furnish statistics to reduce this mental barrier before it is expressed by the prospect. You might even voice the objection for the prospect: "You may wonder about the effect of so much glass in this home on your electricity bill. Be assured that all glass you see is thermal glass designed to reduce heating and cooling expense." You should also be prepared with testimonials, statistics, and other forms of risk-reducing proof to support your answers to anticipated major objections. In this way you will show professionalism. Even though objections are anticipated, avoid the temptation to answer too quickly and without protecting the prospect's feelings.

Programming and Timing Objections

Objections can come at any time during the interview, and two-way communication can become side tracked away from the main issue. During some presentations it is best to use tactful ways to reduce the prospect's tendency to ask questions and ruin interview tone. Demonstrations during which most of the prospect's questions will be answered anyway go smoother without unprogrammed participation. The prospect can be given a writing pad and pencil and encouraged to write down any questions that might come to mind while the uninterrupted demonstration is in progress. Prospects should then, as promised, be given a chance to ask their questions after the demonstration is over. The question and answer part of the interview is thereby controlled by the sales representative and conducted at an ideal time.

Clarifying Objections

Before answering an objection, the sales representative must be sure the objection is completely understood. The prospect may be asked to state it again if it is unclear, or the sales representative may restate it in slightly less objectionable words if the objection has been understood. The prospect may say: "Why is the price for this car so unreasonable?" You might respond by asking *why* the prospect regards the price as "unreasonable." Questions are sometimes a good way to find the root of sales resistance. You might also rephrase the objection: "Are you asking why this car is slightly more expensive than some models in the same size bracket? It is because of the superior quality shown in the following advantageous features." (You then proceed to explain these features.) In most cases it is better to pay attention than it is to draw attention to the objection by having the prospect repeat it or by restating it. If your restatement, however, helps to clarify the objection for both parties and shows prospects that you are concerned about their need for information, it is worth this risk.

ALTERNATIVE WAYS TO HANDLE OBJECTIONS

There are several standard ways of meeting objections that have been proven effective in the field. Each method can be used to answer many different kinds of objections and protect the prospect's ego. These methods are:

- The "yes, but" method
- The boomerang method
- The counterbalance method
- The denial method
- The question method
- The failure-to-hear method

The "Yes, But" Method

The format for the "yes, but" method is to protect the prospect's feelings in the first phrase or sentence but gently to take issue with the statement in the last part of the response. This method exemplifies the right attitude to objection answering, if executed properly. It is also called the indirect denial method, the "yes, however" method, and the "yes, until" method. The opposing conjunction (but, however, until, unless) may be left out altogether without changing the basic strategy of protecting the prospect's feelings initially and then disagreeing. The prospect may say, "I've heard that the fuel injection system on these cars is a real source of trouble."

You might answer, "Yes, although this is a great fuel-saving feature, we did have some problems on our older models until our engineers corrected the defect. You can be assured that you needn't anticipate that kind of trouble with *this* model." Notice that the word "until" is softer than either "but" or "however" in this statement.

In the same spirit you might leave out the connective altogether, and start a new sentence. The prospect says, "I don't like plastic grilles on cars because they have a tendency to crack with age." You might reply, "I know exactly how you feel. I've had garbage cans and water buckets break on me ... this is not the cheap plastic that you and I are accustomed to. This plastic will resist as much impact as certain metals even after it is ten years old. If it does break under a heavy blow, it can be replaced for one-third the cost of metal. And it stays new looking at all times with minimal care." The prospect says, "This suit looks nice, but it is too expensive." You might answer, "Yes, this really is a quality suit, isn't it? It will outlast cheaper suits almost two to one! Considering the executive image it gives you and the longer life, you will be happy with it long after the price is forgotten."

The Boomerang Method

The sales representative using the boomerang method turns the objection into a reason for buying (see Figure 12.1). The prospect says: "We can't afford this machine right now, since we are planning to hire additional staff in the office next month." You might reply, "A new clerk will cost you about $500 per month, while this equipment rents for less than $300 a month. With it, your existing staff can handle your bookkeeping and have time to spare. In addition, the new K-7000 will generate valuable report information for you that will tell you where all accounts stand at any time." Another prospect might say, "This house is too far from town." You could answer, "This house will retain its value for years to come when houses nearer town will be incorporated into the city, be subject to higher taxes, and be in a deteriorating neighborhood. The Oakwood Shopping Center only a mile away has an excellent assortment of stores with reasonable prices." Again, be careful not to make the prospect appear ignorant or dense for raising the objection—the boomerang can wind up hitting *you*.

The Counterbalance Method

In many cases a prospect's objection is valid and cannot be truthfully denied, but in most cases it can be compensated for by some other

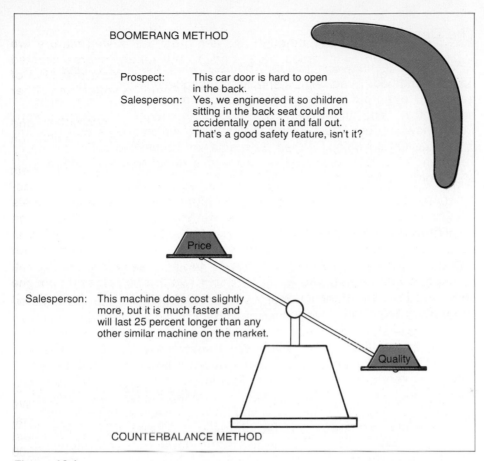

BOOMERANG METHOD

Prospect: This car door is hard to open in the back.

Salesperson: Yes, we engineered it so children sitting in the back seat could not accidentally open it and fall out. That's a good safety feature, isn't it?

Salesperson: This machine does cost slightly more, but it is much faster and will last 25 percent longer than any other similar machine on the market.

Price

Quality

COUNTERBALANCE METHOD

Figure 12.1

overbalancing benefit (see Figure 12.1). The small car may be harder to drive on long highway trips, but it uses less expensive gasoline. Electric ceiling heat may be more expensive to maintain, but it is cleaner and quieter than certain other kinds. National brands of merchandise may have less margin of profit for the retailer, but they are nationally advertised and sales may be greater. The prospect may say, "This typing unit is noisy." You might reply, "While it may make a little more noise, you can remove it to clean it and have much greater flexibility by interchanging type elements." The prospect says, "This house is too far from my work." You could say, "Have you considered that it is within just four blocks of the finest elementary school in town? Your children could walk to school."

The Denial Method

The denial technique should only be used when the prospect leaves you no other method. Even then, it should be used with respect. The prospect says, for example, "I heard that your company is on the verge of bankruptcy." You might reply, "Oh no, sir, someone misinformed you. I can show you our latest financial statement, which proves that our firm is in excellent condition." When prospects are requesting contradiction or verification like this, they may regard a less direct reply as sidetracking an important point.

The Question Method

Questions can be used not only to clarify an objection but also to answer the objection. Sometimes prospects will talk themselves out of the objection when the question method is used. Questions can be used to transfer the responsibility of conversation back to the prospect and allow the sales representative a chance to strategize. "I don't think this car is stylish looking" might be answered with: "What specifically about it makes you say that?" The prospect says, "I can't afford it now." You could say, "If it could save you money every day, could you afford to be without it?" The prospect says, "I'm not interested in offering my customers bankcard service." You say, "If I could show you how you could save more than the service would cost, would you be interested?" The customer says, "I'm too busy to talk to you. See the assistant manager." You might reply, "What I have to offer you will allow you more free time every day. Could you invest just a few minutes to save hours?" The prospect might come out with a strong remark, "I will never buy anything from your company again." You might ask, "Why do you say that, Mr. Templeton?" Whenever the prospect leads with an ambiguous, judgmental statement, a question is suggested for the response. Many times the prospect *expects* you to request an explanation. Through asking the prospect a thoughtful question, you show that you are interested and intend to listen to what the prospect has to say.

The Failure-to-Hear Method

Sometimes prospects offer excuses under their breath or make little comments about which they are not really serious. Salespersons sometimes act as if they never heard the comment or ignore it as if it had not been said. This is poor strategy if the prospect thinks it is really an impor-

Figure 12.2 Methods of Answering Objections

METHOD	STRATEGY
"Yes, but"	Protect the prospect's feelings in the "yes," or agreement response; then gently take issue with the statement.
Boomerang	Turn the objection into a reason for buying, but be careful not to make the prospect appear ignorant for raising the objection.
Counterbalance	Overbalance an objection that cannot be denied with a more important buying benefit.
Denial	When the objection is invalid or when the prospect leaves you no other alternative, tactfully deny the objection.
Question	Use this method to clarify objections and to "answer" objections indirectly.
Failure-to-Hear	When superficial or unimportant comments are made under the prospect's breath, the salesperson may pretend not to hear. This should not be used often, and objections repeated twice should not be ignored.

tant point. If the prospect raises the question again, it is best to meet the objection and handle it in the best way possible. Only superficial comments by prospects should be disregarded. (See Figure 12.2 for a summary of methods of answering objections.)

EXAMPLES OF HANDLING COMMON OBJECTIONS

There are almost too many kinds of objections to classify, but there are some objections that are so common that sales representatives expect to hear them during nearly every interview. You should be prepared to handle these reoccurring objections with responses that work. Customers object to price, particular product attributes, taking time for the interview, not having a need, not having the money to buy, and to making a decision now. (Figure 12.3 shows hurdles that must be met to make the sale.)

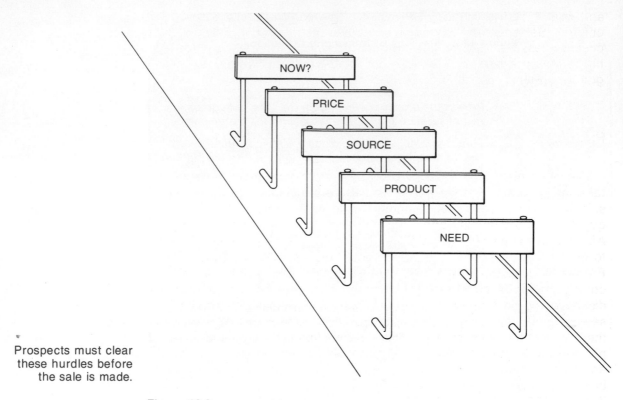

NOW?

PRICE

SOURCE

PRODUCT

NEED

Prospects must clear
these hurdles before
the sale is made.

Figure 12.3

Price

An objection to price can be expected, because to many customers it is a routine way to bargain and perhaps get a better price, and customers expect the salesperson to justify the price if they are interested. Prospects will always think the price is too high until it is overbalanced in their minds by value to be received. This is why questions about specific prices should be postponed until the benefits are understood. Price is only relevant when compared to quality and the useful life of the product. With cost-saving devices or demand-creating programs, cost is only relevant in the light of money to be saved or sales to be made.

Prospects often attempt to bargain by contending that a competitive price is lower. In most cases, it is better to sell the quality of *your* offering rather than make statements like, "Well, I guess they know what their machine is worth." Again, when price is an issue, the customer should be reminded that the offering can be purchased on the installment plan or by rental and that it should be examined with respect to the durability and quality of the product. Prospect: "We can't afford a $10,000 machine." Salesperson: "If you look at it over the life of the machine, it will cost you less than five dollars a working day; and if it can save you from hiring an extra person, it will pay for itself within two years. Isn't that a good long-term investment?"

Product

Like price objections, product objections stem from many reasons and take many forms. Retailers and wholesalers are likely to question the salability of the product to customers, and final consumers are likely to question product quality and suitability to their particular need situation. After all, this is part of the bargaining process, and the salesperson needs to be prepared to substantiate all product claims when objections arise. Frequently, product objections come in the form of an unfavorable comparison with an alternative product or a reference to someone's disappointing past experience. If the prospect is seeking information, the salesperson should furnish proof to reassure. If the objection is real and the product has that deficiency, the weakness should be overbalanced by price or other offering advantages. If the objection is to suitability of use, arrangements should be made to modify the product if possible to fit the buyer's specific need. Fewer objections to product should be encountered if you ask use questions and then recommend the product or products in your line best suited to the buyer's use requirements. Such consideration often forestalls unnecessary opposition, focuses customer attention on the real issues, preserves interview tone, and saves valuable interview time. Examples of product objections and answers are:

Objection: My brother bought a Fastgo outboard motor last summer and has had to have it repaired six times since he bought it.

Answer: Can I talk to him? Repair frequently varies with conditions of use and running time. But this study (hands prospect repair-frequency table) shows that our repair frequency is 20 percent less than our nearest competitor and repairs are rare within the first 500 hours of running time. Your brother's motor is under a two-year guarantee, and we are quite interested if he has had a problem.

Objection: I don't like that color van.

Answer: Come look at our color chart. This model comes in twenty-one different colors and you can select just the color you want.

Objection: Our customers don't ask for your product, and our present brand is moving quite well. Why should I try something new that might not sell?

Answer: Read this letter from Mr. Jacob Goldsmith. He put our product side-by-side with the brand you now carry and reports ours outsold the old type by a 20 percent margin. Will you try the same experiment with no risk to your profits?

Taking Time for the Interview

Since time is money to the busy prospect, the salesperson should be prepared to answer the standard objection, "I just don't have time to see you today," or "I'm too busy." This may be a "put-off" in the form of an excuse, or it may be the truth. If it is the truth, the salesperson usually should respond, "I certainly understand. Would next Friday afternoon at two o'clock be a more suitable time?" or "When would be the best time to see you, Mrs. Hanley? It will only take a few minutes to show you how installation would save you $25 a month on your natural gas bill and make the President happy." After replies like this, the prospect usually reveals whether the first answer was an excuse or not. If it was an excuse, it will likely be followed by another objection like, "To tell the truth, I'm really not interested." In which case the salesperson had better have a good approach answer ready, like, "Would you be interested if I could prove that fifty merchants in this area alone have averaged a $100 a month net with only the investment of some previously wasted store space?" Remember, always respect the prospect's time, and the next time you visit you will be more likely to be heard again.

Not Having a Need

What do you do when the prospect meets you at the door with, "Sorry, we don't need any," or "We are overstocked now"? Again, the best answer may be an attention-getting opening or a question that will make him or her review the need. Perhaps the following responses will give you some ideas:

- Did you know that customers will double their purchases from you the first really warm month of summer?
- How many hammers do you have in stock, Mr. Smith?
- Last week, Mr. John Patterson of Maury City lost his whole house to fire because his fire extinguisher gave out before the fire did. Are

"I'll be brief . . ."

THE SATURDAY EVENING POST

Reprinted by permission of the artist, Joseph Zeis.

Sometimes you can anticipate objections and forestall them before they arise.

you sure the one you have is the right capacity to put out more than a superficial fire?

■ This chart shows the recommended inventory stock according to weekly store volume. Is your present stock adequate according to this?

Not Having the Money to Buy

When the prospect says, "I can't afford it," this usually means, "I don't believe that your product is worth the money you are asking me for it." Even businesspeople will plead that they don't have the money to buy an industrial product that can be justified on the basis of paying for itself in two years in cost savings or extra sales. There are ways to buy products other than the immediate pay-out of current cash. Products can be rented, and products can be bought on the installment plan. This objection immediately suggests that the prospect is not yet sold and needs to be persuaded that the product is worth the sacrifice. For example, the prospect says, "I don't have the money to buy it now," and the salesperson replies, "Just for 10 percent down, we can arrange for you not to have to make a payment until two months from now. Would that help?" or "You can see that this equipment will save you $200 a month. Did you know that you can rent it for only $85 a month?" If the product can be justified in the mind of the consumer as being worth more than the price, a way can usually be found to buy it.

Making a Decision Right Away

Buying emotion and desire can fade if the sales representative fails to close the sale during the interview. It is natural for the prospect to say, "I'd like to think about it," or "I'd like to wait until next week to decide." The person then has time to think of all the other things that can be done with the money, and a competitor may sell him or her before "next week." The salesperson must always be armed with some reason why the prospect should buy now instead of later—the price will increase, the product won't be available, a special is available if you buy now, or you want it to start saving (or making) you money right now. This is one objection you can expect with every interview. If you are selling a one-of-a-kind product, like a particular home or plot of land, a standard answer is, "Someone else may buy it before you have another chance." Even with products that are standard, you can always answer, "I know we have some available today, but we may not tomorrow. If you like it, get it while we have it!" In giving a reason for buying now, don't yield to the temptation to misrepresent or fabricate a reason when none exists to get a quick decision.

SUMMARY

Skill in meeting sales resistance and answering objections is vital in selling. Objections from prospects are natural in the selling process and should be expected and welcomed. The salesperson should, in fact, try to draw out hidden objections so that any barrier to the sale may be dealt with openly. Two main reasons why objections occur are: prospects wish to find out more information without asking questions that might weaken their bargaining positions, and prospects wish to end the interview if they are not interested. The salesperson should try to determine if objections are real or just an excuse. All real objections must be overcome or they remain barriers to the close. Excuses, on the other hand, may be passed over with less attention.

Salespersons should convey a helpful attitude, protect the prospect's feelings, anticipate objections, and determine the real nature of the objection before answering it. Every effort should be made to promote a harmonious interview tone, and the sales representative should not lose control of the interview by showing anger or resentment, even if the prospect exhibits a combative attitude. If you can anticipate objections before they arise and answer them satisfactorily, you may prevent prospects from committing themselves to opposition and defending their negative positions.

There are six standard techniques for answering objections. The "yes, but" method uses the strategy of agreeing with prospects initially to protect their feelings and then taking issue gently without antagonizing. The boomerang method turns an objection into a reason to buy. The counterbalance method overbalances the objection with a stronger benefit. The denial method meets the objection head on and should be used only in certain circumstances. The question method can be used to find out the motive behind the objection. The failure-to-hear method should be used only in the case where the objection is just an excuse or is superficial.

Objections to price, product features, buying now, paying for the product, and taking time for the interview are common. Prospects will also tell you that they don't need the product. An innovative sales representative should have several good answers for each of these objections and never be caught off guard when they come up in the interview.

REVIEW QUESTIONS

1. How are answering objections and closing the sale related?

2. What is it about the nature of the selling situation that makes prospects raise objections?

3. What are some other reasons prospects raise objections?

4. What is meant by "anticipating" and "forestalling" objections?

5. How can sales representatives clarify objections?

6. Name and give an example of each method of answering objections. Which do you think is the best method? Why?

APPLICATION QUESTIONS

1. Give several examples of excuses that are not real reasons for refusing to buy.

2. Give words for interview attitudes that provide the right interview atmosphere and will help you answer objections without being offensive to the prospect. Give words for bad interview attitudes that make it hard for you to answer objections without making the prospect mad.

3. Identify the objections that are expected in nearly every interview. Select a product and make up standard objections and answers based on the product you select and the objection raised.

4. Give several ways to answer an objection to buying now.

5. Cut out three advertisements for automobiles, articles of clothing, houses, or other products. List two objections that might be raised for each product. Supply a good answer to each objection or let another student supply the answers.

INCIDENTS

12–1

Roosevelt Watson sells Sun-Trap solar heating systems dealerships. He is calling on a contractor and building-materials dealer, Harry Summers, in northern California. The secretary has admitted him.

Rosy: Mr. Summers, I'm Rosy Watson with Sun-Trap Corporation, and I would like to explain the profit opportunities in our solar heating systems dealerships.

Summers: Rosy, I'm glad to meet you, but I'm not interested in solar heating, and I'm very busy today.

Rosy: In twenty minutes I can show you how you can earn profits of up to $40,000 per year. You are in a better position than anyone in this area to profit from this opportunity. Can you give me just twenty minutes?

Summers: Okay, but solar energy is new right now, and solar energy storage is too short to take care of total energy needs.

Rosy: Yes, it is true that storage with water systems is too short, but our solid storage batteries can hold heat and supply heat much longer, making the system practical.

Summers: It still is not effective as a sole supply of building heat.

Rosy: It's true. The system does work best with other heating systems, but it can pay for itself in five years for most of your customers when used as an auxiliary system. It lasts a lifetime . . .

Summers: But it takes up a lot of space and looks ugly with conventionally styled homes.

Rosy: Many people are proud of their solar furnaces. It is a status symbol standing for energy conservation and the look of the future. While not everyone may want to install it, you would want to have it available for those customers who need and want it, wouldn't you?

Summers: It sure makes the initial cost of houses higher, and as you know, people feel houses are too high out here anyway.

Rosy: Energy costs are going up every day too, and with the threat of water shortages affecting hydroelectric power, there is the possibility that electric heat may be shut off for periods.

Summers: Even if it were a good investment, I don't have extra capital to invest in a dealership right now.

Rosy: We have a plan that requires an investment of only $5,000 and having on hand only five complete units. Last year a dealer in southern California made $30,000 by just keeping a minimum stock and suggesting these auxiliary units to his customers. We can supply you rapidly with additional units in case you have a sudden big demand for them.

Summers: It would cut my sales of standard heating units.

Rosy: He found that his standard heating unit sales did not decrease since the solar system is an auxiliary system.

Summers: Well, leave your folders and I'll think about it—give me a few weeks to consider it.

Rosy: We feel that you have the best dealership in the area, but it is important to Sun-Trap to get a dealer in this area soon. Call Mr. Guy Malon in Sacramento. He is a dealer who can tell you all about the extra profits the furnace generates. We don't want to approach your competitors with this offer, but we do need to have your consideration and answer soon. Could I see you next week and until then not offer it to anyone else in this area?

Summers: Well . . . where can I see a unit in operation?

QUESTIONS

1. Evaluate Rosy's use of objection-answering techniques.

2. How many methods did he use?

3. Did he use them effectively?

4. What should he have done better?

12–2

Jerry Nunn sells automobiles for the Riverside Agency, and a customer is looking at one of the medium-sized models.

Jerry: Hello. I'm Jerry Nunn. This is a nice car, isn't it? Would you like to drive it?

Customer: No, I'm just looking. I like Merlin automobiles, but my neighbor has one and it stalls on him often and he has trouble getting it started again. I've heard that most Merlin cars have that trouble.

Jerry: I never heard that one before. Maybe it needs a tune-up.

Customer: He got a tune-up and it still didn't help the stalling. He likes the car except for that. Another thing that worries me about Merlins is that last year they had to recall quite a few because of a steering difficulty. Has that been corrected in this year's model?

Jerry: Yes ... uh ... I feel sure that they have corrected that. Why don't you drive it, and you'll see that it has good steering response.

Customer: Well, I guess I'll give it a try if you'll go with me.

Jerry: Sure, here are the keys.

Customer: (*After getting into the car*) I wish there were a little more head room. I have the seat all the way back and I feel as though I'm almost touching the ceiling!

Jerry: You just have to get used to a new car. They all sit differently until you drive them a while.

(*The car starts sluggishly.*)

Customer: It doesn't start too well, does it?

Jerry: It's just been sitting for a couple of days and needs running.

(*The car runs fairly well on the demonstration drive except for one hesitation at a stop sign upon acceleration after the stop.*)

Customer: It almost stopped on me. What do you think is wrong?

Jerry: Well ... you know these new cars are idled down so much in order to get better mileage out of them.

Customer: Yeah, but I've heard that this model gets much worse mileage than the ratings on the sticker.

Jerry: It depends on how you drive it, but you're right. All new cars get about four miles per gallon less than the government ratings for normal driving.

(*Back on the car lot.*)

Customer: What would you really take for this model? I see you have some advertised for $7,295.

Jerry: The advertised cars don't have power windows and FM radios like this one. Do you want to make a straight cash deal, or do you have something to trade in?

Customer: Yes, I have something to trade in and it's over there (*pointing to his car*). What would it be worth?

Jerry: Um . . . the body looks like it's in bad shape. Assuming that it runs well, we could sell the new Merlin to you for $7,000 and your old car.

Customer: I would just be giving you my car at that price!

Jerry: Well, it's seven years old you know. Why don't you sell it yourself if you think it's worth more?

Customer: It looks like you want too much for your car, and you won't give me anything for mine!

Jerry: But . . . we have to make a profit, you see.

Customer: Well then, you can just make your profit on someone else! Thank you for showing me the car. (*Customer leaves.*)

QUESTIONS

1. Classify and identify each objection raised by the customer and point out Jerry's mistakes in answering.

2. Suggest better answers for each of the customer's objections that you feel deserves a better, more thoughtful answer.

12–3

Mel Franklin sells business forms to commercial customers. The new purchasing agent for Cenco Corporation, Dexter Harrihan, transferred Cenco's business to a competitor in spite of Mel's best and most courteous efforts. Mel could not understand why Harrihan went to so much trouble to change suppliers (and consequently forms) so quickly after becoming purchasing agent—the competitor's forms were no cheaper. After eight calls over a period of a year, Mel confronted Harrihan directly and asked him what was wrong. Harrihan simply explained that Cenco was now ordering from a new supplier and that there was no reason to change back to the old.

When Mel called on Cenco again four months later, he found a new purchasing agent, Robert Linton, and was able to secure a $400 order. Linton was very cordial and explained that he had replaced Harrihan, who had been fired when it was learned that he was purchasing only from salespersons who gave him a kickback.

Did Mel handle the situation correctly?
Did he wait too long to ask Harrihan what was wrong?
What would you have done?

13 Closing the Sale

Closing is the climax of the sale, the part of the selling process that directly affects the outcome. All other efforts can be carefully accomplished, and the prospect can be mentally prepared to accept your offer, but you can lose the opportunity to sell by failing to close or by a weak closing effort. If you are a good prospector, a few customers will recognize a need and consider your product. If you are a good approacher, the prospect will listen to your presentation. If you make a good presentation, you will create a desire for the product. Then, if you are a good closer, you will sell the product. No one expects to get an order every time a prospect is visited, but a good closer gives the prospect a real opportunity to buy whenever an appropriate buying circumstance is recognized. The essentials of becoming a professional closer are:

- Developing a good closing attitude
- Timing your close
- Having command of many closing techniques
- Learning to handle recurring closing problems
- Customizing the close
- Knowing what to do after the close

DEVELOPING A GOOD CLOSING ATTITUDE

The sales representative should be confident, enthusiastic, and sensitive at the time of the close. Whether you are aware of it or not, you project

333

your attitude to the prospect, your attitude can cause you to lose the sale, and there are ways you can improve your attitude.

You Project Your Attitude

You project your attitude by what you do and what you say. If you have confidence that you will get the order, you will convey this to your prospect by the tone of your voice, the words you choose, and your nonverbal communications. Buyers will feel that you believe you are giving them a fair offer and expect them to buy. Your attitude alone will convey that buying is the reasonable thing to do. On the other hand, if you begin to perspire from fear as you approach the big moment, and if your voice breaks and your hand trembles, your prospect will receive negative signals. Prospects may think; "You are about to ask me for the order and you're afraid. Perhaps you are not accustomed to getting orders because your product is bad." At best, the prospect's buying mood and enthusiasm are diverted to concern over what is wrong with you, and the prospect may be embarrassed for you, because of your inexperience. Yes, it *is* hard to avoid showing concern, particularly when some single sales can mean over a thousand dollars in commissions for certain salespersons. Nevertheless, the professional learns to expect positive results and channels emotions into optimism instead of fear.

You may be loaded with confidence and enthusiasm but still turn your prospect off by being insensitive. The prospect may have been sending you verbal and nonverbal signals, but you have been dominating the conversation without sensing that something is wrong. Perhaps it is an unanswered question. Perhaps you are making such a grand finale of the close that the prospect has become apprehensive and resistive. Perhaps the prospect thinks you are just going through a routine without any concern for his or her feelings. Closing the sale is a time when the salesperson should be most sensitive to feedback clues.

Your Attitude Can Make You Lose

Your attitude not only affects your prospect, it also affects your actions. Your attitude may be so bad that you fail to ask for the order until your prospect has already been sold by your competitor. Sales representatives fail to ask for the order because they are afraid of being rejected or disappointed. They may be afraid that if prospects say "no," they will be committed to maintaining a negative position. Some salespersons have deep reservations about asking another person to make a decision. Just remember that when you leave an interview unfinished because you have failed to close, you have been unfair to your prospect and unfair to yourself. You have taken opportunity away from your prospect and allowed a potential buyer to lose the buying mood. Your customer may fall prey to a competitor who might sell an inferior product for more money. You have also been unfair to and taken opportunity away from yourself, because you risk losing the sale, thereby wasting all previous selling efforts. Your company is certainly a loser. Suppose you come back to sell this prospect and invest $200 more in effort—you could have used that effort to call on other prospects. Few sales representatives make the mistake of closing too soon or too often. Most make the mistake of closing too late.

Ways to Improve Your Attitude

You can improve your closing attitude through belief in yourself and your product; through knowledge of your products, prospects, and selling techniques; and through preinterview practice. If you really believe you are helping the prospect by selling your product, you can develop confidence and enthusiasm. If you *don't* believe this, you are going to have to be an excellent actor to hide your feelings both verbally and nonverbally. To increase your belief in your product, imagine how satisfied the prospect could be using the product. You can also increase your belief in yourself through self-suggestion or reprogramming yourself as suggested in Chapter 4. If you study your product's benefits and your selling techniques (especially closing techniques) thoroughly, you should be able to go into the interview with closing confidence. Preplanning and preexperiencing an interview in your imagination before you go into it and reviewing the types of closes that would probably be appropriate under the circumstances should give you more self-assurance. It should also allow you to devote more attention to being sensitive to your prospect. It is normal for even experienced sales representatives to feel pressure in closing, but the very good ones have learned to look forward to this exciting point in the sale and channel their emotions into enthusiasm.

TIMING YOUR CLOSE

When you ask for the order is just as important as *how* you ask. A good salesperson has to know how to tell closing time (see the closing clock,

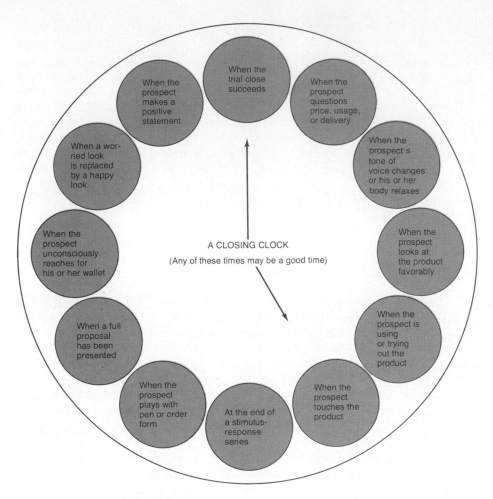

When the trial close succeeds

When the prospect makes a positive statement

When the prospect questions price, usage, or delivery

When a worried look is replaced by a happy look

When the prospect's tone of voice changes or his or her body relaxes

When the prospect unconsciously reaches for his or her wallet

A CLOSING CLOCK
(Any of these times may be a good time)

When the prospect looks at the product favorably

When a full proposal has been presented

When the prospect is using or trying out the product

When the prospect plays with pen or order form

At the end of a stimulus-response series

When the prospect touches the product

Figure 13.1   A Closing Clock

Figure 13.1). While there may be one best time to close during every sales situation, there are usually several times when closing would be appropriate. The keys to sensing closing time are trial closes, verbal closing signals, and nonverbal closing signals.

Trial Closes

Good closers are said to close early and many times in a single interview, but how soon and how often you close depends on what you are selling and the receptiveness of your prospect. If you are selling a product that your prospective customers can understand and they look receptive, it may be appropriate to try an early close. If, on the other hand, you are selling a complex and expensive product that your prospect has difficulty understanding, you should try to resolve buyer questions before you attempt a final close. If you feel that all important buyer questions—the need, the product, the source, the price, and the "time to buy" are resolved, try a trial close, even if you don't receive a definite closing signal. After all, if you keep trying to find the perfect moment to close, it may have already passed.

A trial close is an attempt to find out if the prospect is ready to buy without actually insisting on a final decision on the total offer. You might ask how interested the prospect is in the color or some other minor point. You might say, "Do you like this beige or the blue one best?" If the prospect shows real interest, even on this minor point, an order-clinching close would be your next step. "Could we deliver a blue one for you this Wednesday?" If the trial close fails to get even a partial commitment from the prospect, continue to sell benefits and attempt another trial close after you have given more reason to buy.

You may not say anything to attempt a trial close. You might simply take some nonverbal action that would induce the prospect to volunteer an opinion. You might run your fingers back and forth over a carpet sample watching the prospect's expression or waiting for a verbal comment. The trial close is a method of leaving yourself the option of easily and harmoniously continuing the interview. If there is any barrier in your prospect's mind, the trial close may bring it out. If the customer should say, as you run your hand over the carpet sample, "I'll bet that would feel good on my bare feet," you have induced your closing signal. If the response is: "That would probably show dirt," you have another barrier to the sale to overcome before you try another trial close, but at least the barrier has been identified.

Verbal Closing Signals

Every good salesperson learns to recognize both verbal and nonverbal closing signals. If prospects ask questions that indicate interest, such as inquiries about price, delivery, or care of the product, they are sending positive closing signals. When the usage, the warranty, or the storage (placement) of the product is questioned, a trial close is indicated. Any compliment to the product, the company, or the sales representative may signal a close. Objections to product features that are really questions and can be turned into a positive feature benefit may also merit a close. The prospect may say, for example, "I'll bet that wouldn't last me five years." Your reassurance that it will last much longer might be followed by a close.

Nonverbal Closing Signals

Nonverbal signals can include practically any change in voice, posture, or expression that indicates a change in attitude. The prospect may simply raise or lower her voice, or lean forward or backward in her chair indicating a change of mind. Suppose a prospect who has been crossing his arms or legs uncrosses them and opens his hands. In body language he is indicating a more receptive frame of mind. Some sales representatives pay particular attention to the face. When the prospect's face relaxes, they try a trial close. Of course, smiling, affirmative nods, or looking at the product admiringly indicates a ready-to-buy attitude, especially if these gestures have been absent before. Attempts to use or operate the product are positive signals. Touching or handling the product with respect nearly always indicates interest. Resisting your efforts to leave or collect sales materials may be the signal. Picking up a pen or reading the sales contract usually has significance. Again, look for any change that could mean the prospect is becoming more receptive or less defensive. When prospects change their minds, they usually change their verbal and nonverbal signals (see Photo 13.1).

You must understand that there are times when it is not good to try a close. You may show insensitivity by asking for the order when the prospect has practically no information about a technical product, has

Photo 13.1

This prospect is leaning forward, playing with his pen, and exhibiting a favorable facial expression. Perhaps he is ready for you to ask him for the order.

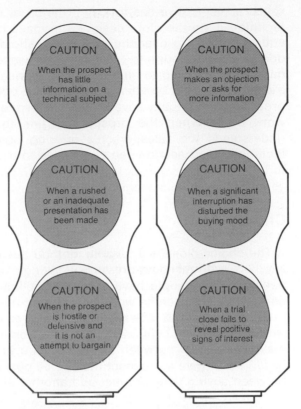

In these instances something more should be added before you attempt to close again.

Figure 13.2 Closing Caution Lights

indicated great disinterest or hostility that can't be interpreted as an attempt to bargain, or has major questions unresolved. To close on a negative indication without resolving the problem is to be unresponsive to the prospect's need for more information. If the prospect looks worried and says: "I don't understand how to change programs on this machine," show how easy it is and *then* close. Sales representatives seldom have a problem recognizing the wrong times to close, but they often fail to recognize real closing opportunities (see Figure 13.2).

HAVING COMMAND OF MANY CLOSING TECHNIQUES

Buying involves risk and prospects don't like to make risky decisions. Most of the time the prospect has a lot more to lose from buying than the sales representative has to lose if the order is not signed. Good closing techniques are therefore designed to make it easier for buyers to decide and to help them over the buying threshold. Closing methods are seldom powerful enough to sway the unconvinced or resistant prospect who has been subjected to an incomplete or weak sales presentation. While trial closes should be attempted early and often in the interview (for most products) and usually several times after the prospect says "no," closes work better when the prospect begins to send closing signals and understands the salesperson's offering benefits. The tested methods included in this section can all be used to make it easier for the prospect to buy.

Choice Close

The choice close is a favorite method because it leads the prospect to say "yes" without heavy pressure. Making choices is reasonable, everyday behavior, and people have a natural inclination to express their preference. "Which machine would you prefer, the one with a tape recorder or the one without the tape recorder?" The customer will tell you "The one with the tape," and you have led the customer right into the sale. Always make the choice between something you have and something else you have. Never give a prospect the choice between buying or not buying or between buying your product and another alternative.

Choice closes often bring positive results.

"Oh, I think one will be enough."

THE SATURDAY EVENING POST

Reprinted by permission of the artist, Joseph Zeis.

You might give a choice between two or three different styles, colors, features, models, or amounts. You should always narrow down the choice by recommending that the selection be made between two or three products. Some ice cream parlors offer two dozen different flavors, and patrons are sometimes confused by the decision range. This confusion is increased when complex, high-value, or style products are involved, so make sure the choice is among a few *desirable* products. If the prospect has trouble deciding, you may be asked to recommend the choice you feel is best. You might say, "Why don't you take this one. I honestly believe it's best for you."

Remember that a series of choices by the customer on color, features, and amounts leads to a specific product and the sale.

Minor-Points Close

No one likes to make big decisions, so the sales representative who can get the prospect to make decisions on minor points can effectively lead up to acceptance of the total offer. This is a natural method to use with the choice method in getting the decision. Once prospects have committed themselves on one or a number of minor points, it becomes harder for them to back out of making a major choice. The sales representative might ask, "If you were to buy a car, what color would you want? Would you want tinted or regular glass? Do you want bucket seats or standard? Vinyl or plush interior?" The prospect, after expressing preference on all these points, will find it easier to accept the whole car. You want the prospect to establish a mental pattern of making selections and commitments.

The Assumptive Close

The sales representative assumes that the prospect is going to buy, and the prospect must consciously resist in order not to buy. You may get out the order blank or point to the signature line or start processing the sale; and if the prospect doesn't stop you, he or she has decided, without having to make a verbal commitment, to buy. You may say, "Do you like this gold one?" If the prospect agrees, you can start preparing the papers for signature assuming the sale is made. The assumptive close works best if you really do have the attitude that the prospect will buy and you express this in your nonverbal communications and your words. You might say, "When you own this house, you will enjoy this view of the lake." While it may be unwise to be too presumptuous at the start of the interview, gradually assume that the prospect will accept as you furnish more and more benefits and you see that you are not offending by this tactic.

Summary Close

When the presentation is nearing the climax, it is good to summarize all of the benefits the prospect will enjoy from accepting the offering. This repetition is allowable and prepares prospects to make decisions, particularly if there are many benefits and the ones that mean the most have been emphasized. "This tree is hardy in this climate. Its roots go far below the surface and won't bother you on top of the ground. The leaves do not have to be raked but will rot and make your soil rich, and it is not susceptible to most tree diseases. This tree will furnish you with shade and maintain a symmetrical shape. Can we plant it in your yard this afternoon?" Sometimes with sophisticated prospects you might use a more balanced summary containing a few disadvantages in what is called a "T"-account close or balance-sheet close (see Figure 13.3). You might list the benefits on one side of a sheet of paper and the disadvantages on the other side, showing that the advantages outweigh the disadvantages. The prospect, seeing the logic and fairness of this method, can mentally justify signing the order.

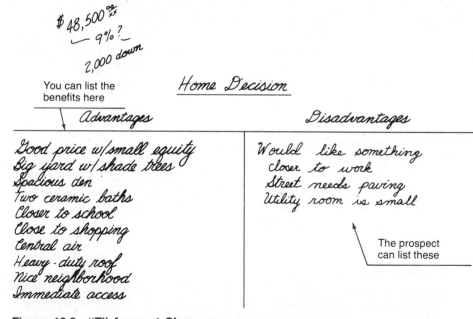

Figure 13.3 "T"-Account Close

Standing-Room-Only Close

One of the biggest barriers to buying is the option of putting off the decision until later. Perhaps the strongest support for buying is the knowledge that the product is so good that it is scarce, and it's possible to lose the opportunity to buy because "everybody wants it and is buying it up." The Standing-Room-Only close (SRO) not only gives a strong reason for buying now, but it supports the prospect's decision by indicating that if everybody else is buying it, it must be good. This close works especially well on one-of-a-kind items like houses, farms, and antiques. You indicate that the prospect may not be able to get the same offer later. You may say, "Another couple was looking at this home, and they said they were coming back this afternoon to let me know what they decided. It is an excellent buy, so I'd advise you to take it now. It may not be here tomorrow" or "We have one demonstrator left in this model at 20 percent off. If you like it, buy it!" or "You won't be able to find a lot like this ever again. There are only three left on the waterfront, and the price could double in two years, even if you should decide to sell it."

Special-Deal Close

Perhaps your presentation has been good, but your prospect is still undecided after you have tried to close several times. The prospect wants to wait and decide later. If you can, you might make a special offer to tip the scales. "If you will order this color TV today, we will sell you an aerial at wholesale price and install it free. This is in addition to giving you the break in price we have already discussed" or "This week only our company is giving a $200 rebate on compact cars. Won't you let us order this model you like now and take advantage of this saving?"

Closing on Resistance

If you can turn the prospect's objection into a reason for buying, you can close on it. Suppose the prospect says, "I'm too busy to change over my office to a mechanized accounting system." You can close after assuring the prospect that even while the system is being changed, bills will go out much faster. Suppose the prospect says, "I don't have the money to buy." You might reply, "Your labor savings of $60 each month will more than cover the payments of $50 a month. Give us your order today, and you can start enjoying this extra profit next month." Suppose the prospect says, "I like it, but I want a compact with automatic transmission." You might reply, "We can get you this model with automatic transmission. Which color would you like?"

Stimulus-Response Close

The stimulus-response strategy has already been treated in an earlier chapter. In this close the salesperson may ask a series of leading questions or get agreement on several minor points before closing. If the prospect is programmed to say "yes," to say "no" to the close would require the prospect to willfully resist the pattern of saying "yes."

Success-Story Close

The salesperson can tell the prospect about a customer who had the same problem and solved it by buying the product. By giving specific details such as names and events in the narrative, the salesperson enables prospects to put themselves in the place of the satisfied customer who bought. It seems natural to follow the example and buy. "Sam Allison thought the same as you do about compacts but bought one because of the gas mileage. Because his car was more maneuverable, he was able to avoid a head-on collision with a big truck. He says he feels as safe in his little car now as he did in his big gas user. You will be delighted too, with this peppy smaller model. Can we fill it up and let you drive out in it?"

The Contingent Close

In the presentation, the sales representative makes the sale dependent on proving some point to the prospect. You might say, "If I can show you how this equipment can pay for itself in two years, will you buy it?" You then proceed to outline proof based on the cost and productivity of the machine. The prospect may feel the obligation to disprove your claims or buy. An aluminum-siding sales representative may say, "If I can prove to your satisfaction that this siding will save you enough in paint and electricity to pay for itself three times over in the next ten years, will you order it?" Or the car sales representative might ask, "If I can get you $1,000 for your present car, will you invest in this new model?" Such contingent statements set up easy closes if the prospect agrees.

The Turnover Close

Sometimes when a salesperson and his or her manager visit a prospect together (or a junior salesperson and a senior salesperson), the prospect may not respond to the closing efforts of one of the team. The junior

Figure 13.4   Summary of Closing Techniques

TECHNIQUE	EXPLANATION
Choice Close	Give customers a limited choice and lead them into the sale
Minor-Points Close	Decisions on minor points are easier to obtain and lead to the acceptance of the total package
Assumptive Close	Actions assuming the sale is made downplay the significance of making a buying decision
Stimulus-Response Close	A series of leading questions makes it easier for the prospect to say yes when asked for the order
Summary Close	Summarize benefits before asking for the order
"T"-Account Close	A summary close on paper, arranged in balance-sheet fashion
Standing-Room-Only Close	A statement suggesting that the opportunity to buy is limited because demand is great and few are left
Special-Deal Close	A "special" offer is made to get prospect to buy now
Success-Story Close	Prospect is told of a buyer who had a similar need or problem who solved it happily by buying the product
Closing on Resistance	Answer the objection or turn the problem into a benefit and then ask for the order or close using any of the closing methods
Contingent Close	Get an agreement by the prospect to buy if the salesperson can substantiate the benefits promised or the contingency happens as predicted
Turnover Close	Turn the closing over to another person present, who has a better chance to make the sale
Ask for the Order	Simply ask for the order directly or indirectly; this can be straightforward and honest
Trial Close	This is usually a question or a nonverbal action designed to elicit some commitment on the part of the buyer without harming the chances of continuing with the interview
Pretend-to-Leave Close	The salesperson pretends to leave but "just happens to remember" another benefit or special offer after the prospect has relaxed sales resistance

sales representative, for example, may turn the prospect over to the senior by saying something like, "Mr. Robbins is more familiar with that application than I am." Under usual circumstances, however, it is best for the team leader who has presented most of the selling points to close. There is often an interruption in interview mood during a turnover.

Ask for the Order

Asking for the order can be the simplest and most natural of all closing methods. This should not be done in a blunt manner like, "Sign the order." The word "sign" can frighten prospects and make the decision seem so legally binding, and, of course, you never order a prospect to do anything. It is better to be a bit indirect, like, "Is there any reason why you shouldn't affirm this order and allow us to get this to you as soon as possible?" or "If you will write your name here, you will start realizing these savings right away," or "Since this will pay for itself within three years, will you authorize us to deliver it to you immediately?" Remember that prospects *expect* you to ask for the order because you are a salesperson. (For a summary of closing techniques see Figure 13.4, p. 345.)

LEARNING TO HANDLE CLOSING PROBLEMS

Common closing problems confronting the sales representative include: leading up to the close in the presentation; handling the uninvited guest; getting around "no's"; and introducing the order form and getting the signature.

Leading Up to the Close in the Presentation

Everything you do during the presentation should lead up to the close. The entire interview tone should promote harmony and lessen the feeling of pressure and tension. Even if the stimulus-response strategy is not consciously used, verbal agreements and affirmative nods from the prospect should be encouraged by leading questions. Objections should be answered and barriers to the sale such as inadequate information should be overcome. Prospect risks in buying should be minimized through assurances. The salesperson may get the prospect to agree that if a barrier to the sale is removed, then the prospect will buy. Remove the barrier or answer the objection and ask for the order. Avoid hasty presentations.

Handling the Uninvited Guest

The sales interview should be held in as private a place as possible. If another person comes in and interrupts the presentation just before the close, the mood of the presentation may be lost. Worse than that, the third party having not been present to learn the benefits of the offering may say something to make the "ready-to-buy" prospect reconsider and cool off. A couple had almost decided to buy a carpet for their dining room when one of their friends interrupted and said she thought the carpet would look out of place between two different colors of existing carpet. They didn't buy. If there is no way you can keep the third party from taking part, direct a little of your selling effort to him or her and use a summary close. If everyone is not on your side when you ask for the order, you can easily lose the sale (see Photo 13.2).

Getting Around "No's"

Prospects know they can say "no" many times and change their minds and say "yes." After they say "yes" once, they're committed. So "no" is

Photo 13.2

If necessary, direct a little of your selling effort to the third party, and use a summary close.

the most flexible and safest position for the prospect and the one with the most bargaining potential. The prospect understands that a few "no's" may soften you up and get a better trade-in or a better price. Prospects actually *expect* you to continue in most circumstances and you'll never be a good salesperson if you leave after the first "no." Good sales representatives pretend that the "no" is not heard and continue with other positive selling benefits. This is why you should always keep some selling benefits in reserve to use if the first attempt to close fails. You can keep going beyond each "no" if you still have something else to say. One tactic after a particularly meaningful "no" is to pretend you are leaving and say something like this, "Oh, yes, I forgot to tell you, this equipment is subject to a price increase next week of 10 percent. You can save $100 by buying today, and you can't buy a finer desk computer for the money!"

Introducing the Order Form and Getting the Signature

The best practice is to introduce the order form early in the presentation, so customers can get used to it, and it will not weaken your close. Making a decision is hard enough, but "signing" a legal contract is a real commitment, and you don't want to make it easier for your prospect to back out later by saying, "You can cancel if you change your mind." Try to provide a proper closing atmosphere, so that buyers will not feel they are being pressured into signing. An "X" near the signature line and pointing to the signature line is good suggestive psychology. As mentioned earlier, using a statement such as "Just put your name here, and we can have it in the hands of your secretary by next week," may be better than using the more legal term "sign here" or "put your signature here," which may sound more formal and binding.

CUSTOMIZING THE CLOSE

You can have a decided competitive advantage over the average salesperson if you have the right closing attitudes, if you know when to close, if you understand several good closing techniques, and if you can handle closing problems. Expert closers, however, must also select the most appropriate closing method to use in each selling situation. While the application of closing methods is largely learned through selling experience, certain writers have contributed insights into matching closing methods with the following situations:

- Closing by type of prospect
- Closing purchasing agents
- Closing in systems and industrial selling
- Closing when not in the presence of the prospect

Closing by Type of Prospect

Prospects are different, and what may be perfect for one may not work well on another. Alan Schoonmaker and Douglas Lind contend that prospects can be divided into "dominant people," "dependent people," and "detached people."[1] Dominant people are identified by their attempts to assert themselves over you and by their desire for esteem. The walls of their offices are crowded with diplomas, awards, and trophies that show their accomplishments. They would prefer to be looked up to than to be accepted as a friend. They will continually try you to see if you are a good sales representative, and if their attempts to "test" you by interrupting and controlling the sales situation succeed in revealing that you are not professional, they will write you off as a weakling. Dominant people expect you to be seasoned and firm. They expect you to ask for the order often and may not buy until you prove your selling maturity by closing the sale several times.[2] You would probably use a direct close or a pretend-to-be-leaving-and-then-return-with-another-point close on dominant types but not assumptive or minor-points closes.

Dependent people are friendly, and they try to identify with you and be nice to you. They are warm and thoughtful and their offices convey a relaxed nonformal atmosphere. Their offices may abound with pictures of family or acquaintances and not reflect neatness or coldness. Such prospects are gracious and hospitable and expect you to be friendly and exhibit the social graces in return.[3] The strategy with these prospects is to minimize the closing decision as much as you can. Use choice, minor-point, and assumptive closes with this type. Statements like "Shall we order five boxes then?" work well with dependent people.

Detached people, according to Schoonmaker and Lind, are very cold, businesslike, and unfriendly—and they don't want you to be overly friendly or domineering. They are interested in facts and logic. They are not interested in small talk or your attempts to establish rapport. Like most introverts they like to position themselves at a comfortable distance from

[1] Alan N. Schoonmaker and Douglas B. Lind, "One Custom-Made Close Coming Up," in *Closing the Sale* (special report), *Sales & Marketing Management*, 118, no. 8 (June 13, 1977).

[2] *Ibid.*

[3] *Ibid.*

you. Their offices are neat but cold, with very little on the walls. They don't like emotions and prefer rational arguments. Don't use pressure selling with this type but support all product claims with evidence. Give them reasons for acting now. The "T"-account or balance-sheet close is an ideal close to use with such prospects.[4]

Charles Roth in *Secrets of Closing Sales* writes that it is important to set your talking pace to correspond with that of the prospect. He advises that the indecisive buyer and the silent prospect be pushed a little harder than the others and that you compliment the egotist and listen to the griper in setting up for the close.[5] The important thing for the salesperson is to be conscious of using different closes appropriately.

Closing Purchasing Agents

You should assume that most purchasing agents are seasoned buyers and that many who see sales representatives day-in and day-out have been subject to good closing techniques by many professionals. While purchasing agents may not always be high-ranking executives, they are nearly always experienced. Barry Hersker and Thomas Stroh write that these expert buyers put sales representatives into three classes—"the top closers, the mediocrats, and the bottom rung."[6] Top closers give good service to purchasing agents. They know their product applications and their competition, they see nearly all buying contacts in a company with the knowledge of the purchasing agent, and they bend over backwards to fill every request and need of the buying company. They are eager for business and close more sales. The "mediocrats" give ample service, but the *buyer* has to be the creative one, shoulder the hard work, and not expect too much. The "bottom rung" consists of those salespeople who do not study the prospective firm before calling, make excessive promises in order to close, waste time, are unfair to competition, and won't listen to find out the buyer's problem before rendering a solution. Professional buyers get rid of these people quickly and do not grant reinterviews.[7] With professional buyers the close is not as important as the selling-service style.

Purchasing agents are trained not to overbuy and purchase higher

[4] *Ibid.*

[5] Charles B. Roth, *Secrets of Closing Sales* (Englewood Cliffs, N.J.: Prentice-Hall, 1953), pp. 57–63.

[6] Barry J. Hersker and Thomas F. Stroh, "The Purchasing Agent Is No Patsy," in *Closing the Sale* (special report), *Sales & Marketing Management,* 118, no. 8 (June 13, 1977).

[7] *Ibid.*

quality goods than the company needs, so many sales representatives oversell quality.[8] It is best to listen and close by recommending a quality that is just good enough to meet the purpose of the buying firm. Since purchasing agents are more educated and sophisticated than ever before, they expect you to ask for the order but to lead up to the close in a professional way and build a good case for buying.

Closing in Systems and Industrial Selling

Systems and industrial salespersons often sell complicated, high-unit value products to a buying team of many people, and negotiations for a period of many months usually precede the closing or loss of the sale. Selling strategy may entail making contact with and persuading several persons in the prospective firm who might have influence on the buying decision. Frank Burge advises that the top executive is the place to start, because the top person can get the representative in to see everyone who can help with the study of present operations necessary to assess needs.[9] The systems sales representative who is busy working within the firm's operating structure to lay the groundwork for the proposal and the close usually wins out over the less aggressive competitor who is unwilling to work within the firm's structure.

In industrial selling the salesperson does not concentrate on the close. On expensive and complex items the primary focus is on a mutual understanding that the product is right for the particular application. According to Charles Bergman, the industrial buyer feels a great weight of uncertainty and risk when deciding to commit capital funds. He advises sales representatives to root out hidden objections and concerns and deal with them.[10] The close for industrial products should come as a matter of course after a series of low-risk decisions diminishes the apparent uncertainties of the final decision. He maintains that some good industrial salespersons do not ever ask for the order at all, that the order is implied after all the sales barriers are removed.

The NCR Corporation has found an innovative way to shorten negotiation time, reduce risks for the industrial prospect, and facilitate sales closes for systems equipment.[11] The NCR sales representative can carry a

[8] Ibid.

[9] Frank Burge, "In Systems Selling, the Close Is Systematic," in Closing the Sale (special report), Sales & Marketing Management, 118, no. 8 (June 13, 1977).

[10] Charles Bergman, "Secrets of the Industrial Close," in Closing the Sale (special report), Sales & Marketing Management, 118, no. 8 (June 13, 1977).

[11] Thayer C. Taylor, "Closing by Computer," in Closing the Sale (special report), Sales & Marketing Management, 118, no. 8 (June 13, 1977).

portable computer terminal into a prospect's office and attach it to the telephone line. The prospect and the sales representative can then communicate with the main computer in Dayton, Ohio. During the first call, the computer can ask the prospect important questions about present operating procedures and equipment and analyze need. During later calls, the computer can answer technical questions with authority and even communicate all the alternative ways the proposed systems equipment may be obtained. The prospect gets customized answers and can make a more assured decision with less negotiations, and the sales representative's statements are backed by competent authority.[12] This is a computerized version of the systems presentation.

Closing When Not in the Presence of the Prospect

Decisions in corporations today are being made by people who never see the sales representative. Jim Rapp calls closing procedures designed to face this situation "closing by remote control."[13] He recommends the following for reorder buyers and other buyers you can't face directly in asking for the order: (1) influence someone inside the organization to represent your cause; (2) write out a proposal with a cover letter specifying the time and date you will call for the order, and have your advocate present this to the decision maker; (3) in this proposal establish that a decision must be made by a certain date; (4) give evidence that you are knowledgeable about your products by furnishing credentials or references; (5) work out a complete package offering including all details about price, delivery, warranties, etc., in advance; (6) try to communicate with the decision maker by telephone or in some other way in addition to the message proposal; and (7) follow up by finding out if everything is going according to your plan.[14] You can close accounts in this way without seeing inaccessible prospects.

AFTER THE CLOSE

Remember to control your post closing emotions. You must remain professional in your attitude whether you win or lose the sale. If you get the order, you may feel so elated that you make buyers feel they have lost

[12] *Ibid.*

[13] Jim Rapp, "The Remote-Control Close," in *Closing the Sale* (special report), *Sales & Marketing Management,* 118, no. 8 (June 13, 1977).

[14] *Ibid.*

the contest. Or you may exhibit the letdown (relaxation) that comes from goal accomplishment, and the buyer may wonder why you are not more pleased to have the business. Analyze yourself and do not let your strong victory emotions cause you to lose image or detract from your customer's satisfaction from having decided to buy your product. Also, do not allow yourself to feel so proud of yourself that you do not accomplish anything else the rest of the week. Direct your enthusiasm toward interviewing and closing other prospects.

After prospects have committed themselves and signed the order, reassure them that they did the right thing and thank them: "Mr. Chapman, you couldn't have bought a better home for the money. You'll always be glad you invested in this one." Prospects who have committed themselves usually lose their resistance attitude and are eager to prove that they have made the right decision in buying. If the order is signed, you might suggest that the buyer purchase additional products needed with the primary product (like service policies or insurance); but even if you practice suggestion selling here, you should not go into another lengthy presentation. If the sale *is* lost, shake the prospect's hand and thank him or her anyway for listening to your presentation. The refusing prospect may well be one of your best customers in the future when needs change. Above all, do not stay around and fail to end the interview for a long time after the sale is made. Do not give your prospects opportunity to reconsider while you are there, and do not talk them out of the sale. Make a graceful exit, realizing that you have the order. You have reassured and been courteous, and you can only lose by remaining too long. GOQ—Get Out Quickly!

SUMMARY

For most salespeople closing is the most important skill required during the interview. If you expect the prospect to buy and convey this by your verbal and nonverbal communications, your chances of making the sale should increase. A good time to close is when prospects understand your offer and when they give you signs that indicate an interest in the product. If the prospective buyer relaxes, regards the product favorably, touches the product, or asks questions that reveal an intent to own the product, you might try a trial close to gauge the extent of interest.

There are many different closing situations, but a closing technique exists for every closing circumstance. *Choice closes, minor-points closes, assumptive closes, stimulus-response closes, summary closes, "T"-account closes, standing-room-only closes, special-deal closes, success-*

story closes, closings on resistance, contingent closes, turnover closes, and *directly-asking-for-the-order closes* are field-tested ways to make the sale.

Leading up to the close in the presentation, handling third parties, getting around "no's," and introducing the order form are common problems in closing. Standard strategies for handling these problems should be thoroughly understood. Salespersons should also be aware of specific closing methods and strategies to use in dealing with dominant prospects, dependent prospects, and detached prospects. Closing purchasing agents, industrial buyers, and closing when not in the presence of the prospect also require tailored techniques. After a successful close, reassure and thank the buyer, possibly suggest additional products, and leave quickly.

REVIEW QUESTIONS

1. What are the main requirements for expertise in closing a sale?

2. What attitudes should a good closer project? What attitudes should not be projected to the prospect? How can you cultivate good closing attitudes?

3. What effect does the kind of product that you sell have on when you should close?

4. What is a trial close? What is the purpose of a trial close? Give an example.

5. List as many verbal and nonverbal closing signals as you can.

6. List the closing methods given by the text and put an * by the three that you feel are most effective.

7. Give an example of: a choice close, an assumptive close, an ask-for-the-order close, a standing-room-only close, and a success-story close.

8. What is the difference between a stimulus-response close and a summary close? Give an example of each.

9. Describe the contingent close.

10. How can you prepare the prospect for the close in your presentation?

11. How do you handle the situation when someone comes into your prospect's office just before you plan to close and stays around?

12. Why is it natural for the prospect to say "no"? What should you do when the prospect says no?

13. If your prospect must sign an order to accept the product, when should the order form be introduced? How else can you make it easier for your prospect to sign?

14. Schoonmaker and Lind contend that you should vary your closing methods by the personality type of your prospect. Describe the three prospect types and the closing methods that can best be used on each. What does Charles Roth add to closing by prospect types?

15. Give the seven suggestions Jim Rapp promotes for closing when you can't close in the presence of the prospect.

16. What should you do after the prospect has signed the order? What attitude should you convey?

APPLICATION QUESTIONS

1. What considerations are important in closing purchasing agents?

2. Using some of the closing methods you have learned, try to persuade a friend to go somewhere with you or help you do something. Describe this experiment. Did the closing methods work?

INCIDENTS

13-1

Janet Brothers is a real-estate agent who is showing a house to Kermit Stokley. Kermit has told her he wants three bedrooms, a den, a kitchen, and two full baths and desires a larger-than-average yard with shade trees. The house that Janet is showing him meets these requirements.

Janet: This house seems to have every feature you requested plus a low-interest loan. It will make a beautiful home, won't it? And from what you have told me, your furniture should fit into it perfectly . . . It's a beautiful place, isn't it?

Kermit: Well, it's nice, but the price tag sure is high. We would have liked a larger utility room.

Janet: The price is considered reasonable for this neighborhood. Brentwood School is just three blocks away, and the shopping center is just a mile out Grove Road. Remember, that low-interest loan will make your payments under $500 per month, and that's good for a home like this. Did you know that the utility room can be enlarged later without much problem? Let's go out in the yard, I want to show you something.

(Out in the yard on a pretty summer day.)

Kermit: This grass needs mowing, doesn't it?

Janet: Yes, it's healthy isn't it? But look at these two trees, aren't they beautiful? Isn't it nice to stand out here in this cooling breeze and enjoy this beautiful setting? Your two boys will love to play out here, and your wife and you can sit out here in the afternoon and enjoy the peace and quiet. I sure wish I had trees in my yard like this. You may find another house, but I don't know where you will find one with trees like these.

Kermit: I notice that there is a place I could put my garden on the back of the lot. What kind of dirt is this?

Janet: It's rich loam. You can tell the richness of the soil from the health of the trees. Mr. Stokley this house just seems tailor-made for you. It has room inside and out, it has a low-interest loan, and it is near one of the finest junior high schools in the city. Most of all, it has this beautiful yard with these heritage oaks which take 100 years to grow. Could it be any more right for you?

Kermit: Well, I do like it, Mrs. Brothers, but Sally couldn't come with me this time and although she liked it when we drove by, I'm afraid I need to consult with her.

Janet: The problem is that this house has so much going for it that it may not be here tomorrow. I know that one of the other salespersons plans to show it to another prospect this afternoon. Let's put a sold sign on it, before it gets away from us. I know you wouldn't want to lose it. If you give me a check for $400, you can reserve it and we can work out the details tomorrow.

Kermit: Well, Sally loves the yard, and, you're right, I wouldn't want to lose it . . .

QUESTION

1. Identify all trial closes in this conversation. Identify all closing "signals" by the prospect. Identify and evaluate the close given by Janet.

13-2

Dan (Red) McDougal worked many hours detailing a proposal for a minicomputer for the Deltoid Construction Company. He felt that he had the business, but when he presented his proposal to Robert Cringler, controller of Deltoid, he learned that he had lost the sale to a competitor. Dan lost his cool and angrily expressed his disappointment. He said, "At least you could have waited to make the decision until after you had seen my proposal." Mr. Cringler ordered him out of the office. Dan was sorry he had lost his temper, although he still felt that Cringler had treated him unfairly, and he had lost the sale anyway.

One month later Dan uncovered another good prospect in the building material business, Ronald Solsburg, of the East Frasier Materials Corporation. The proposal this time was for a larger minicomputer, and Dan did an exceptional job of both the survey and the groundwork necessary to sell Mr. Solsburg. The presentation went exceptionally well, and Mr. Solsburg was impressed with the detailed proposal. The sale would mean an amount equal to two months' quota for Dan, and it looked like Mr. Solsburg understood all the details. Mr. Solsburg had asked about the price and delivery, but Dan waited to ask for the order until he was sure Solsburg understood the payback period and the service contract advantages. He was about to climax his efforts with a choice close based on two similar minicomputers with slightly different memory capacity when the intercom buzzed. Mrs. Coppers, the secretary, informed Mr. Solsburg that Mr. Robert Cringler of Deltoid wanted to see him and was waiting in the outer office. "Well tell Bob to come in now, Mrs. Coppers. Maybe he knows something about computers. He just bought one a while back."

How should Dan handle this interview problem?
What mistakes has he made in the past that jeopardized this closing effort?
Does he have a chance?

13–3

LK&G Furniture Manufacturing Company had been a good customer of Bayside Plastics for seven years. Bayside had averaged selling LK&G about two-thirds of their total plastic resin input needed for both furniture coverings and structural furniture. Allen Redgraves serviced the account. Allen retired, and a rookie, Claude Knowles, took the LK&G account. Claude called on Ted Talbert, the purchasing agent, for about a year. Talbert is a highly experienced purchasing agent, more of a "dominant" buyer than a "dependent" buyer. He was not unfriendly, just highly professional.

Claude made mistake after mistake in serving the account and dealing with Talbert. He would move his chair too close and, without being invited, call Talbert "Ted." He failed to give good service, could not answer technical questions about the resins, and was responsible for several late deliveries by not turning in the order on time. He had used off-color jokes in an attempt to establish rapport, but the jokes just embarrassed Talbert, who was deeply religious. Claude used choice, minor-points, and assumptive closes to ask for the order, which irritated Talbert. Talbert kept buying from Bayside, however, and simply "overlooked" Claude's personality until six months ago. During a sales contest, Claude tried to overstock LK&G, and when Talbert failed to order the recommended amount, he tried to bribe Talbert with three twenty-dollar bills. This was the last straw for Talbert, who was highly ethical. He found a new supplier and quit ordering from Bayside altogether. Claude quit the company.

How would you reinstate the LK&G account?
What kind of presentation would you use?
What kind of closing technique would you use on Talbert?

14. Special Selling Situations

Persuasive talents and techniques are required in many specialized fields of selling. While most basic strategies and methods are similar, there are important differences in approach and tactics in retail selling, industrial selling, intangible selling, and public relations. This chapter is designed to point out some of these differences and suggest customized techniques for each of these specialized selling situations.

RETAIL SELLING

In retail selling the customer usually visits a store or place of business with interest in a particular product or group of products. While route sellers, door-to-door salespersons, telephone salespersons, and home-service salespersons do contact the customer, they comprise only a small part of the total retail sales force. In a retail situation, customers often have already decided that they have a problem or need before they enter a store, but this does not mean that the prospect is ready to buy or that retailing is mere order taking. Since many retail salespersons can't actively prospect, they must make the most of every potential buyer who enters the store and sell with such diplomacy that the customer will keep coming back. Retail salespersons, in fact, must be expert strategists and closers. Customers, especially those desiring consumer durables and style goods, can be substantially influenced by effective selling methods. Retail management is such an important activity that it leads to positions involving six-figure salaries. Store ownership can mean even greater earning potential. Therefore it is important that the requirements for retail selling, the techniques for serving customers, and the methods for handling special retail selling problems be understood. Even industrial sales representatives sometimes serve walk-in trade and should be acquainted with in-store methods.

Requirements

Successful retail selling requires complete stock knowledge, store policy knowledge, and a tactful, service-oriented sales personality. Salespersons should be prepared not only to present the merchandise to customers but to care for stock, watch for thefts, wrap packages, keep records, make reports, give information and directions, handle returns, and deal with customer grievances.

Floor sales personnel sometimes send customers away with, "I'm sorry, we don't have that in stock," or "I don't think we carry that" when the product is available in inventory. It is important to know all the benefits of all the stock and to be able to demonstrate every product whose application is not obvious. The challenge of answering customers' questions about a variety of products can be met by salespersons who study the merchandise.

Photo 14.1

Even industrial sales representatives sometimes serve walk-in trade, and successful selling requires complete and in-depth stock knowledge.

Customers will complain about merchandise, return products, or ask for special favors. The salesperson must know all about lay-away, discounts, credit, check cashing, return, delivery, exchange, and special-request handling policies of the firm. A store might, for example, have a policy of meeting the price of all competitors when proof (newspaper advertisement) is given. The salesperson must know how to handle and record these special sales and how to manage other recurring situations.

Retail sales personnel help to create the image of the store. Their dress, appearance, and behavior is therefore always important. Customers return to friendly, helpful representatives who know their merchandise and know their customers. The retail salesperson must have extra tact and patience, must be willing to listen even to angry customers, and must know how to suggest merchandise without seeming to pressure customers.

The selling situation requires perception of needs and the adjustment of presentations to serve widely differing personality types. An attitude of prompt service is essential.

Techniques for Serving Customers

Since most retail salespersons have little opportunity to prospect outside of the store or place of business, nearly every person who enters the establishment should be regarded as an important customer. The salesperson should notice and evaluate nonverbal communications immediately—appearance (especially clothes), apparent mood, walking speed, and focus of attention. Some customers come to look and should not be approached too rapidly. Others are in a hurry and want immediate service. Some want to bargain and appear disinterested when they really are interested. Some come in to complain or to assert their egos. Many come in with the intention of getting more information and making a purchase.

The Approach. Customers who simply want to look may leave early if approached too aggressively by the salesperson. Their body language—evading eye contact and leisurely browsing without indicating any need for assistance indicates that they want to consider the merchandise without pressure. The salesperson should be available but should not insist on dogging their footsteps. Most of the time, however, it is good practice to offer service. It is important to smile. "May I help you?" is a standard approach that indicates a service attitude but is weak from overuse. The temptation is for the customer to say: "No, I'm just looking." "Is there something I can show you?" is more suggestive and may receive an answer pointing to the customer's needs. "Good afternoon, Mrs. Jones, may I help you today?" has the personal touch. Customers feel important if you have remembered their names, and with this approach you also show politeness and a service attitude as well. Of course, if you know the customer well it is best to be less formal by calling him or her by the first name. A very good approach is to draw near the customer who, by his or her body language, appears interested, and say something meaningful about the product the customer is inspecting. "Customers tell us those pants are very comfortable, and this is the first time they have been offered on special," or "This car is not only beautiful—it gets over 25 miles per gallon in mileage tests," or "That blue coat certainly would look good on you. Here, let me help you slip it on." It is usually better to say something than it is to just follow the customer around without saying anything. Always think about *your* body language when you approach the customer, and make sure you convey genuine interest and pleasure at being able to be of service. When customers are in an obvious hurry, approach them promptly and respect their lack of time.

The Presentation. After the approach greeting, it is usually best to be silent and listen carefully to the customer's response. If customers indicate that they want to know more about the product, you should proceed to explain the benefits. The more you can customize benefits to needs and match customer self-image to product image, the more buying response you are likely to get. It is sometimes good strategy to admit certain faults in the merchandise to win prospect confidence. This is especially true when you are dealing with more intelligent clientele. If clothing doesn't look good on the customer and doesn't match eyes, hair, and complexion, or you can tell that the customer doesn't like an item, you might explain that you have something better and show that to the customer. Two important things to remember when dealing with the customer: always attempt to get the customer to try on or try out the product, and handle the product as if it were valuable (unless you are trying to demonstrate its durability). The customer who touches the product or takes part in the demonstration tends to feel possession and is usually more convinced about its worth. If you handle the product as if it were valuable, you will convey value to the customer. Show the product against the proper background and use words that convey image. "You would be proud to get the morning paper or even welcome guests into your home, wearing this robe."

An important question in retail selling is whether you should show the customer the more expensive merchandise, the middle-range merchandise, or the less expensive merchandise first. Nonverbal signals such as clothes and other appearance clues can indicate what level you should show. It is best, however, to listen to the customer and bring out the quality level of merchandise expressly requested. If the prospect doesn't voice a preference, you can either trade up or down if you show merchandise

BED DEP'T

"I lose more customers that way!"

THE SATURDAY EVENING POST

Reprinted from *The Saturday Evening Post* © 1957 The Curtis Publishing Company.

It is also important for the retail salesperson to have control of the demonstration.

in the middle range. Usually, it is best to start with merchandise of slightly higher-than-average quality and come down a bit. Quality merchandise is remembered after the price is forgotten, and more profit is gained from higher-priced merchandise.

It is important to ask questions to determine customer needs, but be particularly careful about what you ask. Asking questions about the intended use of the product is safer than asking questions about specific styles, colors, and brands unless you have an almost limitless selection. You can make recommendations more often from products you *have,* from responses to questions like these: "For what occasions would you want to wear this dress?" or "How do you intend to use your boat?" or "What kind of materials do you need to glue together?"

Good retail strategy is to allow the customer choice, but *limited choice.* Help the prospect to decide by narrowing down the selection to just a few items—probably not more than three. Don't bring out too many goods at once, and remove goods that are "out of the running" so that the customer can focus on those remaining. Never give the customer a choice between something and nothing—always try to make it a selection between something you have and something else you have.

Closing. Retail salespersons should close early and often and watch for closing signals. Customers often give their intentions away by the questions they ask and the way they look at or handle the merchandise. A customer who keeps coming back to a product, who compares other products to it, or who concentrates main interest on a product is usually ready to be asked for the order. Trial closes such as: "That looks good on you, doesn't it?" or "Isn't that a pretty color?" should also help you in timing the request for the order. Choice closes, minor-points closes, and assumptive closes are especially good. "Do you prefer the four-door sedan or the elegant model with bucket seats?" or "Would you like to add both the blue and the gray suit to your wardrobe?" or "Having your initials on the suitcase will help keep it from getting mixed up with someone else's. May I write it up for you?" or "May I gift wrap this for you?" The assumptive close must be done with skill and at the proper time, or the customer could resent the closing effort and become resistive.

Suggestion Selling. The retail sales representative can increase sales substantially by suggesting a greater quantity of merchandise or additional merchandise that may be used with the product or products just purchased. New merchandise, items like ties and shirts that compliment a new suit, merchandise on special sale, and merchandise that is obviously needed are often suggested. The service-station employee who asks: "Fill 'er up?" is practicing suggestion selling. This same alert employee may inspect the vehicle for deficiencies such as dirty air filter, low oil, low transmission fluid, treadless tires, weak battery, or burned-out lights and suggest that these problems be corrected. Not only will the station get more business, but the customer will travel more safely.

Salespersons should consider that most retail products suggest other products that might be needed:

- We will be glad to write up a homeowner's policy on this new house.
- A racket cover and press will protect your new racket.
- This tie is great with your new suit, isn't it?
- With this grass catcher to go with your new lawnmower you will have instant fertilizer available for your mulch bed.
- Why don't you buy a dozen golf balls, Sir, and get a 20 percent discount?
- At this sale price, would you like another pair of shoes?
- How about some extra batteries? It might save you a trip back.
- If you buy two of these smoke detectors you can get a discount on your house insurance.

Sometimes nothing need be said. To suggest the product, the salesperson simply brings out a tie, or a shirt, and puts it against the suit the customer has just purchased—the customer will usually make a comment. While forcing unwanted merchandise on the customer is wrong and may endanger future business, it is just as wrong to let the customer leave without suggesting that their total needs be fulfilled through your offerings. The customer shouldn't have to go down the street to look for blouses and other accessories to go with the new skirt because you wouldn't meet the obvious need to match the apparel while it was available in the store. You will nearly always sell more if you practice suggestion selling.

Postsale Courtesy. Thank customers whether they buy or not. Never indicate by nonverbal communication that you are upset or displeased because the customer didn't buy. That customer is a walking advertisement for or against you and the retailing establishment you represent, and you want that prospective buyer to return and consider you again. In most retail situations, it is much less important for you to lose the sale than the customer and all the other people that person is likely to influence. Before the customer leaves make sure that he or she knows how to operate and use the product to get maximum satisfaction from it. Too many buyers leave the store and come back to complain that the product didn't live up to expectations, because they were never shown how to care for it and operate it properly.

Retail Selling Problems

The retail salesperson faces challenges that require patience, perception, and intelligence. The following problems arise in many retail selling situations: (1) serving two or more customers at a time; (2) serving the customer who shops with friends or relatives who advise; (3) handling out-of-stocks; (4) handling returned merchandise and complaints; (5) turning over customers to a more experienced salesperson.

Serving Two or More Customers at a Time. At rush times or when other personnel are on a break, the retail salesperson may be called upon to serve more than one customer at a time. The customer on whom you are waiting has first right to your time and you should continue to serve that customer fully (in most circumstances), unless he or she indicates that it is permissible for you to give part of your attention to the newly arrived customer. In many instances your present customer will see the situation and indicate that you may give some attention to the new customer. If you are convinced that the present customer needs more time to look and consider and the new customer seems impatient and neglected, you might *ask* permission: "Would you mind if I take just a moment and show him where he can find the sports coats in his size?" It is always good practice to show you are aware of a new customer you see waiting. You might say: "Someone will be with you in a little while." You should never make your present customer feel rushed or pressured into leaving without deciding. If another salesperson is immediately available, see that the new customer is waited on by him or her. Skilled salespersons can often handle two or more customers at once if each is in a different phase of the sale. The first customer will have time to consider and decide, while you are showing the new customer requested merchandise. This way customers feel less pressure, and all customers get enough attention. This is better than having customers leave the store because of the inability to get service, even when they know what they want. When two or more customers are waiting, the salesperson should keep track of who is next, because customers can become angry if not served in turn.

Handling the Customer Who Shops with Friends and Relatives. It is usually better to talk to the interested customer without the presence of a third party. While husbands or wives sometimes will not buy style goods without the opinions of the other, it is nearly always harder to sell to two people than to just one. The advice of friends is usually against buying; so, if you can steer the third party to look at other merchandise or get another salesperson to occupy his or her interest, your chances of making a sale are usually better. If you must, give the friend attention and watch for closing signals from both. If the friend says, "I like that on you, Susie," that is a perfect time to close. If you can get the friend or relative to sell with you rather than against you, you have an important ally in making the sale. You must cater to both customer and adviser. Sometimes leading questions like, "Doesn't that look good on her?" get positive participation from the adviser.

Handling Out-of-Stocks. Few stores can satisfy all customers' direct requests for merchandise. In most cases it is better to express regret, show the nearest substitute, and/or promise to order that exact item for customers if they are willing to wait for it. Some salespersons even tell the customer of a competitive store (often one not in direct competition) where the product may be purchased. This kind of unselfish service is usually noted and wins the customer's confidence. If you are out of the item and the substitute you have is just as good or better, you should try to persuade the customer to buy the acceptable alternative; but selling a product that will not serve the purpose injures goodwill. If you are out of merchandise too often, you will lose customers permanently, because they have already formed the image that the store is always "out of every-thing." Tell the buyer who is responsible for ordering about merchandise frequently requested but not on hand. Don't say, "We're out" unless you are sure you're out. Being out of merchandise advertised on special is particularly image-destructive. Always suggest an acceptable substitute if you have one. Above all, don't make the customer feel ignorant or embarrassed for having asked for the item.

Handling Returned Merchandise and Complaints. This will be discussed more fully in the next chapter, but proper handling of these problems is essential to increasing business. You must first know the policy of the store—some stores will even exchange merchandise bought in another store. The main thing to remember is to serve the customer's needs within store policy with as much pleasantness as possible. Customers stay away from salespersons who make exchanges and returns grudgingly. If you are eager to serve return and exchange customers and treat them with the same courtesy you treat present prospects, they will remember and come back to you. You have successfully reduced their risks in buying. Listen to customers with a complaint. They have "honored" you by telling you what is wrong, given you an opportunity to reestablish a good relationship, and helped you correct something that might offend other customers. It is, after all, the customer who never returns and complains to friends and relatives who hurts retail trade.

Turning Over Customers to a More Experienced Salesperson. Retail selling is a team effort at times. Your image may clash with certain prospects, and they may not identify with you because of your age, sex, or size. More often, you may not have the knowledge they require about particular merchandise. You may simply not be able to make a sale with the prospect for some reason or another. If you realize you can't close and you feel another salesperson could make the sale, tactfully turn the customer over with a statement such as, "Mrs. Lacy, I would like you to speak to Mrs. James about that problem. She is our expert on antique furniture" or "I would like you to speak with our buyer [another salesperson who also buys]. I believe she can order for you exactly what you want."

Closing Comments

The key elements of success in retail selling are customer needs recognition, product knowledge, cheerfulness and enthusiasm, genuine attitudes of helpfulness, and honest service. An important test to apply is: would you want to come back and buy again from someone who treated the customer as you did?

INDUSTRIAL SELLING

Most of the selling methods and examples covered in previous chapters also apply to industrial selling. However, because industrial sales is such an important job alternative for college students and because there are some differences in emphasis and procedure, separate consideration is given here. Industrial sales representatives sell major equipment and installations, accessory equipment, services, raw materials, and operating supplies to businesses, institutions, and governments. This type of selling usually requires salespersons to go to the prospect to create interest. Often, there are a limited number of important customers buying significant dollar amounts of products, after careful, rational deliberations. Quite often, too, there are several persons the salesperson has to satisfy before an important industrial sale is made. Installation, operator training, maintenance, delivery, and other services may be furnished with the tangible product and are important parts of the offering. Because of these characteristics, the market commands high-level and expensive sales personnel, requires certain customized selling techniques, and generates particular selling problems that must be solved.

Requirements

The educational and personality requirements for industrial salespersons are high, because they are the points of contact between an important supplier and important buyers. Moreover, the product line offered may be technical and complex. Since there are often just a few prospects, each must be carefully cultivated, and each must have a favorable image of the supplying firm. Often, many departments of the prospective corporation are involved in the purchase decision. Then, it becomes necessary for the salesperson to understand all aspects of the buying firm's operations. Because of these characteristics, the higher dollar amounts involved, and the fewer orders generated, there is usually pressure with each selling situation. Complex proposals are necessary in many systems sales. Sometimes formal education in engineering, accounting, data processing, or other technical areas is necessary because technical knowledge of prospect business problems and product applications can be extensive. Customers have great respect for industrial salespersons, and many consider them professional consultants, particularly when thousands of dollars of capital goods are purchased. It is not hard to understand why good industrial salespersons command high compensation. It is difficult to find people who have personalities that can project the best image for the firm and who have the educational background necessary to sell complex products.

Selling Techniques

Prospects and Preapproaching.   Industrial sales representatives should know the characteristics of firms that might need their product and locate those firms in their territory.   Change is often the key to need.   Expansion plans, new-product promotion, operation and equipment changes, and changes in personnel may indicate a new requirement for an industrial product.   The salesperson should cultivate people inside the firm to learn when new industrial purchases are being contemplated, or call on the customer often enough to be considered when the need arises.   Good preapproach information about the financial, operating, and policy characteristics of prospective firms is strategic in approach planning.   It is especially good to know the buying policies and the names of all personnel in the concern who might be brought in on the buying decision.   Receptionists and secretaries may volunteer contact information, but if the representative goes through the purchasing agent or a top corporate official, it may be necessary to ask permission to contact certain other members of the buying team.

The Approach.   The industrial salesperson often sells the prospect on doing a study of operations to see if there are problems and opportunities for new techniques and products.   An approach may be, "Mr. Hartly, Alamo Corporation has a new metal-stamping machine that has increased the speed of operations like yours by as much as 30 percent.   May I have your permission to meet with your engineers and study your exact procedures? This equipment could save your firm thousands of dollars each year and speed your products to your customers," or "In one minute this new chemical will clean surfaces that required thirty minutes under the old process.   May I show you exactly how it works?"   Industrial approaches are usually rational and to the point so that important executive time is not wasted.

The Presentation.   Presentations are seldom made without study and material preparation.   Although sales are frequently made by appealing to emotional motives (especially pride), nearly every sale must be justified by practical considerations.   The industrial salesperson must remember that each person on the buying team is looking at the product in respect to what it will do for them—will it help their position in the company or help them by helping the company?   Presentations are often made before several persons and with the help of prepared visual aids such as films and portfolios.   All applications and benefits must be customized to fit the needs of the buying firm.   Often an important part of the presentation is the explanation of a detailed problem-solution proposal well justified by cost and benefit figures.

Closing. The standard closes all work well in industrial selling—even closing on a minor point. An excellent close for equipment and other complex products is the choice close. Prospects become absorbed in selecting between two or three alternatives all within the salesperson's line of products and hopefully lead themselves into the sale. "Either of these machines, Mrs. Landry, will do an excellent job in all four applications. This one is capable of generating two extra reports, while this one is slightly less expensive. Which one would you prefer?" The assumptive close is also widely used, "We could deliver this model within ten days. Is that all right?" With capital and accessory equipment, stimulus-response and summary closes are also popular, because there are so many features and benefits to talk about. Because so much money is involved in many industrial deals, the special offer is often used. "We have a demonstrator model in this machine that has never been out of the wrapper—it just has a lower serial number and has been declared a demonstrator on that basis. This would be available for 15 percent less than the price on the proposal, but we have only one, and I'm sure it won't be here long. Can I deliver it to you this week?" After a lengthy and technical presentation, the close is often assumed by the prospect. Some industrial sales representatives claim that they seldom have to ask for the order, because the prospect will usually comment at the end of the interview when the detailed proposal is presented. A tested closing method is still the best strategy. (See Chapter 13 for more about industrial sales closing.)

Industrial Selling Problems

There are four main industrial selling problems: (1) getting in to see the right prospect, (2) selling against competition, (3) reciprocity, and (4) delivery. Getting in to see the right prospect in the beginning has already been treated. Selling against competition is critical because of the longer negotiation time and the importance of considering all alternatives on large capital or long-term purchases. The salesperson's effectiveness in this regard depends on the professional image he or she exudes, the knowledge of product, relative advantages over competition and competitive deficiencies, and the time span between the prospect's recognition of the problem and the close. Reciprocity or the obligation to purchase from another firm must also be met with proof of the relative superiority of the salesperson's product. Delivery is a problem, because complex products that are custom-made or programmed take time to be prepared for the specific prospect, and the prospect wants the product as soon after the order is signed as possible. The best practice in most instances is to explain to the buyer exactly why the product requires the specified delivery time and to assure that you will do everything necessary to deliver it as soon as possible. Sometimes normal delivery channels can be by-passed if the sale depends on it. Know the facts and tell the truth.

Closing Comments

Industrial selling requires a great effort from the salesperson in every respect. The problems are more complex than in most selling jobs, but the pay is usually higher and the opportunities better.

SELLING INTANGIBLES

Insurance, investments, services, ideas, and images represent intangible offerings that touch the lives of everyone. The lack of a tangible product needn't handicap the creative salesperson. Actually, the opportunity to build visualizations and images in the mind of the prospect is greater, because no definite picture already exists. Because an intangible product doesn't command the attention of the potential buyer, the personality and communication abilities of the sales representative become very important. The professional image builder who can sell an idea can command high rewards.

Selling techniques used in selling intangibles are generally like those used in other selling situations. The emphasis is on making sure the prospect can visualize the benefits of the offering. This is even true in life insurance. When buyers purchase a policy, they are reinforcing their present self-image of amply providing for loved ones even in the event of death. Visual aids that show what could happen if the insurance is not purchased (fire burning up a home) or charts that illustrate the benefits from buying certain investments substitute for the tangible in the presentation. Because the salesperson can show what could happen if the intangible were not bought and contrast this with what could happen if the intangible were bought, the prospect can imagine extremes that, while not likely to happen, could happen. This furnishes important buying emotions for the decision. The pressure to buy now instead of later should be built into the presentation in some way. Generally, life insurance costs more per year as the prospect becomes older; house or health insurance when not in force leaves the prospect unprotected; investments can't earn interest when not possessed; and ideas can't materialize unless supported by acceptance of the offer. Elements should also be included in the close to get the buyer to make a decision now rather than put it off.

PUBLIC RELATIONS

Public relations, which differs from other persuasive fields in techniques, is growing in importance and providing an increasing number of positions for educated young adults. Public relations includes those activities designed to sell corporate images and build good relationships with all organizational publics. Organizational publics include such groups as the public at large, customers, employees, stockholders, and legislators. Public relations is selling an intangible, organizational image and goodwill to everyone able to influence the success of the firm. Some representative must see to it that the organization's reputation is maintained and enhanced by interpreting feedback from the public and promoting policies and communications designed to advance the firm's progress. Public relations will be discussed under the following headings:

- Gaining internal cooperation
- Communication methods in public relations
- Dealing persuasively with specific publics

Gaining Internal Cooperation

The image and reputation of an institution is influenced by every person connected with the firm. A basic function of a public-relations representative is to sell the importance of promoting the institution to both management and employees and secure cooperation in protecting and projecting a good impression. This can be accomplished through good internal communications—meetings with management and employees, house publications, posters, and other methods that might impress all personnel with the importance of promoting the firm's good name. The P.R. representative must frequently make suggestions to the organization's executive personnel who may be undermining employee morale through poor policies or who may be making careless public statements that reflect on the firm's image. A company executive may say, for example: "My company comes first and the country's energy problem second," and may thereby damage the firm and the industry's image. Since the executive outranks the public-relations representative, the representative must use diplomacy and creativity in handling the situation. Perhaps forwarding the executive the resulting press clippings appraising the speech without comment would impress that executive with the seriousness of such unguarded statements without causing emotional reaction against the representative. Employees, too, should become P.R. conscious. A bulletin board slogan such as: "What people think of Dell Company affects its sales. The good impression you make for the company is important," is an example of a public-relations communication to get everyone behind the vital image-selling effort.

Communication Methods in Public Relations

Advertising, audio-visual aids, organizational publications, speeches, prestaged events, and publicity are important communication methods associated with building an institution's reputation. Every good public-relations person must be skilled in using them.

Advertising. Public-relations representatives work with advertising specialists inside and outside the firm and help them develop themes, identify organizational features that can be promoted, and approve final ad campaign plans and copy details (see Figure 14.1, p. 374). Energy companies, for example, have often used the media to correct mistaken ideas about their profits and operations. Corporations are frequently explaining how their products benefit society, increase the standard of living, strengthen the free-enterprise system, and even help save lives. Organizations also help sponsor public-service advertisements that are designed to help improve dental hygiene, prevent fires, encourage patriotism, and accomplish other purposes for the public good. Notice institutional copy in newspapers and magazines and on television. You may be impressed by how much advertising is public relations in nature.

Audio-Visual Aids. The P.R. representative often originates and coordinates the production of films, photographs, and records that dramatize the ideal organizational image. Here again, the representative should help uncover the most beneficial and most communicable features of the institution. A university, for example, may find through research that location and size, curriculum offerings, reputation for high-quality education, ability to help students get financial aid, favorable social climate, and physical facilities are its most important features and seek to promote these benefits in a film for high school students. Questions that might help identify selling points include: How does the firm benefit the area economically, culturally, and environmentally? How do its products contribute to the quality of life? How do its employees serve the community? Scenes and sounds that best convey these benefits must then be captured on films, tapes, and records, and the P.R. representative must plan their coordination with presentation opportunities. The representative should also suggest executive actions and institutional improvements that will help make the firm salable to its publics. Many films sell the organization less directly by treating topics of public interest under firm sponsorship.

The Electric Economy requires four vital resources. Technology's one.

America is on its way to the Electric Economy. And The Southern Company has the resources needed to get there.

The fuel. The management. The investors. And the technology.

Our technological experts are at work pioneering a process called solvent refining — removing pollutants from coal before it's burned. This could be the best way to make full use of the country's most abundant fossil fuel.

The Southern Company has the other three resources, too.

The fuel: Coal already generates more than 80 percent of the electricity produced by the four operating companies in the Southern electric system.

The management: The system's management is continually looking for new cost- and energy-saving techniques, like introducing energy-efficient home building concepts to help customers reduce their electric costs.

The investors: The Southern Company has over 294,000 common stockholders. Investment dollars like theirs help build the facilities for the operating companies' customers.

The Southern Company: The company with the resources to meet the demands of the Electric Economy.

The Southern Company
P.O. Box 720071
Atlanta, Georgia 30346

Southern Company ◣

the southern electric system

Alabama Power Company
Georgia Power Company
Gulf Power Company
Mississippi Power Company
Southern Company Services, Inc.

Figure 14.1

Source: *Forbes*, August 1, 1977, p. 42.

Organizational Publications. Company newspapers and magazines can far outreach the internal organizational family and help form public opinion in the community at large. Wider public readership is fostered by including contents of general interest in firm publications and mailing them to publics, like legislators, who are in a position to help promote company interests. Sometimes articles originating in company publications are sent to and republished by newspapers where they receive favorable free publicity. P.R. representatives must also help shape the image-building contents of annual reports, stockholder magazines, and customer publications. Such publications should always be carefully examined before they are circulated to evaluate their probable impact on the public. People form their impressions by all contacts they have with the organization, and many organizations print periodicals for their most important publics.

Speeches. Civic organizations, schools, clubs, and other groups ask for and welcome speakers recruited from the organization's executives, staff, and workers. The public-relations representative may organize intrafirm conferences, speakers' bureaus, and lobbying efforts. The organization may be set up to help select speakers, help train speakers, furnish speaking guidelines to insure that good images are projected, and coordinate speaking engagements. The public-relations staff is expected to influence and guide personnel representing the firm in public. They do this through creative persuasiveness, to protect the organization's reputation.

Prestaged Events. Public-relations staff arrange plant tours, employee social functions, special days, awards, dedications, parade participations, and sporting events. Universities have special visitation days such as High School Seniors' Day, ROTC Day, and Band Day, when prospective students can come and form an impression of the school and its atmosphere. Manufacturers invite the public to the plant occasionally to impress them with the care, cleanliness, and efficiency of their manufacturing methods. Whenever the public is invited, someone must make sure that property and personnel are ready to receive guests and put the institution in a good light. The coordination of such events by the public-relations representative should produce a favorable, low-key persuasive impact.

Publicity. Publicity is considered free, but it can be influenced by the public-relations representative. The representative can foster "good press" by meeting with reporters, writers, and editors and by assuring that all favorable acts of organization receive good coverage. The function includes sending in photographs and edited news stories, inviting the press to special events, and seeing that expansion plans or plans involving other changes that affect the community are expressed properly. Such releases should be truthful, concise, newsworthy, interestingly written, and timely. Even when reporters seek information about events that would harm institutional image, it is better to see them and try to influence them to print the institution's side, thereby keeping damage to a minimum. Reporters will seldom kill a story, but many will accept the institution's view of the situation if it is an honest view. Press conferences, press dinners, news releases, and frequent contacts with important press representatives are ways of assuring that the press is informed and that the corporation will receive image-building coverage.

Dealing Persuasively with Specific Publics

Corporations and other organizations have employees, customers, stockholders (owners), suppliers, the government, universities, and the public in general to consider as their influencing publics. The public-relations representative should be familiar with the interests of each public and the methods whereby each public can be persuaded that the firm is a valuable member of the community.

Employees. Employees want to feel that they are an important part of their firm and that their organization plays a valuable role in the public welfare. They want to feel "included" and especially want to be informed about changes that affect their welfare. They want to be sure that their voice is heard when complaints are justified. When they are denied information, they sometimes rely on distorted sources—the grapevine or the rumor mill. Information given to employees should be truthful and clear, and it can be communicated by several methods. Planned meetings, house organs, public-address systems, letters, bulletin boards, and personal visits by superiors are mediums for spreading important news. Employees' opinions should be solicited by questionnaires, suggestion boxes, editorial space in the company newspaper, committee meetings, and executive access. All of the firm's officials should be good listeners, just like the public-relations representative, and the "presentation" to sell the firm's image and team spirit should include information and assurances through the best communications media available.

Customers. Customers want good products and service and are the heartbeat of profit institutions. When they contact the corporation, make inquiries, or express complaints, they should be given much more than just passive consideration. Customers "spread the word" about the corporation and influence prospects for the firm's products. Nonprofit firms should be just as responsible to the publics they serve as profit enterprises. When information on new products or new safety information becomes available, customers should be informed by direct mail, advertising media, or other channels. Customers should be encouraged to visit the plant, and every employee should be recruited by public relations to be a sales representative and win new customers. Word-of-mouth advertisement by satisfied customers and good reputation with the consuming public are valuable assets that should be promoted by the P.R. representative.

Stockholders. Stockholders want accurate, truthful information about their investments, and corporations want their stockholders to be convinced that their organization is doing an efficient job in maintaining their interests. The public-relations representative should know what kind of people own stock in the corporation and should be personally acquainted with big-block investors such as security analysts, bank-investment officers, and insurance-investment officials who require even more information from stock-issuing organizations. Like other important publics, the stockholders can be sent feedback questionnaires and should be mailed publications and information folders to help them keep up with all the important happenings in the firm. The annual report, the annual stockholder's meeting, letters, personal visits (to important investors), and tours help stockholders keep in contact with the firm. Remember that stockholders not only help finance the corporation and vote on officers and policies, but they are also prime customers for the corporation's products, since their ownership interests give them incentive to buy and increase profits for higher dividends.

Suppliers. Suppliers furnish the raw materials and other inputs for businesses and are sometimes in a position to allocate their scarce materials and affect organizational survival. Suppliers' sales representatives should be treated with respect—almost any buyer's market can turn into a seller's market on short notice. Organizations should invite important suppliers to visit the plant and understand operations so they can better serve the organization's interests. Communications between suppliers and firms should be made more routine. Visits to suppliers' plants also foster two way communication and good understanding. Suppliers will give better service to and cultivate customers who don't demand excessive service, pay their bills, and treat their representatives well when they come to call.

The Government. Government regulations are an increasing consideration for all businesses. Public-relations representatives may advise in lobbying matters or personally participate in persuasive efforts to gain support with local, state, or national legislators. Government bureau personnel who feel that the firm is not complying with employment or reporting laws can seriously affect organizational survival. Such inspecting personnel should always be welcomed and treated cordially on visits to the company. Information should be given them on request. One of the important functions of public relations is to maintain a good public image and so discourage efforts to pass new legislation that could be damaging.

Universities. Colleges and schools are the nesting places for the "publics" of the future. Research bureau personnel, academic consultants, and teachers are in a position to help the organization through research and suggestions. These researchers and student influencers should be received cordially by the organization's officers and be given appropriate information for their research when it is requested. Corporations furnish many kinds of teaching aids to build good relations with this public. Classes can be taken through the plant on field trips, organizational speakers can serve as guest lecturers at the school, and company literature can be given for distribution to classes. Scholarships are often contributed by organizations to deserving students, to increase public and student interest in the firm.

The Public in General. Large organizations can establish favorable images with the public in general, by sponsoring community athletic teams, helping to build and maintain parks, and initiating cultural programs. The P.R. representative and the firm officers should encourage their employees to get involved in community affairs and organizations. Corporations should help keep the local environment healthy and clean. Open houses, plant tours, employee speeches, sponsored social events, and other community-serving events cost time and money but pay dividends through enlarged public support. They make people feel that the organization is a contributing part of the community. The P.R. representative must be creative in devising effective ways to gain public support.

Closing Comments

Public relations requires a diplomatic persuader who influences others through an image-reflecting personality and various devices that directly or indirectly cast the organization in a favorable light. You must show creativity and leadership in influencing employee groups to sell the institution. Selling image involves using visual aids, communicating with advertising media, and dealing carefully with several publics. While public relations does not usually require strenuous closing efforts, it does require the use of social sensitivity and tact.

There are many different kinds of sales jobs open to sales aspirants who want to use their personalities persuasively. Four different selling fields have been treated in this chapter to give the student a better idea of how methods and requirements vary.

Retail selling can lead to lucrative positions in commission sales, store management, and store ownership. Retail salespersons should know their merchandise and present it cheerfully with a service attitude. Most retail approaches should exhibit a spirit of helpfulness and use questions and suggestions that are designed to find customer needs. Offering customers a limited choice among merchandise items and suggesting additional products are keys to increased sales. Retail selling problems include handling more than one customer at a time, handling customers' friends who advise, handling out-of-stocks, handling complaints, and handling the turnover of certain customers to more experienced salespersons.

Industrial selling may require a highly professional sales image and an extensive knowledge of product and prospect problems. Sales often require rational justification, detailed proposals, and selling to more than one person. Gaining access to the right persons, overcoming competition, selling against reciprocity arrangements, and effecting timely delivery of the product are standard problems encountered by most industrial salespersons. Intangibles, which include insurance, investments, services, ideas, concepts, and images, provide opportunities for salespersons to build visualizations and images in the minds of prospects. Sales representatives selling intangibles must possess personal qualities and communication abilities that can make the difference since competitive offerings may be similar.

Public-relations positions require creativity in selling institutional images, but high-pressure closing is not usually necessary. Public-relations representatives should be able to write persuasive letters, press releases, and advertisements; to edit publications, films, and speeches; and to influence the many publics of the corporation diplomatically.

REVIEW QUESTIONS

1. What are the differences between retail selling and industrial selling?

2. What are the duties and requirements of retail salespersons?

3. How can you distinguish customers who want to come in and look from customers who want immediate service?

4. Review several approaches to customers and tell which one you like best for most circumstances. Why do you prefer that approach?

5. Why is it important to get the customer to handle the product?

6. Should a salesperson show the most expensive type of merchandise first? Explain.

7. What are the special requirements for industrial-equipment salespeople?

8. Explain the special selling ideas connected with selling intangibles.

9. Define public relations.

10. Suggest several ways to gain internal cooperation in promoting the firm or organization.

11. What special communication aids are available to help the P.R. representative sell the organization?

12. What techniques can be used to influence the firm's employees?

APPLICATION QUESTIONS

1. Make up three good questions to ask a customer to find out what kind of car he or she wants.

2. The customer has bought a new suit. Using proper suggestion-selling techniques, suggest several items to the customer that go with the new suit.

3. List the five retail selling problems given in the text and suggest a strategy associated with each.

INCIDENTS

14–1

Sara Morgan needs help in finding merchandise and has been waiting for ten minutes for Elaine Winter to finish her conversation with her boyfriend. Jane Bloom, who is the floor manager, usually waits on Sara but has been on another floor temporarily.

Elaine: What would you like?

Sara: Could you show me where to find suits in my size?

Elaine: What size are you, about a twenty?

Sara: No, I wear a sixteen. Do have something for about $100?

Elaine: We don't have a good selection in that price range. Try this $200 rack. These suits would do much more for you than what you have on.

Sara: They do look good, but my budget is tight, and I need the suit to work in. Do you have any on special or on sale?

Elaine: No, I don't think so.

(*Jane has entered the department and overheard the last two lines.*)

Jane: Elaine, we do have some on the rack by the elevator . . . some $150 suits, which have been marked off a third. I'm sure that Mrs. Morgan would want to see those.

Elaine: I forgot about those, and these $200 suits will probably be reduced in August.

Sara: This one is my size.

Elaine: Why don't you buy it?

Sara: I'd like to try it on. (*later*) How does it look?

Elaine: Try this one on. I like it better.

Sara: That's not my size.

Elaine: Well, buy the one you have on. It's O.K. It looks better than what you have . . .

Sara: I would like to take it home and show it to my husband. Can I return it if he doesn't like it?

Elaine: Sure, if you don't get it dirty.

Sara: Do you have any accessories that might go with it?

Elaine: It's my off time now. Jane will write this up for you. Nice to meet you. Jane, will you help this lady?

Jane: I'll be glad to help Mrs. Morgan, Elaine. That is a beautiful suit you have selected, Mrs. Morgan. It goes so well with your hair (*puts scarf and blouse against suit*). Aren't this blouse and scarf pretty with it?

Sara: They certainly do go well with it.

Jane: Can I show you something else before I write these up?

Sara: No, this is fine.

Jane: The store has an excellent sale on shoes in our shoe department. Thank you for shopping at the Style Center again, Mrs. Morgan. I know you'll like your new clothes. Please excuse Elaine, she's new. Come back soon.

Sara: I always like to have you wait on me, Jane.

QUESTION

1. What retail selling mistakes did Elaine make? What did Jane do correctly?

14–2

Paula Merrimore sells carpets at a large suburban department store. Mrs. James Hardwick (June) and Mrs. Brent Newcastle (Mary) are looking at samples.

Paula: (*Approaching*) That's beautiful carpet, isn't it? We've just had that in for a few weeks, and it's a good seller!

June: It is nice, but I need something less formal.

Paula: What room did you want it for?

June: Well, James and I have two girls, 7 and 12 years old, and we have just added a bedroom onto our home. We want to make the old bedroom into a playroom for the girls.

Paula: You would need something that would wear well then and would stand up under heavy use. What colors are you considering?

June: Shades of green or brown.

Paula: (*Pointing to sample stand*) These carpets wear well and because of the texture, most colors won't show dirt. Do you like this desert sand?

June: That *is* very nice. What do you think, Mary?

Mary: I think that is a little light. Why don't you keep what you have, June, and buy curtains to match?

June: Well, I want them to have a fresh new room. I plan to redecorate the whole thing if I can find what I like. How about this April leaves?

Mary: That light green will probably show dirt.

Paula: She's right about that color, I'm afraid. It will show dirt more than these two. (*Paula takes two new samples of green and brown from a different sample rack and lays them on top of the other sample stand. Looking at Mary she says,*) Either of these would be very practical, would wear well without showing dirt, would not crush down, and would bring out furniture and curtains. (*To both*) These would look beautiful in the girls' playroom, wouldn't they—and either would look beautiful for years.

June: How do you like this early autumn beige, Mary?

Mary: It's prettier than the green, June. Do you like it? It's *your* room.

June: How much is it a yard?

Paula: It's first-quality material and only $15.95 a yard, which is two dollars less than the first carpet you saw. That price includes installation and we will send someone out to measure your room. Could you tell me the approximate size?

June: The room is about 14 by 16.

Paula: Would you like to charge this then at those dimensions, and I will make adjustments later for any differences?

June: (*Gives Paula charge plate . . . signs charge slip . . . and says to Mary*) I like that color; let's go find some drapes.

Paula: (*Looking at name on charge plate*) Thank you, Mrs. Hardwick. Please come back. I know you will like your new carpet.

QUESTIONS

1. Do friends like Mary risk less by giving negative advice rather than positive advice? Why?

2. Did Paula handle the "friend's advice" problem correctly? What other alternatives did she have? Comment on Paula's selling methods.

14–3

Marcia Gomez graduated with an average record and a marketing concentration from a New York-area community college. She was very popular at college and well liked by everyone. Her flair for getting along with all kinds of people and her attractive looks are important in her new job, a public-relations position with the Empire Metal Products Company. Marcia's superior and head man at Empire Metal is Barry Morris. Morris hired Marcia because he realized that Empire Metal needed a better image with all of its publics, but especially with its employees. Labor problems have plagued the company since Morris has been president. Many of the workers are relatively uneducated, and Morris thought Marcia could start a house magazine and use other public-relations devices to help. Morris simply does not understand lower-level workers. He has a tendency to remain aloof, furnish workers with little information, and never side with employees in grievances and disputes. Union officials are particularly upset with Morris' attitude, and if he appears to have little time for the lower-level workers, he is openly hostile to union officials. The corporation has a high incidence of expensive labor turnover, although it pays better-than-average rates. Morris' attitudes often show up in his nonverbal communications and in statements he makes. He is very nice to Marcia and does not seem to regard her in the same way he sees lower-level workers because of her education and personality. Nearly all of Morris' tactless statements leak into the rumor mill that thrives in the Empire corporate atmosphere. In a recent address to a Rotary Club in the area entitled "Industrial Problems in the New York Area," Morris said that his work force was inefficient because of the "dumb hired help I'm forced to employ." The speech was also blatantly antiunion and antigovernment control. Word of the speech quickly reached the workers of Empire Metal Products, and Marcia is well aware trouble is brewing in the firm.

How can Marcia persuade her boss to improve internal public relations in Empire Metal Products?
What public-relations tools can she use?

Insuring Future Opportunities

Part III examines long-run career success in selling. Career sales representatives must build service reputations in their territories, deal ethically with their companies and their customers, and understand the viewpoints of their managers. The chapter on goodwill and ethics concerns your interpersonal dealings inside and outside of the firm. The chapter on sales management is designed to help you understand the thinking of your superiors and to make yourself eligible for this next possible step up the promotional ladder. The last chapter should give you ideas for approaching the job market and selling your professional services to corporate recruiters. All units are written to help you with the important decisions that affect a future career in persuasion.

15 Goodwill and Ethics

The salesperson who uses fairness and good service to promote the long-range patronage of customers and who gains a favorable reputation through ethical dealings is building for the future. A satisfied customer is a triple asset because: (1) a satisfied customer becomes a preferred prospect for future business; (2) a satisfied customer will often furnish referral leads and preapproach information; and (3) a satisfied customer will often promote the reputation of both the salesperson and the product to other potential buyers. Customer cultivation and ethical procedures that lead to customer satisfaction and confidence are important considerations for any sales representative.

GOODWILL

Goodwill is an intangible asset. It is an attitude customers and prospects have about you and your company that assures that your offering will be favorably considered in the future. It occurs when you have established good public relations with your customers and the general public because you have shown positive service attitudes in your business dealings. While there are many practices that build goodwill, some of the more important ways will be treated in this section.

Sell the Right Product in the Right Amounts

It is better to lose a sale than to lose a customer. Customer orientation means that you have the customers' best interests in mind in recommending products. In the short run you may make more commission by selling a customer a model with too much capacity and a higher price, or by overstocking a dealer with a slow-moving product that will stay in inventory. You may also profit temporarily by selling something that doesn't really coincide with buyer needs, such as a certain product in your line, because you are trying to win a contest or push a special. In the long run, however, you will sell more and keep the confidence of your customer, by selling the product you would buy yourself if you had the same needs.

If you overstock a customer (sell a dealer too much of an item) you will have to wait a long time to get a reorder, and you may never sell to that customer again. If you gain a reputation for overstocking customers in your territory, your future selling potential may never be fully realized. Underselling (selling less than is needed), on the other hand, can be worse than overselling. The retailer or wholesaler who doesn't have enough in stock because you recommended too small an order loses sales and customers by being out of the demanded item. You lose also because you could have gotten a larger commission on the order you should have recommended. Insurance customers who don't have adequate coverage suffer loss when their houses burn down. Materials shortages in factories can stop assembly lines and embarrass purchasing agents. Put yourself in the customer's place when recommending specific models, qualities, and quantities. Think of every prospect as a long-term customer.

Assure Maximum Customer Benefits from Product Use

You have the important responsibility of seeing that your customer gets maximum satisfaction from owning and using your products and services. This begins with your presentation and the product you recommend. You should not yield to the temptation of giving your prospect unrealistic expectations of product performance when emphasizing the benefits of buying. You also need to inform the buyer about the total uses or applications of the product, the best procedures in operating or enjoying the product, and the proper care of the product. It is important for the new car salesperson, for example, to explain to the purchaser where the hood-release lever is located and how to refill the windshield solvent container. The operator of the new typewriter should know the easiest way to take the typing unit out for cleaning and how to change the ribbon without soiling fingers. Consider the operator of the copy machine who hasn't been told that certain plastics or paper can't be used without melting in the machine and catching fire. A salesperson who doesn't explain safety precautions may be negligent and face legal involvement if someone is injured.

It is good practice to watch the customer use your product, if possible, and make sure the optimum usage is understood and practiced. If you do a good job training equipment operators, your customer will realize maximum production speed and quality of output. You never want the buyer to be able to say, "Why didn't the sales representative tell me about that?"

Maintain Open Communication Channels with Customers

Customers feel more assured when they have an open line of communication to contact you if they have questions about your product or if something is not satisfactory. Moreover, the salesperson who thoughtfully takes the time to call customers and inform them that the product will be delivered at a specific time gives those customers a chance to prepare to receive the order. The customer may want to make special physical arrangements, such as moving furniture or otherwise preparing to absorb the new product into the work routine. If the order cannot be delivered on schedule, it is best to notify the customer of the delay. Customers who wait with eager anticipation for the product to be delivered and who are not notified that the delivery promise has to be broken may feel that the salesperson didn't care enough to call and explain why the product would not arrive as expected.

It really is not enough to expect the customer to call you if something is wrong. An important device that allows buyers to express their attitudes about their experience with the product and service is the questionnaire. Some motels, for example, leave a questionnaire and a self-addressed, stamped envelope on the dresser inviting the customer to evaluate the lodging accommodations. Few customers take the time to complete the questionnaire unless something needs attention, but all customers feel more assured knowing that the motel ownership cares and wants to provide good service (see Figure 15.1, p. 390, for a sample questionnaire).

Give Customers Attention

Customers appreciate any kind of thoughtful attention. Follow-up calls after the sale is made show that the salesperson is interested in more than just the commission and give the customer an opportunity to ask questions or express a need. Some sales representatives make it a practice to be present when the product is delivered to the customer to help place the product in use and to explain the care and operational specifics on the working site. The buyer might see a need for additional units or other

Figure 15.1   Sample Questionnaire for Feedback

Dear Customer:

YOUR OPINIONS ARE VALUABLE TO US. Would you mind taking time to fill out this brief questionnaire so that we might serve you better in the future? Our customers mean a great deal to us, and we want you to keep coming back.

Were all Travel Ways Inn personnel courteous to you?
Courteous _____ Fairly courteous _____ Discourteous _____

Did you find your room clean and well supplied?
Yes _____ No _____ (If no, please tell us what was wrong) _____
_____

Did all lamps and appliances operate properly?
Yes _____ No _____ (If no, please explain) _____
_____

Were you bothered by noise of any kind?
Yes _____ No _____ . . . . _____

Was your bed comfortable?
Yes _____ No _____ . . . . _____

Was the pool and playground area clean and properly maintained?
Yes _____ No _____ . . . . _____

Please rate our restaurant facilities.
Excellent _____ Good _____ Poor _____ (If poor, please tell us why)
_____

Additional Comments _____
_____
_____

Thank you,
Travel Ways Inn

products in your line at this time while the enthusiasm of physically possessing the new product is high. This can also be a good opportunity to set up for the next sale by reminding buyers about when they might need to replace or replenish the item(s) just purchased. If you find out at delivery that the product is not suitable for the buyer's operation or setting, you may prevent a lost commission by exchanging the delivered product for a more suitable model. Products are not really sold until the customer is satisfied and pays for the order.

Using the telephone and direct mail are inexpensive ways to assure customers that you are remembering them between calls. Using these communication devices requires a minimum investment in time and money, and both make it easy to inform customers of new products, keep the name of the company in customers' minds, and make sure customers feel remembered on special occasions. Many salespeople acknowledge birthdays, special holidays, and business expansion occasions by a personal card or a phone call (see Figure 15.2 for an example of a goodwill contact letter).

Figure 15.2   Goodwill Letter

March 17, 1979

Mr. Fred Latham
173 Larkspur Drive
Travathan, Oklahoma 33908

Dear Mr. Latham:

Thank you for purchasing your Wellbuilt tractor from us. This garden tractor is every bit as durable and versatile as our larger models, and it comes with a full range of auxiliary attachments that are available at our South Elm Dealership.

When you bought the Wellbuilt, you also bought a year's free maintenance service with it. It is very important to us that you are satisfied in every way, so please call us if you have any problems at all. You may reach me at 275-4871.

Thank you again for becoming our customer. We are grateful for the privilege of serving you, and we hope that you enjoy your Wellbuilt tractor so much that you will tell your friends about it.

Sincerely,

Walter James

Walter James
Wellbuilt, Sales

Enclosure

Give Good Service with What You Sell

Retailers are buying more than inventory from you. They are buying prompt delivery, display arrangement, return privileges, advertising, and a whole package of services. Insurance companies and their beneficiaries expect prompt and courteous payment of claims with a minimum amount of red tape and a maximum amount of attention. Machine and equipment customers expect the product to operate without frequent breakdown. They expect you and your company to do everything possible to keep equipment running through preventive maintenance, proper servicing, and prompt repair. Think about it. Would you keep your insurance with a company that "drags its feet" in settling legitimate claims? Would you buy another tractor from a salesperson or firm whose repair personnel are slow to respond to service calls and seem not to care that your harvesting is disrupted because of malfunctioning equipment? Seeing that the customer gets satisfactory service over the life of the product *is* the responsibility of the sales representative as well as the company service personnel.

A customer who had recently purchased a bookkeeping machine called the firm's zone manager and threatened to put the equipment out on the sidewalk unless something was done quickly to make it work properly. The sales representative who had sold the machine was notified immediately and went to see about the problem. He found that the control had been improperly set, and the customer had struggled for days trying to do an accounts receivable operation on the malfunctioning equipment. Careful installation of the machine and adequate customer attention after delivery would have prevented such an embarrassing situation. Some customers will suffer a long time before they complain, but when they do, they are usually emotional.

Help the Buyer by Offering Advice

The salesperson is in a unique position to furnish consulting advice to customers, since they visit hundreds of customers each year and are familiar with solutions to common problems. Because of their wide exposure to many operations, salespeople often know the best way to accomplish business goals. While it is risky to advise in areas where you are inexperienced, you are in a sense obligated to suggest ideas to your customers that will help business, cut costs, or help them enjoy the product in areas where you are competent. Your company will probably furnish brochures that deal with operating problems your customers might face. Learn the solutions to common problems from as many sources as you can, and when you see something that needs to be corrected or done more efficiently, tactfully give your customer the benefit of your advice. Advice should be given only in the form of a suggestion or upon the request of the customer. If the customer is cool to your ideas, it is a mistake to insist that your suggestion be implemented.

Handle Customer Complaints Fairly

Customers are not always satisfied with products or services as received. Sometimes products are deficient on delivery, have latent defects, are damaged in shipment, or for some other reason are unsuitable for the intended use. The customer should know how to get in touch with you in cases like these, because dissatisfied customers not only cease buying, they damage the salesperson's reputation in the territory. Your firm may be liberal in accepting the customer's word in exchanging merchandise, or it may insist that each claim be clearly substantiated. Regardless of the position of your firm's management on returns, it is the best practice to listen and communicate with all disgruntled customers.

The customer's claim can usually be investigated through company records, product inspection, and questioning and listening. Listen attentively and quietly to the customer's side, even if he or she is excited and angry. Many times after customers explain the complaint, they lose their initial anger or emotionalism and are able to talk in a sensible manner.

"Hi, Mr. Shultz! How did that plant vitamin work on your garden?"

THE SATURDAY EVENING POST

Reprinted from *The Saturday Evening Post* © 1957 by Al Johns.

Sometimes products do not perform as customers expect. Listen carefully to the complaint and, if possible, see that the customer goes away satisfied.

Being able to explain the matter to a receptive listener also seems to help the customer see all sides of the situation and feel that the sales representative is interested in a fair settlement. Mistakes like billing errors, incomplete contents, defective merchandise, wrong sizes, wrong colors, and wrong mechanical adjustments of equipment can often be corrected immediately. Problems that stem from improper customer care and usage, on the other hand, are harder to adjust, because few firms are willing to subsidize customer abuse of products, especially if the customer was given proper instructions on maintenance.

The main objective in handling claims is to make the customer feel satisfied that you and your company have done all that can be done in an effort to be fair. Even if the problem arises from the customer's negligence, it may be best to take some good-faith action to restore lost confidence. Suppose, for example, that minor damage is done to the paint on the fender of a new car. It is simpler to have it touched up in the service facility than it would be to argue whether the scratch occurred before or after the customer drove the car out of the lot. One practice customers especially dislike is being referred from one person to another when they come to settle a claim. It is better that the person who first listens to the complaint or problem stay with the customer until the matter is resolved. If you need to get help from someone else in the organization when handling a customer claim, get assistance without completely turning over the customer to someone else. Remain responsible until satisfaction is achieved or the matter is closed.

It is important to reach a mutually acceptable solution to the customer complaint on the first interview and to make sure the customer understands all the particulars of the agreement. Even more important is that any promised follow-up action be taken as soon as possible. Delays in problem solutions and claims adjustments are disturbing to customers who may feel that you were insincere in not following up your promises with quick action. Why not follow up at the earliest possible moment and show your customer your dedication in making the mistake right. When problems are resolved quickly, the customer feels important, remembers your eagerness to serve, and is predisposed to buy from you again.

ETHICS

Ethical behavior is an important factor in promoting customer goodwill and fostering long-term relationships between sales representatives and employers. Such conduct proceeds automatically from attitudes of honesty, loyalty, fairness, and consideration for others. But because these dispositions are not perfected in any of us, a study of ethical problems in selling should remind us of the qualities we should exhibit. There are many practices that, while legal, promote distrust, anger, and suspicion in interpersonal dealings. Ethical practices, on the other hand, promote harmony and trust in transactions with the customer, shorten bargaining time, and strengthen the customer's disposition to buy by reducing the risks of buying. Today, because of public suspicion of the entire business community and a noticeable lack of ethics in political and business dealings, corporations and buyers are seeking out salespersons with moral character and ethical attitudes. It is therefore important that every sales representative understand the major areas of ethical problems and build a reputation for having high standards of personal integrity in all situations. The major ethical problem areas may be classified as follows:

- Your ethical duty to yourself
- Ethical responsibilities to your employer
- Ethical dealings with your customers

Your Ethical Duty to Yourself

You owe it to yourself to maintain an ethical self-image and a moral belief in the products and practices of your employer. Self-image theory

For your selling career, select a company that has good ethical standards.

"To close on an upbeat note, I'm happy to report we received twenty-two per cent more in kickbacks than we paid out in bribes."

Drawing by Dana Fradon; © 1976 *The New Yorker Magazine,* Inc.

emphasizes that what you think of yourself is critical to your relationship with others and to your ultimate success. There will doubtless be many occasions in a selling career when you will be tempted to act against your standards of conduct. At times there will be pressures in the bargaining situation to shade the truth and close a sale. If compromise with your ethical standards for short-run gain causes you to begin to view yourself as a dishonest person, your damaged self-image can lead you to even lower levels of practice, and the ensuing guilt can erode your personality. A few theorists feel that the answer to guilt feelings is to eliminate conscience and suppress standards through the rationalization that "everybody's doing it" rather than to suffer the frustrations of denying self when tempted. However, this approach can lead to long-run failure for a salesperson trying to build a reputation in a territory. One misrepresentation can undermine the ability to sell in an area, while hundreds of legitimate transactions may not restore the confidence of prospects. A self-image of honesty is not only useful in projecting sincerity but is necessary for personal satisfaction.

Your ethical responsibility to yourself in selling begins with the selection of your company. (See Figure 15.3 for a company's ethical policy statement.) If selling the firm's product would be against your moral scruples, you should not sell for that firm. Also investigate the operating procedures and selling techniques of your prospective employer. Your self-respect (which is a valuable personal asset in self-image theory) will suffer if you attempt to please an employer who expects you to misrepresent, trick, or otherwise deceive prospects to get orders. While it is true that it is possible to make money selling socially questionable products in a deceitful way, consider the nonmonetary advantages of selling one of the thousands of beneficial lines that you can promote with full confidence. Even in the most respected of companies, enough situations arise to test your character, but you can minimize your ethical problems by a careful selection of your work environment.

Ethical Responsibilities to Your Employer

Since close supervision of personal selling is impractical, every sales representative is placed in a position of trust. However, there are many situations in which your loyalty to your employer will be tested. Ethical problems commonly arise in these areas:

- The use of assets and expense accounts
- Time accountability and reporting
- Defending and promoting your firm's image
- Loyalty to firm personnel

Figure 15.3 An Ethical Policy Statement by Johnson & Johnson

JOHNSON & JOHNSON POLICY STATEMENT

1 No corporate or subsidiary funds or assets shall be used for any unlawful purpose. Nor shall any Johnson & Johnson company engage in the practice of purchasing privileges or special benefits through payment of bribes, illegal political contributions, or other forms of payoff.

2 No undisclosed or unrecorded fund or asset of the corporation or any subsidiary shall be established for any purpose.

3 No false or artificial entries shall be made in the books and records of the corporation or its subsidiaries for any reason, and no employee shall engage in any arrangement that results in such prohibited act.

4 No payment on behalf of the corporation or any of its subsidiaries shall be approved or made with the agreement that any part of such payment is to be used for any purpose other than that described by the documents supporting the payment.

5 Any employee having information or knowledge of any unrecorded fund or asset or any prohibited act shall promptly report such matter to the general counsel of Johnson & Johnson.

6 All managers shall be responsible for the enforcement of and compliance with this policy, including necessary distribution to ensure employee knowledge and compliance.

7 Appropriate employees will periodically be required to certify compliance with this policy.

8 This policy is applicable to Johnson & Johnson and all its domestic and foreign subsidiaries.

Source: *Sales & Marketing Management*, 116, no. 7 (May 10, 1976), 38.

- Switching jobs
- Accepting gifts or bribes
- Contests

The Use of Assets and Expense Accounts. A good test to apply when using the firm's money and materials is, "If it were mine, would I use it or spend it that way?" If the stationery, the car, the visual aids, the advertising materials, the electricity, the paper, the packaging, or the telephone were yours, would you tolerate the same degree of waste? If the company were yours, would you want another employee to appropriate office supplies for personal use? A careful use of seemingly inconsequential company assets communicates that you are loyal to the firm and interested in the concern's profitability.

Expense accounts present special temptations. It is almost impossible for managerial accountants to devise "unpaddable" expense accounts and still allow the salesperson flexibility. The salesperson must be trusted to make the correct odometer reading and to deduct any miles driven for personal convenience. Meals, tips, and taxi fares are often misrepresented, because receipts are not always required for these minor items. The salesperson may be tempted to eat hamburgers and falsely claim the entire meal allowance of six dollars. When motel accommodations cost over the limit in large metropolitan or resort areas, some sales representatives add more to mileage turned in or other less expensive motel rooms to cover the difference. Sometimes other salespersons show fellow sales representatives ways to get by the company accountants. Such falsifications, whether advised by other persons or not, can eventually lead to outright expense-account cheating—violating the spirit of trust as well as the actual rules. While your employer probably does not want you to starve yourself or stay in dirty motels, you are not expected to waste money either. More than likely, your expenses will be compared to other sales representatives' to determine your profitability and your loyalty.

Time Accountability and Reporting. The salesperson who works on a straight salary or a salary base and wastes time is in a sense stealing profits from the company and failing to sustain sales support personnel such as clerks and mechanics whose jobs depend upon your sales. Even if representatives work on a commission basis, the company still loses if too much time is spent over coffee, if extra-long lunch periods are taken, and if the territory is left early. Another more conscientious salesperson could be taking advantage of the lost sales opportunities. Sales representatives who are dissatisfied with their salary should talk the situation over with superiors rather than purposely waste time in retaliation. Salespersons who handle another line of products other than those known to their employers are engaging in an unethical practice. Employers have the right to expect full-time work from salespersons selling products they are hired to sell. If your employer *agrees* that you can handle the line of another company, then you have fulfilled your obligations by disclosing your intentions.

Reporting is a clerical task that many salespersons dislike, and some sales representatives pad daily reports with fictitious calls and demonstrations. The temptation exists to overstate the number of real calls made in a territory. A real call has not been made if the salesperson was refused an interview, and a full demonstration is not a brief glimpse of the product by the prospect. The sales report can easily be distorted by sales representatives who don't write down events when they take place and who "fudge a little" in an effort to justify time expenditures when time has been wasted.

There is also an ethical responsibility for off-time if it affects job performance. Some salespersons work a second job, and without proper rest, they fail to do either job well. Salespersons who party too much or drink too much and report to work tired are not giving their employers full measure.

Defending and Promoting Your Firm's Image. Some customers will speak out against your firm, and you will be tempted to take their side in an effort to be agreeable and win their confidence. While it is permissable to admit errors and mistakes made by your company, it is disloyal to speak against your superiors' motives and attitudes. Your customer will respect you more if you support your employer. If the customer says uncomplimentary things about your sales manager, for example, you might reply, "I'm sorry you feel that way about Mr. Conners. I have worked for him for years, and he has always been fair to me." Sometimes it is wiser just to listen and ignore the prospect's negative comment. Even if you feel that the accusations are just and you agree with them, don't reinforce them with a statement like, "You're right, we do have inept repair pesonnel, but good help is hard to get." This increases the chances of the prospect not buying from you. It would be better to say, "We didn't repair your equipment properly last time, Mr. Anderson. I will inspect it personally next time before it leaves our shop if you will let me know when it is sent in again. Our service personnel are human and occasionally make a mistake like this, but we will make it right."

Loyalty to Firm Personnel. In nearly all large organizations there are cliques or informal groups of employees who seem to agree on certain issues. Often such groups become politically active and seek to promote the good of the clique members above the good of the organization. Clique members and certain independent persons may attempt to tear down the reputations of other members of the firm to gain advantage. It is unethical to join in character assassinations of persons above and below you in the firm hierarchy, especially when evidence is skimpy that such backbitings are true. Efforts to tear others down to increase your own position can win you many enemies, while justifiable support in defense of criticized supervisors, peers, and subordinates can gain you respect and trust.

Sales representatives are sometimes tempted to sell to prospects who are outside of their territorial boundaries. The representative may know these prospects personally, run across them accidentally, or actually make an effort to find them. Territory jumping, like claiming credit for ideas or efforts not your own, lessens respect and support by other members of the selling team.

Switching Jobs. It is usually improper for sales managers to attract (proselyte) sales representatives from their competitors. While it is usually acceptable for a salesperson to advance by taking a better job with a competing firm, this kind of job switching does raise many ethical questions. Such persons have had access to confidential information and competitive secrets in their former employment. Under strict standards of ethics, it is unprofessional to take advantage of having been with the former employer by trying to switch old customers right away to the new firm or to use the old firm's competitive secrets strategically. Certainly, it is wrong to destroy the image of your previous employer with the customers you used to cultivate for that employer. Another consideration in switching jobs is to give adequate notice of intentions to leave. You can leave your old firm with problems, unless you give them time to replace you without hurting their customer relations. Someday you may need a good reference from every firm you ever represented.

Accepting Gifts or Bribes. Occasionally, buyers will attempt to bribe sales representatives to obtain special bargaining concessions such as lower prices, higher trade-in allowances, and larger allocations of products in scarcity situations. Such gifts should be refused tactfully, allowing the sales representative to act in the best interests of the employer and in fairness to all customers. This kind of artificial inducement in the marketplace distorts the operation of fair bargaining, and any kind of preferential treatment in response to bribes endangers goodwill with all customers—even those who successfully make the bribe.

Contests. Contests are designed to motivate the sales representative to make more sales of all products or to make more sales of specific products in the line. The pressures to win tempt some sales representatives to sell the wrong products to customers—products that will yield points in the contest but are not the best match for customer needs. Sometimes order dates are falsified so they fall within the contest period, or pressure tactics and trickery endangering goodwill are initiated as part of the extra effort to win. Cheating in contests is unfair to the company and unfair to other salespersons participating in the contest.

Ethical Dealings with Your Customers

Considerable pressure exists for sales representatives to lower their ethical standards when dealing with customers, because sometimes there is a large, short-run monetary gain from making small moral compromises and because a few customers and competitors are sometimes unethical in their strategies. Often a small bribe to a purchasing agent or a half-truth representation of a product can mean gaining rather than losing a large order. Representatives see competitors resort to unethical tricks in selling against them and are tempted to retaliate in kind. Prospects who seem otherwise upright may relax standards of moral integrity in the bargaining situation and misrepresent competitive offers to try to get special price and delivery concessions. Even purchasing agents for reputable companies may drop hints that personal gifts will influence their patronage. Strong moral character is required to play by the rules when the opposition is cheating. But long-run gains from ethical dealings in terms of goodwill, reputation, and projected self-image outweigh short-run temporary advantages. Ethical areas in dealing with customers include:

- Misrepresentation of products
- Gifts and entertainment
- Special treatment
- Keeping secrets confidential
- Competitive fairness

Misrepresentation of Products. Intentional misrepresentation of important facts about products to induce buyers to purchase is fraud, but misleading half-truths and withholding certain kinds of information can be a question of ethics. Prospects expect sales representatives to emphasize the strong points of their offerings and realize that few salespeople are going to stress product weaknesses. Many salespersons feel that it is up to the prospect to find the disadvantages of buying, and while they will answer questions truthfully, they will not volunteer negative information hurting their bargaining positions. While pointing out a few minor weak features of the product offering in an attempt to promote a balanced argument is good selling strategy, it is not productive to emphasize offering deficiencies. Any words or actions that are intentionally designed to deceive the prospect are unethical, however true they are on the surface. Suppose, for example, that a sales representative says that a copying machine will easily make transparencies from printed copies but knows that special expensive materials are necessary for this process, making it impractical. The truth has been told, but the buyer has been deceived. A car sales representative may declare that the compact automobile will pull a heavy trailer but fails to add that it will wear out the motor even on a short trip. Few buyers could forget much less harmful deceptions, and most who have suffered the consequences of having been "told the truth" in misleading words will spread the word to other buyers not to patronize the products of companies employing such sales representatives.

Salespersons who take advantage of customer trust and ignorance to overload inventories, sell more expensive products than are necessary, or recommend repair items when the original equipment parts are not worn are acting in bad faith. The more the customer trusts and the less the customer knows, the greater the responsibility of the seller to be fair. The building-materials dealer who purposely overestimates the number of bricks needed for a house, knowing that they are not returnable, or the mechanic who installs unnecessary parts in an automobile just to sell them are examples of sellers violating prospect trust. On the other hand, if the customer insists on buying the product with greater capabilities than are apparently needed, against the salesperson's recommendations, the responsibility for consequences rests with the buyer.

Gifts and Entertainment. Buyer decisions should be based on the worth of the offering and not on the efforts to buy the customer's patronage. Small gifts in appreciation for business can be considered legitimate promotion, but gifts and bribes to corporate buyers to induce them to act in their own interests rather than in the interests of the firm they represent are competitively unfair. It is hard for legitimate sellers to compete for business when decisions are based on the personal gain of the buying agent and not the value of the products to the company. Many purchasing agents resent any attempts to unduly influence them or obligate them to buy from a particular supplier. Even the few that are "on the take" respect the salesperson who tactfully declines to participate in wrongdoing to get the business. Lavish entertainment can become unethical if the sales representative is substituting it for good selling techniques in order to obligate the prospect or if representatives are spending the firm's money primarily because they can participate along with the prospect in enjoying the entertainment.

Special Treatment. Affording some customers special treatment can generate ill will with customers who didn't get the extra concessions. Many customers try to take advantage of their customer status to make excessive demands on the sales representative's time. Suppose a customer requests that an equipment salesperson stay long after the equipment is working properly and the operator has learned the procedures. The salesperson should diplomatically decline, if possible, and remember that the first priority should be to spend time productively for his or her employer. It is possible to become so service-oriented that other ethical obligations are forgotten.

Keeping Secrets Confidential. Telling customer's and employer's secrets is a fast way to ruin a selling career and helps sell few products. Leaking strategic information to competitors or betraying confidences is a serious selling "sin" and is an unfortunate personality habit with some sales representatives. Customers know that if you tell them things that you shouldn't, you will also tell their confidences to others. A professional image requires confidential communications.

Competitive Fairness. You should be familiar with unfair competitive tactics to be on your guard against them. Unethical salespersons may bribe secretaries to learn the amounts in secret bids, pattern their selling calls behind the calls of a competing salesperson, rearrange competitive displays, and even sabotage competitive products. They have even been known to pay confederates to pose as customers and complain about competitive products. Most often they name your product and put it down viciously and unfairly in front of their prospects. This type of activity reflects on their professionalism and can even help "advertise" your product. Wise prospects know that any product pointed out by competition and given attention must be good, and often they investigate and find out the truth for themselves. In the last analysis, ethical selling is fair to everyone and promotes long-run business over short-run temporary gains.

SUMMARY

Goodwill is a long-term asset to the sales representative and the company and must be earned by careful customer cultivation. It is important to sell the right product in the right amounts, to make sure the customer knows how to use and care for the product, to give the customer attention and see that the product is giving the intended satisfaction, and to see that the customer gets every purchased service due and expected. Repair service is a very important part of the product offering to customers of mechanical products, and fair and rapid claims adjustments are important in the insurance industry. Sales representatives are expected to act as consultants to help the customer with problems concerning the product offering.

Customer complaints can be an opportunity to increase the loyalty of buyers. Customers expect to be heard, prefer not to be referred to different adjustors, want quick and positive action, and desire fair and courteous treatment. Customers will long remember how they were treated in problem matters.

Ethical conduct proceeds naturally from attitudes of honesty and fairness and is a prime factor in long-run customer relationships. High ethical standards promote a professional self-image that is projected in all dealings with the prospect. A salesperson's first duty to self is to select a firm with product and standards in marketing compatible with his or her ideals. The salesperson can gain respect in the company by using assets and expense accounts fairly, by spending time efficiently, by accurately reporting selling activities, by creating harmony in the firm through loyalty to all employees, and by following the rules in sales contests. Proper notice should be given before leaving a company, and secrets learned in that employment should remain safe. Sales representatives who use deceptive methods to produce sales in the short-run ruin their reputation and lose customers in the long-run. The more the customer trusts, the more obligation there is to deal ethically. Special treatment in the form of large gifts, lavish entertainment, bribes, and unwarranted service is a substitute for good selling methods and a good product offering and is competitively unfair. While the bargaining situation produces temptations on both sides, the buyer's decision should be based on the worth of the offering instead of personal gain. Confidence-keeping and competitive fairness are essential to the professional selling image.

REVIEW QUESTIONS

1. Why is it important to satisfy customers?

2. Define goodwill in terms of a selling asset.

3. How do you lose from overselling a customer? From underselling a customer?

4. List ways you can insure that your customer will derive maximum satisfaction from the product.

5. In what way can you maintain communications with the customer after the sale? Why is this important?

6. When and how can you give customers attention after the sale? How can you use the telephone and direct mail after the sale?

7. Why is ethical conduct important to your self-image? Why is an ethical self-image important in selling?

8. What ethical problems arise in selling for an employer?

9. Which expense items are most likely to be falsified? Why?

10. How do some salespersons misrepresent their daily call reports? Why do they?

11. How can you promote your firm's image when other persons criticize?

12. In what ways can sales representatives "cheat" in sales contests?

13. How is bribing a purchasing agent unfair to the agent's company and unfair to your competition?

14. How can your prospects tell that you are professional about keeping confidences?

15. List several unfair competitive tactics given in the text.

APPLICATION QUESTIONS

1. Explain why quick repair service is important to customers.

2. How can the salesperson help the buyer as a consultant?

3. Construct a step-by-step procedure for handling customer claims. Which element in this procedure do you think is most important? Why?

4. Do you know of any cliques that make a point of tearing down persons not in the group? Explain.

5. Explain how you can tell the truth and misrepresent a product to the customer. Give an example.

INCIDENTS

15–1

Steve Hall is returning a gasoline-powered lawnmower to the Grass Master Lawncare Center. Finally, he gains the attention of Fred Hearn, the salesman.

Steve: I'm returning this excuse for a lawnmower. The durn thing quit on me five times before I got halfway through with my front yard. I don't know what's wrong with it, but I don't want it.

Fred: Well maybe it's your fault. What kind of oil did you put in it?

Steve: (*Angrily*) The blasted oil they sold me for it here, that's what. I wasn't shown anything about it, but I followed the directions they told to me, and it won't work. So here it is. Give me my money back.

Fred: Well it wasn't my fault it didn't work. Why don't you bring it back this afternoon when Mr. Beecham is here? It's a used mower now with all those grass stains on it!

Steve: I want my money back now, and I haven't got time to come back this afternoon. If you don't give it back to me I'm going to call the Better Business Bureau.

Fred: Go ahead, I don't care. I just work here. Say, there's Mr. Beecham coming in now. Why don't you tell *him* your troubles. Maybe he can do something about it. Hey, Mr. Beecham, this man is mad about his mower and wants to get his money back.

Tom Beecham: What seems to be the matter, Mr. Hall?

Steve: This mower doesn't work properly, and I want to return it.

Tom: We certainly want you to bring it back if it is not satisfactory. But tell me everything you did before it acted up on you.

Steve: Well, I filled it with the oil you sold me, and I put in some gasoline I had kept through the winter for my old mower.

Tom: That might be what's wrong. Sometimes water gets in those cans. If you can leave it here for about two hours, I'll have it working perfectly for you or give you a brand new mower. You have always been one of our good customers, and we want to keep it that way.

Steve: Sure . . . I have to have a mower, and I have to get the grass cut. Will you show me how to take care of it? I didn't even get a book of instructions with it when I bought it.

Tom: I apologize that no one showed you how to maintain it, but you can rest assured I can show you how to get maximum service from it. Thank you for giving us a chance to satisfy you with it.

Steve: Thank you, I'll be back in a couple of hours.

QUESTIONS

1. Contrast the way Tom handled Steve with the way Fred handled Steve.

2. Since it was probably Steve's fault that the mower didn't work, should Tom have insisted that Steve pay for servicing the mower?

3. What violations of maintaining goodwill were shown?

4. What principles for maintaining goodwill were shown?

15–2

Nathan Tamm has called on Phil Collier for several years and sold him two accounts-receivable posting machines for his expanding business. Collier, a public accountant, specialized in taking care of the accounts-receivable (billing) operations for several medical doctors and dentists. The two small-capacity machines had enabled Collier and his wife to do an excellent job for their clients, but both machines were being operated to capacity and could not handle the increasing volume. Collier called Tamm, explained his need, and inquired about a machine that has much greater capacity and costs four times more than a new, smaller-capacity machine like the one he presently uses. Collier liked the large machine because of its automatic features and magnetic memory capabilities. Tamm explained to Collier that the large machine could save some labor time but that another smaller machine would do his additional work well and recommended the smaller machine. Tamm knew that the larger equipment required very expensive forms (magnetic strips for memory), was designed primarily for bank posting, and had experienced considerable downtime (mechanical trouble) in use. He stood to lose $500 commission by recommending the smaller machine, but he was trying to do what he felt was best for Collier. Collier's answer to Tamm's recommendation was, "If you won't show me the big machine, I'll look at your competition." Tamm arranged for Collier to come down to the branch sales office for a demonstration, and Collier was fascinated with the automatic qualities of the posting equipment. He bought the machine, but two weeks after delivery sent for Tamm to complain bitterly about the form cost and the downtime.

What ethical problems are involved in this situation for Tamm?
Did he do rightly to sell the customer the bigger equipment?
How would you suggest he handle Collier now?

15–3

Robert Ransom sells for General Distributors, which offers a full line of plumbing and electrical supplies to contractors, builders, and the ultimate consumer. He is on the road three days each week and in the office on Tuesdays, Thursdays, and Saturday mornings. Six months ago Robert had an especially pleasant interview with a Mr. Merlin Cochran, who was interested in two fiberglass tub-shower combinations for the upstairs addition that he planned to make. Robert quoted a price for the two fiberglass units, and Cochran seemed pleased and promised to call him when his construction progressed to the point that the units could be installed. There was no commitment made to buy the units. Sure enough, five months later, Cochran called and told Robert to deliver the two units. By this time, however, there had been a price increase of 5 percent. The units were delivered to the site and partially installed in the upstairs addition. Cochran received a copy of the bill a few days later reflecting the price change. Robert had never experienced a customer reaction any more heated than Cochran's—he had changed from "Dr. Jekyll to Mr. Hyde!" Robert just listened as Cochran swore at him and General Distributors over the phone, but Robert kept his composure. After Cochran had steamed for about five minutes, Robert tried to explain to him that price increases during the last few months were not unusual and that he was certainly sorry that there had been any misunderstanding. Cochran's last words were, "Come get these two units and if you scratch anything getting them out, you are responsible." Robert talked the whole thing over with his sales manager, Mr. Taylor, who agreed that Robert could offer the units at the first price quotation, although that price had been out of the catalogue for four months.

Robert went to the construction site and found the two tub-shower units walled in. He explained to Mr. Cochran that General Distributors would sell him the units for the old price and that he was sorry for the misunderstanding. Cochran's answer was, "I'm done mad now. Come get these units and you had better not harm anything. Within two more days they are going to get the staircase up, so you had better get them today!" Robert could see that it would be impossible to remove the units without tearing out part of the already constructed wall and possibly marring the subfloor. Cochran had specifically said that the subfloor had better not be scratched, but Robert could not understand why that would hurt anything. Robert tried again to get Cochran to accept the order at the lower price and finally had to leave with the issue still unresolved. There was no way to get the units out without hurting the units or disturbing the already completed construction.

What would be the best way to handle this customer grievance?
Do you think Robert and General Distributors did the right thing in permitting the customer to pay the old price?
Have negotiations reached the point where General Distributors should take legal action against Cochran, irrespective of the possible loss of goodwill, or should they simply absorb the $400 cost?

15–4

Charles Mulder has been a salesman for the Easy-Plane Boat Company for two weeks, since leaving Aqua-Queen, a competitor that also sells a line of speedboats to dealers. He is calling on Lewis Werne, an account he had formerly cultivated for Aqua-Queen.

> *Lewis:* Come in, Charles. I guess you want to talk about your new boats for the spring, don't you?

Charles: Yes! But I'm with a new company, Mr. Werne. I'm now with Easy-Plane. These are better boats than the ones you handle now. Believe me, I know both lines very well. Easy-Plane is rapidly taking the market from Aqua-Queen. I want to show you why it would be good strategy for you to switch. You have been a good customer, and I know you can gain profits from handling this more popular line.

Lewis: Wow! This is a surprise! What about those new Aqua-Queen models for the coming season, which you were talking about just two months ago?

Charles: Have you seen Easy-Plane's new model? Confidentially, before I left, I found out from the sales manager that Aqua-Queen has been losing its market position for several years now and is presently in a very weak financial state. But Easy-Plane is increasing its market share every year. The boats have a stronger hull, look better, and will move faster with the same power. When five of my best accounts switched, I got wise and changed companies. You have to believe in the products you sell, don't you?

Lewis: But I built up the Aqua-Queen name with my customers. What will I tell them if I switch lines? Besides, I understand that Tyson, your new credit manager at Easy-Plane, is hard to deal with.

Charles: I'll admit he's a pain, but I'll handle him for you. Say, I found out something before I left "Queen." I saw a memo on Ned Dunstan's desk—he's the "Queen" dealer nearest you. It indicated that he planned to spend over ten thousand dollars on an advertising campaign this spring. Easy-Plane has a plan whereby they would pay for half of your advertising. That would help you ward off Dunstan's challenge in this area without costing you nearly as much. I'll tell you what . . . if we can do business, we will take a weekend in the Bahamas together with our families to celebrate. I'll see that it won't cost you a thing. I'll just leave this material with you. Think about it!

Lewis: I'll consider it, Charles. But it would be a big step for me to change lines.

QUESTIONS

1. What are the ethical and goodwill issues involved in this incident?
2. Which of Charles' actions, if any, would you consider to be unethical?

16 Sales Management

Promotion to the job of sales manager is a logical step up the company ladder for most sales personnel. The representative who becomes an assistant or zone sales manager may later advance to higher paying positions such as branch sales manager, district sales manager, and vice-president in charge of sales. Many corporate presidents are selected from sales managers because they have been trained through sales experience to project good images. They are able to persuade people, and they can promote good public relations within and outside of the organization. Even if you don't aspire to be a manager, you will be better prepared to be a good sales team member by understanding the responsibilities of your "captain." Understanding this position, in fact, will mean better communication between you and your immediate supervisors. It will also enable you to have greater knowledge of your working environment.

Sales managers must plan, organize, lead, control, and secure personnel for the activities of the selling team. Managers set selling objectives, and they devise selling strategy. They also assume responsibility for salesforce results. They research the market, forecast sales, set territorial boundaries, fix quotas, help salespersons with problems, and select, train, and motivate the sales force. They take part in product planning, market expansions, sales-policy formulations, and the development of selling control and evaluation methods. Most managers are expected to sell important prospects and help persuade problem accounts that other sales representatives find difficult to close. They are well paid for all of these responsibilities and, in addition, receive many indirect rewards, such as club memberships, travel, and opportunities to express their ideas. Sales managers are selected from individuals with proven sales ability, communication talents, product knowledge, loyalty to the organization, and a leadership personality. Managers must, after all, set an example for sales personnel and project a positive image capable of inspiring greater selling effort. The manager's responsibilities will be examined in detail under the following headings:

- Approaching the leadership challenge
- Planning
- Recruiting and selecting
- Training
- Motivating
- Evaluation and control

APPROACHING THE LEADERSHIP CHALLENGE

A fundamental decision area for new sales managers is determining how to establish leadership image and example. The respect of the sales force can be won by showing competence, fairness, positiveness, decisiveness, and acceptable supervisory style.

Competence

To appear competent, the manager should exhibit superior knowledge of products, policies, and selling techniques. Many sales-manager development programs are designed to meet this competency requirement by having potential managers make example demonstrations at sales meetings and introduce new products at company branches. Aspiring managers must study new products and applications thoroughly and be able to sell in problem situations. They must learn to convey the competency image that salespersons expect of their leaders.

Fairness

To show fairness, the manager must be careful in deciding which representatives get the largest salary increases, the promotions, the praise, and the prizes. The manager who plays favorites by giving greater increases to lodge brothers or selecting certain persons over others for superficial reasons is dissolving the glue that holds the selling team together—the expectation of gain from belonging. Every decision, in fact, should take into consideration firm members' expectation of gain.[1] Young firm members who find no chance of advancement quit, and old firm members become demotivated when they lose hope of promotion. A fairness image can best be initiated by establishing definite standards of evaluation for greater compensation—standards such as quota attainment or profitability—and using them in rewarding personnel. Personnel must realize that intangible factors such as leadership qualities enter into promotional decisions for supervisory positions, but other rewards should be based almost entirely on merit and experience. Patterns of bias and favoritism are quickly noticed and resented.

Positiveness

A positive, enthusiastic atmosphere inspired by the sales manager must prevail for maximum results. A primary responsibility of every manager is maintaining a working environment that inspires productivity. Negative attitudes have no place in motivating salespersons who must face many disappointments in selling situations. While it is foolish to be overoptimistic or unrealistic, a "can-do" attitude must dominate. Uncertainty, pessimism, or setting goals too low can infect the sales force and undermine confidence. Positive, realistic goal setting and approaches apply the principles of cybernetics and contagiously stimulate sales force self-images. This primes each individual's mental capabilities for success.

Supervisory Style

Supervisory style concerns the assumptions managers make about their salespeople and the basic approaches they take to motivate them. One manager may assume, for example, that sales personnel are basically lazy, don't like responsibility, and will not work well unless closely supervised or threatened with dismissal. This manager is likely to set rigid work policies and be very restrictive in giving information to the selling team. The opposite of this supervisory style is the manager who assumes that personnel are responsible, creative, and capable individuals who desire to participate in decisions and who work best when fully informed and included. This type of manager promotes full communications with team members and tends to motivate through positive incentives.[2] This style includes trusting members of the sales force with responsibility and

---

[1] Wroe Alderson, *Marketing Behavior and Executive Action* (Homewood, Ill.: Irwin, 1957), p. 38.

[2] Douglas McGregor, *The Human Side of Enterprise* (New York: McGraw-Hill, 1960), pp. 33–48.

creating an environment with few restrictions. It is generally conceded that with today's shortage of qualified sales applicants and the inclination of sales representatives to resent close supervision, the dictatorial, threatening, overly restricting, and noncommunicative style is "out." The participative, trusting, and positive incentive style is "in." Most salespersons consider being their own boss and working their territories with relative freedom part of their job benefits. The greater the intelligence, education, resourcefulness, and selling experience of the persons managed, the less restrictive their work environment should be. While parttime, lower-level salespersons might need tight supervision and restrictive policies, professional industrial sales representatives require more freedom.

There is evidence, however, that the benevolent good-friend style of leadership has been taken too far. It is almost a proverb that the super salespersons who have risen from the ranks and want to be popular with their subordinates fail as managers. Too often, these new managers are overconcerned with popularity, bend rules for too many individuals, exhibit indecisiveness, and show irresponsibility by putting the firm's welfare in second place.[3] The friendly manager often fails to delegate and dodges the hard decisions that need to be made. Managers should recognize the aspirations of subordinates, but they should also apply a reasonable amount of discipline and put the good of the firm first.

The leadership model. The leadership model is the impression leaders make on their followers. It involves maintaining leadership image and providing good examples in order to inspire the sales-force members' willing compliance with supervisory requests. Managers must be aware that they are continually under close observation by sales personnel. If the manager wears certain clothes, handles a demonstration in a certain way, or shows particular ethical standards, sales representatives will likely take the cue and copy.

A primary principle of leadership is to give subordinates the *authority* they need to carry out their responsibilities. This means that managers who expect results from territorial operations should see that salespersons have flexible expense accounts, latitude to make sensible decisions, and general resources necessary to carry out their responsibilities.

Management by objectives. Management by objectives is a particular way of insuring that sales personnel participate in decisions. MBO entails joint determination of goals by the manager and the salesperson. In situations where conflicting goals occur, however, the manager is expected to apply some pressure. For example, if a salesperson purposely sets low

[3] David C. McClelland and David H. Burnham, "Good Guys Make Bum Bosses," *Psychology Today Magazine,* 9, no. 7 (December 1975), 69–70.

yearly goals in order to look good at the end of the year, the manager can pressure for higher goals. MBO also requires setting up definite times to compare progress with goals. If salespersons can be persuaded to set realistic goals, they will have fewer excuses for not obtaining them, and the detailed objectives will be able to guide their activities. MBO is particularly popular as a leadership device in selling because of the ease in measuring results—sales made, demonstrations given, interviews accomplished, expenses entailed, and profits generated.[4]

Managerial expectations. Managerial expectations are a powerful force in meeting the leadership challenge. This does not mean setting unattainable goals, but it does suggest that sales managers should communicate a high opinion of their personnel's capabilities. If managers indicate they feel that every member of the selling team has high potential, each member will be motivated to live up to that potential. The manager's expectations build up self-images, and improved self-images focus the mental resources of sales personnel on the success path (self-image theory).

PLANNING

Since sales managers are responsible for their sales force's success, they must make organizational decisions, forecast sales, plan products, establish territories, set quotas, and help finalize budgets. Each of these planning functions will be discussed below.

Planning Organizational Relationships

Organization is essential in coordinating effort. Every person on the selling team should know his or her responsibilities, the work load should be divided appropriately, and authority should be defined. The steps involved in organizing are: (1) reviewing objectives; (2) determining the activities necessary to accomplish the objectives; (3) grouping activities into job designations; (4) assigning the right person to each job designation; and (5) providing for easy control.[5] Job descriptions are detailed listings of all the activities, responsibilities, and authorities associated with each job position. They should be put in writing. The total work load of the sales force can be divided by separating groups of job positions by product, geographical area, customers, or combinations of these. When grouping activities, it is important to have the right number of subordinates

[4] Donald W. Jackson, Jr., and Ramon J. Aldag, "Managing the Sales Force by Objectives," *MSU Business Topics,* 22, no. 2 (Spring 1974), 53–58.

[5] Richard R. Still, Edward W. Cundiff, and Norman A. P. Govoni, *Sales Management Decisions, Policies, and Cases,* 3d. ed. (Englewood Cliffs, N.J.: Prentice-Hall, 1976), p. 135.

reporting to each superior. If a manager or supervisor controls too few people, expensive executive time is wasted. But if too many personnel are put under one manager, that manager's time may be spread too thin. A manager can supervise more salespersons if they are intelligent, well trained, have fewer selling problems, and sell uncomplicated products.

Organizations may be centralized or decentralized. Centralized organizations, like the Armed Forces, have a few people at the top making most of the decisions, while subordinates operate under strict policies or rules. This promotes coordination and tight control and assures uniformity of procedures, but it also discourages individual freedom in accomplishing results. Under decentralization, field personnel are made responsible for results, but they have more freedom in achieving those results and in meeting selling problems on their own initiative. While most firms set down important policy guidelines for some matters, such as meeting legal requirements, they usually allow considerable freedom in selling practices.

As firms grow larger, managers may find it necessary to create "staff" or advisory positions. Lawyers, product specialists, and research experts are examples of staff people who gather information and give advice to sales-force personnel but who have little authority over them. Such specialized advisers can free managers and salespersons from research, technical aspects, and other nonselling assignments and allow them to spend more time in the field. When there are *too many* staff personnel, they tend to generate unnecessary reports and can actually increase the nonselling time of sales-force members.

Sales managers can use organizational planning to keep the work environment healthy. A top-heavy organization with too many supervisors and too few workers can be prevented by including fewer top-level positions in organizational charts. Cliques or informal groups can develop that spread rumors, cause dissension, and damage morale. Cliques can be discouraged by having fewer persons under one supervisor and by improving information flow in the organization. The better the organization is managed and the more highly motivated the employees, the less important these informal groups will be. When cliques do develop, they should be influenced by the manager to work for organizational purposes, instead of against the formal structure. (See Figure 16.1 for a sales organization chart.)

Territorial Estimates and Sales Forecasting

Sales and territorial estimates are the basis for most of the firm's budgeting and planning. There are two basic methods for estimating territorial potential: the build-up method and the buying-power method.[6]

[6] Philip Kotler, *Marketing Management,* 2nd ed. (Englewood Cliffs, N.J.: Prentice-Hall, 1972), pp. 204–224.

Insuring Future Opportunity

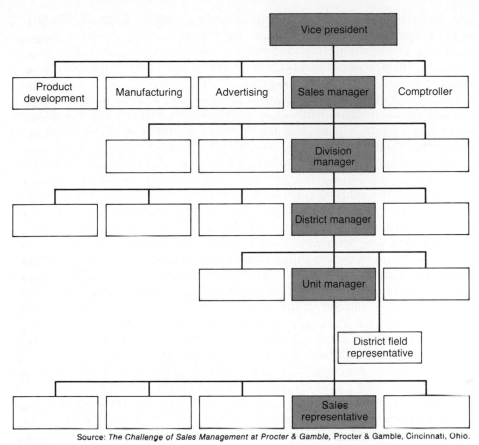

Source: *The Challenge of Sales Management at Procter & Gamble,* Procter & Gamble, Cincinnati, Ohio.

Figure 16.1   Procter & Gamble Sales Structure for a Typical Product Line

The build-up method is useful when there is a list of potential buyers and accurate estimates of what each will buy. This method entails identifying possible customers, finding out how many are in the territory, and determining the average amount each can be expected to purchase. If the firm is selling to manufacturers, for example, managers can use the U.S. Government Census of Manufacturers to find the number of particular establishments in a certain geographical area, annual sales figures, and net worth data—all of which help make good estimates. In the index-of-buying-power method, purchasing power and credit availability are put together in an index and used to estimate potential. Consumer companies have too many customers to use the build-up method, so most use the index method. Since a market is people with money to spend, who are willing to spend it on your product, buying power and number of people are important measurable factors affecting sales. *Sales & Marketing Management* magazine's "Annual Survey of Buying Power" gives an estimate of buying power in different counties and cities. But for the individual firm, competitive factors and target-market differences must be used to adjust such gross estimates.[7]

Nearly all company plans depend on estimates of total sales, and sales managers are usually involved in some way in making these aggregate forecasts. There are several methods of forecasting sales of present products. *Customers* may be questioned about their buying intentions if a few prospects comprise the market for the product. *Company officials,* including sales managers, may estimate sales by using an averaging method. All the estimates are added together and divided by the number of executives making the estimates. *Sales representatives* can also give their opinions about how much can be sold at certain prices. However, salespersons are not always aware of the influences affecting sales and have a tendency to underestimate deliberately to encourage the assignment of lower quotas. Sometimes sales of recent years are plotted on a graph and the *trend line extended* (see Figure 16.2). If sales have gone up at a rate of about 6 percent in the previous four years, it might be assumed that sales will rise about 6 percent for the subsequent year. This is not always a safe assumption, however. Factors that affect sales could change drastically in the forecasted year. It is better to find out which factors influence sales, estimate how those factors are going to change in the forecast year, and derive the sales forecast on the strength and direction of change of the *influencing factors.* If the demand for a certain automobile, for example, is influenced by the amount of income consumers have, the price of gasoline, and the relative increase in the price of competitive cars, these three factors could be estimated and the forecast based on them. Sometimes statistical experts examine past years to determine the relative influence of various factors on sales. They then express the relationship in a mathematical *formula* that is used to predict sales for the next year. Some product sales are easily forecast when sales follow behind some other leading factor. If sale of lumber follows construction permits issued, then the number of construction permits would indicate the demand (sales) for lumber.

New product sales are more difficult to forecast. Sales depend on how fast new products will be substituted for the products they were designed to replace, and this involves educated guessing. Usually, new products gain acceptance slowly at first, and at a certain point sales begin to climb, at a rapidly increasing rate, until the market is nearly saturated. Forecasters look at the experience of similar products that were introduced earlier to estimate how well the new product should sell in the coming year. An

[7] "1976 Survey of Buying Power," *Sales & Marketing Management,* July 26, 1976.

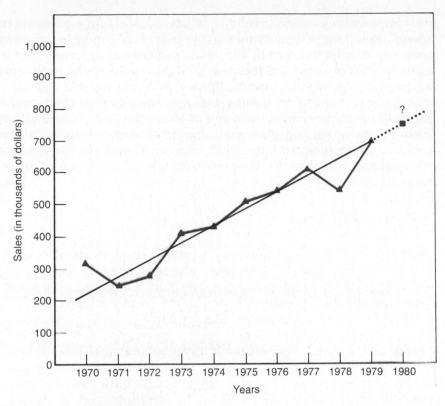

Figure 16.2 Trend Projection

expensive method is setting up test markets in selected cities to find out how rapidly customers will accept the new product before estimating sales for the total market. While these sales forecasts for old and new products may not always be accurate, they have to be made to plan production schedules and gauge what raw materials and personnel will be needed for the year.

Product Planning

Sales managers may not have direct responsibility for product planning, but they are usually deeply involved. Product planning concerns developing new products and modifying or deleting old products to meet the firm's changing markets. The greatest return on investment is usually made during the market-growth stage in the product's life cycle. Thus, many executives feel that they must have products in this stage to maintain market share and make profits. The push for new products and for improvements in existing products is vital to the firm's prosperity and growth. New products must be created that have strong, built-in advantages over existing products. They must be pushed vigorously, or buying habits will not change, and the new product will fail. New products that can be produced with existing equipment and sold without changing the basic sales organization involve less expense and consequently less risk. Sales managers must be aware of these considerations and furnish timely advice in helping plan new product strategy. They must receive feedback information from the sales force and translate this information into workable suggestions for modifying the product line to fit target markets better.

Territorial Planning

As explained, territorial potential is measured in terms of people and their purchasing power. The sales manager must divide and assign territories fairly on the basis of their potentials. Customers who constitute a territory should be located in the same geographical area to make coverage by salespersons easier. Geographical boundary lines should be drawn to make identification and control by management less complex. If areas are too large, unnecessary traveling expenses will be incurred, and if the sales potential is too great, salespersons will tend to call only on the best accounts, leaving much potential business unsolicited. If territories are too small, sales calls will be wasted on poor prospects, and salespersons will become discouraged. Although senior salespersons may be assigned to the best territories, territories and quotas must be assigned on a fair basis. Otherwise, negative morale factors will develop, and potentially good representatives will quit. Territories are established to motivate salespersons, to enable the evaluation and control of selling efforts, and to cultivate customers properly. In some businesses, such as life insurance—where personal friendships and contacts are important or where the total market is small—territories may not be assigned. The product, the customers, the competition, the geographical lay of the area, and the type of salesperson affect territorial divisions.[8] Of course, territorial designations should be reviewed often, to take into consideration any changes in selling conditions.

Setting Quotas

Quotas are set to motivate sales representatives, to appraise selling effectiveness, to form a basis for sales contests and compensations, and

[8] William J. Stanton and Richard H. Buskirk, *Management of the Sales Force,* 5th ed. (Homewood, Ill.: Irwin, 1978), pp. 481–495.

to budget marketing expenditures. Quotas should not be set only in terms of sales goals. Interview, demonstration, profit, and expense quotas should also be established to give salespersons a set of guiding standards.[9] All of these quotas can be determined at the yearly management-by-objectives conference with the salesperson. Quotas should never be impossible to attain. The negative morale factor is immense when compensation plans, contests, and honors are based on unrealistically high quotas. Quotas that are set too low are likewise a psychological hindrance.

Budgeting

Budgets provide monetary standards for control and coordination. The sales budget divides sales expectations into categories by customer, product, and territory. The expense budget is set to reveal cost problems and wasted resources. When actual figures are different from budgeted figures, managers must reconcile actual sales performances with planned performance. The sales budget is based on the sales forecast and territorial potential estimations. The expense budget is determined by estimating the costs required to reach sales goals.

RECRUITING AND SELECTING

Sales managers may have complete responsibility for the total selection process, or they may have an important influence in screening applicants. It would be against good management principles to make sales managers responsible for sales results and not let them participate in critical staffing decisions. There is probably no management activity more determinative of success or failure than picking the members of the selling team. No amount of training or motivation can overcome bad selection decisions, and a strong team of well-selected sales representatives can cover a multitude of managerial mistakes. Recruiting and selection are interrelated and entail the following steps:

- Determining the quantity and kind of personnel needed
- Assessing the sources of applicants
- Screening applicants
- Selecting the right person for the selling job

[9] *Ibid.,* pp. 511–525.

Determining the Quantity and Kind of Personnel Needed

It is very hard to determine the quantity of salespersons needed, because there are so many influencing factors. But good methods produce the best estimates. If too many representatives are hired, selling expenses will go up in relation to sales produced, increased turnover is likely, and profits may decline. It is also bad practice to hire more sales representatives than needed, with the expectation that many will quit, thus leaving only the successful producers. If too few representatives are hired, they will tend to "skim the cream" in their territories (call only on the best accounts), neglect customers, and generally lose many opportunities for sales to competitors. Some of the considerations involved in determining how many salespersons to hire are sales-force turnover, territorial expansion plans, increases or decreases in competitive activity, changes in products, and economic conditions. Many companies simply rely on intuition and past experience to estimate the number of salespersons needed. It is far better, however, to have a more scientific approach because of the importance of the decision.

Still, Cundiff, and Govoni identify three rational methods for approaching quantity determination: *the work-load method, the sales-potential method,* and the *incremental method.*[10] The first step in the *work-load method* is classifying customers into categories by importance to sales volume. Then determine how long interviews should be for each class of customer and how many calls should be made for each class. The total interview time necessary to do a good selling job can be found by adding together the total time that should be spent with all classes. The interview time each salesperson can spend with the customer each year is estimated by subtracting nonselling time (utilizing the number of hours in a typical workday) from the total time. The final step involves dividing the yearly interview time available to each sales representative into the total interview hours necessary in the firm's total territory, and the result is the number of sales personnel needed.

The *sales-potential method* entails dividing the yearly dollar sales volume each salesperson can be expected to accomplish into the total forecasted sales volume, while making allowances for turnover (salespersons leaving the team). This method is too simple since the forecasted sales volume *depends* on how many salespersons are selling for the firm. *The incremental method* involves hiring additional salespersons as long as the estimated sales generated by that additional person, less the costs of the additional person, yield a profit. This method does take into consideration

[10] Still, Cundiff, and Govoni, *op. cit.,* pp. 63–68.

that as salespersons are added to a given territory, other factors being equal, the sales per salesperson will decrease because about the same amount of prospects will be shared by more representatives.[11] All three methods give a rationale for the quantity decision and are better than intuitive guessing.

Written job descriptions and analyses of past experience are very helpful in determining the kind of personnel needed. A complete written job description should be prepared for every sales position. This involves a job analysis to determine what qualifications are necessary for each position. The wide variety of selling situations requires sales representatives with varying backgrounds. A sales applicant who might do very well in one job may fail in another situation. Selling accounting-system equipment, for example, requires a technically competent, highly intelligent sales representative who is both proficient in detail (an introvert characteristic) and able to relate well to customers (an extrovert characteristic). A salesperson with these qualifications would probably be unhappy and ineffective as a door-to-door sales representative. Some salespersons are good closers but may be deficient in service-attitude requirements. They would not do well selling wholesaler's lines to retailers or carrying out the teaching aspects of some selling jobs. An important device used by many sales managers involves carefully reviewing the characteristics of the firm's best sales representatives. It is fairly easy to analyze personnel profiles and determine the age, marital status, education, and work-experience factors that characterize the best sales personnel. However, it is harder to determine attitudes and other personality factors that characterize these stars and harder still to measure these qualities in applicants. It is in this area that managerial skill in the selection process really counts. Usually it can be assumed that sales representatives with whom customers can identify (relate to) because of their attractive personalities have a persuasive advantage. Certainly intelligence, communicating ability, appearance, health, drive, a positive self-image, money motivation, enthusiasm, competitiveness, and determination are important qualities for most successful salespersons.

Source of Applicants

Having several good sources for applicants increases the chances of finding outstanding salespersons and reduces screening costs. The sources used depend on specific qualifications needed for each job

[11] *Ibid.*

description, the current availability of applicants from each source, and the time available to screen and hire new personnel. Some companies fill sales positions from present employees, selecting production or other personnel who have had a chance to learn the company's products, traditions, and policies. Company officials have a chance to observe the personalities of such individuals, but success in other departments does not always transfer to personal selling. An excellent source of talent is *"walk-ins"* who study the company, match their talents with company requirements, and show their persuasiveness by selling themselves to the management official. Unfortunately, there are usually not enough of these qualified aggressive individuals to fill all needs.

Colleges and universities provide applicants with proven intelligence, problem-solving ability, good health, and the ability to communicate well with most prospects. Education can provide technical competence, a confident self-image, and the projected image that company recruiters seek.

Many college seniors reject sales, however, because they fail to consider the opportunities and the requirements. Many feel that sales won't give them a professional image and that they don't fit the erroneous picture of a sales representative that they have in their minds. Therefore, companies that recruit in college markets must prove they can provide the challenge, the image, and the compensation to attract highly qualified college graduates.

Many companies also give special consideration to hiring *salespersons who have experience with other companies* in the same industry. Managers can reduce training costs, provide an internal source of competitive information, and perhaps enlarge the market by letting the new representative bring old accounts into the fold. It is unethical to solicit such salespersons openly, and they usually require higher compensation to make the change.

Employment agencies, private and governmental, can furnish applicants quickly and help in the screening process. Private agencies often charge a fee, though, and both governmental and private agencies are sometimes more concerned with opportunity for the applicant than they are with the needs of the requesting company. Agencies are often used when other sources are exhausted. Blind and full-disclosure *newspaper ads* provide a large number of individuals with widely varying qualifications. Because many applicants apply, screening and selecting costs will be more expensive. Blind ads (ads which don't reveal the name of the company) give recruiters a chance to sell the company before the applicant rejects the employment possibility. Sales managers and the entire selling team can also look for prospective salespersons in their many contacts outside of the firm.

Screening Applicants

The five major tools used in the selection process are the application form, the personal interview, references, tests, and physical examinations. Governmental restrictions forbid using discriminatory hiring practices in regard to race, sex, religion, or age. Screening devices must therefore be justified as important to the selection process and not designed to screen out qualified minorities.

The Application Form. The properly designed application form (Figure 16.3, pp. 426–427) can include a wealth of valuable information about the person. Particularly important are work experience, educational experience, health, interests, special achievements, reasons for wanting to work for the company, reasons for leaving the last position, geographical background, and special abilities. Experience in sales or sales-related activities reveals that the individual has had to learn to adjust to other people and has tried and liked sales. Military experience indicates maturity and the experience of having to adjust. Athletic experience indicates the desire to compete and win in addition to health, enthusiasm, and a confident self-image. Unaccounted-for time, too many jobs in too short a period, a criminal record, or failure to have work experience in school are negative factors. Questions on many application blanks indicate the applicant's willingness to travel, relocate, work unusual hours, or otherwise accept any undesirable working conditions associated with the opening. Questions relating to personal habits (drinking or smoking) may be asked as well as questions about the applicant's spouse. Most firms require a great deal of information and attempt to match the profile of the applicant with profiles of successful sales representatives already employed. The work and educational history sections of the form may provide sources of references who are less biased than the references suggested by the applicant.

The Interview. The interview allows consideration of the applicant's appearance, personality, attitudes, interests, sociability, intelligence, and communications ability. Some firms conduct several interviews before hiring, and most firms pattern their interviews for maximum effectiveness. Nearly all interviewers look for nonverbal indications and realize that they must judge on incomplete evidence. The idea is to give the applicant a chance to express personality variables and the recruiter a chance to see if qualifications match the position. Applicants are appraised through careful questioning. Interviewers should attempt to provide an atmosphere in which the applicant can relax and be natural. Applicants who show nervousness are at least indicating that they care about the interview and should not be judged too harshly for not being perfectly

Figure 16.3

RANDOM HOUSE INC.

EMPLOYMENT APPLICATION

AN EQUAL OPPORTUNITY EMPLOYER

INSTRUCTIONS

1. Type or print in ink.
2. Answer each question fully and accurately. Use additional sheet, if necessary.
3. Do not include information regarding race, color, religion, age or national origin.
4. Read declaration carefully — then sign and date form.

Name	Last	First	Middle	Area Code Telephone ( )

Address	Number	Street	City	State	Zip	Social Security No.

EXPERIENCE

List All Employment - Including Previous RANDOM HOUSE, INC. Employment and U.S. Military Service - Start with Present Employer.

Dates Employed	Employer's Name and Address	Major Duties Performed	
From To			
Starting Position			Starting Salary (Base) $ Per
Terminal Position	Supervisor's Name and Title	Reason For Leaving	Last Salary (Base) $ Per

Dates Employed	Employer's Name and Address	Major Duties Performed	
From To			
Starting Position			
Terminal Position	Supervisor's Name and Title	Reason For Leaving	Base Salary $ Per

Dates Employed	Employer's Name and Address	Major Duties Performed	
From To			
Starting Position			
Terminal Position	Supervisor's Name and Title	Reason For Leaving	Base Salary $ Per

Dates Employed	Employer's Name and Address	Major Duties Performed	
From To			
Starting Position			
Terminal Position	Supervisor's Name and Title	Reason For Leaving	Base Salary $ Per

EDUCATION

Show All Formal Education Including U.S. Military Schools.

Institution and Location	Dates Attended		Graduated		Degree Received	Major and Minor Fields of Study
	From	To	Yes	No		
High School (Last Attended)						
College or University						
Other						
Other						
Other						

1185 10/77

426

LAST NAME

FIRST

DATE OF APPLICATION

EMPLOYMENT INTERESTS

Describe Type of Position Desired

Date available for employment	Salary expected
	$ Per

Will you travel?	Will you work nights?
☐ None ☐ Occasional ☐ Frequent	☐ Yes ☐ No

MISCELLANEOUS

Reason for applying at Random House, Inc. - Referred by a Random House, Inc. employee, private employment agency, newspaper advertising, etc.	Are there any types of jobs you are not able to fully perform because of physical or mental injury, disability or disease? ☐ Yes ☐ No. If Yes, explain. Yes *will not* disqualify you from consideration for employment.
If employed, can you submit proof of U.S. Citizenship? ☐ Yes ☐ No	If employed, can you submit proof of age? ☐ Yes ☐ No	
Have you ever previously applied for employment at Random House, Inc. or other subsidiary companies or locations of RCA? If yes, give place and date. ☐ Yes ☐ No	Are you in the U.S. on a visa which prohibits you from working here? ☐ Yes ☐ No
Have you ever previously been employed at Random House, Inc. or other subsidiary companies or locations of RCA? If yes, give place and dates. ☐ Yes ☐ No	Have you ever pleaded guilty or been found guilty of a crime, civilian or military? (Do not include minor traffic violations.) ☐ Yes ☐ No If yes, explain. Yes *will not* disqualify you from consideration.

Note clerical skills and office machine or technical equipment.

Describe your hobbies or other avocational interests.

Professional Attainments.

Do you have a currently effective agreement with employers or others concerning inventions you have made or may make?
☐ Yes   ☐ No   If Yes, please furnish copy of agreement and indicate the number of months the agreement remains effective after termination.

_____ Months

REFERENCES
List Former Supervisors Not Previously Shown or Others Familiar With Your Work - Exclude Relatives.

Name	Occupation	Address	Telephone
Name	Occupation	Address	Telephone
Name	Occupation	Address	Telephone

The information on this application is accurate and subject to check by Random House, Inc. I understand the furnishing of any misleading or incorrect information will render this application void and will be just cause for termination in the event of my employment. I hereby give permission to Random House, Inc. or its duly authorized representative to contact any persons, companies or educational institutions named in this application other than my present employer. I understand that it is Random House, Inc. policy to respect the rights of other companies in their confidential and proprietary information. In keeping with this policy, I hereby confirm that I understand this policy and I agree that I will not disclose or use, in connection with my employment with Random House, Inc., any confidential or proprietary information of a former employer which is not publicly available from another source.

_____   _____
Signature of Applicant   Date

Random House, Inc. complies with all federal, state, and municipal laws which prohibit discrimination because of age, race, color, religion, sex, national origin, handicap or veteran's status.

poised (see Figure 16.4). The employment interview will be thoroughly treated in the next chapter, and additional interview techniques and responses discussed.

Figure 16.4   Interview Guide

Name of applicant_____

*REMEMBER . . . .

Establish rapport and try to put applicant at ease.
Sell Taylor Company to the applicant.
Get answers but try not to let the applicant feel pressured.
Encourage the applicant to talk by keeping your responses short.

Invite the applicant to sit in a chair facing your desk.
Express appreciation for the interviewee's interest in the company. Ask:

Who told you about Taylor Company? How did you become interested in us?

Why do you feel that you want a career in selling?

Where do you expect to be in your career seven years from now?

I've asked you some hard questions. Now I just want you to relax and tell me about yourself. What do you like and dislike; what are your strengths and weaknesses; and what are some of your important past experiences?

Now tell me why we should hire you as a salesperson.

What kind of a person was your last boss?

If we hired you, when could you go to work, and what kind of money would you expect?

Promise the applicant the company's thoughtful consideration and an early decision on further processing.

RATE THE APPLICANT:

APPEARANCE	Excellent	Poor
POISE	Excellent	Poor
VOICE	Excellent	Poor
COMMUNICATION	Excellent	Poor
LIKABLENESS	Excellent	Poor
OVERALL	Excellent	Poor

RECOMMENDATION:

References. References are more realistic if they are not suggested by the applicant. That is, it is better to question persons not listed by the applicant as references. Few former employers or professors want to give applicants bad references, and references that are not confidential are almost worthless. Interpreting references is a talent, because they must be "decoded" for inferences, indications, and for what is not said. The reference may read: "John Jones will make you a good employee, if you can get him to work for you," or "Sam Smith was not late for work too often." Others condemn by leaving unsaid the comments recruiters expect to read or hear about outstanding talents. When studying the real meaning of the reference, managers must learn to read between the lines and take into consideration the tendency to rate too high.

Tests. Tests can be obtained that are designed to measure the applicant's intelligence, personality, interests, and aptitudes. Intelligence tests indicate verbal and mathematical reasoning capabilities and are useful for qualifying sales representatives for high-level jobs. While very high intelligence is not required for all selling situations, a good intelligence test can gauge the ability to solve problems and the trainability of an applicant. Personality tests are questionable, because qualities and attitudes are difficult to measure on paper, and answers to many questions can be "faked." Personality tests don't always measure what they are supposed to measure, and conclusions may depend on which psychologist interprets the responses. While a test interpreter may conclude that a person is "aggressive" because he or she walks fast, talks fast, and eats fast, this may not always translate into selling "aggressiveness."

Interest tests can also be faked by intelligent applicants who can guess the best answer. However, just because personality and interest tests are imperfect measures does not mean that their careful use can't furnish valuable insights into the applicant's attitudes. Mechanical, clerical, and mathematical aptitudes may be important in selling complex products such as major equipment or accounting systems. Firms often require that a minimum score be attained on tests like these that reflect the applicant's ability to learn and demonstrate the product line.

It is best to use tests to substantiate judgments determined from other selection tools and to eliminate untrainable applicants. It is illegal to use tests to discriminate against minorities.

Physical Examinations. Selling is a rigorous activity, sometimes requiring extensive traveling, lifting heavy products, and enthusiastic presentations. Physical examinations can reveal health deficiencies that preclude investing in an applicant who has or probably will have serious physical problems. Some corporations are too quick to eliminate otherwise qualified persons who have physical stamina but a minor health defect.

If the prospective sales representative is able to show vitality and enthusiasm during the interview—and the defect is not major—it should be weighed against other qualifications that are more important.

Selecting the Right Person for the Selling Job

Selection tools can furnish only information about an applicant—the manager must balance all the factors and make the final decision. For selling situations involving complex products, high-level intelligence and mathematical abilities are required. For most selling jobs average intelligence, good general knowledge, acceptable appearance, and reasonable health are sufficient. The variables that really matter are those that are the hardest to measure—attitudes and character. A few questions every sales manager should ask before adding a new member to the team are:

- Will the salesperson work hard, relate well to customers, and present a good image?
- Does the salesperson indicate adaptability by having work, military, or athletic experience?
- Do references reflect enthusiasm in commending the applicant or contain only a minimum of positive information?
- Do tests reflect that the applicant is intelligent and trainable?
- Am I really impressed with the applicant's personality and social sensitivity?
- Will the applicant enjoy working for the firm and stay, or is the person likely to quit before making a profit for the company?

Every new salesperson is a big investment in training and development costs, and if the wrong individual is trained and quits, the person who should have been hired and developed may be working for the firm's competitor. Hiring the right person is the most important function of the sales manager and the personnel staff, so get adequate information before making a decision.

TRAINING

Training should be planned for new representatives soon after they report for work. Too many companies put the new salesperson in an out-of-the-way corner of the sales office, expecting an automatic orientation because of the sales-office atmosphere. In a few days the new member may be assigned errands in and near the office. The recruit will have a higher image of the new company if definite training periods that provide a real orientation and a sense of belonging are scheduled during the first week. Sales managers must take differences in experience into consideration in training both new and long-tenured members of the sales force. Separate plans should be devised for new representatives without previous experience, new representatives with previous selling experience, junior representatives, senior representatives, and supervisory sales personnel. Good training programs involve four major planning areas:

- Goals of the training program
- Contents of the training program
- Methods and personnel to be used
- Evaluation of the program

Goals of the Training Program

A good training program increases profits by increasing sales volume, decreasing selling costs, smoothing the introduction of new products into the market, boosting sales-force confidence, improving individual self-images, generating enthusiasm, fostering goodwill, and lowering sales-force turnover. Knowledge is the author of both confidence and enthusiasm in selling, and when sales representatives learn the answers through a good training program, their selling time will be more effectively utilized. Specific goals should be detailed in writing before the program is planned.

Contents of the Training Program

The contents of the program should be detailed from the goals. Program content depends on the type of product, the experience and knowledge of the trainee, and the nature of the selling situation. Sales managers responsible for moving complex product lines that frequently include new offerings or new applications to their product systems emphasize product knowledge in their programs. Managers responsible for consumer products that are easily understood tend to stress selling techniques and merchandising principles. New salespersons have to learn everything—company policies and history, product features and benefits, methods of operation, personnel and their place in the organization, selling techniques, and work-planning methods. More experienced sales representatives must master new products, new product applications, new markets, and new communication techniques (such as transactional analysis and non-verbal language). Markets can change dynamically, and the selling environment can also change, necessitating a continual updating of information. Success theory and attempts to restructure attitudes are included in many corporate training sessions to boost confidence and self-image. To many sales managers, training is part of the motivational effort. It is an attention-giving device that lets the trainee know the firm expects continued learning. Learning is growth, and it promotes self-esteem and production and prevents stagnation. While training periods are shorter for the more experienced, sometimes longer-tenured sales-persons must unlearn bad selling habits before the habits can be replaced with modern techniques.

Sometimes the nature of the selling situation indicates special program contents. Missionary sales representatives must learn to be good instructors and teachers to train dealer salespersons. Sales managers who train intangible or system representatives to sell life insurance, securities, franchises, and accounting systems must prepare their selling forces to offer customers consultation in business and legal matters associated with the offering. A certified life underwriter (CLU) insurance representative may study for years to meet the knowledge requirements to qualify as a top consultant salesperson.

Methods and Personnel to Be Used

New personnel can be trained in formal sessions where sales supervisors demonstrate products, simulate interviews, or direct discussion participation and role playing. Some trainees may take formal correspondence courses or attend company-paid college classes. Many trainees are given personal training sessions with their immediate sales supervisor (zone sales manager or senior salesperson) where they may have to give complete demonstrations of products in the line. Some are assigned to read policy manuals to understand company standards. Few methods are more real and exciting, however, as calling on prospects in the field with experienced seniors. A total view of a coordinated sales effort yields insights that can never be explained in the branch office—a holistic combination of personality variables, body language, sales points, and persuasion techniques unified to convince a real buyer can't be fully duplicated in artificial situations. Even more instructive is the new representative's first attempt to persuade a prospect under the senior's watchful eye. Good training programs must include field observation and direct participation, because selling is an art that requires practice, as well as a science, which must be applied.

Companies vary in respect to when they send trainees to the "home office" for formal instruction and to see production lines in operation (for tangible products). Some companies with less complex product offerings don't include home office instruction in their program. Other companies have products of such a technical nature that they require the sales trainee to work in production for months before graduating to selling. Others may allow the trainee to sell less consequential products before working into consulting sales—selling aluminum cookware to the ultimate consumer before selling bulk aluminum to industrial accounts. Senior representatives and junior sales managers do most of the training of new salespersons, although staff instructors are used at the home office.

More experienced sales representatives with well-developed (and sensitive) egos must be approached cautiously to protect their self-images. Sales meetings and yearly conferences that feature their participation refresh their knowledge. Some managers feel that this mature group should be separated and recognized at conferences rather than being included on the same level as more junior sales representatives. This group often learns from sharing sessions where new selling tactics are discussed. Often, these seniors are asked to make demonstrations for which they must prepare.

Visual aids are being increasingly used in training for all levels of salespersons. Films, specially prepared training folders, and programmed instructional materials can be edited and designed to assure that trainees are learning correct techniques. A sample demonstration may turn into a bad example, but training films can be carefully edited.

Evaluation of the Program

All methods should be reviewed for effectiveness and matched with stated objectives to determine if the training program is living up to expectations. Effectiveness can be determined by the time and expense required to raise a trainee to a measurable level of performance or accomplishment. How much have sales increased since the installation of the program? How much are sales expenses down in relation to volume of sales produced? Have customer complaints diminished, and is morale noticeably better as measured by less salesperson turnover? There is no such thing as a perfect program, but constant improvements as evidenced by good feedback can lead to a more effective training operation.

MOTIVATING

Sales managers can substantially affect company profits motivating the sales force. Good motivational practices are almost as important as selecting high-potential sales personnel. Leadership example, sales training, sales meetings, conferences, contests, and compensation plans either stimulate sales-force members to greater efforts or have negative effects at high expense. Motivating will be considered under the following headings:

- The motivational problem
- Usable theory in motivating sales personnel
- Motivational style
- Compensation plans
- Sales contests
- Sales meetings and conferences

The Motivational Problem

Although sales-force members have basically the same motivational drives as customers, there are some notable differences. Sales personnel are more money-motivated than most individuals. The selling job subjects them to emotional highs and lows not experienced in many other occupations. Travel and after-hours work may deprive them from spending as much time as they would like with their families. They work most of the time without supervision and have a special need for managerial attention. Senior sales representatives may fall into routines and find it hard to maintain enthusiasm in territories and with customers that are too familiar.

Motivational profiles point out another basic problem—having to approach individual sales personnel with different motivational techniques. An ideal salesperson should be a blend of achievement-oriented and affiliative-oriented profiles. However, most individuals lean in one direction or the other. The achievement-oriented salesperson has strong needs to complete unfinished work, to excel, and to be given specific feedback. This competitive individual will work hard alone. He or she needs less group involvement than the affiliative type but often lacks the social sensitivity to win complete customer approval.[12] The affiliative type, on the other hand, needs to be with other people, can be told in general terms how they are doing, and have a higher tolerance for unfinished work. While affiliative types may not be as competitive, they may have the social skills to earn acceptance by both customers and supervisors.[13] The needs of various sales-force members are different and require tailored motivational approaches gained from a never-ending learning process.

[12] Saul W. Gellerman, *Motivation and Productivity* (American Management Association, 1963), pp. 122–141, reviewing David C. McClelland, et al., *The Achievement Motive* (New York: Appleton, 1953).

[13] *Ibid.*, pp. 115–141, reviewing Stanley Schacter, *The Psychology of Affiliation* (Stanford: Stanford University Press, 1959).

Usable Theory in Motivating Sales Personnel

The challenge of leadership has already been explored and is important in motivating sales personnel. In addition, work motivational theory indicates that because of their independent working conditions, sales-force members need more individual supervisory attention, more group participation meetings, and more training opportunities than less independent workers. Supervisory and group support is needed to recharge self-images assaulted by refusals and the self-subjection that is a part of selling. The sales manager should provide an encouraging work environment that includes such basics as good products, good prices, a realistic territory, a competitive compensation level, realistic training opportunities, and suitable training aids. Sales personnel who are well-compensated and have their basic and safety needs met are released (according to Maslow's theory) to pursue fulfillment of social, esteem, and self-actualization needs. Accordingly, praise and supervisory approval, special recognition, and promotional progress can mean more than money in stimulating greater production.[14] A letter from the president of the company, a commendation certificate, a quota-maker pin are incentives that satisfy higher need levels.

Motivational Style

The full information management approach is a motivational style compatible with today's sales force and selling environments. It features consultations with sales personnel before changes are made, reprimands that are made in person to maintain good communications with the salesperson, and communications involving adult-adult (transactional analysis) ego states. Managers should always praise good work either personally or through a personal letter, and appropriate disciplinary actions should be taken when necessary or sales personnel will lose respect.

Compensation Plans

Trends are away from straight-salary and straight-commission compensation plans, and most feature a salary plus an incentive in the form of a commission or a bonus. Table 16.1 indicates the types of plans commonly used and the direction of change from 1976 to 1977. Public-relations positions are more likely to be compensated by the straight-salary method, while insurance and other intangible selling is more likely to have higher commission elements in the pay package. In straight-salary plans, there

---

[14] Abraham Maslow, *Motivation and Personality* (New York: Harper & Row, 1970), pp. 35–58.

**TABLE 16.1 ALTERNATIVE SALES COMPENSATION AND
INCENTIVE PLANS**

| METHOD | PERCENT OF COMPANIES USING PLANS—1977 | | | | |
| | ALL INDUSTRIES | | CONSUMER PRODUCTS | INDUSTRIAL PRODUCTS | OTHER COMMERCE/ INDUSTRY |
	1977	1976	1977	1977	1977
Straight salary	23.5%	25.1%	15.7%	23.4%	36.6%
Straight commission	—	0.9	—	—	—
Draw against commission	7.4	4.2	11.9	6.8	3.7
Salary plus commission	27.0	24.4	20.9	29.1	24.4
Salary plus individual bonus	29.8	32.5	39.6	28.1	24.4
Salary plus group bonus	3.3	2.8	3.0	3.7	1.2
Salary plus commission plus individual or group bonus	9.0	7.7	8.9	8.9	9.7
More than one method of payment	—	2.4	—	—	—
Total	100.0%	100.0%	100.0%	100.0%	100.0%

Note: Some year-to-year differences reflect changes in the organizations reporting data.

Source: American Management Associations, *Executive Compensation Service*, in *Sales & Marketing Management*, February 27, 1978, p. 60.

is little incentive to push a salesperson to greater effort, and straight-commission sales representatives become so intent on orders or volume that they tend to forget goodwill, service, firm image, and the profitability of the transaction for the company. In most sales situations there should be a floor under the representative's income to assure that the grocery bills and other necessities will be paid. The more significant the salesperson's skills are in getting orders (creative selling), the higher the incentive part of the pay package should be. Incentive pay should be made frequently (monthly or weekly) for better results, and it should be based on a salesperson's individual accomplishments.

Smaller firms that don't have good training programs for inexperienced salespersons may pay high salaries or commissions to attract more experienced sales personnel. Larger firms, which may offer more opportunities for advancement, may pay less in actual money but may have better fringe benefits. When firms heavily overpay salespersons, they may have difficulty in persuading good persons to leave the field and take managerial positions. When salespersons are underpaid, the best ones quit to take more attractive opportunities elsewhere (sometimes with a direct competitor), leaving the low producers in the selling force. High turnover is a waste of resources and is upsetting to customers. A pay level slightly above the competitive level is just a little more expensive to the company in terms of pay rates, but it attracts and retains better personnel, which pays dividends in the long run.

Sales Contests

Sales contests call for special selling efforts and offer special rewards. As such, contests can lift slumping sales and generate new enthusiasm in the selling force. However, themes must be mature, promotion of the contest must be timed correctly, rules should be fair to all, prizes should be desirable, and there must be many winners. Contests can generate bad morale when themes are embarrassingly childish, when rules encourage cheating, when competition among salespeople becomes cutthroat, when prizes are undesirable, and when certain sales personnel are unduly handicapped by territorial or product restrictions. Prizes include such incentives as products, cash, travel opportunities, or special recognition symbols such as certificates of commendation from top management. If prizes are too significant, salespersons may be tempted to overstock customers or cheat, and the contest may be too expensive for the company. If prizes are not worthwhile, there may be little incentive to participate.

Sales Meetings and Conferences

Local sales meetings should take place several times a month to promote better training, motivation, and communications. New product knowledge, analysis of recently experienced selling successes and failures, recognition of achievement, review of future plans, review of market and business conditions, and discussion of special problems are sample topics. Sales managers should avoid the temptation to dominate the meetings and should encourage participation and communication of ideas. All meetings should be positive and encouraging, even when it is necessary to point out mistakes and problems. A manager should not appear to be a critical parent-boss (transactional analysis) and should hold meetings on an adult-adult basis with the "I'm O.K.; you're O.K." position prevailing. Salespersons should be allowed to interact with each other in regard to mutual problems. Special training for new products, new product applications, and new selling ideas motivates salespersons by arming them with knowledge about their offerings.

Yearly national conferences assemble salespersons at a central place and feature prominent speakers, top company personnel, and entertainment personalities. Such large group meetings can promote contagious enthusiasm and interaction among salespersons from all parts of the country. Local salespersons are given a chance to meet company officers and top sales "stars." Such meetings are costly in terms of travel expense, elaborate facilities, and territorial neglect and may be regarded by personnel as an opportunity to have a good time rather than to learn.[15] Regional meetings are apt to be taken more seriously as working meetings, but they require the company's top executives to travel more and usually fail to engender the same enthusiastic spirit as the national meetings. Aggregate travel costs are less because sales personnel travel shorter distances, but it is often impractical to have well-known sales trainers and motivational speakers at each regional meeting.[16]

Speeches by very successful sales personalities and audio-visuals featuring success theory can be inspirational at meetings. Salespersons have an opportunity to evaluate the mannerisms, the tone of voice, and the personalities of successful persons, and this is stimulating. Testimony from a star salesperson is worth much more than reading words in a sales manual. Records featuring the ideas and voices of America's top sales personalities are available for local meetings, and the personalities themselves are often available for the big national get-togethers.

EVALUATION AND CONTROL

The sales manager must check, by means of feedback information, to see if planned goals are being achieved. It is not hard to determine if sales representatives are reaching their quotas, if territories are yielding expected potentials, if expenses are being kept within limits, or if total sales are reaching forecasted levels. Computers can be programmed to analyze reported sales and yield sales results. They can analyze results by sales representative, by product, by geographical area, by customer, and in relation to other factors. Sales results can be compared with objectives set for each factor. Such analysis can quickly reveal which products and which salespersons are living up to expectations and which are not. Further analysis can sometimes indicate why. Daily call reports, turned in by sales personnel, show how many calls, interviews, demonstrations, prospecting attempts, collection attempts, and other activities were completed. These, in turn, can be compared to MBO subgoals and provide an indication of effort to produce sales. Sales dollars generated per interview show how effective a salesperson has been in getting results. Actual expenses can also be compared with planned expenses to partially determine the costs of supporting sales.

When salespersons are evaluated solely on the basis of sales, problems can arise. Salespersons may be so intent on making short-run sales that they may neglect other important matters such as prospecting, reporting, introducing new products, selling the full line, learning, and account profitability. Many companies have therefore devised more elaborate

[15] Still, Cundiff, and Govoni, *op. cit.*, pp. 316–317.

[16] *Ibid.*

evaluation techniques, including subjective (opinion) evaluation scales to judge salespersons. Subjective forms are especially useful for new salespersons and those being primed for managerial positions. Sales managers are most often given the responsibility of making these judgments. Salespersons should not feel, however, that they are under continual scrutiny for the minutest details. All evaluation criteria should be selected carefully, and the salesperson should be informed about the criteria used to evaluate. The evaluation points used will channel sales-force efforts in that direction to win approval, and the areas that are not evaluated are likely to be neglected. Overevaluation can hinder salespersons by restricting their freedom, and too much subjective evaluation encourages bias and hypocrisy.

SUMMARY

It is important to understand the functions of the sales manager because it will help new salespersons understand supervisors, the working environment, and the next possible step in promotion. Sales managers are responsible for providing a productive work environment and maintaining a leadership image. They should be competent, fair, informative, and encouraging. They should bolster the self-images of their sales personnel by expecting them to do well. Sales managers set up organizational relationships, estimate territorial potential, and forecast sales. They help with product planning by crystallizing information from the field into suggestions for new products and product features.

Selecting salespersons is the most important responsibility of most sales managers. The work-load method, the sales-potential method, and the incremental method are three ways to determine how many new salespersons should be hired. Important from the very beginning, too, is writing out detailed job descriptions of all sales-force positions to indicate the types of sales recruits needed. Applicants can be found from "walk-ins," at colleges and universities, in other companies, through newspaper ads, through recommendations of personnel, and through employment agencies. The sales hopefuls can be screened by effective use of the employment application blank, the personal interview, references, tests, and physical examinations. The application form can yield the socioeconomic characteristics of an applicant, past work experience, education, interests, and it can be useful in initial screening. The personal interview can reveal an applicant's personality attributes, poise, image, and sincerity. References, even from supposedly unbiased sources, must be carefully interpreted to discern the true opinion of the person giving the reference. Tests, especially intelligence tests and aptitude tests, can be valuable selection tools. But care must be used in testing, so that minorities won't be subject to discrimination. Physical examinations should be used to screen out persons with physical handicaps that would hinder performance in strenuous selling work but should not eliminate those with minor physical defects who are otherwise highly qualified. Final selection rests with the judgment of the sales manager or the top corporate official who is responsible for hiring the applicant.

Training should be segmented to fit the experience of new and tenured sales personnel. The amount of training and the type of training depend primarily on the nature of the product and the professionalism required in the selling situation. Most firms use home-office training for beginning salespersons and on-the-job training under senior supervision. Experienced salespersons and seniors learn about new products and developments in sales meetings and at conferences. It is important to let senior salespersons participate in training sessions.

Motivating salespersons is important because selling is emotionally demanding. Sales managers should maintain a good leadership example, treat salespersons like responsible professionals, and appeal to belongingness, esteem, and self-actualization levels. A salary plus a commission or a bonus, if well-devised, can help insure sales and service. Sales contests, meetings, and conferences are widely used motivational tools. A sensible mixture of comparing sales and work methods with planned objectives and a minimum of subjective evaluation can provide valuable bench marks, letting managers know how well the sales force is doing. Managers have a great deal of influence on the success of the sales force. They are the ones who must initiate new directions when problems arise.

REVIEW QUESTIONS

1. Why should a new salesperson know about the sales manager's job?

2. What are some of the more important functions of the sales manager?

3. How can a sales manager maintain a good leadership image according to the text? What would you add to this?

4. Explain why a manager should expect professionalism, competence, and hard work from sales personnel in terms of self-image theory (cybernetics).

5. What are the steps involved in organizing?

6. What type of staff personnel can help the salesperson and the sales manager with expert advice?

7. Name the important ways of forecasting sales for existing products and for new products.

8. What part does a sales manager have in product planning? How can the salesperson help the manager in this function?

9. Why is it important to be careful in assigning territories? Setting quotas?

10. Explain three methods of determining how many salespersons are needed.

11. What is a written job description, and why is it such an important early step in the selection process?

12. List and tell how each of the selection tools are used to select good salespersons. What are some of the problems in using references? Tests? Physical examinations?

13. Name and evaluate the methods used for training a new and inexperienced salesperson.

14. What methods and considerations are important in training experienced senior salespersons?

15. What are the four major decisions involved in devising a good training program?

16. What is the motivational problem in motivating salespersons?

17. How would you motivate a person with an achievement-oriented motivational profile? An affiliative profile?

18. What insight does Maslow's theory give in regard to motivating sales representatives?

19. What precautions should be taken in devising sales contests?

20. What are the advantages of national sales conferences? Regional sales conferences? Local sales meetings?

21. Explain methods by which the sales manager can evaluate and control the sales force.

APPLICATION QUESTIONS

1. What supervisory style would you recommend for sales managers of door-to-door salespersons selling encyclopedias? For a manager managing salespersons selling computer systems? Should there be different styles in these two situations?

2. Explain what takes place in a management-by-objectives session between the manager and the sales representative. How should the manager "pressure" salespersons to agree on good objectives and subobjectives?

3. List the sources of sales applicants. Which do you feel is the best source? Why?

4. Assuming you had all of the information gathered, what factors would be most important in selecting a new salesperson?

5. Explain the different compensation plans and the advantages and disadvantages of each. Which would you recommend for an insurance salesperson? A public-relations representative?

INCIDENTS

16–1

Edward Kappel, the sales manager, is about to interview Sarah Calhoun for the annual management-by-objectives conference:

Ed: Come in, Sarah, and sit down. Now that we've assigned you to a territory it will be necessary to set some goals for next year. Ted Orniwitz sold $112,541 last year in that territory. What do you think you can do this year?

Sarah: I'm not sure, Mr. Kappel. How does the total sales forecast for this next year compare with last?

Ed: We expect to sell at least 10% more this year. But you know one of the reasons that Ted is no longer with us is that he never cultivated his territory as he should have.

Sarah: Well, I could shoot for $125,000, but remember, I'm a rookie.

Ed: How about putting you down for $130,000?

Sarah: I'll try.

Ed: Now we have to set the number of calls and demonstrations you will need to gain that volume. You've been averaging seven calls a day and just two demonstrations helping John Frazier. Could we boost that up to eight and four demonstrations? It would help.

Sarah: I'd better not commit myself to make more than seven calls a day, but I will try to make four demonstrations. I like to spend selling time with my prospects.

Ed: How about seven account calls and one or two *prospecting* calls?

Sarah: Well, I'll try, Mr. Kappel.

Ed: Now that you will have a territory, you realize you will have to make at least two collection calls a week, so I'm putting you down for that—O.K.? Now to sell $130,000 you will have to get orders for over $2,500 per week. You will probably have to sell about three typewriters and a calculator each week. I think that's reasonable, don't you?

Sarah: I'll work hard to do it.

Ed: I know you will, Sarah. I'm expecting you to develop into one of our star salespeople. Remember to keep your expenses within reasonable limits. It will help to plan your routing and avoid backtracking. Do you plan each day ahead of time?

Sarah: Oh, yes. I plot my itinerary on the map.

Ed: Well, Sarah, I guess we've got it pretty well set down. It's just a question of doing it now, isn't it?

Sarah: Yes . . . I'll do my best.

QUESTIONS

1. Who controlled this MBO conference, Ed or Sarah?

2. What other points should have been discussed?

3. Did Mr. Kappel do a good job?

16–2

Peter Daniels has been working as a salesperson for the Delmar Chemical Company for about three years and has worked more than a year and a half under Bob Merideth. Pete has a good overall sales record but has failed to make quota for the last three months and has seemed to be a little depressed and low in morale. He has come into Bob's office with an announcement.

Pete: Bob, I know this is going to be a suprise to you, but I've talked it over with Belinda and I'm giving my two weeks' notice. Things just aren't working out for me with Delmar this year.

Bob: Pete, I *am* surprised! You made $18,000 last year and surpassed your quota. I thought you were doing well. What's wrong?

Pete: I'd rather not say. You have been very fair with me, but I feel that I may not be cut out to sell chemicals. I'm down quite a bit this year.

Bob: I've been in this business for several years, Pete, and I can tell you that everyone has their ups and downs in selling. It's like football. No team does it all every game, but when you get discouraged, it makes it doubly hard to get orders. You're a good salesman, Pete, with a lot of potential. We've invested over $20,000 in training you, and I need to know what's wrong so I can correct it. So . . . What is it? You won't hurt my feelings!

Pete: O.K., here it is straight. I don't like my territory, and I think my quota is too high for the potential. I like to excel! I like to make quota! Competition is getting rougher every month in the city territories. Delmar makes good products, but our prices are high. If I keep on going at the rate I'm going this year, I won't make $15,000. Frankly, Bob, I can do better than that. I can make at least $20,000 selling for another supplier.

Bob: Other people have told me about the increasing competition, Pete. As a matter of fact, Mr. Cook at the home office and I have talked about it, and he plans to recommend several measures to counteract it—one of which will be a softening of prices on three products. The company plans to introduce two new products into the line within three months and, while the details on these are secret now, Cook feels like they will more than counter our competitive problems. Keep this under your hat; I haven't told any of the others about this yet. As for the territory problem, I plan to make a thorough restudy of territorial potentials and quotas next month. As you know, the more senior salespersons with the best records are given better territories as a reward for their achievements. That's an important reason why you should reconsider. We feel that you have potential, and I'm sure you will be reassigned in the future if you want.

Pete: I didn't know that the home office was trying to do something about the competition problem, Bob. I like you and the other folks here at Delmar, but . . . well . . . maybe I'm just getting a bit impatient to make better money. You know how it is when you get in a sales slump at the first of the year.

Bob: Would you like to go to the home office for a week? Cook mentioned a refresher course that includes competition. I was going, but I would just as soon you do it and take notes for all of us. I'll help out in your territory while you're away.

Pete: Let me talk all of this over with Belinda. Do you really think those new products will push us back to where we were?

Bob: We've been in the chemical business a long time. Delmar may get behind temporarily, but never permanently. Think it over, Pete. We would sure like you to stay with us.

QUESTIONS

1. Salesperson turnover is a serious problem for many firms. Do you think Bob acted wisely to try to talk Pete into staying? Did he use the right appeals?

2. What other things can the sales manager do to assure better retention of salesforce personnel?

3. Do you think Pete was sincere in offering his resignation? Should he have discussed the problem with Bob before attempting to resign?

16–3

Richard Brighton has been zone sales manager for three months. One of the first changes he made was to institute a "thorough" evaluation system that involves an evaluation by the sales manager every four months and an evaluation by other fellow salespersons. Both questionnaires were designed entirely by Brighton with no help from anyone and no input from the sales force. Each form contains more than fifteen questions. In addition to the two new evaluations, Richard has installed a one-way mirror between his office and the large sales office room where all of the sales representatives have their desks. He can watch what is going on in the sales room at any time, but his office cannot be seen from the sales room. Richard has explained to the sales-force personnel that they will be evaluated very strongly on the number of interviews and demonstrations they make. Reported interviews and demonstrations have increased considerably in the last month, but sales have slightly declined. Included below are sample entries from the sales manager's evaluation form:

The salesperson's personality is: Poor _____, Average _____, Good _____, Very Good _____, Excellent _____.

The salesperson's attitude is: Poor _____, Average _____, Good _____, Very Good _____, Excellent _____.

The salesperson's appearance is: Poor _____, Average _____, Good _____, Very Good _____, Excellent _____.

The salesperson's self-evaluation and "team-member" evaluation form contains the following sample elements:

Rank each salesperson (do not include yourself) in regard to selling effectiveness from most effective to least effective.

Rate each of the salespersons in the zone (listed below) as to company rules and regulations (A = Excellent, B = Very Good, C = Average, D = Poor).

Rate each of the salespersons below as to promotability: 1 = Very promotable, 2 = Promotable, 3 = Perhaps promotable, 4 = Not promotable.

Now rate what you consider your own value to the company: Very Valuable _____, Valuable _____, Fairly Valuable _____, Probably not very valuable _____.

Since the first evaluations were made under the new manager two months ago, a strong clique has developed among the sales-force personnel. One salesperson has resigned stating the inability to work under the new manager as the reason, and two senior sales representatives have complained openly about the new evaluations, especially the self and team-member evaluations.

Evaluate Richard Brighton's evaluation program from the information given. How would you improve it?

17 Starting a Selling Career

Persuasive knowledge becomes the power to achieve goals when it is used in your own business or when you are a representative of an established organization. One way you can develop your persuasive potential is to initiate your own firm. This has always been a good way to become wealthy. It entails a substantial amount of risk, however, and usually requires a great deal of patience until your idea gains momentum. If you select this success path, you should research possible opportunities carefully, read several good books on small-business management, take courses, and gain experience by working for a similar business, to minimize the risks of failure.

Most people choose to begin their careers in selling with an established organization to get experience under seasoned supervision, to begin making money from the start, and to take advantage of training programs and other available benefits. Very few people, however, know how to approach the important career step of finding the right job. Many students, in fact, work hard for years—studying diligently, making good grades, and participating in many outside activities—only to lose these advantages by an unrealistic approach to the job market. Others, with lesser qualifications, study the art of job finding and attain higher success by beginning with the right company. There are many ideas that can give you a distinct competitive advantage in the job market. This text would be incomplete if it failed to assist you with one of the more important prospecting and sales assignments in your career—selling your services to the right employer. This final chapter discusses:

- Selecting a good organization
- Finding an opening
- Writing résumés
- Selling yourself in the interview and on tests
- Selling yourself on the job
- The future in personal selling

447

SELECTING A GOOD ORGANIZATION

The first step in career planning is to establish definite written employment goals. It is never too early to begin research that will help you do this. The basic idea is to determine what you really want, assess what you have to offer and are willing to sacrifice, and match your potentials realistically with the job type that gives you maximum satisfaction. This process does not always involve searching for sales work you think you would like regardless of its profitability, rather, it involves being open to opportunities for work that you might *learn* to like. While one approach is being willing to adjust yourself to jobs paying the highest monetary benefits, there are some employment situations you should avoid, simply because you would never be happy in them, even with higher pay. Although many of the better opportunities require expertise in specific areas and entail hard work, after the expertise is gained, the job is interesting and profitable. The process of matching your employment needs and your abilities with specific organizational positions can be accomplished if you:

- Do a self-analysis
- Decide the specific area of persuasion
- Write a prospective job description
- Research specific companies that could meet your requirements

Do a Self-Analysis

Make a thorough list of your likes and dislikes. Make another list of your assets and liabilities, highlighting any strong relative advantages that you might be able to offer an employer. Decide how important money, location, traveling, and working hours are to you. Review Chapter 1, which explains why some persuasive positions pay more than others. Ask yourself if you are willing to become an order-getter and qualify for the higher-paying jobs. Try to translate your preferences into actual job features.

Decide the Specific Area of Persuasion

You may wish to reread Chapter 14 and review the characteristics of public relations, retail selling, intangible selling, and industrial selling. Consider again the sacrifices you must make to be successful in the higher-paying selling jobs. Consider the technical training necessary, the selling problems involved, the length of apprenticeship periods, the relocation demanded, the travel required, and the long or irregular working hours associated with each of the major types of persuasive opportunities. Consider the pay, the indirect rewards, and the promotional opportunities, and make a tentative decision on the specific area of selling.

Write a Prospective Job Description

Now write a detailed job description that you feel would realistically balance rewards, sacrifices, and abilities, and that might be available within the selling area of your interest. Put factors like "travel 500 miles per week" and "relocation in region" in your description if you would be willing to do those things for the probable extra compensation involved. Also, clearly state the features you would insist on having, and you might rank these features in the order of their importance to you (see Figure 17.1, p. 450, for an example of such a job description).

Research Specific Companies That Could Meet Your Requirements

After you have written your tentative job description reflecting your qualifications, what you want, and features that you would accept for extra compensation, you can make a search for specific firms that might be able to supply such a selling job. Do not be concerned at this point whether or not the firms have "openings"; be concerned with considering all firms that might have persons employed with job descriptions similar to your tentative description. A good place to look for companies is in the latest *College Placement Annual* at your college placement service office or at a university placement service near you. The *College Placement Annual* has firms listed under such headings as public relations, merchandising, retail management, banking, and sales that regularly search for graduates interested in persuasive careers. The *College Placement Annual* also carries detailed information on specific companies, including products, number of employees, and the kind of graduates they seek.[1] You may also find firms in trade directories, the Yellow Pages, chamber of commerce lists, and trade association lists. When you have selected perhaps five to ten firms, you might find more information about them in Dun and Bradstreet or Standard and Poors publications. They provide data on corporate financial conditions.

If you learn how to evaluate organizations before you enter the job

[1] *College Placement Annual* (Bethlehem, Pa.: College Placement Council, P.O. Box 2263, 1978).

Figure 17.1 Future Job Description

1. Location

   Strongly prefer to locate in New England-New York area for family reasons. Prefer not to locate more than 400 miles from Hartford. Will not accept overseas location for more than one year.

2. Pay and Benefits

   Prefer salary plus commission or bonus. $12,000 second-year minimum with over $24,000 potential in five years. Prefer good training program and promotion potential.

3. Customer

   Prefer to sell to executive business customers or professional-type customers. Prefer not to sell to ultimate consumer customers.

4. Product

   Tangible or intangible product but prefer high-unit value. Must be beneficial to society. Prefer quality product even if priced above competition. Complex product or concept preferred.

5. Travel

   Willing to travel but prefer not to be overnight more than once per week. Prefer auto to air.

6. Call Frequency

   Prefer to make from 8–10 calls or less per day in full interview-type selling. Prefer extra compensation for irregular interval calls rather than service selling at regular intervals.

7. Type of Selling

   Willing to do creative selling for possible extra compensation involved. Prefer to make programmed presentations based on researched proposals on a professional, consultative selling level. Prefer extra compensation of problem-solving selling.

8. Nonselling Duties

   Willing to do extensive reports and analyses. Willing to collect accounts but prefer not to collect on a regular basis. Delivery, installation, research, and public-relations work (such as trade fairs) acceptable if compensated.

market, you will be able to select a firm instead of letting a firm select you. Reflect on the products of the firm and how they will fare in the markets of tomorrow. Consider the firm's research and its ability to market new products to meet dynamically changing environments. Consider everything that will bear upon long-run profit potentials. Find out the firm's reputation and standing in the industry. Trade associations or trade journals may have this information, or you might ask prominent business executives who might know. Does the firm have significant operations in the geographical area in which you wish to locate? What are its employee policies? Does the firm retain its employees, or does it have considerable salesperson turnover? Is the company basically stockholder-centered, upper-management-centered, or personnel-centered in its distribution of earnings? What are the organization's ethical standards? A good idea is to talk to people who buy from the firm, sell to the firm, or work for the firm. Talk to people (if you can) who previously worked for the firm and find out what they think of the company. Write to public relations and ask for publications such as annual reports and institutional brochures that will give you more information. See if your college placement service has annual reports or packets concerning the company. After you have collected as much information as you can find, write down the advantages and disadvantages of each company in reference to your employment needs. Next, rank the companies in respect to your preferences.

FINDING AN OPENING

Several months before you plan to be available for your selling job, you should begin the second important phase of your investigations. You should remind all of your relatives, friends, and acquaintances that you are in the market, and get them to help you. Tell as many people as you can about your availability. Although you may plan to approach your selected firms first, you need to have many alternatives and an open mind about changing your preferences. Go to a college placement office and solicit their help. Find out which firms are going to conduct interviews on the campus and when. Read some of the books and pamphlets at the placement office and at the library that are written expressly to give you inside information on how to approach the job market. Even go to the college alumni office and see if you can get names of recent graduates who have found selling jobs. You might ask your professor for names of recent graduates who have found good jobs. Recent job finders can tell you about the job market, and they may give you valuable leads. Remember that starting out with the right employer is worth the extra effort.

Newspapers

It is also a good idea to read the many ads for selling jobs in newspapers to get some idea of salaries and the market. Some of the ads will not give the name of the company, but even blind ads will help you assess the needs of employers. It is possible but unlikely that you will find a top job through the newspapers. Primary reliance on this source may be a mark of an unsophisticated job seeker. You should regard newspaper ads more as a research source, although reading the ads will give you a better "feeling" for opportunities.

Employment Agencies

Another natural consideration is employment agencies, both private and governmental. Many employment agencies represent the employer rather than the employee, and some charge large fees for helping you if you get the job. You should probably use agencies only after trying a more direct approach or in case you need a job in a hurry. The best jobs are won by resourceful job seekers who take the initiative and search for opportunities. Jackson and Mayless, in *The Hidden Job Market,* estimate that up to 90 percent of the available jobs are never advertised and never reach employment agency files.[2] Other books suggest the futility of going through long waiting lines after responding to newspaper ads or paying high fees only to have access to a small, highly competitive portion of the job market. Nearly all authorities caution that it is important to understand the fee arrangement before signing with an employment agency.

A Direct Approach

Before you respond to "openings," try this approach. Take the firms selected from your previous research and investigate them closely. Eliminate those firms that require grade-point averages, experience, or health standards that you cannot meet. Go to the library and do more extensive research on the remaining firms. Look at their advertisements; look at their annual reports; talk to their employees; look at their trade journals; talk to chamber of commerce officials about them. After this second, more thorough research, rerank the firms in order of their attractiveness for employment. Don't consider whether or not the company has an opening at this point. Nearly all large firms with an active sales force have

[2] Tom Jackson and Davidyne Mayless, *The Hidden Job Market* (New York: Quadrangle Books, New York Times Book Company, 1976), pp. 95–122.

turnover from retirements, deaths, dismissals, and resignations. Firms that are really prospering need additional personnel to expand their product lines and territories. Good sales representatives are so scarce that if you do a good job of convincing them that you have what they want, recruiters may create an opening for you or consider you first when an opening does occur.

You can approach the firms in which you are interested either through a written résumé or by direct contact. How to write a professional résumé and how to impress recruiters in a persuasive interview are subjects of the following sections. If you try the direct-contact method, which is probably the best method, you may want to circumvent the employment manager and interview the person who will make the final hiring decision. In many cases, the sales or branch manager decides with the approval of the home office. Find out the name of the sales or branch manager and make an appointment or simply walk in the branch and ask to see the sales manager. Remember this person is sales-oriented and interested in people with initiative and a degree of aggressiveness. Most managers will not be offended by your direct approach and will appreciate a qualified walk-in who is interested in selling for the company. After all, if you can do a good job of selling in the future, hiring you will mean more money or a better position for them. Good managers are always looking for high-potential stars who can sell. If the manager won't see you and refers you to personnel, go through channels as directed. *Your biggest danger in sales-job hunting is being hired by the wrong company, not being turned down by several good firms.* Unless you are highly qualified, it is normal to get turned down several times. By using the direct approach, you have at least proceeded in true selling fashion. If a firm does turn you down for some reason, ask them about other firms that might need you. You might pay special attention to firms on your preferred list that are going through expansions, are changing product lines, or have definite openings as reported by one of the many persons you have job hunting for you. If the firms in which you are most interested are located at a distance, you might try the résumé approach.

WRITING RÉSUMÉS

A résumé is a concise summary of your experience and characteristics, an advertisement for your services, and—it is hoped—a ticket of admission to an interview. Big corporations get hundreds of résumés each week and discard most of them after a superficial look. Writing a good résumé and cover letter can improve your chances of surviving this initial weeding out and winning an interview.

A résumé should be short and preferably contained on one normal-sized sheet of white bond paper. It should never be over two pages. It should be typed on an electric typewriter with carbon ribbon and contain no mistakes in spelling, grammar, or punctuation. It should contain action words and omit personal pronouns. It should be arranged attractively with neat margins and white space. There are two main styles of résumés: historical and functional. The historical résumé features a listing of your work and education experiences in reverse chronological order (last situation first) and is the most acceptable and popular format.[3] The functional résumé is arranged (structured) by listing skills the applicant possesses that are associated with the job. It is sometimes used by applicants with unexplainable gaps in their work history. The functional style is not very suitable for most selling résumés and arouses the suspicion of many résumé reviewers. An example of a historical résumé is shown in Figure 17.2. Note the concise style and yet the quantity of detailed information.

In addition to your education and work experience, a résumé should contain your name, your address, your telephone number, your marital status, how many children you have, academic honors, and your height, weight, and age (only if you think these last three items would help). Remember, a résumé is an advertisement. You should not include items that might hurt your chances of being considered unless you feel it would create suspicion to leave them out. It is considered best practice *not* to include a photograph, even for a selling job. Also, leave off the names of your wife and children, references, salary requirements, and reasons for leaving previous jobs.[4] Names of wife and children mean absolutely nothing to the reader; references would be overworked if you sent out several résumés; it's too public and too early to reveal salary requirements; and any reasons for leaving previous jobs would introduce a negative element. When you have finished your résumé, proofread it several times and read it aloud to others at least once, listening to their suggestions. As you read it aloud, ask yourself: "Would I hire the person who wrote this?"

It is permissible to send your résumé to as many employers as you wish. Some applicants send it to dozens of firms, hoping to find an opening this way. While this shotgun approach is probably not necessary for selling positions, if you do send out multiple copies, have the résumé printed or reproduced on expensive paper. You want to avoid the appearance of someone looking for just *any* job. A basic strategy in hunting for the right employer is to appear discriminating. You want your

---

[3] Adele Lewis, *How to Write a Better Résumé* (Woodbury, N.Y.: Barron's Educational Series, 1977), pp. 6–8.

[4] *Ibid.*, pp. 27–29.

Figure 17.2   Sample Résumé

John A. Ballantine	Age: 21	Single
142 Sand Road	Ht: 6' 1"	Wt: 190 lbs.
Raging Creek, Texas 89720	Date available: June 1980	
(817) 527–0000		

CAREER OBJECTIVES: To be a successful industrial salesman and to be a sales executive within reasonable time.

EDUCATION: B.S. in Business Administration from the University of Middle Texas. Courses include Sales, Advertising, Sales Management, Public Relations, Public Speaking, and Physics. Grade Average: 3.1 on a 4.0 scale.

ACTIVITIES: Debating Team. Vice-President and Treasurer, Sigma Alpha Theta Fraternity. Letterman varsity basketball, two years. Sales Manager, Yearbook, Raging Creek High School.

EXPERIENCE:
Summer 1979   Sold dictionaries and children's story books for Middlewest Book Company; leading salesperson in section.

1977–78   Sold men's clothing at retail for Tamm's Men's Wear, Raging Creek, during summers and vacation periods.

1975–76   Sold ads for Raging Creek High School Yearbook. Surpassed sales or previous year by 50 percent.

1973–75   Paper route for *Daily News*; increased circulation by 20 percent.

INTERESTS: Team sports of all kinds, camping out, bronco riding, guitar, debating, and public speaking.

future employer to feel that you selected the company because it is a superior company, and you have much to offer. Sending out cheap copies does not convey this impression.

A cover letter should accompany the résumé, typed on the same kind

Figure 17.3 Cover Letter

142 Sand Road
Raging Creek, Tex. 89720
March 17, 1980

Mr. Robert Wellerman
Branch Manager
Duraco Oil Equipment Company
Houston, Tex. 71701

Dear Mr. Wellerman:

Oil-rig equipment is an exciting product and vital to our country's future with growing demands for energy. I am interested in becoming a part of a sales force that would see that this important equipment is put to work.

I plan to graduate in June, and as the enclosed résumé shows, my academic curriculum and my work experience have helped prepare me for sales work. The physics, sales, and management courses should be valuable in selling rig equipment. The competition of varsity athletics and debating has taught me the thrill of winning and being a team player. The sales experience in books, clothing, ads, and newspapers has taught me how to sell and convinced me that personal selling is my occupational choice.

Could I talk to you in person about employment opportunities in the oil-equipment industry? Harvey Lyles, your sales representative in this area, has me very interested in Duraco and in meeting you. I will call you next week and try to arrange an appointment at your convenience.

Yours truly,

John Ballantine

cjc

Enclosure

of paper and with the same type as your résumé.[5]   It should be an original and never a copy.   It should not be over five paragraphs or one page long, nor should it be just one or two sentences.   While your résumé is your advertisement for employment, your cover letter should be customized and directed specifically to the company to which it is addressed.   Re-

[5] Melvin W. Donaho and John L. Meyer, *How to Get the Job You Want* (Englewood Cliffs, N.J.: Prentice-Hall, 1976), pp. 43–63.

Insuring Future Opportunity

member that the company reviewer is judging you with limited evidence—only by what you send. The first paragraph of your letter should explain why you are petitioning that company for an interview. The middle paragraph(s) should point to your main selling features (qualifications) as featured in your résumé that would interest that specific employer. Your closing paragraph should suggest possible arrangements for an interview (see Figure 17.3).[6] More examples of cover letters and résumés can be found in the *College Placement Annual* or in one of the many books on the subject. If you plan to send out several résumés, keep good records and keep track especially of the interviews you are given. Contact the company immediately, and accept the interviews you plan to attend. Express regrets if, for some reason, you can't make the scheduled appointment.

SELLING YOURSELF IN THE INTERVIEW AND ON TESTS

The interview is the main event for persuasive positions. Personality is the most important factor in most selling situations, so you cannot expect a company to hire you without talking to you in person. Grades are an indication of your ability to be trained and your determination to excel. Some employers with technical products look carefully at grades because grades reflect self-image and intelligence. Most companies, however, are more interested in personality factors.

Prepare for the Interview

Research the company again and find out all you can about its history, its products, its size, its operations, and its problems. Know about its credit standing, its sales record over the last ten years, its training programs, and its policies. The company wants salespeople to help it solve problems. Decide what you believe the company would want in a salesperson. Companies, like customers, have a dominant buying motive—a main reason for hiring new salespeople. Dress for the interview in the same kind of clothes you would expect to wear on the job. Never wear any pins, emblems, or other indicators of political or ideological preferences that might be controversial. Dress conservatively and wear your hair conservatively. Men with long hair and bushy beards enter most

[6] Lewis, *op. cit.*, pp. 237–250.

interviews with a decided handicap. Manicure your fingernails and be as neat and clean as possible. Women should dress modestly for the interview. You are asking to reflect the image of the firm—to represent the firm as a salesperson. If you are dressed and groomed properly in conservative and coordinated colors, you will enter the interview with extra poise and self-assurance. The interviewer will form an important first opinion of you the first second you appear.

There are other ways you should prepare yourself. You should be ready to answer standard interview questions and to ask intelligent questions. You should also be prepared in your attitude. Determine to be honest and consistent. Trained interviewers will test your consistency and reject you if they think you are being deceptive. Figure 17.4 contains examples of questions that you might be asked. Expect these questions in one form or another and plan good answers. More will be added about key questions later. If you are a minority member or a woman, never indicate the attitude that the interviewer must hire you because it is the law. Interviewers are looking for applicants who want to work and profit the firm and are pleased to find qualified minorities and women who stand on their qualifications, not their legal hiring advantages.

You are expected to show enthusiasm in the interview and perhaps even a little apprehension and nervousness. Sales interviewers like least of all the quiet, reserved, extra "cool" types, who seem withdrawn and answer questions too briefly. This does not mean that you should overdo it with frantic nonverbal gestures and artificial theatrics. It does mean that attempts to appear extra reserved will probably be misinterpreted as boredom or disinterest.

If you seem overanxious for the job and willing to take anything, it is human nature to discount your qualifications. Project to the interviewer that you are selective because you are highly qualified. And because you are selective, you are interested in the company.

A final note on preparation is that you should role-play the interview before you actually experience it. Find a friend or relative who will play the part of the interviewer, or at least go over the interview in your mind and "synthetically" experience it (psychocybernetics) before actually experiencing it.

Sell Yourself from the Beginning

Never arrive late for an interview. Arrive two or three minutes early. You will be observed as soon as you enter the building or as soon as the interviewer meets you, so be alert. The sales job required in the screening interview is necessary to win a hiring decision interview later on with a higher company official. Some of the screening interviewers are unskilled

Figure 17.4   Questions You Might Be Asked in an Interview

What made you consider us for employment?

Why did you select selling as a career?

What are your short- and long-range objectives?

Where do you expect to be in your career, and what do you expect to be earning four years from now?

Why did you leave your last job?

What do you consider to be your greatest strengths?

What do you consider to be your greatest weaknesses?

What advantages do you have to offer our company; that is, why should we select you over other applicants?

Tell me about yourself.

How would someone who knows you quite well describe you?

What makes you work your hardest—what motivates you?

What qualities do you think are important to selling success?

How would your previous work experiences help you sell?

What do you know about us?

Are you willing to relocate? Travel?

What have you learned outside of the classroom that would help you in selling?

What specific elements or features do you want in a selling job?

What college subjects did you like least? Best?

What makes you mad?

What do you dislike the most in other people?

What do you feel are the three greatest problems of the United States as a country?

If we would hire you, when could you go to work? What is the minimum we would have to offer you to hire you?

at interviewing and are not highly paid corporate officials. This does not mean that you should not be respectful to them, but it does mean that unless you are careful, they may evaluate you incorrectly and not give you a full chance to express your qualifications. This is why you should see the person who can hire you in your first interview, if possible. Fortunately, your selling strategy is the same for the screening and the depth (hiring) interview—to sell yourself and give yourself the option to accept or reject the offer. The interviewer is viewing you for the selling job and is looking for someone who is extroverted, attractive, pleasant, optimistic, and interested in other people.

Practice Persuasive Principles

Greet the interviewer as you would a prospect with a firm handshake, good eye contact, and your name. Wait for an invitation to sit down, but try to arrange it so your chair is close enough to the interviewer for good two-way communication. Sit straight in the chair with your arms and legs not defensively crossed, but with an open body-language position in a poised but relaxed manner. Remember that the interviewer is just as much on trial as you are, and the worst thing that can happen is that you will be hired by the wrong firm. There are hundreds of other firms that will hire you. If these thoughts don't relax you, then maybe you should take a public speaking course and cybernetically practice under conditions that are not as significant to you. The interviewer's job at this point is to get you relaxed—to get you so relaxed, in fact, that you will reveal your true self.

Be Prepared to Answer Standard Questions

The interviewer might ask you a few harmless rapport-establishing questions at first, like "Did you have a nice trip over" or "Did you find a good place to park?" Interviewers want to get you talking about yourself and also want to sell you on the company situation if you are qualified. Eventually, you will probably be asked depth questions to ascertain your attitudes and motivations. Included below are questions you might expect and suggestions for replies.

"What about our company made you consider us?" This question presents an unusual opportunity to show your knowledge about the specific company that you gained from your research. Answer this question specifically. An answer might be: "I have always wanted to sell for a firm whose products I can believe in. I am particularly impressed with your research and new products, especially the new Z copier. I believe the XYZ Company has great growth potential, and I want to get with a dynamic growth company with a future."

"What are your ambitions?" "What are your long-range goals?" "Where do you want to be seven years from now?" Seven years from now, you want to be somewhere *reasonably* up the corporate ladder. You won't impress the interviewer by stating that you expect to be president of the firm in several years. You might answer like this: "I expect to be a high-producing senior salesman in the next few years and by seven years possibly a zone sales manager, with recognized potential for branch manager." Actually, your response should reflect what you know about the company's promotion policies.

"What are your strengths and weaknesses?" Express your strengths in terms of the selling personality. "I have always had the ability to get along with other people and influence them. I like to work hard, and I enjoy the challenge of competition and problem solving." Make your answers to questions like this meaningful but concise. Giving answers that are too long are worse than giving answers that are too short. Boomerang your weaknesses into a selling point. "I have a tendency to become overconcerned about doing a good job, but this makes me more careful." Don't admit too many or too serious faults in an attempt to appear overly honest and humble.

"Are you a conservative or a liberal in your philosophies? Explain." You should probably lean to the conservative side politically, morally, and socially. Sidestep questions like this by answering, "I believe in the free-enterprise system, and the American form of government, and high moral standards, but I'm tolerant of the beliefs of others."

"Why did you leave your last job?" You may have left your last job because you couldn't stand your boss and you thought you were treated unfairly, but it is inappropriate for you to express this to the interviewer. It is best to be positive and answer, "I didn't feel that the growth opportunities were sufficient, and I wanted to represent a company with greater potential for advancement" (which may be the better of two true reasons).

"Do you like to be with people, or would you rather work alone?" As a potential salesperson, you like people—rich, poor, foreign, fat, and lean. You especially like the kind of people who are the customers of the interviewing firm. You might answer: "Yes, I like to be with people very much; but I don't mind traveling by myself, since this will be necessary in selling."

Nearly all good interviewers ask a simple and effective depth question that is designed to throw the applicant off guard, and it usually does. "Tell me about yourself." Many people have a tendency to ramble and show their disorganization when answering this question. Others relax and in an effort to appear humble confess too many shortcomings. David Knight, in his excellent short book, *How to Interview for That Job and Get It,* calls this the "killer question."[7] Write out your answer to this one before entering the interview. Portray yourself as human, but overbalance a few admitted minor weaknesses with strengths that count in selling.

[7] David N. Knight, *How to Interview for That Job and Get It* (copyright by David N. Knight, printed by Commercial Printing Services, News Examiner Company, Connersville, Ind., 1976), pp. 43–44.

Watch for Tricks

A few interviewers will test you by purposely trying to make you mad and noting your response. Handle this properly, but consider this a very negative approach for that company. You may not want to work for them. Some interviewers will request a light or a pen. They want to see if you fumble around to get one, if you respond immediately with one, or if you say that you don't have one. Others may tell you a joke and watch your response. Some interviewers are more interested in how long it takes you to respond; long waits indicate deceptiveness. Don't let interviewers trick you by pretending to hold views that they don't hold or getting you to join in a critical attack on some person or institution. Interviewers are looking for honesty and consistency, and you want to cast yourself in a favorable but believable light. You don't want to smoke in the interview unless you are invited to do so, and you want to use titles like "sir" and show social sensitivity and courtesy.

Ask Intelligent Questions

You will have a chance and probably be invited to ask questions in the interview. Ask intelligent, appropriate, and prestudied questions. Ask about profits, growth potentials, policies, and opportunities.[8] Ask what progress you might make with the firm if you do a good job. Don't ask about salaries or paid vacation days near the beginning of the interview. Ask about the training program and what you would do the first year if you are hired. You want to join a company with a good training program for two reasons. You want to learn, and you want that company to have a substantial investment in your success. Companies without a training program will be less patient with you because they have less investment in you.

Watch for Important Decisions at the End of the Interview

Near the end of the decision interview, you may be asked questions that could be hard to answer. What would you reply if the interviewer says: "I've decided to employ you, John. When can you go to work?" You must either accept the job or bargain for time if you are not sure. You

[8] *Ibid.,* p. 113.

"I'd like to hear more about the retirement plan."

THE SATURDAY EVENING POST

Reprinted from *The Saturday Evening Post* © 1961 The Curtis Publishing Company.

Watch the interviewer for nonverbal clues.

might answer: "I'm very interested, Mr. Bell, but I would like to talk it over with my family. Could you give me until Monday?" Or you might answer with a question bearing on the decision: "Could you tell me what salary or commission I might expect?" Another hard question to answer is: "What are your minimum salary requirements?" Before you answer this question, you should have a very good idea about what the firm pays new salespeople from your preinterview research. To state a figure too low is to sell yourself short and lose image with the interviewer. Interviewers are also unimpressed with sky-high expectations. Ask for a salary slightly higher than average or respond that it depends on fringe benefits and advancement possibilities. You might turn the question back around and ask for salary ranges for new recruits. If you have sold yourself and if they really want you, the firm may meet your compensation requests. Most often, however, salary and commission schedules in selling are uniform and depend on how much you produce. You might also avoid answering the minimum salary question by asking about bonuses and contests. Remember, you want to play a little bit hard to get.

Forms and Tests

You should be honest, complete, and neat in regard to your application blank, but what about tests? If you know what tests will be given, and you can find out sometimes by asking employees and other applicants, you can actually prepare. You can get mechanical, verbal, and math intelligence tests and practice. Experience taking these tests may give you a slight but significant edge over other applicants. Personality tests are another matter. Personality and preference (interest) tests are of questionable value and interpretation. Many such tests were designed to detect mental and emotional problems in abnormal people, and they have been incorporated into tests for job applicants. Some were designed to pry deep into your attitudes and motivations. Because they all are often invalid, questionable, and sometimes unfair, you might attempt to avoid taking them. If you take them and you are absolutely honest, you may be at a disadvantage in competition with others who deliberately fake answers; or if you try to slant your answers, you may appear inconsistent. There *are* right and wrong answers to the questions, and many vocational experts feel that in this case it is not unethical for you to use your intelligence and give the "right" answer as long as it is not untrue, but be consistent.

A college professor who formerly worked for a personnel agency confided that he once advised a shy applicant who was applying for a bill collector's job to imagine himself to be a tough army general and answer all the questions from that viewpoint. The applicant scored extremely high on the personality test and was ushered into the company with great expectations. He was released later when his true, gentle nature revealed that he was unfit for the job.

The "right" answers to most sales personality tests are that you are aggressive but not overaggressive—you walk, talk, eat, and work faster than most people. You are socially active and participate in group activities more than most. You are *not overly* interested in theater, music, art, or other "impractical" subjects unless they are associated with the job for which you are applying.[9] You are more conservative than liberal or radical. You are not overly critical or introverted.[10] You are money-motivated and achievement-motivated, but you are able to get along with all kinds of people. You do not read a lot, but you are active in competitive sports. You like to socialize, but you can be alone enough to travel. Use your intelligence, of course, and consider the job for which you are applying. A public-relations profile is different from an insurance-sales-person profile.

Don't Get Discouraged

Few applicants get the first job for which they apply. You may not be offered the job for many reasons: the organization may not be growing;

[9] *Ibid.,* pp. 136–140.
[10] *Ibid.*

there may not be any opening; the interviewer may have felt that you were over- or underqualified for the job description; or the interviewer may have been inexperienced or inept and may not have evaluated you correctly. Most applicants can expect to participate in many interviews before being offered a job, just as most salespersons expect to make many calls before making an important sale. Don't lower your self-image and decide to take a situation beneath your reasonable aspirations. Relive your interviews and testing situations just long enough to profit from your mistakes and successes. Recognize your mistakes without branding yourself as a failure. Regardless of the outcome, write a letter to the company, thanking them for the interview. Company recruiters have been known to change their minds in response to such courtesy.

SELLING YOURSELF ON THE JOB

When you arrive at the sales office, you will probably be introduced to the office, sales, and repair personnel. Don't be surprised if the other sales representatives don't receive you with enthusiasm. You are their competitor. Some of them may have to accept smaller territories so you can have a share. Others may have to sacrifice selling time to help train you. Some of the sales team will probably be very nice to you, and some won't. It is your place to be friendly, helpful, and respectful toward experienced sales personnel. Most salespeople are friendly by nature, and when they get over resenting having to share with you and get to know you as a person, they will receive you as one of the team.

In your first days with the company, you will still be closely scrutinized by management. Dress well, be dependable, and make good use of your time. Be aggressive and indicate that you would like to go out and sell as soon as you are allowed and that you want to learn as much as you can about the products and company. Ask questions without being a bother, read the policy manuals, see problems, and volunteer to solve them. Be willing to run errands, prepare products for demonstration, and study hard to catch up with the established sales force. Show that you are no stranger to hard work and do everything cheerfully and enthusiastically. Above all, never, never, never criticize or speak ill of anyone—especially your superiors. Courtesy always pays. Be your own public-relations representative and cultivate all of your publics—office staff, sales-force members, repair personnel, managers. Learn everyone's name as quickly as you can, but show respect for everyone, including the maintenance personnel.

It is good to be ambitious, but don't be a threat to your immediate supervisor. You can gain more by supporting your sales manager and following him or her up than you can by tearing him or her down to gain position in the firm. Remember that everyone is vitally concerned with his or her position in the company. Watch out for those who might pull you down to get ahead of you. This is why you must be careful what you say, even around your best friends in the company.

You can show that you are concerned about firm profitability by being careful with firm property and being reasonable about expense accounts. Since your managers do not see you all the time, they judge you by the actions they do see and the things they hear about you. Be willing to do things other employees do not want to do, and solve problems other salespersons do not want to solve.

In every organization cliques or informal groups exist. Many cliques are very divisive and exclude those not in the clique while advancing the interests of clique members. Be sure you want to be identified with the clique before you "join." Joining is not a formal act. It is simply conforming to clique norms, acknowledging clique leadership, and being accepted by the group. It is possible but difficult to remain neutral. This often requires acting as an individual while being friendly to people who belong to the informal group. It can be dangerous to engage in any of the "political activities" of the clique such as putting down some people and pushing up others (especially supervisors). Fortunately, many salespersons work such separate territories that cliques are seldom as active as they are in situations where persons work in closer proximity.

Learning the names of organizational personnel and being friendly to everyone will pay big dividends. Write letters of appreciation. Work hard to make your goals, especially in the beginning of your selling career, and do more listening than talking in the sales office. The same persuasive principles that count in selling and public relations can gain you the respect of your peers and your supervisors.

Sometimes, political and organizational pathologies are irreversible, and the company loses its potential for providing any promise of future opportunities. If you find yourself in a sick power structure and someone above you is really out to get you, you must have the patience to wait or the sense to find another situation. Continually assess your future with the firm and be willing to find new opportunities when the company loses its long-run potential for furnishing you with a healthy working environment.

THE FUTURE IN PERSONAL SELLING

Adele Lewis, who has had extensive experience in helping people find jobs, writes in her book, *How to Write Better Résumés,* that sales work is "recession proof," that openings always exceed applicants, and that excellent opportunities exist in this growing occupational area.[11] If the past is indicative of the future and you gain expertise in persuasion, you will be able to find lucrative employment in almost any geographical area and under almost any business conditions.

No one can really see into the future, but there appear to be many trends and innovations that will affect tomorrow's marketplace.

- Personal selling is becoming more professional and enjoying a higher image.
- Salary-plus-bonus plans and other profit-sharing plans are growing in popularity.
- Telephones that allow visualization of the conversants will have a big impact on personal selling.
- More and better visual aids such as holographic three-dimensional projections will improve the prospect's ability to preexperience ownership.
- Women and minorities will continue to enter the field in greater numbers and enjoy increasing acceptance.
- Salespersons may have to assume an allocation role when temporary shortages occur in product lines because of raw material scarcities.
- The population will become older, more affluent, and enjoy increasing leisure time.
- Appeals will increasingly be directed to higher motivational levels.
- Fewer people will actually be working.
- New transportation and housing products will significantly affect lifestyles.
- Consumerism and environmentalism will produce more laws affecting selling.
- The trends toward socialism and lower moral standards will suffer only temporary setbacks and will continue.

Finally, opportunities in personal selling will increase because fewer applicants will have the personality, willingness, achievement motivation, and success characteristics required to fill an increasing number of public-relations and selling positions. The future holds promise for those who prepare for it.

[11] Lewis, *op. cit.,* p. 292.

SUMMARY

Selling yourself to an employer is one of the most important sales you will ever make in your career. Find an employer who is employee-centered, who has salespeople working under job descriptions that match your aspirations, who has a good training program, and whose products promise future growth. Select the employer rather than letting the employer select you. Secure an interview with the branch or sales manager after you have done thorough research on the firm and have decided that it presents you with optimum long-run opportunity. If you sell yourself properly, there is a good chance the manager will make an opening for you, since promising sales aspirants are in demand. You may want to try the résumé method if employers in which you are interested are located in another region. Realize that a professional-looking résumé is your advertisement to secure an interview and should be written carefully in accordance with an acceptable format.

A successful interview is the key to obtaining an excellent sales opportunity. Before entering the interview, you should be appropriately dressed and groomed to reflect the desired image of the firm. You should be thoroughly prepared to reflect your specific interests in the firm and to answer standard questions designed to help the recruiter learn about you. Always be ready to justify why the firm should hire you over other applicants, and always be prepared to tell the interviewer "something about yourself." Be on your guard at all times to present your ideal self, and watch for interviewer tricks. Prepare yourself in case you are accepted, in case you are rejected, and in case you are asked to answer questions about what kind of compensation you expect. Be prepared to *ask* good questions, too. If you try to supply the "right" answers to personality tests, be consistent and answer as you expect yourself as an ideal salesperson would answer.

When on the job, make good use of company assets, especially time. Learn the names of all company personnel and speak well of everyone, never criticizing anyone. Watch out for cliques and positional-behavior motivations.

The future will be characterized by many new markets and products, but there will always be a great need for professional persuaders in a free-enterprise system.

REVIEW QUESTIONS

1. What kind of selling job do you think you would like best? Why?

2. What factors should you consider in evaluating organizations for employment?

3. Evaluate newspapers and employment agencies as sources of selling jobs.

4. Explain the "direct approach." Why should you first try to interview the manager who will make the final decision?

5. According to the text, what is the worst thing that can happen to you in your search for a job? Do you agree? If not, what do you think?

6. What is a résumé?

7. What should résumés always include? Exclude?

8. What is the difference between a functional and a historical résumé? When should you use the historical structure? The functional?

9. Why is it permissible to send out good copies of the résumé but bad practice to send copies of the cover letter?

10. How long should the résumé be? The cover letter?

11. What should be in the cover letter?

12. Why do employers put so much stock in the interview? What are they looking for?

13. How do you prepare yourself for the interview?

14. List five important questions you might expect to be asked in the interview.

15. What kind of tricks might interviewers use to find out about you?

16. Why should you want a good training program as part of the company offering?

17. What important decisions might you have to make near the end of the interview?

18. Do personality tests have "right" and "wrong" answers? Explain. How can you supply the "right" answers?

19. What should you do if you are turned down in the interview?

20. What factors will help you sell yourself on the job?

21. List seven important trends that might affect personal selling in the future.

APPLICATION QUESTIONS

1. List the features you would like to have in a selling job.

2. What sources of information might you consult to find companies that might have a selling job such as you described above?

3. Outline an answer to the question: "Tell me about yourself."

4. Make up five intelligent questions you might ask an interviewer.

17–1

Robert Dunning is applying for a sales job with the Stable Life Insurance Company after having completed two years of college. He is wearing a leisure suit and is fairly well groomed except for dirt under his fingernails and a 26-hour beard. Mr. Juan Rodriguez represents Stable Life.

Juan: Hello, Robert, I'm Juan Rodriguez. Come in and have a seat.

Bob: Hi, Juan. I was free this period, so I thought I would come over and find out what you guys have on tap.

Juan: Would you care for some coffee?

Bob: No, but you don't care if I smoke, do you? It keeps my jitters down.

Juan: We are looking for life-insurance agents who want a future with a growing company. Do you think you might be interested in selling insurance?

Bob: Maybe. How much does it pay, and how much time off do you have?

Juan: We pay a straight salary of $850 per month during the four-month training period, and after that, it depends on how much life insurance you write. You are on your own as to working hours after the training period, but some night work and weekend work is involved, because that's when people are home. I see you're a history major. Why did you choose that major?

Bob: I'm not sure, really. I have a pretty good memory, and ole Dr. Hacklestack is fairly easy to get by. I'm a hard-rock fan, and that major gives me time to take in concerts.

Juan: I see you are not married.

Bob: Well, you know, Juan. All that responsibility is not too cool. That's one institution I don't care for.

Juan: I just want you to relax now and tell me about yourself.

Bob: *(Slumping down in the chair and enjoying his cigarette)* Well . . . there's not much to tell. You already know about my major. I have about a 2.2 average. I play a bass and did pretty well with the "Fire Ants" group, but they started to go on the road too much. I belong to the Student Freedom Club, which is dedicated to getting grass legalized in the state and getting a bar in the dormitory. I did a little selling once. I sold records for the "Fire Ants" before I started playing bass for them. Dad is in Alaska, and Mom lives here. I've had two good trips to Alaska since I've been here. One time I made it clear down to Florida on my cycle. Like I said, Juan, not much to tell.

Juan: It sounds like you've had an interesting time in college. Have you had any business courses?

Bob: Nope, sorry. You have to have accounting and "sadistics" as prerequisites over there. I'm not much with the numbers.

Juan: Robert, I'm going to be honest with you. I don't think life-insurance selling is your thing. A lot of it takes place in the evening hours and would probably interfere with your interest in music.

Bob: Are you telling me no, man? Come on. I can do it—at least for four months.

Juan: Well, we are looking for someone who will stay with us and has preferably had business interests and selling experience. But we sure appreciate your coming in.

QUESTIONS

1. This dialogue is exaggerated, of course. Few applicants would make as many mistakes as Robert Dunning. Identify Robert's mistakes.

17–2

Howard Cashdollar also has an interview with Mr. Juan Rodriguez of Stable Life that was scheduled after Robert Dunning's interview. Howard also has two years of college. He is dressed neatly in a conservative suit, has recently had a haircut and a manicure, and has on well-shined shoes. He is clean-shaven except for a neatly trimmed moustache.

Juan: Hello, Howard, I'm Juan Rodriguez. Come in and have a seat. (*Shakes hands firmly with Howard*)

Howard: Thank you, Mr. Rodriguez. I appreciate the opportunity for this interview. I've always had a great deal of respect for Stable Life Insurance Company.

Juan: Why do you say that, Howard?

Howard: Our neighbors, the Mitchells, had a policy with your company. Mr. Mitchell died five years ago, and Mrs. Mitchell was able to keep her home because of the insurance settlement. She remarked how prompt and courteous the company was in settling the claim. I understand, too, that Stable Life has grown at a rate of about 15 percent a year over the last five years in total life underwritings. That's an excellent growth rate in today's competitive market.

Juan: I appreciate your interest in us, Howard. Our company *is* doing very well. Won't you have some coffee?

Howard: (*Who doesn't drink coffee ordinarily*) Thank you, sir.

Juan: We are looking for potential life-insurance agents who want a future with a growing company. Do you think you would be interested in selling insurance?

Howard: The insurance field is certainly one of my considerations. I realize that it is challenging, but I've always liked a challenge.

Juan: Good agents do very well in insurance, Howard. Those who stick with it and earn their CLU, certified life underwriter, certificates do especially well. We start trainees out at $850 per month during a four-month training and orientation period. After that period, our average salesperson earns fourteen thousand the first year with the company. I see you are a business major. Why did you select that major?

Howard: My father has a retail store in Madison, and I had a chance to talk with many of the salespeople who came in. I decided that I wanted to be a salesperson, so I took business with a concentration in marketing. I like to move around and meet people.

Juan: I see you are not married.

Howard: No sir, not yet.

Juan: Howard, you make a very good first impression. I would like you to just relax now and tell me about yourself.

Howard: I grew up in Madison, where I threw newspapers while I was in junior high school. At Madison High I concentrated in Distributive Education and lettered in baseball my last two years. I worked summers and holidays with my father, selling men's wear in his shop. I was vice-president of the senior class and graduated in the top third of my class. Here at college I'm playing baseball again, I'm working in the bookstore, and I'm maintaining about a "B" average. I'm president of the Business Club and treasurer of OET, a service fraternity. Last summer I sold dictionaries door-to-door and made about $2500. I like to play the guitar and sing at campouts, and I love swimming and the out-of-doors. Is there anything in particular you would like to know about me, Mr. Rodriguez?

Juan: Well, I have your application and references, Howard, and they look good. Can you come down to the agency next week? I would like you to meet some of our underwriters and show you what you can really accomplish as a career underwriter. Can you come Monday about eleven o'clock? I want you to have lunch with me and some of the agents.

Howard: Yes sir, thank you. I'll be there.

QUESTIONS

1. Which do you think were Howard's best answers in this interview?

2. Which answer would you have handled differently?

3. Evaluate his answer in response to Juan's invitation to tell about himself.

4. Pretend you are answering that question. What would you say?

17-3

Patricia Milhouse started to become concerned about employment a month before she graduated. She has a 3.0 average in marketing and was vice-president of the senior class at Woodruff Community College. She is attractive although she is about twenty pounds overweight. The first thing Patricia did in her search for a job was to go over to the employment office and find out who was going to interview during the next two months. She also read the newspaper ads every morning. She has had interviews with five national companies, three on campus and two she found in the want ads. Two of the on-campus interviewers seemed very interested until she explained that she would never consider traveling or moving more than 100 miles away from Woodruff, where her parents lived and her boyfriend worked. One of the two companies she interviewed from newspaper ads has a branch located in Watertown, only fifty miles from Woodruff, but the recruiter became concerned when Pat told him he needed to hire her since she was a woman applicant and his company had to hire more females or run into trouble with the law. He found an excuse to turn her down. Pat is a little discouraged at this point. She thinks that part of her lack of success is that sales managers and recruiters don't really want to hire women. The national companies that seemed interested wanted her to be willing to relocate and do some overnight traveling. She is contemplating going to an employment agency and explaining her problem or sending out about twenty-five résumés.

Do you think Pat's approach to the job market is correct?
What mistakes has she made?
What should she do now?

Appendix:
Selling Real Estate

A real-estate broker sells an intangible service to the owner of real property—the ability to find and persuade a qualified buying prospect and the expertise necessary to transfer the property. To the prospective buyer, the broker sells tangible, real property, as an agent for the owner. The prospective buyer uses a broker because the broker has a selection of properties, can help the buyer find the right property at the right price, and can give expert and reputable advice about transferring titles and financing. Both sellers and buyers use realtors because they feel inexperienced and unsure about making such an important and infrequent transaction.

Real-estate selling is an exciting field offering many challenges and opportunities to an innovative salesperson who wants to work in a certain geographical area. Before a real-estate commission can be earned, three separate "sales" must be made: (1) an owner must be sold on listing with the agency; (2) the buyer must be led to buy or make an offer; and (3) the seller-owner must be persuaded to accept the buyer's offer or make a reasonable counteroffer (see Figure A.1, p. 476). The salesperson must use diplomacy in getting sellers and buyers to compromise on real estate. Usually, a great deal of money, sentiment, and emotion are involved in negotiations. Sellers are leaving a property that has been part of their life experiences and memories. Buyers are looking for a home or a working space that will serve their future aspirations. Because of the emotional involvement and the risks, the salesperson must be a good listener and select words that build positive images. Salespeople must also understand the legal requirements for exchanging real property. The salesperson must see that all transactions are ethical and fair to all parties, since real-estate agencies depend heavily on their reputations.

Real-estate selling offers excellent financial potential for creative sales-

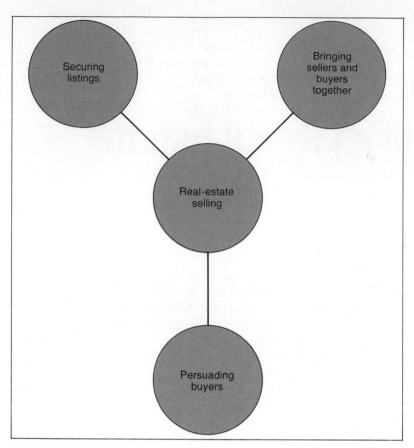

Figure A.1

persons willing to meet the challenges. A new salesperson usually goes to work as an apprentice to a licensed broker selling residential property. During this apprenticeship, the new agent receives valuable experience and a designated part of the broker's commission for each transaction. Some salespersons choose to stay with this arrangement and are given increasing responsibilities by the broker. Others enroll in special courses and take the state examination to become a licensed broker. Only a broker is entitled to full commissions. Brokers may establish their own agency and hire their own sales personnel. Often, because of their experience and expertise, brokers invest in real property and take title to some of the properties that they buy and sell. Small-town brokers may become auctioneers and receive commissions in estate and farm-equipment auctions. Many brokers offer insurance and other services related to property exchange. Some brokers become involved in developing and subdividing huge land tracts. Some move from selling residential to selling industrial properties. Industrial properties frequently must be justified by locational research, so many of these brokers must learn locational theory. The United States has enjoyed a rising market in real-estate values for a long time, making many brokers and investors who know what they are doing very wealthy.

Real-estate selling will be treated under the following headings:

- Securing listings
- Prospecting and selling properties
- Negotiating and getting offers accepted
- Special problems in real-estate selling

SECURING LISTINGS

Securing listings involves (1) determining sources of listings; (2) precall preparations; (3) approaching and persuading owners to list their property for sale or lease; and (4) getting a signed listing agreement from the owner. Buyers are more interested in contacting real-estate agencies that have a large selection of properties. In most markets, securing listings is the most important facet of real-estate selling and requires the greatest part of the broker's time.

Sources of Listings

Approximately 20 percent of Americans move from their homes each year, and most of them list their homes with some agency. With this much turnover, a lot of business can be generated by a salesperson skilled in finding listers. The *newspaper* is a three-way source of potential listers. Owners who advertise in the newspapers can be persuaded to list with the agency. Newspapers contain legal notices, estate-settlement notices, birth and death notices, plant closings and layoffs, and other information directly related to the transfer of real property. The agency can also use newspapers and other media to advertise directly for listings. In addition, owners who see the agency's advertisements for other property for sale will sometimes contact the agency and list their own property.

Files in the real-estate office can result in new listings. One of the best sources of listings is a satisfied buyer or seller who has had a good experience with using the agency. Satisfied buyers and sellers can advise other property owners in their old or new neighborhoods to list with the agency. Both sources should be asked if they know anyone planning to move or sell property for any reason. Owners who previously listed with the agency and were not successful in selling within the contractual time frame may want to relist and try again. Perhaps the price that they established previously is more reasonable now and the house or property will sell this time.

Friends and acquaintances can help the real-estate agent with information. It is important for salespersons to let it be known that they are in the real-estate business and need information that could lead to clients. Many listing agents make it their business to join clubs and associations and to interact with other people who can furnish leads. An agent may have many spotters, who can give direct leads on prospective listers who have been retired, been promoted, gained an inheritance, or moved into a higher income bracket. They can also give information about plant closings or layoffs that may mean people will move. Persons who are promoted into a higher income bracket may want to move and find a more luxurious home than the one they now own. Your spotters may tell you about a family who has outgrown their old house because they have more children or their children are getting older. People contemplating a local move are prospects for both a listing and a new home and can provide a double benefit to the salesperson.

Canvassing in neighborhoods or prospecting by telephone can furnish listing leads. You can ask people not only about their own intentions but also about intentions of their neighbors and friends. Such leads can be developed long before any competitors find out about them. It is probably best to use the telephone to *spot* listing prospects only; attempts to *close* listing prospects over the phone often result in losing the prospect.

Precall Preparation

Once you have the name of a potential lister and before you visit a prospect, it is important to get as much precall information as you can. You should review selling strategy, set selling goals, and prepare a sales kit. You need to find out why the owners wish to sell the home or business. Some people wish to move immediately and are willing to take any fair offer, while others are not really anxious to sell. Some owners wish to list at a price far above market only on the chance someone might buy at that price—such listings may be unprofitable for the agency. They require diverting selling time and attention from other listings, give the agency the reputation among buyers of listing at high prices, and hurt the company's record for being able to move real estate in a reasonable length of time. Before you call, you also want to make some preliminary evaluation of the property to determine a reasonable list price.

A 6 percent commission on a $50,000 home is worth $3,000, so many owners are tempted to try to sell and advertise themselves to save the commission. Thus, you need to devise selling strategy before you call. You must convince the owner that your services are worth the commission to get the listing. Most owners feel unsure of their asking price, their selling abilities, and their expertise in handling the legalities of closing. They realize that they are at a disadvantage in knowing the market and in bargaining directly with buyers. Buyers might be suspicious of the owner's evaluation of the property and of the owner's good faith unless the advice and reputation of a reliable agency is involved. It is necessary, then, that the salesperson appear to the prospect to be an informed professional and capable of doing a competent selling job. Because of this expectation, real-estate salespeople should not drive an older car, dress too casually, or give evidence of representing an unprosperous agency.

The salesperson usually sets the goal of persuading the owners to list exclusively with the agency. Under an *exclusive brokerage listing*, the owner reserves the right to sell the property without paying a commission, but the broker gets the commission if an agency salesperson accomplishes the sale. Under an *exclusive right listing* agreement, the owner must pay the agency commission, even if the owner does the selling and the property is sold to a relative. Under an *open listing*, the property may be listed with many realtors, but the one who sells the property gets the commission. Under a *multiple listing agreement*, any realtor may sell and get a larger share of the commission, but a part goes to the multiple listing service (which keeps track of multiple-listed properties and sales), and a part goes to the agency that secured the listing. Under a *net listing,* the agent gets all above a specified price (see Figure A.2).

There are advantages to the owner listing exclusively with one agency. The agency that is certain of getting commissions on their own prospects tends to work harder to make the sale than if the property were open-listed. Nearly every salesperson has experienced developing a sale only to have the property closed by someone else just before their prospect would have signed the papers. Another advantage of an exclusive listing to an owner is that showings can be coordinated better by one agency so that they don't inconvenience the tenants. Salespersons wishing to have the owner sign an exclusive agreement would do well to stress the advantages of listing with just one agency rather than bring out the exclusiveness of the contract.

Finally, before you approach buyers and sellers, you should have a sales portfolio (or briefcase) complete with such items as real-estate forms, maps, charts, related real-estate newspaper and magazine articles, testimonials from satisfied customers, measuring devices such as tape measures or rulers, and photographs of houses currently being listed with the agency at various selling prices. Having statistics and information in a professional-looking briefcase can help your image with buyers and sellers.

TO: _____, REALTORS   DATE: _____ 19____

In consideration of your agreement to use your best efforts to find a purchaser and to submit the property with the MULTIPLE LISTING SERVICE OF THE KNOXVILLE BOARD OF REALTORS. I hereby grant you sole and exclusive right to sell my property located _____
_____

This agency is given for _____ months from date. The price is to be $_____
Upon the following terms: _____
_____

I agree that if this property is sold by myself or anyone else during the above stated period of time, I will pay _____% sales commission of the total price at the time of closing from the proceeds of the sale.

I further agree, if necessary, to pay a discount not to exceed _____%, and to furnish a letter stating the termite condition as required by the Mortgagee.

You are hereby authorized to place a "FOR SALE" sign on the property and to remove all other signs.

If a sale or exchange is made within _____days after the expiration of this agency, or any extension thereof, to any party with whom Realtor negotiated during the agency period and Realtor notifies the under-signed in writing of such negotiations within _____days after the termination of this agency, the under-signed agrees to pay Realtor the commission herein provided.

PRICE	ADDRESS	TYPE	ROOMS	BDRMS	BATHS	AREA	MLS NO.

Lot Size _____ Legal Descrp. _____ Square Feet

Listing Realtor _____ Realtor No. _____ Phone_____ Up _____

Listing Salesperson _____ Phone_____ Dn _____

Owner's Full Name _____ Phone_____ Total _____

Type_____Dishwasher_____	ROOM SIZES	CRPT	DRPS	Possession _____
Const._____Range_____	Entry _____ x _____			Mort. Bal. _____
Age_____Disposal_____	Liv. _____ x _____			Equity _____
Sewer_____Compactor_____	Din. _____ x _____			Payments _____ Maturity_____
Driveway_____Intercom_____	Kit. _____ x _____			Int. Rate _____ Type_____
Roof_____Washer_____	Den _____ x _____			Escrow _____
Garage_____Dryer_____	Rec. _____ x _____			City Tax _____
Carport_____Walls_____	Bdrm. _____ x _____			County Tax _____
Patio_____Floors_____	Bdrm. _____ x _____			Mortgagee _____
Deck_____Frpl._____	Bdrm. _____ x _____			Aug. Utility Costs _____
Windows_____Bar_____	Bdrm. _____ x _____			El. Company _____
T.V. Ant._____Heat_____	_____ x _____			Water Co. _____
Bus_____Air Cond._____	Utility _____ Basement _____			Gas Co. _____

School: GR. _____ BUS_____ JR _____ BUS_____ HI_____ BUS_____

REMARKS: _____
_____

DIRECTIONS: _____

Owners _____ Res. Phone _____ Bus. Phone _____

Information regarding this property is from sources deemed reliable, but is not guaranteed by us and is subject to correction, prior sale, or withdrawal without notice.

It is understood that this listing is placed on the Multiple Listing Service of the Knoxville Board of Realtors.

AGENT _____   OWNER _____

Send Original to Board Office

Figure A.2

Persuading Potential Listers

While your preapproach information and selling goals should give you direction for specific approach tactics, you should leave yourself flexible to adjust after you meet the owners. First, you should introduce yourself, identify your agency, and ask if the owners are planning to sell their property. A skilled salesperson learns to question, listens attentively and with patience, and bases the presentation appeal on an evaluation of communications feedback from the prospects. It is important to find out who will probably make the decision. Usually, the owner who dominates the conversation and answers the questions is the decision maker. It is also important to find out why the owners want to sell. A good agent can frequently detect the real reason why the owners might agree to list.

Strategies and appeals center around seven benefits the realtor can offer the owners: (1) the agency's superior selling position and selling power; (2) the agency's ability to handle the "red tape" associated with financial and legal arrangements; (3) the agency's superior advertising power; (4) the knowledge and expert advice of agency personnel; (5) the agency's file of potential buyers already looking for property; (6) the agency's ability to move property rapidly; and (7) the agency's ability to move property confidentially.

The Selling-Power Strategy. When a salesperson talks with the owners, observing their situation might reveal a reluctance to show property and persuade prospects. Therefore, the owners have a real need for sales professionals to accomplish that function. The potential listers are reminded of both the negotiation position of the agency and the skilled selling effort that professional realtors are able to make. Many buyers have a tendency to trust an agent more than an inexperienced owner. The salesperson might say: "Mr. Leverson, if you list with our agency, you will have seven expert sales professionals showing your home to prospects who are already interested in your house. We could get the top-market price your particular property can command because we are trained in persuading people to make such big decisions. We put our reputation on the line, and buyers have confidence in us."

The Red-Tape Strategy. Most owners are awed by the legal papers and mortgage commitments associated with property transfers. Many owners who try to sell their own homes do not understand the alternative financial arrangements available to prospective buyers and may fail to interest prospects by talking in terms of total selling price rather than monthly payments. Many sellers, too, have a suppressed fear that they might not be able to protect themselves legally—that some mistake might be made in drawing up legal papers. The agent may say something like the following to prospects who seem to have a fear of real estate "red tape." "Mrs. Dunstan, buyers are interested in more than just the selling price of your house. They are also interested in borrowing money and arranging for a good mortgage. Without the advice of realty experts, they don't feel that they are being offered the best possible loan for their particular situation. In addition, people who are not accustomed to handling the important legal paperwork associated with property transfers sometimes make expensive errors or omissions and can even leave themselves open to lawsuits. Contracts and deeds must be carefully considered and prepared. Let us handle all this red tape for you. We will get the top-market dollar for your property and arrange all of the complicated details involved in transferring real estate."

The Superior-Advertising-Power Strategy. Many owners realize that they are not skilled in writing ads or in painting signs for the front yard. The agency has advantages in several respects: their yard signs are recognized, neat, and well appointed; newspaper ads are skillfully worded; buyers are attracted by their total advertising effort and the reputation of the agency; and prospects who call the agency about one property can be diverted to other properties. The agent might say: "We will put your house in the limelight, Mrs. Statler. Not only will we enter a well-worded ad in the newspaper, bringing out its best features, but we will put out well-known signs in your yard so prospects will know we are staking our reputation on treating them and you fairly. All of our salespeople will have a color picture of your attractive property to show prospects, and it will be displayed down at the realty office for all new potential buyers to see. We can give your house maximum exposure to the market."

The Expert-Knowledge and Advice Strategy. If the salesperson makes a good, professional impression, the prospective lister might realize the advantages of superior experience in offering the property. The sales agent can go over some of the complications of the sale and instruct the owners in real-estate procedures and terms. If the potential listers are impressed by the complexity of the selling situation and the personality of the agent, they may be more willing to put the sales job into more competent hands than their own. "Mr. and Mrs. Mostello, your potential buyer may want an abstract, an expensive appraisal before buying directly from an owner, and special legal papers. Some prospective buyers want to know about such things as easements affecting the land. Sometimes owners who don't know about these things scare off the better prospects, and then it becomes doubly hard for even a knowledgeable realtor to move the property. We can answer buyers' questions, and they usually trust our advice. Our presence in the transaction takes a great deal of the risk out of transferring real estate for both parties. Let an agency with experience and expertise handle your sale for you."

The "We-Already-May-Know-a-Buyer" Strategy. This approach can take two forms. The salesperson can explain that the agency already has lists of prospective buyers looking for property like that of the sellers, or the salesperson can speculate on just what kind of buyer would most likely be interested in the owner's property and remark that the agency has many such buyers in that classification. The sales agent can even go further and say that he or she knows of a specific buyer who is looking for property such as the owner plans to sell. "This property with its built-ins and spacious yard would be ideal for a family like your own with several children. I know just such a family that would be interested in seeing this house. It would be ideal for their children. If you list with us, I will try to get them to come over and look at it this week before they buy something else."

The "Move-It-Quickly" Strategy. Some sellers have a pressing need to sell their property in a hurry. Owners who are moved to another locality by their employers and owners who have found another property and need a down payment right away fit into this classification. A skillful salesperson can determine this from careful questioning and listening. The salesperson can explain to these potential listers why full-time salespeople or special listing services can give property maximum exposure and sell it quickly. "Mr. and Mrs. Whitney, it is to our advantage to sell your property as soon as we can. We may be able to sell it before you leave and provide you with an equity for your new home in South Dakota. You will have a full sales force working every day representing your interests, and we already have prospects who may want to buy your house. Prospective buyers, buying through a realtor, are less likely to hesitate and engage in lengthy investigations after seeing your property. It would be advantageous if you could have your cash in hand and the deal legally closed before you leave, wouldn't it? Even if it takes a little longer than the three weeks you have left here, we could still handle the entire transfer without your having to be concerned about it."

The "We-Can-Keep-It-Confidential" Strategy. Sometimes sellers need to keep their move confidential until it is made. Persons who plan to quit their job and move, for example, may not want their superiors to learn of such plans, because it would give their superiors a chance to perhaps dismiss them prematurely. An executive may not want subordinates to know that he or she is being transferred until the executive's replacement arrives to take over the responsibilities. It is possible for realtors to sell the property before it becomes common knowledge that the owners plan to leave, but it is almost impossible for an *owner* to advertise without word getting around. Such a sale might take a little longer because the realtor can't identify the home in newspaper advertising or use on-premise signs. But salespersons can discreetly show such property to prospects without fanfare and often without even neighbors suspecting. The agent might say: "Mr. Swain, it would be almost impossible for you to advertise in the newspaper, put a sign on your premises, or even tell your neighbors that your house is for sale without your employer's getting wind of it. We have prospects looking for homes like yours, and we can show your house without making your departure common knowledge. If you want to be especially careful, we can restrict showings to prospects coming to this locality from out of town. Won't you let us get things rolling and list with our agency now so we can handle this for you as quietly and as quickly as possible?"

Securing a Signed Listing Agreement from the Owner

Good approach strategy should end up in a close with a signed listing agreement from the owner. Usually, before owners will sign any kind of agreement, some understanding about the list price of the property is necessary. Owners who are willing to list only because they think they can get more for the property than its normal market value will quite naturally opt for an unrealistic price. Other owners realize that they are not experts and that they might overvalue or undervalue their property. They may rely heavily on what the salesperson advises in pricing their property. For all these reasons, sales representatives must acquire experience in evaluating property. They don't want it to be valued too high and be a drag on the market or valued too low and rob the owners of potential equity.

The value of any property depends primarily on its location. Residential houses located in neighborhoods with responsible neighbors and near schools, parks, and shopping centers are worth more, other things being equal, than equivalently constructed houses near industrial settings. Business property located near the intersection of busy traffic thoroughfares with plenty of parking space has locational assets. The pleasantness of the surroundings and the stability of the people in the area are important. Site characteristics such as air pollution, airport noise, access to waterfronts, dead-end streets, and traffic make a difference. Residential property located near trailer parks or near neighbors who don't keep up their yards, have vicious dogs, and have junk cars around has environmental defects. Property that is not well drained and is subject to forest fires, mud slides, avalanches, earthquakes, and floods might not be worth as much. Evaluation also depends on the amount of square-foot space in the property; the quality of construction; the age of the buildings; the quality of built-ins; the type of heat, air conditioning, and insulation; and the attractiveness of space arrangements and landscaping. As you can see, there are so many factors involved in evaluation that even very experienced realtors can make misestimations of thousands of dollars.

While the real-estate salesperson must have some idea of the worth of the property, it is up to the owner to decide on the listing price. Property is often sold for about 5 percent less than the asking price. Since the broker usually has a percentage commission stake in the transaction, it is to the broker's advantage to list the property at a price that will attract a reasonable number of buyers. Some owners may even want a professional appraiser to set the price, but even professional appraisers vary in their estimations. Most owners who will list with a broker either already have in mind what they want or are willing to rely on the salesperson's advice to some degree. This is why salespeople must have a reasonable idea about the evaluation.

It is a natural time to close once a listing price is decided. The market may eventually determine the actual selling price, unless it is set too low. Salespersons should probably try to sell some type of exclusive agreement with the appeals of "concentrating marketing power" and organizing showings so they won't disrupt household or business routines. "Mr. Higgs, you have decided that you should list your house for about $59,500. That seems a reasonable figure to me, considering all factors. If you will sign an agency agreement with us, we will apply a concentrated marketing effort to move your property as quickly and efficiently as possible. This agreement would let you reserve the right to sell your own property should you find the buyer, but it will give us six weeks to move your property at its top-market value. What could be fairer than that?" Of course, any of the standard closes discussed in Chapter 13 could be applied to the situation. Remember that the lister is buying an intangible service and remember always to find something you can admire about the property, because it has emotional significance to people who have lived or worked for years in it.

Before you leave the seller with listing agreement in hand, make sure you have a clear understanding about showing the property and the date of possible occupancy by new owners. It is important to the sale of the property to be able to show it at times convenient to the buyer as well as to the owner. Every effort should be made to impress the owner that the grass should be neatly cut and the property in display condition. The buyer may receive a bad image if property looks its worst at the time of the showing. You might also remind the owner again that the buyers in the market ultimately determine the fair price of the property, especially if the list price seems high. Don't spend too much time after the listing agreement is signed. As advised before—GOQ (get out quickly) and do not talk yourself out of the contract.

PROSPECTING AND SELLING PROPERTIES

The nature of the market determines the relative importance of securing listings and finding buyers, but it is always important to have a good market for listed properties. The "persuading buyers" phase of the real-estate selling process consists of:

- Prospecting and selling a showing
- Showing the property
- Closing and getting a signed offer

Prospecting and Selling a Showing

Prospecting involves finding potential buyers, qualifying buyers, and determining what buyers are really looking for in properties. If you are selling residential property, you should talk to buyers in terms of a "home" instead of a house. While owners must break ties with their former properties, buyers are buying the physical arrangements of their future homes. You are now selling a tangible investment for the lister, and it is essential that you know all the selling points and match selling points with the dominant buying motives of prospects.

Sources of Prospects. After you secure a listing, you should knock on several *doors in the immediate neighborhood* and announce that the property is for sale. Residential and business tenants have an important stake in who moves in as their new neighbors and will prospect for you. Almost everyone on *your lister file* will have to move, and some of them may want to move in the same community, especially if they are moving because they want a larger or more desirable home. There are many sources from which you can compile a list of people who need new property. *Friends and acquaintances, club members, and other spotters* can constantly be on the lookout for people planning a move or coming in from out of town. Organizations that are hiring more people or turning over employees rapidly are a source of prospects. Persons who have been transferred in, just married, or who have suddenly come into more money are good prospects for a new home. Because people move so often, *former customers (listers and buyers)* can be contacted. They may be moving or know of someone who is moving and they might recommend your agency. *The real-estate office and on-premise sign* can attract walk-ins. Some of the best prospects, however, are the ones who see the *"for sale" sign* on the property, because they show interest in the specific location and the specific house through their inquiry. Skillfully written *newspaper ads* interest many people in the agency's offering. Planned "open houses" can be used but attract many hard-to-qualify "lookers" with no intention to buy and require a lot of selling time. If prospects are fairly scarce in a buyer's market, a salesperson can *call people* who are coming into the community or plan to move and determine their intentions. *Direct-mail campaigns, bulletin-board advertising, special displays in heavily trafficked areas* and even *billboard advertising* can uncover prospective buyers who would be willing to buy real property. Every realtor should have a *list of people looking for investment property* to take advantage of new listings suitable for that particular purpose. If the realtor has a good reputation, prospects from all of these sources will be easier to find.

Questioning and Qualifying Prospects. Many people look at real estate for entertainment. They may plan to buy some day, but for right now they are just educating themselves. Such "lookers" can waste a lot of valuable selling time if indulged, while real buyers will buy from some other agency if neglected. Lookers should be treated courteously because many of them will buy in the future and because not even the most experienced brokers are ever sure that lookers are not really planning to buy. Skilled salespersons can separate lookers from buyers by good questioning, listening, and observing. Real buyers are usually less evasive, more willing to answer specific questions, and less defensive when pinned down. Ask your buying prospects specific questions about what size home, what style, what kind of neighborhood, landscaping, location, appliances, heating, and air conditioning they want. Find out what price range they can afford, the reason why they are looking for a new home or business property, and the type of furniture and cars they have. Find out, if you can, how long they have been looking and when they want to move if suitable property is found. Buyers will be more willing to give specific answers than lookers, and the person who answers most of the questions is usually the dominant buyer who will ultimately make the decision. While questioning buyers, *remember to be a good listener.* You must gain some idea of the main features buyers are searching for in property to show them the most suitable property and get an offer. You must also find out about their financial positions.

Selling a Showing. Few people will buy real property without seeing it. You must convince potential buyers that it is worth their time to see property. You must sell them on the possibilities that it could very well fit their specific needs and is a good investment. Some realtors feel, however, that you should not show the best property for their needs first but should show a less suitable listing to give a positive comparison. If you can, make an appointment for a specific time for more than one showing. Make sure that the time is suitable for the owners and that the property can be made ready to show by that time.

Showing the Property

Plan everything about showing property. It is best if the buying prospects ride with you in *your* car, because you can have time to talk and listen on the way. You can take the most scenic route and show off the best environment and approach to the property. You can also park where your clients have the most favorable first impression. You want to show off shopping centers, schools, fine homes, and other desirable features as much as you can on your drive to the property. Ask prospects questions and listen attentively to learn more about them and their real wants. Remember, too, that buyers need to know that you are sincere and honest. For most buyers, you would do well to admit some of the obvious negative features, but you must know all of the good features to overbalance negative aspects. Houses that have nice furniture already in them are more impressive, so it is better to show the house before the owner leaves if you can. The owner should not participate very much in a showing, however. It is best if *you* do the showing since owners are amateurs and may ruin the sale by what they say or show.

Leading questions and positive statements woven around features for which prospective buyers have already expressed a desire are in order. But listen, and *listen carefully* for the response and reaction. "You can buy anything you need at this shopping center, and they have an excellent supermarket, Mrs. Thrasher. ... Aren't the trees in this neighborhood beautiful, and this is one of the best elementary schools in the city for Mary. Those certainly are nice children playing on the swings, aren't they? ... This spacious den is where you will spend many restful hours, Mr. Thrasher; and I want to show you the basement where you can do the woodworking you said you liked to do so much." You need to create images by what you say. Remember that people are looking for a home— a future. Place them positively in that future by helping them see themselves enjoying that future on that property.

Closing and Getting a Signed Offer

Real property is unique in that most of it is one of a kind, and most of it can be sold at any time. The pressing reason to act now is that some other buyer can buy it, and your prospect can lose it. Nearly all closes have an element of "standing room only." Buyers who know that other buyers are looking at and are interested in the same property are especially impressed that a decision should be made. A rising market, too, continually pushes property prices higher and higher. If you have established the buyer's confidence in you, explained all financial and other contingencies of the sale, have thoroughly informed the buyer about all aspects of the property, and have built up desire by getting the buyers to see themselves enjoying the future intangible benefits of owning the property, you should ask for action. "Now, this excellent home that is so well located and with such nice neighbors can be yours if you reserve it. It's very reasonably priced, isn't it? It has plenty of space, and the trees in the yard are beautiful. If you will just O.K. this deposit receipt, no one will be able to take it away from you." If you can close for the full amount required by the owner, you have a sure sale. If you can't, you should try to get the buyer to make a reasonable offer. "Remember, Mr. Thrasher, I showed you other houses in the neighborhood and their selling prices, so the asking price for this home is well in line. Why don't you make the owner an offer? There is a chance that the owner would be willing to take a little less. This is a good buy and a good investment, and houses like this don't stay for sale long. This one has only carried a sign for eight days. If you make a reasonable offer, I will see what the owner says."

Remember that when dealing with real estate, oral promises are useless— any commitment by the buyer must be in writing, so get a signed deposit receipt (see Figure A.3). Remind the buyer that a signed offer does not have to be accepted and that your real challenge will begin with the offer. Try to encourage buyers to raise offers that are more than 10 percent less than the asking price, but transmit every written order to the seller.

NEGOTIATIONS AND GETTING OFFERS ACCEPTED

Every written offer must be transmitted to the owners and should be carried in person. It is best practice to see all of the owners together when presenting the offer. Usually, this is husband and wife for residential property or the partners in business property. Make sure that you come at a time when there is no hurry and you can review the situation thoroughly. The owner-listers may have had many people look at the house and reject the house at the asking price. Review this problem with the owners. Let them know if you think the offer is a realistic one under the circumstances and in line with the range of market values for the property. The offer should seldom be presented without a rational discussion of some of the reasons other prospects have rejected the property and the problems of getting buyers with the financial capacities to buy. Sometimes, it helps to describe the prospective buyers and their side of the transaction. People are especially sentimental about their houses and who will move into the neighborhood to take their place. They have an emotional attachment and are interested in selling to people with

SALES CONTRACT AND RECEIPT FOR DEPOSIT

1. The receipt of the sum of $_____ as earnest money from _____ of _____, hereinafter called "purchaser", is hereby expressly acknowledged by the undersigned Realtor and shall be held by said Realtor in escrow pursuant to the terms hereof. Said sum is a part of the purchase price of $_____ payable on the following terms: _____ _____ _____ _____

for the purchase of the following premises, hereinafter called the "property", located in _____, _____ County, Tennessee: House Number _____, Street _____, Lot _____, Block _____, Unit _____, Subdivision _____ _____ _____

Purchaser hereby offers to purchase the property on the terms and conditions herein contained and acknowledges receipt of a copy hereof.

2. The above stated purchase price shall be paid fully in cash and this transaction shall be closed on _____, or, in the event a mortgage loan has been or is to be applied for and is so indicated above, then such payment shall be made and this transaction closed on the day said mortgage loan is closed. It is agreed that the property will be delivered to purchaser (A) on the day of the closing, or (B) within _____ days after the day of the closing. (Strike out one.)

3. If a mortgage loan has been or is to be applied for and is so indicated above, then this contract is conditioned upon purchaser obtaining such loan and if said loan is not approved, this contract may be cancelled at purchaser's option and the earnest money will be refunded, provided, however, that purchaser shall make a good faith effort to obtain said loan.

4. Seller shall convey the property to purchaser by a warranty deed free and clear of all encumbrances except restrictive covenants, easements of record and _____

If marketable and merchantable title cannot be given, if title insurance cannot be secured, or if the improvements are destroyed or substantially damaged by fire or other destructive force, the purchaser shall have the option of enforcing this contract or cancelling the same by written notice to seller within thirty (30) days after the receipt of written notice from seller of said defect or destruction. If cancelled, the earnest money will be refunded to purchaser. The conveyance shall describe the grantee(s) as follows: _____

5. Property taxes are to be (A) pro-rated between the purchaser and seller as of the date of closing or (B) assumed by the purchaser and paid when due. (Strike out one.) If taken over by the purchaser, insurance (shall) (shall not) be pro-rated between the purchaser and seller as of the date of closing. (Strike out one.)

6. Upon seller's acceptance of this offer by signing the acceptance herein contained, this contract between the parties hereto shall become effective, provided ,however, that if the seller does not sign said acceptance and notify purchaser within _____ days from the date purchaser signs this offer, or if seller for any reason declines to execute this agreement or approve the terms set out herein, then this offer is void and any contract is terminated, in which case the earnest money shall be returned to purchaser. The date on which seller signs the acceptance herein contained shall be the date of this contract.

Figure A.3

7. No representations or warranties about the condition of the property, title or title condition have been made unless stated herein. It is agreed that the purchaser is buying the property on an "as is" basis and has inspected said property unless otherwise stated herein: _____

8. If purchaser fails to carry out and perform the terms of this contract, except for some permissible reason specified herein or other reason satisfactory and acceptable to seller, purchaser shall forfeit all amounts advanced as earnest money, together with all other amounts deposited with the undersigned Realtor or seller, provided however, that such forfeiture shall not preclude seller from pursuing any other remedy available to him including specific performance of the contract and an action for damages. If seller defaults in the performance of this contract, purchaser may reclaim his earnest money payment and pursue any remedy available at law.

9. This contract shall be binding upon the parties hereto and their respective heirs, executors, administrators or assigns, and, when approved by the seller, shall contain the final and entire agreement between the parties hereto, and they shall not be bound by any terms, conditions, statements or representations, oral or written, not herein contained.

10. Other terms and conditions: _____
_____
_____
_____
_____
_____
_____
_____
_____
_____
_____

REALTOR: _____   PURCHASER: _____

_____   _____

DATE EXECUTED: _____   DATE EXECUTED: _____

The undersigned seller accepts the foregoing offer and agrees to sell the property to purchaser on the terms and conditions therein set forth. Seller further acknowledges receipt of a copy hereof.

Seller agrees to pay _____,
the Realtor who negotiated this sale, a commission pursuant to the listing agreement between the seller and said Realtor. If purchaser shall default, said Realtor shall be entitled to one-half the earnest money or his full commission, whichever shall be smaller

DATE EXECUTED: _____   SELLER: _____

_____

whom they can identify. When the salesperson does get around to announcing the offer, it is extremely important to be alert for verbal and nonverbal reactions. The verbal comments may be negative because the owners are still bargaining, but the nonverbal signals may indicate relief or an otherwise positive attitude, indicating that the offer will be met with a reasonable counteroffer. The salesperson should suggest that a counteroffer be made if complete acceptance is not achieved at that time.

Eventually, it may be necessary to get sellers and buyers together to talk over details, but it is usually best to compromise offers and counteroffers until the price has pretty much been settled. Getting bargainers together in the same place can often result in personality clashes, emotionalism, and unyielding positions. When major issues *are* settled, a contract will be signed, and the house will be sold to the new owner.

SPECIAL PROBLEMS IN REAL-ESTATE SELLING

When special problems or challenges exist in any selling area, opportunity is greater for people who are willing and able to solve the problems correctly. Three special problem challenges in real estate that need more understanding are:

- Learning real-estate vocabulary and using the right words to sell
- Managing husband-wife and other group-buying situations
- Knowing real-estate law and mortgage arrangements

Learning Real-Estate Vocabulary and Using the Right Words to Sell

Real estate involves the use of many technical terms that describe the property itself or are used in connection with a legal property transfer and mortgaging. If you sell homes, you should know the difference between a Georgian and a colonial-style house, a split-level and a tri-level, and an abstract and a guaranteed title. If you want a professional image, you must know what prospective buyers mean when they describe what they are looking for, using real-estate terms. While listers and buyers may not fully understand technical terms like "escrow," "easement," and "amortization," you should be able to explain all words associated with the particular sales situation. Your understanding of the vocabulary and the technicalities behind the terms is an important reason why sellers and buyers use the services of the agency.

Using the right *descriptive* words in the right situation is also critical to selling real estate. All descriptive words should suggest positive, pleasant images. You should first of all be a good listener, but when you speak, you should use words that build the sale. Here are a few suggested words and phrases:

- Use "home" instead of "house" when talking to prospective buyers.
- Use "agency agreement" instead of "exclusive agreement" when talking to listers.
- Use "landscaped" rather than "planted" in referring to trees and shrubs.
- Use "young willow-oak shade tree" rather than "tree."
- Use "flowering azalea" rather than "bush."
- Use "sun-room" or "Florida room" rather than "glassed-in porch."
- Use "patio" rather than "concreted-in area."
- Use "children" rather than "kids."

Managing Husband-Wife and Other Group-Buying Situations

Many times in buying a home, one of the group of people you have to convince is more enthusiastic or "sold" than the other. The temptation is to direct all of your attention to the enthusiastic person, and it is good to get them even more sold. Do not, however, neglect the partner or spouse who is still unconvinced. Direct a fair part of your questions to them and include them in the communications. It is, after all, the unconvinced buyer-decider that can cause you to lose the sale. It is good strategy, too, to let the husband-wife team or partner-buyers have time together to "talk it over." If the wife, for example, is really sold on the property, she can do a much better job than you can in convincing the husband that he ought to buy. The same is true of partners or groups of any kind. Just make sure that you have at least one enthusiastic person on your side when the deciders go into conference, or the verdict will probably be "no!" In negotiations between two families or partnership groups, it is best to keep the groups from meeting together (in the same place) until most differences have been resolved. When you get many people who are amateurs at bargaining negotiating directly with each other, emotions may get out of hand, and harsh words may raise resistances that will kill the sale. The salesperson must concentrate on maintaining an atmosphere of harmony at the critical point when bargaining parties meet face-to-face.

Knowing Real-Estate Law and Mortgage Arrangements

Keeping abreast of the law is not easy, and a complete course in real-estate law is usually required before a person can obtain a brokerage license. Every real-estate salesperson who sells any property needs to realize that since the Open-Housing Law of 1968, it is illegal to refuse to sell to a potential buyer on the basis of race, color, religion, or national origin. Brokers in today's market must also know the latest developments in the interest rates and mortgage arrangements that can change daily. Many brokers call up mortgage houses every Monday to find out what the interest rate is at that time. Interest rates vary with the percent of down payment made by the buyer and, of course, with economic conditions. One of the big advantages of having a real-estate agency handling the sale is that the prospect can be told almost exactly how much the monthly payments will be, and the prospect is more interested in knowing about monthly payments than in knowing the total asking price of the home.

SUMMARY

Selling real estate is a three-part challenge and involves selling both an intangible and a tangible product. The salesperson must persuade the owner to list, the prospective buyer to buy or make an offer, and then handle negotiations diplomatically. In most states obtaining a brokerage license involves working as an apprentice to a broker and taking an examination. Brokers can also sell related services and make lucrative investments in real property.

Listing prospects can be found by advertising in the media, contacting owners who have advertised their property for sale, having friends and acquaintances watch out for people who plan to move or who have come into more money, watching plant transfers and lay-offs, outright canvassing in neighborhoods, and using the telephone. Salespeople should try to find out why the owners wish to sell, and they should review possible selling appeals and strategies. They should set goals about the exclusiveness of the listing agreement, and they should make up a sales briefcase before contacting potential listers. Most potential listers are unsure of their ability to sell and their technical knowledge about real-estate transfers and mortgage arrangements. Their impression of the professionalism of the salesperson is critical. After salespersons have asked questions about the property and listened attentively, they should decide on the right selling strategy. Suggested appeals include the selling-power strategy, the red-tape strategy, the advertising-power strategy, the expert knowledge and advice strategy, the "already-have-buyers" strategy, the move-it-quickly strategy, and the "we-can-keep-it-confidential" strategy. Before you can close a listing, it is usually necessary to talk about the list price. The owner should decide this, but the salesperson should be expert in evaluating property to advise the owner and secure a realistic listing price.

Buying prospects are looking for a "home" or a business property that will be instrumental in their future lives. After you get a listing, let the neighbors know the property is for sale. They may help you find a buyer. Prospective buyers can also be found through lister files, friends and acquaintances, organizations with employee turnover, old customers, signs, newspaper and other media ads, open houses, and investment-property prospect lists. Prospects should be carefully questioned to find out what they want, and they must be persuaded to look at listed property. Since location is the most important factor in real-estate value, the salesperson must sell the neighborhood as well as the specific property. The salesperson should not talk too much about the property before the prospect sees it and then should carefully note the reaction. Well-selected words promoting positive images should be used in describing the real estate's assets. Real-estate prospects have two reasons for buying now—the fact that they could lose the property to another buyer and a rising-price market. Summary and standing-room-only closes are particularly well-suited if skillfully done. The salesperson should get the asking price if possible or a reasonable offer.

The written offer should be transmitted to the owners in person and announced after a careful review of showing experiences and market indications. Owners and prospective buyers should be kept physically apart until major differences are resolved, because personalities may conflict in the bargaining situation during face-to-face negotiations. The salesperson must try to maintain harmony when negotiators come together to sign the contract.

Three problems in real-estate selling are learning real-estate technical terms and using image-building words, managing group-buying situations, and knowing real-estate law and mortgage alternatives. A glossary of real-estate terms will help you with the first problem. In selling groups, get someone in the group on your side and then let the group "talk it over." Make sure that some members of the group are enthusiastically sold before you do this. Knowing real-estate law requires course study, and keeping up with mortgage alternatives requires frequent inquiries to local lending agencies.

REVIEW QUESTIONS

1. What does a real-estate broker sell in terms of tangibles and intangibles?

2. What are the three selling phases of a real-estate salesperson's job?

3. In what other respects can the job be said to be challenging?

4. Describe other ways besides selling real estate that brokers can make money.

5. In what three ways is the newspaper a source of listing prospects?

6. In what other ways can the salesperson find listing prospects?

7. What should be done before the listing prospect is approached?

8. Name and describe five different listing contracts.

9. What items might real-estate salespersons carry in their briefcases?

10. Name and describe seven different selling strategies that can be used to persuade owners to list with the agency.

11. Why should a real-estate salesperson be able to appraise property?

12. What is the main factor to be considered in evaluating real property?

13. List at least twelve other important factors in evaluating real property.

14. What should a salesperson do if the owner wants to list at a price about 20 percent higher than the market value?

15. After you obtain the listing agreement, what other understandings should you have with the owners?

16. What are the best sources of buying prospects?

17. Why is it important to differentiate between qualified buyers and "lookers"?

18. What are five important things that you might do to impress the prospect when showing property?

19. Why should a prospect buy property now instead of waiting until next week?

20. If you can't get the buyer to accept the owner's price, what should you do?

21. How should you present the offer?

22. Why should bargainers be kept apart during initial negotiations?

23. Mention three good rules or ideas that can help you sell in group-buying situations.

24. How can brokers learn about the latest developments in interest rates and mortgage arrangements?

1. Look up in a dictionary seven real-estate terms mentioned under "Special Problems" and write out the meanings.

2. Using the picture of a house or a farm, make up a list of selling features that might be used to persuade a buyer.

A–1

Kyle Kemp has worked as a salesperson for the Triple Star Agency for about seven months. He has noticed a "For Sale by Owner" sign in the front yard of an attractive ranch-style house and has found out that the house belongs to Mr. and Mrs. Henry Dodd. The sign has been in the yard for two weeks. Kyle is ringing the Dodd doorbell at 7:15 p.m. on Tuesday.

Kyle: Good evening, Mr. Dodd. I'm Kyle Kemp with the Triple Star Realtors, and I see you have offered your house for sale.

Henry: Yes ... You're the second real-estate salesman to come by. I'm afraid we're not interested in listing with an agency. We think we can sell it without paying a high commission.

Kyle: I can understand your thinking about that, Mr. Dodd. But tell me, have you had many people come in and look since you have had your sign up?

Henry: We have had about six or seven. I don't know. Maybe we want a little bit too much for it. I tell them the price, and they just look and leave.

Kyle: How much are you asking for it?

Henry: I'm asking $43,000. The Breedland house down the street sold for $39,500, and our house is worth at least $5,000 more.

Kyle: How much down, and how much would the monthly payments be for someone who bought your house?

Henry: I don't know. I figure that's up to them and their bank. I just need the cash to buy another house.

Kyle: I don't think your price is too high for your property, Mr. Dodd. When do you plan to vacate?

Henry: Well, we need to be gone by three weeks; but I feel like we'll get a buyer by then.

Mrs. Dodd comes to the door.

   Alice: Why don't you invite the young man in, Henry?

    Kyle: Thank you, Mrs. Dodd. I'm Kyle Kemp from the Triple Star Realtors. I'm glad to meet you.

   Alice: I told Henry he should give up this idea of trying to sell our home by himself. Don't you think so?

    Kyle: Well, I can understand how he feels, Mrs. Dodd. But I do believe you would have better results if you let us sell it for you. I believe we could get you what you want for it.

Henry: How's that, Mr. Kemp?

    Kyle: A reputable realtor has many advantages over an individual, Mr. and Mrs. Dodd. Our agency has eleven experienced sales representatives, and we already know prospective buyers who would be interested in your home. We would advertise it in the paper and put an attractive sign in your front yard. We would arrange to show it at your convenience. I would recommend that we list your house for $44,500, which I feel is in range. You see, while buyers are interested in the list price, they are more interested in how much they have to pay down and how much each month. We could quote a monthly price and give the prospect alternatives in financial arrangements. You would be surprised what a difference this would make in response. We should be able to sell it before you leave. If you should be able to sell it by yourself, you won't have to pay the commission anyway. What could be fairer than that?"

Henry: We'll think about it and let you know, Mr. Kemp.

   Alice: Henry, I think Mr. Kemp is right and knows what he is doing.

    Kyle: Mr. and Mrs. Dodd, why don't you talk this over while I take another look at the outside of the house.

Ten minutes later.

Henry: Could I see that agreement, Mr. Kemp? Maybe Alice and I will let you try your hand at it if you think we could get $42,000 for it net.

QUESTIONS

1. Evaluate Kyle's approach tactics.

2. Did he ask the right kind of questions?

3. Should he have tried to sell an exclusive rights agreement in this case before approaching with an exclusive brokerage listing agreement?

4. Was he wrong to suggest selling the house at about the same price the owner was asking for it before listing?

5. What did Kyle do right? What could he have done better?

A–2

The Galloway house has been a real problem for the Highland Realty Company. Several people have looked at the house, but in the last five months, no one has even made an offer. It was well built but it is close to the expressway, and the neighborhood has deteriorated as many of the more affluent families moved to the suburbs. The house is also large and thus more expensive than other houses in the midtown neighborhood. Mrs. Galloway's refusal to lower the asking price hasn't helped matters either. The house is worth more than the asking price structurally but less locationally.

Bob Callis showed the historic-looking house to a couple who seemed interested, John and Lynda Davidson. They were interested in a great deal of room at a bargain, and Bob could tell that both of them liked the possibilities of redecorating the old home. They had inherited some antique furniture and needed a larger place. After they looked at the house, they went back to their apartment to think about it. Two days later, a middle-aged couple, Mr. and Mrs. Tom Overton, also saw the house. Bob mentioned in his closing tactics that another couple was extremely interested in the house. The next day, Mr. Overton called to say that he would buy the house at Mrs. Galloway's asking price. Bob called the Davidsons and told them that the house was sold. They were disappointed, but said that although they had decided to buy the Galloway house, there was another house that suited them almost as well that was listed with another realtor. Bob then went to Mr. Overton with a deposit receipt for him to sign. "My wife and I have changed our minds," he said, "We just don't feel we can invest that much in a midtown home." Bob immediately called the Davidsons, but they had already signed a deposit receipt for the other house that they were considering.

What was Bob's mistake?
Should any real estate be considered sold without getting a signature?
Is fostering buyer competition a good closing strategy?
When should he have informed the Davidsons that the house was sold?
Should he try to get the Davidsons to reconsider and make Mrs.
    Galloway an offer that reflects their loss of the earnest money?
Would the above action be ethical?

Glossary

The following selected terms are commonly used in selling. The definitions are based on general acceptance and are related to selling. In some instances the definitions have been extended to include the practices connected with the terms.

Not all the terms or definitions included in the text appear in this glossary; only the most important or commonly used ones are given.

Above Market   A basic price policy of selling at a price above competitive prices and implies that more services and guarantees will be offered with the product and/or that the product itself has superior qualities.

Acceptance   The communicated agreement to the terms of a legal offer.

Amortize   Putting money aside for gradual payment of a debt (in real estate a mortgage payment that reduces the principle owed).

Appraisal   An evaluation of the real estate's worth. An appraisal implies a certain amount of formality and expertise of the evaluator.

Association   A propaganda technique that encourages a prospect to accept an idea or item by relating it to something already accepted or to something desirable. The technique can also apply negatively by encouraging a prospect to reject an idea or item by relating it to something already rejected or to something undesirable

Attitudes   An individual's feelings or opinions that may be projected verbally or nonverbally.

Baby Boom   A population group born right after World War II that has an overproportionate number of members. Because of its huge size, this group affects the selling of most products.

Bandwagon   A propaganda method that implies that everyone else is buying the product so the prospect should buy too.

Below Market   A basic policy of selling below competitive market prices, and it implies that fewer frills and services will be offered with the good.

Bird Dogs   Persons who "point out" or designate prospects for the salesperson.

Breadth of Consideration   The range of alternatives contemplated by a person. It expands the choice of selection or the depth of inclusion.

Buffer   A person who screens salespersons to protect the time of a superior and who can be a barrier to obtaining an interview with a prospect. A buffer can also be an ally in obtaining an audience with an important prospect.

Build-up Method   A method of estimating territorial potential that entails identifying possible customers, finding out how many are in the territory, and determining the average amount each is expected to purchase. Multiplying the number of customers by the average amount each is expected to purchase gives the potential for that territory.[1]

Buying-Power Method   A territorial-potential-estimation method based on buying-power indices of the territory under consideration.[2]

Canvass   A method of prospecting that is not selective and involves knocking on every door to assure that every possible lead is uncovered.

Card-Stacking   A propaganda method that involves getting one-sided arguments for a product; a failure to give a balanced evaluation of your product or your competitor's product.

Closing   A distinct verbal and/or nonverbal attempt by the salesperson to get prospects to obligate themselves to buy the product.

Communications   An exchange of information, feelings, or emotions among individuals or groups based on common spheres of experience.

Communications Structure   The means by which messages are transmitted from the power unit to the members of a behavioral system and vice versa to effect coordination of activity toward a common goal or goals.[3]

Consideration   Money, written promises, or goods given to show intent to enter a contract.

Conspicuous Consumption   A term coined by economist Thorstein Veblen, who used it to describe the tendency of people to be motivated by status; the tendency of people to buy to "show off."

Contract   An agreement that can bind you and your company to perform that which you promised. A valid contract usually involves an offer, acceptance of an offer, consideration in the form of money or promises, parties with the capacity to contract, and a legal objective.

Customer Orientation   The marketing philosophy and attitude that all marketing efforts should be directed toward satisfying the customer while making a profit or satisfying the firm's goals.

---

[1] Philip Kotler, *Marketing Management,* 2nd ed. (Englewood Cliffs, N.J.: Prentice-Hall, 1972), p. 205.

[2] *Ibid.,* p. 207–208.

[3] Wroe Alderson, *Marketing Behavior and Executive Action* (Homewood, Ill.: Irwin, 1957), pp. 35–50.

Cybernetic Model A simplification comparing the mind and nervous system to the control and computing mechanisms of data-processing machines, such as computers.[4]

Decoder The person interpreting the communications message for the receiver.

Deposit Receipt A receipt for the buyer's earnest money that is given to show intent to buy the property. Signing the deposit receipt is similar to signing a purchase order for the real property.

Distinctiveness The first phase of the fashion cycle, in which the product is popular with an elite, first-accepting group.[5]

Dominant Theme A main plan; a unified pattern or purpose that is recognized as more important than secondary goals.

Early Adopter A person who is not the first to accept a new product or idea but accepts it soon after the first accepters do. They are usually opinion leaders in the local social system.[6]

Early Majority (Adopter) The first half of the majority of people who accept a new idea or product.[7]

Easement A legal right or permission that one person has concerning the land of someone else (the landowner).[8]

Economic Emulation The phase of the fashion cycle in which most socioeconomic groups have accepted and can afford the style. The style may be mass-produced and lose its distinctiveness as a mode of expression.[9]

Ego State A role reference out of which a person acts and communicates to produce recognizable patterns of behavior. In transactional analysis the person acts and communicates out of the child, the parent, or the adult.[10]

Emulation The phase of the fashion cycle in which a style is popular in middle socioeconomic groups. They wish to copy the elite group who first accepted the style as fashionable.[11]

Encoder A person who formulates or expresses a communication message for a sender in order to promote its effectiveness.

Enthusiasm Inspired zeal, interest, or conviction that is communicated to others and that may be promoted by increased knowledge, positive attitudes, health, or more noticeable nonverbal activity.

Ethical Conduct The practice of conforming to accepted standards of conduct.

---

[4] Based on Maxwell Maltz, *Psycho-Cybernetics* (Englewood Cliffs, N.J.: Prentice-Hall, 1960).

[5] Jerome McCarthy, *Basic Marketing*, 5th ed. (Homewood, Ill.: Irwin, 1975), p. 235.

[6] Everett M. Rogers, *Diffusion of Innovation* (New York: Free Press, 1962), pp. 169–171.

[7] *Ibid.*

[8] *Webster's New World Dictionary* (New York: World Publishing, 1966), p. 455.

[9] McCarthy, *loc. cit.*

[10] Eric Berne, *Transactional Analysis in Psychotherapy* (New York: Grove Press, 1961), pp. 17–22.

[11] McCarthy, *loc. cit.*

Exclusive Brokerage Listing A listing under which the owner reserves the right to sell the property without paying a commission, but the broker gets the commission if an agency salesperson accomplishes the sale.

Exclusive Right Agreement An agreement for selling real estate under which the broker gets the commission regardless of who sells the property, if the sale is made within the time limits of the agreement.

Feedback Indications from the receiver of a message whether or not the purpose of the message has been carried out.

Feminism A belief that women should have rights equal to men in all respects.

Goal Definition An expressed determination of purpose, preferably in concise writing, that can be used as a planning basis for goal achievement.

Goal Visualization The practice of seeing yourself achieving goals in your imagination.

Goodwill A favorable attitude customers and prospects have about you and your company that assures that your offering will be favorably considered in the future. Goodwill is worth money and is an asset to a business.

Hardware The physical product as opposed to the intangibles such as programming and maintenance services that are sold as part of the total offering. Services are designated as software to distinguish their importance.

"Hot Doorknobs" The salesperson's fear, before approaching a prospect, of being rejected.

Hot Prospect A prospect who is ready to buy now and deserves immediate attention.

Ideal Self How a person would like to be ideally.[12]

Incremental Method A method for determining the number of salespersons needed. This method involves hiring additional salespersons as long as the estimated sales generated by that additional person yield a profit.[13]

Innovator A person who is one of the very first to accept a new product or idea. Innovators are usually wealthier, younger, and more willing to take risks than later accepters. Usually, innovators are more interested in social systems outside of their home social systems and might be characterized as being cosmopolitan or "jet set."[14]

"Insiders" Image The view that certain people belong to a particular group because of their use of words, their knowledge, or their understanding.

Intangible Salesperson A salesperson who sells a service rather than a tangible product.

Internal Environment The political, social, and other environments within the firm or system for which you work.

[12] C. Glenn Walters, *Consumer Behavior Theory and Practice*, 3rd ed. (Homewood, Ill.: Irwin, 1978), pp. 183–185.

[13] Richard R. Still, Edward W. Cundiff, and Norman A. P. Govoni, *Sales Management*, 3rd ed. (Englewood Cliffs, N.J.: Prentice-Hall, 1976), pp. 63–68.

[14] Rogers, *loc. cit.*

Kondratiff Cycles Cycles that indicate an extreme recession or depression every fifty years because of an overburdensome debt structure.

Laggard A person who accepts a new idea only after the majority of people have accepted it or a person who will never accept the new idea or product. Laggards may be old, uneducated, poor, and socially isolated.[15]

Later Majority Adopter The last half of the majority of people to accept a new idea or product.[16]

Lead A person or firm that may be a prospect but has not yet been qualified and put into the prospect category.

Leadership Model The example set by a manager to provide a guide for subordinate personnel.

Learning A permanent change in behavior usually caused by repetitive experience or practice.

Listing Real property that is offered by a real-estate agency that has a signed agreement authorizing the agency to sell the property (a listing agreement with the owner).

Lookers People who want to look at the product but who have little intention of buying at the present time.

Management by Objectives or MBO The joint determination of goals by a manager and a subordinate that usually entails subgoal setting or definite plans about how to reach the major goals.

Manufacturer's Salesperson A salesperson directly employed by a manufacturer to sell products.

Market People who have a need or want for a product and who can get the money to buy it.

Marketing Those activities necessary to assure that the right goods and services are moved efficiently to satisfied customers through the right channels, at the right price, and using the right promotional combinations.

Mediocrat A closer who has given ample but not superior service to an expert buyer.[17]

Missionary Salesperson A salesperson who trains *dealer* sales representatives who are not employed by his or her company.

Motive An inner mental state that causes a person to act. A motive usually results from a dissatisfaction or a recognized need.

Multiple Listing Agreement A real-estate contract under which many brokers may sell the property. The realtor who sells usually gets a larger share of the commission, but a part also goes to the multiple listing service.

Name Calling A propaganda method that involves associating a competitive product with something undesirable by giving it a bad label.

[15] *Ibid.*

[16] *Ibid.*

[17] Barry J. Hersker and Thomas F. Stroh, "The Purchasing Agent Is No Patsy," in *Closing the Sale* (special report), *Sales & Marketing Management*, June 13, 1977.

Nest-Builders Recently married persons establishing their product needs for their new stage in the life cycle.

New Listing A listing agreement under which the agent gets all above a specified price.

Objection A communicated resistance to buying that usually consists of a specific reason for not complying with a salesperson's suggestions.

Offer A proposal to another person or group of people that constitutes a contract when accepted.

Offeree The person or persons to whom the offer is made.

Offerer The person or entity making the offer.

Order-Getting Representative A salesperson who must frequently employ skilled persuasive efforts to convince prospects and make a sale.

Order-Taking Representative A salesperson who sells to customers without extensive persuasive efforts or creative closing techniques.

Other-Directed Prone to consider social pressures and influences or reference groups in making buying decisions.

Overmotivation Motivation or ambition so strong that it causes a deterioration in effective action or health.

Performance Features Features relating to a product's abilities to accomplish its purpose or capabilities.

Personality The sum total of traits, attitudes, and other attributes that characterize an individual and determine the reaction of other people toward that individual.

Personality Factor Any element that characterizes an individual (such as attitudes and traits), that is projected through verbal or nonverbal communications, and that is important in determining how others react toward that person.

Personal Selling Leading people to buy by reducing their risks through information and assurances in an atmosphere of harmony rather than conflict.

Persuasion An open appeal to reason or emotion in an effort to influence someone to do or believe something.[18]

Plan A preformulated pattern of intended actions. Planning is the act of prethinking and prescheduling activities.

Planning by Objectives The act of preformulating activities in accordance with clear and concise objectives that are set by an individual specifically for the purpose of making effective plans.

Positional Behavior Competitive behavior among members of a firm or behavioral system for higher positions in the firm or maintaining a position in the firm. Such rivalry can be a detriment to the firm.[19]

---

[18] *Webster's New World Dictionary, op. cit.*, p. 1092, "Persuade."

[19] Alderson, *op. cit.*, p. 46.

Power Principle Acting in such a way as to promote the power to act.[20]

Power Symbol A representation of status of power in a system such as the large office of a superior.[21]

Power Unit A group of people (or a person) who make the decisions in a behavioral system and coordinate the activities of the members toward a goal.[22]

Preventive Maintenance Giving attention to a system on a regular basis to prevent a breakdown that might disrupt operations.

Privacy Bubble An imaginary space surrounding the body. A person can become uncomfortable if this space is penetrated by another person who is not a close acquaintance. The space varies with different cultures but extends about two feet for most Americans.[23]

Product The entire unit offering to the customer that includes the services and warranties associated with the product.

Prospect Book A record where prospect information is recorded for future use.

Psychocybernetics The application of the principles of cybernetics to the human brain. (See Cybernetic Model).[24]

Public Relations Those activities designed to sell corporate images and build good relationships with all organizational publics.

Purpose Tremor Nervousness caused from the fear of approaching a challenging task.[25]

Quadrant One of four equal parts into which a scene may be divided for observation purposes.

Qualifying a Prospect Determining whether a prospect has a need or desire for the product, the means to buy it, and the eligibility to buy it.

Rapport A harmonious relationship.

Real-Estate Broker A person licensed by the state to sell and transfer real property and receive a commission.

Real Self The way people really are as opposed to what they think about themselves or what others think about them.[26]

Reciprocity A mutual business exchange that usually precludes competition from influencing either of the participants. A reciprocity agreement would be one in which one firm agrees to buy the products of another firm if the second firm will, in turn, buy the products of the first firm.

[20] Ibid., p. 51.

[21] *Ibid.*, p. 42.

[22] *Ibid.*, p. 36.

[23] Julius Fast, *Body Language* (New York: M. Evans, 1970), pp. 45–49.

[24] Maltz, *op. cit.,* p. 159.

[25] *Ibid.,* p. 17.

[26] Walters, *loc. cit.*

Reduced Cues Incomplete indications or cues that require the individual to fill in the gaps mentally to get the picture. If the filled-in parts are wrong, the wrong image or interpretation results.

Reprogramming A redirection of attitudes and habitual mental approaches to a problem or task to effect results that will be superior to those gained using older habitual mental sets.

Résumé A concise summary of your experience and qualifications sent to a prospective employer. A résumé should also be regarded as an advertisement for your services and a possible ticket for admission to an interview.

Retail Salesperson A sales representative who customarily sells to customers who are buying goods for ultimate consumption.

Sales-Potential Method Method for determining the number of salespersons necessary to serve on the sales force. The method entails dividing the yearly dollar sales volume each salesperson can reasonably be expected to obtain into the forecasted sales volume, making allowances for salesperson turnover.[27]

Self-Image The sum total of the personality traits, attitudes, and other qualities people attribute to themselves.[28]

Showing A demonstration of real property. A persuasive tour of real property given by the salesperson to the real-estate prospect.

Signal The way the message is sent and the clarity of communication.

Skimming A price policy for new products that indicates a strategy of selling the product initially at high prices to get as much as possible from those willing to pay top-dollar for the new product. Later, prices are expected to be lowered.

Software A term used in the computer and complex-equipment industries to refer to the services, programming, and maintenance elements of the total offering as opposed to the physical product (the hardware or machine itself). The software is important in determining the total effectiveness of the equipment in use.

Source The originator of a communications message.

Spotter A person who "points out" or designates prospects for the salesperson.

Star Salesperson An outstanding or favored salesperson in the firm, usually distinguished by a superior selling record.

Supervisory Style The projection of a manager's leadership qualities stemming from assumptions managers make about their subordinates and the basic approaches they take to motivate them.

Supporting Sales Representatives Salespersons who are more involved in sales-supporting activities than in actually closing sales.

Synthetic Experience Visualizing and preliving an experience through the imagination as a substitute for actual experience.[29]

---

[27] Still, *loc. cit.*

[28] Walters, *loc. cit.*

[29] Maltz, *op. cit.*

Testimonial A verbal or written endorsement of a product, service, or idea by someone other than the salesperson. Testimonials are usually solicited from satisfied and respected customers.

Title The evidence of ownership, usually a printed deed, that a buyer of property obtains upon purchasing real property.

Tradition-Directed Prone to consider long-standing and traditional influences in buying products.

Transactional Analysis The attempt to identify the ego state people are using as references when they communicate in order to formulate suitable strategy to improve communications.[30]

Trial Close An attempt to find out if the prospect is ready to buy without actually insisting on a final decision on the total offer.

Walk-In An applicant who applies for a sales job in person at the place of employment, without an appointment or previous communications.

Warranty A guarantee or assurance about a product or service.

Warranty Deed A deed to real estate containing a guarantee of title.

Wholesale Salesperson A sales representative who works for a wholesaler. Usually such representatives sell service with the product.

Work-Load Method A method of determining the amount of salespersons needed. The method involves classifying customers into categories by importance to sales volume, determining how long interviews should be with each class customer, and determining how many calls should be made on each class. The number of salespersons needed is derived from dividing the interview hours one salesperson might be expected to spend in the field in interviews into the number of hours necessary to serve the market.[31]

Youth Image The view that a person is young because of projected appearance and actions.

[30] Berne, *loc. cit.*

[31] Still, *loc. cit.*

Index

About the Author

Walter Gorman is Professor of Marketing at the University of Tennessee at Martin, where he has taught personal selling, advertising, and other marketing courses for twelve years.

He has had seventeen articles on selling and other subjects published in books and journals, and he has written five correspondence courses while with the University of Tennessee.

Professor Gorman has a Ph.D. in marketing from the University of Alabama, where he was supported by a scholarship from the Birmingham Sales Executive's Club and later by university teaching fellowships. He received his M.S. in marketing from the University of Tennessee and did his undergraduate work in economics at Southwestern at Memphis, where he participated in varsity basketball and track.

He is a member of the American Marketing Association, Southern Marketing Association, Phi Kappa Phi, Beta Gamma Sigma, and Gideon's International. He has worked as a salesman for the Quality Stamp Company of Memphis and as an accounting systems salesman for the Burroughs Corporation.

Professor Gorman has served as Stores Officer of the *U.S.S. Newport News* and Supply Officer of the *U.S.S. Guyatt.*